JŌDO SHINSHŪ

Religion in Asia and Africa series
Judith Berling and Patrick Olivelle, editors

The memorial hall to Shinran (foreground) and the Amida Buddha hall (background) at the Nishi Honganji temple in Kyoto.

JŌDO SHINSHŪ

Shin Buddhism
in Medieval Japan

BY

JAMES C. DOBBINS

INDIANA
UNIVERSITY
PRESS
Bloomington and Indianapolis

Manufactured in the United States of America

Library of Congress Cataloging-in-Publication Data
Dobbins, James C.
Jōdo Shinshū : Shin Buddhism in medieval Japan.
(Religion in Asia and Africa series)
Bibliography: p.
Includes index.
1. Shin (Sect)—History. 2. Buddhism—Japan—History—1185–1600. I. Title. II.
Series.
BQ8712.6.D63 1989 294.3'92 88–45098
ISBN 0-253-33186-2

1 2 3 4 5 94 93 92 91 89

To S.W. and I.M.

CONTENTS

Acknowledgments

This book has passed through several incarnations over the course of which numerous individuals and organizations have lent their support. It was conceived amid the rigors of graduate education at Yale University under the tutelage of Stanley Weinstein. He endowed me with the scholarly skills necessary for research in Japanese Buddhism, and he shepherded the project through the dissertation stage. Yale supported me for what seemed like an interminable graduate career, primarily with scholarships donated by the Sumitomo Group of Japan, and it provided a felicitous environment for my initial forays into this topic. My teachers and fellow students at Yale in Religious Studies, History, and East Asian Languages and Literature proved to be sympathetic companions throughout my years in New Haven.

The actual research for this book was conducted in 1978–80 at Ryūkoku University in Kyoto. Professor Ishida Mitsuyuki oversaw my work there, and demonstrated boundless patience during my first precarious attempts at understanding Shin doctrine and its development. I am also indebted to the Japanese Ministry of Education, which was my financial sponsor during this period, and to the Ryūkoku faculty, the Bukkyō Bunka Kenkyūjo, the Ryūkoku Library, and the Ryūkoku Translation Center for their hospitality and constant assistance. Their kindness throughout that initial period of research forged an enduring bond which has drawn me back to Ryūkoku for subsequent research visits in 1985 and 1987.

The last revision of this work was undertaken at Oberlin College with the encouragement of friends and colleagues in the Religion Department and the East Asian Studies Program. I am grateful to them for the broader vision they have nourished in me and for the confidence they have shown in my work. The college was generous in providing assistance for the production of the final manuscript.

Finally, I want to thank my family—my parents, my wife, and my children. They have indulged me the time and energy to see this project through to completion, and they have supported me in countless intangible ways, day in and day out, for lo these many years. My wife, Suzanne Gay, who is an accomplished scholar of Japan in her own right, has been of particular assistance. She is my best reader and critic. I am deeply indebted to her and to all those who have had a hand, direct or indirect, in making this work possible.

Abbreviations

BDJ	*Bukkyō daijiten*, 10 vols.
BGDJ	*Bukkyōgo daijiten*, 3 vols.
BGJ	*Bukkyōgaku jiten*
BKDJ	*Bussho kaisetsu daijiten*, 13 vols., *Bekkan*, 1 vol.
GSZ	*Gendaigoyaku Shinran zenshū*, 10 vols.
HSZ	*Shōwa shinshū Hōnen Shōnin zenshū*
JDJ	*Jōdoshū daijiten*, 4 vols.
JZ	*Jōdoshū zensho*, 20 vols.
RSG	*Rennyo Shōnin gyōjitsu*
RSI	*Rennyo Shōnin ibun*
SDJ	*Shinshū daijiten*, 3 vols.
SSS	*Shinshū shiryō shūsei*, 13 vols.
SSZ	*Shinshū shōgyō zensho*, 5 vols.
ST	*Shinshū taikei*, 37 vols.
SZ	*Shinshū zensho*, 74 vols.
TD	*Taishō shinshū daizōkyō*, 85 vols.
TSSZ	*Teihon Shinran Shōnin zenshū*, 9 vols., *Bessatsu*, 1 vol.
ZST	*Zoku Shinshū taikei*, 20 vols., *Bekkan*, 4 vols.

JŌDO SHINSHŪ

CHAPTER

1

JŌDO SHINSHŪ

Japan's Kamakura period (1185–1333) marked a revolution in the development of Buddhism. New forms of religiosity—specifically, Pure Land, Zen, and Nichiren Buddhism—rose to prominence and eventually spread throughout the population. The simplified devotions and practices that they advocated offered an appealing alternative to the strenuous and complex systems of discipline that dominated Japanese Buddhism up to that time. So profound was the impact of these teachings and so dramatic was their departure from the past that Japanese scholars have come to describe them as New Buddhism (*shin Bukkyō*) in contrast to the earlier eight schools of Old Buddhism (*kyū Bukkyō*). The significance of these new teachings is that they at last created religious paths that virtually any person could follow, and in doing so they culminated the long process of adapting Buddhism to the Japanese context. The formal schools of Kamakura Buddhism that emerged ultimately became the largest and strongest religious organizations in Japan.

Because of the profound consequences of this religious revolution, there is a tendency to assume that these new Buddhist schools emerged from the beginning as formal sectarian organizations and that they immediately overshadowed their predecessors. Belief systems, ceremonies, ecclesiastical hierarchies, formulas for legitimating authority, and institutional structures are often projected back in time onto the incipient Pure Land, Zen, and Nichiren schools. Such projections tend to distort the complexities of sectarian evolution. Each of the new schools followed an extended and sometimes tortuous path of development. There were moments of creativity and rapid expansion, as well as periods of isolation and retrenchment. Sectarian development was, in short, long and protracted rather than sudden and immediate. This study, predicated on this gradualist viewpoint, is an examination of one of those schools, the Jōdo Shinshū. It traces the stages of Shinshū development from its embryonic teachings in the Kamakura period through its ascendance three centuries later as a dominant school of Buddhism. Throughout this study the underlying assumption is that no one event or individual created the Shinshū. Rather, it was the product of a multiplicity of occurrences in which many people participated.

This study therefore addresses the broader question of how organized religions unfold from core beliefs and rituals. The Jōdo Shinshū exemplifies that process.

Jōdo Shinshū, known popularly in the West as Shin Buddhism, literally means "Pure Land's true principles."[1] As the name of the sectarian organization it denotes "true Pure Land school," and is commonly abbreviated to Shinshū, or "true school." Historically, the Shinshū derives its strength from the great number of ordinary people drawn to its simple doctrine of salvation through faith. It is built on the conviction that through faith one will be born during one's next lifetime in a transcendent realm known as Pure Land (*jōdo*) where the liberating experience of Buddhist enlightenment will occur swiftly and effortlessly. The Shinshū's rise to prominence occurred over a period of time extending from Shinran (1173–1262), the originator of its religious tenets, to Rennyo (1415–99), his tenth-generation descendant.[2] Shinran's teachings provided the inspiration for the movement, and Rennyo's ministry marked its emergence as a major school of Japanese Buddhism. The success of the school is frequently attributed to the ingenuity and energy of these two figures. But the individuals and events of the intervening centuries were likewise contributing factors. The net result of this entire evolutionary process was that the Shinshū outstripped most other schools of Buddhism in the number of converts it made and by the sixteenth century stood as a formidable religious and political force in Japanese society. As much as any other school, it became the creed of the masses. For this reason the Shinshū epitomizes the popular forms of Buddhism that became dominant in Japan from the medieval period on.

PURE LAND HISTORY IN THE EYES OF SHIN BELIEVERS

The perception that the Shinshū sprang into full-bodied existence under Shinran is nurtured in part by the image that Shin believers preserve of their religious roots. They idealize Shinran and the rise of the Shinshū as the consummate event in Pure Land history. He is presented as the crowning figure in a long line of Pure Land patriarchs, and all Shinshū developments subsequent to his time are interpreted as the unfolding of his teachings. Thus, Pure Land history, both prior to Shinran and after his death, is made to pivot around his founding of the Shinshū in the Kamakura period. Hardly any other Buddhists perceive religious history with this same Shinshū slant. Nonetheless, it is crucial to understand the content of that view of history if one is to understand the Shinshū itself, for the view constitutes part of the sacred story on which the Shinshū is built. It embodies the Shin vision of religious truth and how it has been conveyed to the world. This vision was one of the products of sectarian evolution, and it became an essential component of the Shinshū's identity and self-definition.

The Shin view of history begins with the three Pure Land sutras (*jōdo sanbu kyō*) supposedly preached in India by the historical Buddha Śākyamuni, which reveal to sentient beings the supreme Buddha Amida and his promise of salvation in a resplendent Pure Land. From there it proceeds through the so-called seven Pure Land patriarchs (*shichiso*): Nāgārjuna (ca. 150–250) and Vasuban-dhu (ca. 4th cent.) of India; T'an-luan (476–542?), Tao-ch'o (562–645), and Shan-tao (613–81) of China; and Genshin (942–1017) and Hōnen (1133–1212) of Japan.[3] In their wake Shinran is hailed as the culmination of the Pure Land tradition. His teachings are extolled as the true meaning of Amida's message and as the starting point of the Shinshū proper.[4] From him the mantle of Shinshū authority is passed to a temple, the Honganji, and to its leaders, in-cluding Rennyo. Shinran's religious vision is brought to institutional fulfill-ment during Rennyo's tenure as eighth head priest of the Honganji. For his accomplishments Rennyo is remembered as the restorer (*chūkō shōnin*) of the school.[5] After him the Shinshū continues in an unbroken line down to the present as a united body of believers under the guidance of the Honganji and its head priest, the hereditary descendant of Shinran.[6] In short, Shinshū his-tory is perceived as a religious transmission initiated by the Buddha, culminated by Shinran, instituted by Rennyo, and preserved by present-day believers.[7]

Pure Land Buddhism is predicated on the idea that Amida Buddha has provided human beings with a path to enlightenment (*bodai*) or Nirvāṇa (*me-tsudo*)—the ultimate goal of Buddhism whereby one is liberated from Saṃsāra, or the endless cycle of birth, death, and rebirth—without the rigorous religious practices demanded in other forms of Buddhism. Traditionally in Buddhism, one must be disciplined in ethical precepts (*kai*), meditation (*jō*), and cultiva-tion of wisdom (*e*) in order to achieve this goal. Pure Land Buddhism advo-cates instead a simple form of religious devotion aimed not at immediate enlightenment in the present lifetime but at birth in Amida's Pure Land during one's next life. The conditions in Pure Land are wholly conducive to enlighten-ment, so any person born there attains Nirvāṇa quickly and easily. The goal of the Pure Land believer, therefore, is birth in Amida's Pure Land, and the means by which the believer pursues it are the devotions laid out in the Pure Land sutras.[8]

The basic scriptures of the Shinshū are the three Pure Land sutras: the *Muryōjukyō* (Skt. *Sukhāvatīvyūhasūtra*), known as the "Larger Pure Land Sutra"; the *Kanmuryōjukyō*, or the "Pure Land Meditation Sutra"; and the *Amidakyō* (Skt. *Sukhāvatī[amṛta]vyūhasūtra*), or the "Smaller Pure Land Sutra."[9] Of them, the first is the most important, for it contains the forty-eight vows made by Amida in his quest to achieve Buddhahood, to establish his Pure Land, and to save all sentient beings. Among the forty-eight, the eighteenth vow is the crucial one on which Pure Land soteriology rests. As a result, it is called the principal vow (*hongan*). It appears in the "Larger Sutra" in two versions. The first is known in the Shinshū as the causal form of the vow (*ingan*), which Amida framed prior to his Buddhahood. In it Amida made his own enlightenment contingent on the salvation of others:

> Were I to attain Buddhahood, and yet if sentient beings of the ten directions were not to be born [in Pure Land] even though they were sincere in heart,

had faith and joy, and desired to be born in my Pure Land with even ten *nen*, then I would not accept true enlightenment. Only those who commit the five damning offenses or slander the true teachings will be excluded.[10]

The second version is referred to as the fulfilled form of the principal vow (*hongan jōju no mon*), a reiteration of the same promise after Amida has achieved Buddhahood:

If sentient beings hear [Amida's] name and have faith and joy, with even a single *nen*, and if they extend their own religious merit to others with a sincere heart, and if they desire to be born in that Pure Land, then they will attain birth there and will reside in the stage of nonretrogression. Only those who commit the five damning offenses or slander the true teachings will be excluded.[11]

According to these two versions of the vow, birth in Pure Land does not require a long and strenuous career of religious practice. It simply involves sincerity of heart, hearing Amida's name, faith and joy, desire to be born in Pure Land, extending religious merit to others, and *nen*. This last term originally referred to contemplation or meditation on Amida, but over the course of Pure Land history it came to mean uttering Amida's name in the form *Namu Amida Butsu*—"I take refuge in the Buddha Amida." This religious invocation, known as the *nembutsu*, subsequently became the hallmark of Pure Land Buddhism in China and Japan.

The other two Pure Land sutras are generally interpreted in the light of Amida's principal vow. One point drawn from the "Smaller Sutra" is that sentient beings can be born in Pure Land merely by hearing Amida's name (*myōgō*) and meditating on it with singleness of heart (*isshin*) for even one day.[12] The "Meditation Sutra" carries this idea a step further, indicating that even evil persons, if they utter the *nembutsu* on their deathbed with a sincere heart, will be received into Amida's Pure Land, though at the lowest of Pure Land's nine levels.[13] These statements, combined with Amida's vow, depict Pure Land Buddhism as an open and accommodating path to salvation, accessible to believers in virtually any circumstance or religious state.

The seven Pure Land patriarchs venerated by the Shinshū elaborated on the theme of birth in Pure Land to form the basic concepts inherited by Shinran.[14] Nāgārjuna, the first Indian patriarch, delineated two ways of achieving the stage of nonretrogression (*ayuiotchi* or *futaiten*), the threshold of enlightenment from which there is no falling back. The first is by means of difficult religious practices (*nangyō*), which he likened to journeying on land. The second is through easy practices (*igyō*)—that is, simply meditating on the Buddha and invoking his name—which he compared to sailing on water.[15] The latter of these came to be identified as the Pure Land path. Vasubandhu, the other patriarch of India, emphasized singleness of heart (*isshin*) in relying on Amida Buddha, and he enumerated five forms of devotion (*gonenmon*) in which the desire to be born in Pure Land (*ganshō*) is expressed: worshipping Amida (*raihai*), praising his name (*sandan*), vowing to be born in Pure Land (*sagan*), meditating on Amida and his Pure Land (*kanzatsu*), and transferring one's religious merit to others for their benefit (*ekō*). Of these, Vasubandhu valued the transference of religious merit the most, for it is the distinguishing feature of the superior religious path belonging to the so-called Bodhisattva, leading to complete enlightenment and Buddhahood.[16] These concepts constituted the basis of Pure Land thought on which Chinese and Japanese thinkers continued to build.

T'an-luan, the first of the three Chinese patriarchs, characterized the path to Pure Land as based on the other-power (*tariki*) of Amida rather than the self-power (*jiriki*) of the adherent. This other-power he saw vested specifically in Amida's vows to save sentient beings, and he singled out the eighteenth vow, among others, as the repository of this power. T'an-luan interpreted the *nen* of the eighteenth vow to be a meditative act. He considered Vasubandhu's five forms of devotion efficacious not because of the effort the believer puts into them but because they are derived from the power of the Buddha. The important component underlying these devotions is singleness of heart (*isshin*), for therein lies the believer's realization of Amida's power.[17] Tao-ch'o, the next Chinese patriarch, combined the verbal *nembutsu* with the practice of meditation. He also added a historical dimension to these teachings by dividing Buddhism into two categories: the path of sanctification (*shōdō*), predicated on difficult practices and the efforts of the adherent; and the path of Pure Land (*jōdo*), comprising easy practices and the power of Amida. Tao-ch'o maintained that the time has now passed when a saintly life leading to enlightenment can be lived. In this age people are no longer capable of undertaking rigorous religious practices. Thus, Pure Land is the form of Buddhism best suited to the needs and abilities of sentient beings in this last age (*masse*), the period of decline.[18] Shan-tao, the third patriarch of China, stressed for the first time the chanting of the *nembutsu* as the paramount practice making Pure Land accessible to the ordinary individual (*bonbu*). He argued that even the incorrigibly evil person can, according to the "Meditation Sutra," be born in Pure Land. His teachings therefore countermanded the strong exclusionary clause at the end of the eighteenth vow barring from Pure Land anyone who commits the five damning offenses or slanders Buddhism. Shan-tao construed this clause to be a deterrent (*okushimon*) to evil, but not an exclusion of the evildoer. He stipulated five devotional practices that lead to Pure Land—reciting scripture (*dokuju*), meditation (*kanzatsu*), worship (*raihai*), uttering Amida's name (*shōmyō*), and praises and offerings (*sandan kuyō*)—but among them he pointed to uttering Amida's name, the *nembutsu*, as the act truly guaranteeing salvation (*shōjōgō*). The other four devotions he considered secondary (*jogō*).[19] This idealization of the *nembutsu* eventually became the dominant trend among Pure Land Buddhists in Japan.

Genshin, the first of Japan's two patriarchs recognized by the Shinshū, made the *nembutsu* the focal point of his major work, the *Ōjōyōshū* ("Collection [of Scriptural Passages] on the Essentials for Birth in Pure Land"). He praised it as the most beneficial practice for those weary of this tainted world (*enri edo*) and longing for Pure Land (*gongu jōdo*). Genshin believed that the *nembutsu* in its highest form is a meditative practice in which one visualizes Amida and his Pure Land while chanting his name. Meditations of this type had been a long-standing practice in the Pure Land tradition, based on exercises described in the "Pure Land Meditation Sutra." Even for the person incapable of meditation, Genshin recommended chanting the *nembutsu* to concentrate the mind and to focus thoughts on Amida. This was particularly important in the deathbed *nembutsu* ceremony (*rinjū gyōgi*), during which the dying believer envisions Amida coming to usher the believer into Pure Land.[20] Hōnen, the last of the seven patriarchs, also extolled the *nembutsu* as the quintessential Pure Land practice, but he presented it as a verbal rather than a meditative act. In a systematic critique of all types of Buddhist practices, he identified the *nembutsu* as the sine qua non for birth in Pure Land and rejected all others. In the light of this process of selection and rejection, Hōnen adopted the term exclusive *nembutsu* (*senju nembutsu*) to refer to his teaching. He proclaimed the exclusive *nembutsu* to be not only the easy practice but also the superior practice, surpassing any other in Buddhism. The net effect of Hōnen's teaching was to initiate an independent Pure Land movement in Japan.[21]

The seven Pure Land patriarchs reveal a gradual progression away from strenuous religious practices toward simplified ones, the precise direction that the Shinshū emphasizes in Shinran's teachings. In their own times and places, the seven patriarchs' ideas may have been understood differently, but in the context of Shin teachings the seven paved the way for Shinran's ideas. His religious vision is seen as the final step in the patriarchal progression. Shinran was Hōnen's disciple and inherited from him the exclusive *nembutsu*, but Shinran stressed the importance of the state of mind standing behind it—specifically, a mind of faith (*shinjin*). Shinran considered faith the direct cause (*naiin*) of birth in Pure Land, and he identified singleness of heart (*isshin*), mentioned in the "Smaller Pure Land Sutra" and in Vasubandhu's and T'an-luan's writings, as none other than faith. Shinran's concept of salvation is founded on the assumption that there is nothing true or absolute deriving from the believer. All saving power flows from the Buddha. Hence, faith, like the *nembutsu*, is not a product of human exertion but rather the creation of Amida unilaterally bestowed on sentient beings. True salvation comes when people perceive the inadequacies of their own efforts and turn to the unfailing promise of Amida's vow. Shinran's teachings therefore emphasize the absolute power of the Buddha realized in sentient beings in the form of faith.[22]

The successors to Shinran's teachings, specifically his great-grandson Kakunyo (1270–1351) and subsequently Rennyo, gave greater clarity and definition to his concept of faith, and sought to communicate it to others in succinct doctrinal formulas and popular religious terminology. A recurring theme in their writings is that faith is the true cause of birth in Pure Land (*shinjin shōin*) and that chanting Amida's name is an expression of gratitude for his gift of salvation (*shōmyō hōon*). They also interpreted the *nembutsu* as an act in which the believer, who is constricted by limitations, and the Buddha, who is grounded in absolute truth, are united as one substance (*kihō ittai*). To explain the idea of faith, both Kakunyo and Rennyo sometimes employed a synonym for it, the term *anjin*, meaning "a mind at peace." Rennyo went a step further to bring the message of faith down to the ordinary person's level, adopting such popular idioms as "relying on Amida to please save me" (*tasuke tamae to tanomu*) to explicate it.[23] Overall, their teachings couched Shinran's basic tenets in simple and comprehensible language, and fashioned them into a systematic body of doctrine which became the cornerstone of Shinshū orthodoxy. Today their teachings stand as the normative interpretation of Shin doctrine.

This intricate web of religious concepts, practices, and thinkers is the way that Shin believers conceive of the origins and development of their school. From the believer's point of view, the unfolding of religious truth is linear. It is traced as a dramatic progression: the Pure Land patriarchs provide the foreshadowing, Shinran the climax, and Kakunyo and Rennyo the denouement. This perception of the Shinshū's roots is the basis for the believer's sense of a religious heritage. Such a sense adds a historical dimension to the experience of faith, and fosters a sense of commonalty with believers in times long past. This view of Shin history is part and parcel of the sacred story that gives the school definition. Though it is constructed through the interpretive filter of religious convictions, there are indeed conceptual threads that stretch from the Pure Land sutras, through the seven patriarchs, to Shinran, Kakunyo, and Rennyo. Nonetheless, the particular configuration of events and individuals which the Shinshū claims as its history tends to obscure other forces that have likewise contributed to its development.

This study, while following the vertical or diachronic transmission of Shin teachings, seeks also to define the horizontal or synchronic environment in which they evolved and to identify the external influences which also left their mark on the school. The Shinshū has always existed in a multisectarian society, and its ideas have been conditioned as much by interaction with other groups as by internal dynamics. Consequently, the sources of Shin thought, especially during the formative period between Shinran and Rennyo, must be sought in a broader historical context than the strict sectarian boundaries in which the school defines itself.

ORTHODOXY, HERESY, AND SECTARIAN DEVELOPMENT

The most radical ingredient in the making of the Shinshū was Shinran's own teachings. He began with widely recognized Buddhist themes, but interpreted them in such a way as to separate himself from Japan's prevailing religious trends. Specifically, he resisted the all-pervasive tendency to amalgamate Buddhism with Japan's indigenous Shinto tradition, and he turned his back on clerical celibacy and monasticism, which had been a part of Buddhism since its early development in India. Shinran's teachings were not so much a distortion of Buddhism as an emphasis of certain Buddhist principles over others. A similar pattern can be seen in the emergence of virtually every school of Buddhism.

Unfortunately, the particular combination of beliefs and practices that Shinran propounded did not translate easily into a socially viable religious institution. For instance, his idealization of the evil person as the prime candidate for salvation in Pure Land was prey to perennial misunderstanding and misrepresentation. As a result the religious organization created around his teachings was plagued by external criticism and internal dissension. Amid these complexities the concepts of orthodoxy and heresy were constantly at work. Outsiders used them to assail the Shinshū, and insiders adopted them to defend themselves and to hammer out their tenets. Hence, orthodoxy and heresy provide a conceptual framework for examining Shinshū development during its first three centuries of existence.

To understand the dynamics of Shinshū development, it is necessary to recognize the sense of religious persecution that its adherents bore throughout its formative centuries. Because of Shinran's dissent from prevailing religious views, the Shinshū suffered accusations of heresy and outright suppression at the hands of civil and religious authorities. In the face of this adversity Shin believers, convinced of the legitimacy and truth of their teachings, strove to defend themselves against criticism and to preserve their beliefs from distortion. Among them there was constant experimentation in explicating Shinran's ideas. Deviations arose because some diluted his provocative message and others exaggerated it. The process of rendering Shinran's religious vision into an institutionally serviceable body of doctrine, wherein the Shinshū's own claims of orthodoxy would be recognized beyond its own ranks, was long and arduous.

Within Buddhism there have existed from the beginning concepts of orthodoxy and heresy. Denunciations of "wrong views" are attributed to the Buddha himself, and the idea of "assailing heresy and revealing truth" (*haja kenshō*) is traceable to numerous Buddhist classics.[24] Hence, Japan's established schools of Old Buddhism had available to them the conceptual framework for attacking Shinran in defense of orthodoxy. The concept of heresy was invoked again and again to justify repressions against the Shinshū during its early centuries.

The Shinshū also laid claim to the concepts of orthodoxy and heresy. It employed them not only to defend itself against adversaries but also to clarify its own religious doctrines. Criticisms of heresy appear, for instance, in Shinran's magnum opus, the *Kyōgyōshinshō* ("Teaching, Practice, Faith, and Enlightenment"); in the *Tannishō* ("Notes Lamenting Deviations") attributed to Shinran's disciple Yuienbō; in the *Gaijashō* ("Notes Rectifying Heresy") by Kakunyo; in the *Haja kenshōshō* ("Notes Assailing Heresy and Revealing Truth") by Kakunyo's son Zonkaku (1290–1373); and in Rennyo's *Ofumi*, or "pastoral letters." All these works are examined in this study in an attempt to trace the development of the concept of heresy and the formulation of Shin orthodoxy. The particular ideas assailed as heretical vary greatly in these works, but the concern of the authors over this entire three-hundred year period was essentially the same: to defend the true teachings against corruption or distortion. In many senses, the impetus to define orthodoxy in the Shinshū arose out of the necessity to expose and refute spurious teachings circulating in the school.

The causes of heresy have been diverse in Shinshū history. One problem has been the elusiveness of Shinran's teachings. His concepts differed greatly from the dominant form of Buddhism of his day. As a result, elements in them became altered, sometimes out of misunderstanding and other times out of expediency. A second cause of "Shinshū heresy" was the illiteracy of the population that embraced Shinran's teachings. These believers had no access to his writings and were dependent on their local leaders for religious instruction. When misconceptions occurred, there was little means of correcting them, and so they were perpetuated from generation to generation, especially in isolated Shinshū communities. A third complication was the influx of adherents from other religious groups. These new members frequently carried with them beliefs and practices which the Shinshū rejected. Hence, some Shinshū heresies were simply the doctrines of other Buddhist traditions indiscriminately absorbed into the school. All these factors made heresy a perennial concern in Shinshū circles.

The Shinshū's vocabulary for heresy was derived from long-standing Buddhist terminology. No single word was used uniformly to refer to heresy, but rather a variety of Buddhist terms came to have that meaning. The most common were: wrong view (*jaken*), aberrant view (*iken*), wrong path (*jadō*), aberrant path (*idō*), non-Buddhist path (*gedō*), wrong attachment (*jashū*), aberrant attachment (*ishū*), wrong doctrine (*jagi*), aberrant doctrine (*igi*), wrong teaching (*jakyō*), aberrant understanding (*ige*), different understanding (*betsuge*), aberrant intention (*ike*), aberrant learning (*igaku*), wrongness and falsehood (*jagi*), and wrong custom (*jafū*). The Shinshū later coined another word for heresy, *ianjin* or "aberrant faith," which has become the standard term appearing in present-day Shinshū writings. This word first came into usage around 1800, so it cannot be attributed to Shinran or Rennyo.[25] Nonetheless, it indicates clearly how heresy has been perceived in the Shinshū: as a deviation from faith. What makes something heretical from the Shinshū perspective is that it violates directly or indirectly the principle of faith.[26] This is perhaps the most elemental definition of heresy applicable to the Shinshū, encompassing the variety of terminology used and the diversity of heresies raised.

The concepts of orthodoxy and heresy underwent a metamorphosis over the course of Shinshū history. As the Shinshū advanced from a religious vision propounded by Shinran, to an unorganized band of followers, then to a decentralized religious movement, and finally to a unified school of Buddhism, the idea of heresy accumulated new layers of meaning. To Shinran, heresy was a doctrinal abstraction indicating deviation from religious truth. To Kakunyo, it was the misformulation of Shinshū teachings by his religious rivals, prompting a polemical response on his part. To Rennyo, it was the misguided religious inclinations of the masses, inspiring him to evangelical endeavors. Each time heresy took on new significance, it did not cancel out its previous meanings but simply overlaid them. In a similar fashion orthodoxy accrued layers of interpretation, generally in response to the same events that shaped the idea of heresy. Throughout this process, personal conviction was the principle motivating the leaders of the Shinshū. To that extent, their continual redefinition of Shinshū orthodoxy and heresy was not a premeditated effort to build up a school of Buddhism, but rather an attempt over successive generations to explicate the inner logic of faith.[27]

CHAPTER

2

HŌNEN, THE EXCLUSIVE NEMBUTSU, AND SUPPRESSION

During the lifetime of Shinran the idea of Shin orthodoxy existed, if at all, only in the mind of Shinran. It was not an intricately etched concept defining every detail of belief and practice, but rather a broad and sometimes ambiguous exposition of what he considered to be religious truth. As such, Shinran's concept of orthodoxy was essentially private in character without institutional overtones. Those institutional elements came later after the spread of the Shinshū throughout Japan and after the emergence of one temple, the Hongan-ji, as the ascendant religious authority in the Shinshū.

The question of heresy in Shinran's time is complicated by the fact that Shinran himself was an apostate from the organized religion of his day. That religion consisted of the eight schools of Buddhism—Kusha, Jōjitsu, Ritsu, Hossō, Sanron, Kegon, Tendai, and Shingon—or, in short, those schools centered around Nara and the capital Kyoto, which enjoyed imperial or aristocratic patronage and which dominated religious affairs in Japan. In Shinran's mind the Tendai school, located on Mt. Hiei (*Hieizan*), was the most prominent among the eight, since he had spent twenty years there as a Buddhist monk. The religious convictions that Shinran espoused in his writings were in many ways a reaction against the Buddhism propagated at Mt. Hiei. Shinran was not alone in his disenchantment with the schools of Old Buddhism, but was merely one member of the broader religious movement known today as Kamakura Buddhism. It recast Buddhist teachings in forms which were, for the most part, attuned to the needs of the common people.[1] Shinran, like the other innovators of Kamakura Buddhism, presented his own teachings as the true message of Buddhism, transcending the traditional doctrines of the eight schools. Mt. Hiei, on the other hand, and the rest of the religious establishment looked upon Shinran and his lot as religious rebels and their teachings as heresy. Hence, what later became the cornerstone of Shin orthodoxy was, from the point of view of the established schools, the heresy of its day.

HŌNEN AND THE EXCLUSIVE NEMBUTSU

The historical context in which Shinran formulated his vision of religious truth was the Pure Land movement, spearheaded by Shinran's teacher Hōnen (1173–1212).[2] Of all the religious currents in Kamakura Buddhism, the Pure Land movement was the most pervasive. Within that movement Hōnen stood as Pure Land's foremost advocate. Hōnen himself withdrew from Mt. Hiei in 1175. There he had been nurtured for many years on the Tendai interpretation of Pure Land and on the *Ōjōyōshū* ("Collection [of Scriptural Passages] on the Essentials for Birth in Pure Land"), the Pure Land handbook written by the Tendai priest Genshin. Tendai's interpretation integrated the aspiration to be born in Pure Land with Mt. Hiei's concept of personal religious development.[3]

Training at Mt. Hiei was somewhat diversified in Hōnen's time, but at its heart lay the clerical vows in the form of the Bodhisattva precepts (*bosatsukai*) and a twelve-year program of uninterrupted study and practice at the Enryakuji, the Tendai temple complex on Mt. Hiei. Both of these components of training were instituted by Saichō (767–822), the founder of Tendai Buddhism in Japan. The Bodhisattva precepts, as the basis of monastic discipline, consist of ten major and forty-eight minor precepts (*jūju shijūhachikyō kai*). The ten major ones are: 1) not to kill, 2) not to steal, 3) not to indulge in sexual relations, 4) not to lie, 5) not to buy or sell liquor, 6) not to expose other people's faults, 7) not to aggrandize oneself or to defame others, 8) not to begrudge one's possessions or the Buddhist teachings to others, 9) not to hold a grudge against others or to reject their apologies, and 10) not to slander the Buddha, the Buddhist teachings, or the Buddhist order. The forty-eight minor precepts include such injunctions as not to consume liquor, not to eat meat, not to possess weapons, not to be involved in commercial activities, and not to delight in fights, music, games, or sorcery.[4] All priests who received ordination in the Tendai school were nominally obliged to obey these clerical vows.

Over and above the Bodhisattva precepts, Saichō envisioned a twelve-year period of religious training consisting of lectures, study of sacred texts, liturgical recitations, and intense meditation. This program was divided into two tracks, one focusing on Tendai meditation (*shikan*) and the other on esoteric practices (*shana*). The particular scriptures that Saichō stressed included the *Hokekyō* (Skt. *Saddharmapuṇḍarīkasūtra*) or "Lotus Sutra," for those concentrating on Tendai meditation, and the *Dainichikyō* (Skt. *Mahāvairocanasūtra*) or "Great Vairocana Buddha Sutra," for those devoted to esoteric practices. The meditative exercises that Saichō prescribed were the four outlined in the *Mo-ho chih-kuan* ("Great Meditation") written by Chih-i (538–97), the Chinese founder of Tendai. Saichō did not live long enough to see his program of religious training fully realized at Mt. Hiei, but in the decades after his death much of it was actually instituted. Eventually certain elements were elaborated and others eliminated. One of the notable developments in later centuries was the efflorescence of Pure Land teachings under Ennin (794–864), Ryōgen (912-85), and

Genshin. Religious practice at Mt. Hiei was ultimately geared to the cleric and was predicated on the idea that the priest is superior to the lay person in spiritual advancement. Hence, many aristocrats in their old age wanted to take religious vows and to pursue the practices and goals of the clergy. They believed that such efforts would give them an advantage in attaining enlightenment during their next life, or even in the present. This clerical ideal, which existed in Hōnen's time, derived from Saichō's Bodhisattva precepts and from his program of intense religious training.[5]

Hōnen, who grew up under this system of training, began to reassess its value while still on Mt. Hiei, particularly after reading the *Kuan ching shu* ("Commentary on the Pure Land Meditation Sutra") composed by the Chinese Pure Land master Shan-tao. From this work Hōnen came to revere the *nembutsu* as the one religious act which, when practiced exclusively, could lead any human being to salvation in Amida's Pure Land, even the poor or needy (*bingū konbō*), the stupid or ignorant (*gudon gechi*), those who had seen or heard little of the teachings (*shōmon shōken*), or those who had broken the clerical precepts or were without them (*hakai mukai*).[6] The accessibility of the *nembutsu* to believers in any station of life finally led Hōnen away from the rigorous and selective program of religious advancement advocated by the Tendai school and toward his teaching of the exclusive *nembutsu* (*senju nembutsu*). After his departure from Mt. Hiei, Hōnen settled in the Ōtani district on the eastern edge of Kyoto and there preached the exclusive *nembutsu* to an ever expanding community of believers.[7]

Unlike Shinran, Hōnen was a prominent figure in society during his own day. Eminent priests from Kyoto and Nara often engaged him in dialogue, and powerful laymen, including many aristocrats, sought out his religious guidance. The most illustrious among these was Kujō Kanezane (1149–1207), who served as imperial regent (*sesshō kanpaku*) for a decade at the end of the twelfth century.[8] In addition to lay supporters, Hōnen attracted a band of avid disciples dedicated to the Pure Land teachings. In number they totaled at least 190, for that many signed his *Shichikajō kishōmon* ("Seven Article Pledge") of 1204, whereby they accepted certain rules of conduct laid down by Hōnen.[9] These disciples included aristocrats, priests from major Buddhist temples, former samurai, ordinary townsmen, and lowborn itinerant monks from the countryside. Among them there was considerable variation in interpreting the *nembutsu*, from an orthodox view of it as one element in traditional Buddhist training to a more radical conception of it as the panacea for all the ills of the age. Nonetheless, all were united under the leadership of Hōnen. Shinran was one member of this following, but he was by no means the most prominent. Other disciples such as Shinkū (1146–1228), Shōkū (1177–1247), Genchi (1183–1238), Kōsai (1163–1247), Kansai (1148–1200), Anrakubō (d. 1207), and Ryūkan (1148–1227) often overshadowed him during Hōnen's lifetime.

Hōnen, though committed to the *nembutsu*, did not seek to alienate the established schools of Buddhism. He lived the life of a Buddhist monk in strict obedience to the Bodhisattva precepts, and he even administered those precepts to Kujō Kanezane and others who sought ordination.[10] Although Hōnen saw no contradiction between the precepts and the *nembutsu*, he interpreted the *nembutsu* in a much broader context than the traditional schools of Old Buddhism did, and at his deepest level of conviction he embraced the Pure Land teachings to the exclusion of the traditional path of religious exertion. Hōnen summed up this conviction in a series of choices outlined in the concluding section of his *Senjaku hongan nembutsushū* ("Collection [of Scriptural Passages] on the Nembutsu of the Principal Vow Singled Out [by Amida]"), or in short the *Senjakushū* ("Singled-Out Collection"), composed in 1198:

> Upon reflection I realize that, if people wish to distance themselves straightway from Saṃsāra, then out of the two magnificent teachings they should close off the path of religious exertion (*shōdō*) and choose to embark on the path of Pure Land. If they wish to embark on the path of Pure Land, then out of the two kinds of practices, true and indiscriminate, they should cast out the indiscriminate and choose to rely on the true. If they wish to undertake true practice, then out of the two kinds of acts, true and secondary, they should set aside the secondary and choose exclusively the one whereby enlightenment in Pure Land is truly assured. The act whereby it is truly assured is the utterance of the name of the Buddha. If they utter the name, then without fail they will attain birth in Pure Land because this act is founded on the principal vow of the Buddha.[11]

This process of choosing the *nembutsu* exclusively was radical in its ramifications, for it meant rejecting the traditional schools of Buddhism, along with their Pure Land interpretations. The traditional schools also advocated practice of the *nembutsu*, but only as one component in a comprehensive program of clerical precepts, meditation, and study of scripture. Hōnen bypassed these requirements and fixed on the *nembutsu* as the one practice, the exclusive practice, for birth in Pure Land. Hōnen understood the implications of what he wrote, for in the closing passage of the *Senjakushū* he beseeched the reader to keep the work a secret, that is, "to bury it in the wall rather than leave it in the window."[12]

SUPPRESSION OF THE NEMBUTSU

Despite Hōnen's circumspection, his teachings soon evoked a harsh reaction from Japan's Buddhist establishment. In 1204 Tendai monks at the Enryakuji appealed to Shinshō (1167–1230), the head priest there and an acquaintance of Hōnen's, to prohibit the practice of the exclusive *nembutsu* and to expel its adherents from their religious precincts.[13] Hōnen's response to this attack was his *Shichikajō kishōmon* ("Seven Article Pledge"), rules of conduct that his followers were sworn to obey.[14] One year later the Kōfukuji, one of the most influential temples in Nara, petitioned the retired emperor Gotoba (1180–1239) to take measures against Hōnen, and it leveled nine specific charges against him:

1. Establishing a new school without imperial recognition and without proper lineage.

2. Devising a new graphic representation of Amida Buddha called the *Sesshu Fusha Mandara* ("Mandala of Those Embraced and Never Forsaken"), in which followers of the exclusive *nembutsu* are bathed in Amida's light but priests adhering to traditional practices are not.
3. Slighting the Buddha Śākyamuni by worshipping no Buddha other than Amida.
4. Precluding Buddhism's myriad ways of cultivating the good, outside of the *nembutsu*.
5. Refusing to revere the illustrious *kami*, the native deities of the Shinto tradition.
6. Misrepresenting Pure Land by denying that diverse religious practices lead to birth there.
7. Misunderstanding the *nembutsu* by claiming that uttering it is superior to using it in meditation.
8. Inflicting harm upon the Buddhist order by maintaining that violation of the clerical precepts is not an obstacle to birth in Pure Land.
9. Throwing the country into disorder by undermining the teachings of the eight schools which uphold it.[15]

These nine accusations indicate irreconcilable differences between Hōnen and the traditional schools over the meaning of the *nembutsu*, the clerical precepts, the Pure Land movement, and Amida Buddha. They also suggest that Hōnen's followers were involved in disruptive activities that were a threat to the established religious order not only doctrinally but also socially and politically.

The outcries against Hōnen and his band of disciples reached a crescendo in 1207, and resulted in the suppression of the exclusive *nembutsu*, the exile of Hōnen, and the execution of a number of his followers.[16] This was the first in a long series of suppressions which stretched over the next century, extending into the formative years of the Shinshū as well. The following account of the 1207 incident appears in the *Gukanshō* ("Notes of My Foolish Views"), a history of Japan written in 1219 by Jien (1155–1225), the older brother of Kujō Kanezane and head priest at Mt. Hiei in the early thirteenth century:

> Also during the Ken'ei years (1206–1207) there was a religious man named Hōnen. Close to this time, while living in Kyoto, he established the *nembutsu* school and called his teachings the exclusive *nembutsu*. "You should do nothing more than utter [the name of] Amida Buddha. Do not undertake the esoteric or exoteric practices of the eight schools," he would say. Ignorant or unenlightened lay priests and nuns (*ama nyūdō*) of questionable circumstance delighted in this teaching, and it began to flourish beyond expectation and to gather strength. Among them there was a monk named Anrakubō who had been a retainer under [Takashina] Yasutsune (d. 1201), a lay priest. Upon ordination Anrakubō became an adherent of the exclusive *nembutsu*, and in association with Jūren (d. 1207) he advocated singing the praises [of Pure Land] six times a day (*rokuji raisan*), which is said to have been the practice of the master Shan-tao. There were numerous people, among them nuns, who turned to this teaching and placed their trust in it. They were given to believe that, once they became followers, then even if they indulged in sexual relations

or ate meat or fish, Amida Buddha would not regard it as a wrongdoing in the least, and that, once they entered the single-hearted and exclusive way and had faith in nothing but the *nembutsu*, then at the end of their life Amida would come without fail to usher them into Pure Land. As people in both the capital and the countryside turned to this, a lady-in-waiting at the detached palace of the retired emperor, along with the mother of the imperial priest at the Ninnaji temple, also placed their faith in it. Secretly they summoned Anrakubō and the others to have them share their teachings with them, and so he proceeded there, together with his companions, and even spent the night there. Such a thing is unspeakable, so in the end Anrakubō and Jūren were beheaded. Also, Hōnen was exiled, driven from residency in Kyoto.

This affair was dealt with in such a way that it seemed for a short time that things were under control. Hōnen, however, had not been an ally in the plot, so he was pardoned, and he eventually died at Ōtani in the Higashiyama section of Kyoto. On that occasion people were gathered around, and there was constant talk of his birth in Pure Land, but there is no reason to think that it actually came to pass. His deathbed ceremony was nothing like that of the religious figure Zōga (917–1003). Because all of this has occurred, to this day we are pressed from behind. The exclusive *nembutsu*, with its fish, meat, and sexual indulgences, remains largely unchecked, and the monks of Mt. Hiei have risen up saying that they are going to drive out the *nembutsu* priest Kūamidabutsu (1156–1228), who apparently has been put to flight. On the whole, innumerable people have received names such as Kūamidabutsu or Hōamidabutsu in which a single character is added at the beginning of the name Amida Buddha. For instance, the monk [Chōgen] Shunjōbō (1121–1206) at the Tōdaiji temple claimed to be a manifestation of Amida and adopted the name Namuamidabutsu for himself. Hence, there are many priests and nuns who take Amida's name completely intact as their own. In the end Hōnen's disciples have been the ones committing all these deeds. In perceiving this, I realize that, of the two types of obstacles to enlightenment—those from within oneself (*junma*) and those from outside (*gyakuma*)—these unfortunate teachings of his are of the former type, an obstacle from within. In that period when Amida's one teaching will truly benefit all sentient beings and will increase extraordinarily, wrongdoings and obstacles will certainly disappear and people will advance to Pure Land. But at this time the *mantra* of Shingon and the meditations of Tendai are at their height, and there is still no one who can achieve enlightenment by following teachings which are an obstacle from within. It is a deplorable situation.[17]

Jien's account of Hōnen's activities bespeaks clearly the alarm with which traditional Buddhist adherents looked upon the Pure Land movement. Jien was supremely qualified to speak for both the religious and the political community, since he was not only a head priest at Mt. Hiei but also a scion of the powerful Fujiwara family. As a priest, he considered the exclusive *nembutsu* corrosive to the clerical precepts and a detraction from the teachings of the eight schools. As a leader in society, he feared that it would seduce the ignorant and lowly and would erode social values and civil order.[18] In short, he viewed the Pure Land movement as one characteristic of *mappō*, the age of decline, when society would lapse into chaos and the Buddhist teachings would pass into extinction.

Hōnen himself always strove to maintain cordial relations with the civil and religious authorities and to preserve upright conduct among his disciples, but some of his followers were advocates of a radical *nembutsu* teaching which threatened Jien and his level of society. The injunctions in Hōnen's *Shichikajō kishōmon* ("Seven Article Pledge") indicate the kind of unruly behavior that their teachings spawned:

1. Refrain from denigrating other Buddhas and Bodhisattvas and from attacking Shingon and Tendai, for you are not versed in any of their teachings.
2. In your state of ignorance, refrain from indulging in disputes with men of wisdom or when encountering people with other religious practices.
3. Toward people of other persuasions or practices, refrain from saying, with your mind ignorant and biased, that they should abandon their actions. Refrain from wanton ridicule of them.
4. Refrain from saying that there is no practice of the clerical precepts in the *nembutsu* path, from avidly encouraging sexual indulgences, liquor, or meat eating, from occasionally calling those who adhere to the precepts men of indiscriminate practice, and from teaching that those who rely on Amida's principal vow have no reason to fear committing evil (*zōaku*).
5. As an ignorant being who is unable to distinguish between right and wrong, refrain from deviations from the scriptures, from what is not the teachings of your master, from arbitrarily putting forward your own doctrines, from needlessly seeking out disputes, from being laughed at by the wise, and from leading the ignorant astray.
6. In your state of ignorance, refrain from delighting so much in rhetoric, from knowing nothing of the true teachings, from expounding various heresies (*jahō*), and from converting ignorant priests and lay people to them.
7. Refrain from expounding heresies, which are not the Buddhist teachings, and from regarding them as the true teachings. Refrain from the deception of calling them the teachings of your master.[19]

Hōnen's injunction against these actions suggests the kind of behavior that was proliferating among his followers. It included disdain toward the teachings of the traditional schools and derision of their adherents. Over and above this unseemly conduct, the open encouragement of priests to violate the clerical precepts by eating meat, drinking liquor, and succumbing to sexual temptations represents an unveiled attack on both religious discipline and the mores of society. Such conduct left Hōnen's following vulnerable to the charge of preaching licensed evil (*zōaku muge*), an accusation that dogged the Pure Land movement during much of its development and which later resulted in controversies and upheavals in the Shinshū also.[20] Hōnen himself, by using the term heresy in articles six and seven, made it clear that many of the activities and beliefs current among his followers were intolerable in his own eyes, not to mention in the eyes of religious authorities. These heresies, circulating in the guise of Hōnen's teachings, were as much responsible for his 1207 exile as Hōnen's own advocacy of the exclusive *nembutsu*.

Details of the 1207 suppression are contained not only in Jien's *Gukanshō*

("Notes of My Foolish Views") but also in a number of Shinshū sources, including the appendix to the *Tannishō* ("Notes Lamenting Deviations"). The account there indicates that by order of the retired emperor Gotoba two other disciples besides Anrakubō and Jūren were put to death. They were Saii Zenshakubō and Shōganbō. Moreover, a total of eight *nembutsu* priests were ordered into exile: Hōnen to Tosa, Shinran to Echigo, Jōmonbō to Bingo, Chōsai Zenkōbō to Hōki, Kōkakubō to Izu, and Gyōkū Hōhonbō to Sado. Kōsai and Shōkū, the remaining two sentenced to exile, were allowed to remain in Kyoto in the custody of Jien.[21] The banishment of Hōnen temporarily pacified Kyoto of the commotion that the Pure Land movement had generated, but it did not extinguish the movement altogether. Rather, by dispatching Hōnen's followers to different provinces, the authorities unwittingly disseminated his teachings throughout the country, and in 1211, when Hōnen was allowed to return to Kyoto, the movement reappeared in the capital with renewed vitality. The resilience of the Pure Land movement confounded the Buddhist establishment and prompted further suppressions in subsequent decades.

THE PURE LAND MOVEMENT

Hōnen died in Kyoto in 1212. In that year Myōe (1173–1232), an eminent Kegon priest and erstwhile associate of Hōnen's, composed his *Zaijarin* ("Pivotal [Points] Shattering Heresy"), the first major denunciation of Hōnen's *Senjakushū* ("Singled-Out Collection") by an orthodox Buddhist priest. In it he attacked Hōnen on two counts: for omitting the aspiration for enlightenment (*bodaishin*) from his path to Pure Land via the exclusive *nembutsu* and for portraying the traditional Buddhist schools as a band of thieves (*gunzoku*).[22] By this time, however, Hōnen's followers were so firmly committed to his teachings that the exclusive *nembutsu* was assured of survival far beyond Hōnen's time. Shōkū, Kōsai, Ryūkan, Chōsai (1184–1266), and other major disciples were all active in Kyoto and the vicinity. Benchō (1162–1238), who had studied under Hōnen from 1197 to 1204, was successfully propagating the *nembutsu* on the island of Kyūshū to the west. Shinran, who had been exiled to the province of Echigo, was on the verge of moving to the Kantō, the eastern provinces, where he would win an enthusiastic following to the Pure Land teachings. Within another half century Ippen (1239–89), who learned of the exclusive *nembutsu* from Shōkū's disciple Shōtatsu, would be traveling the length of Japan chanting the *nembutsu*, distributing amulets inscribed *Namu Amida Butsu*, and converting people to the practice. These efforts collectively carried the Pure Land teachings to diverse regions of the country and to all segments of society.

Hōnen's followers, though committed to propagating his teachings, were far from united in their understanding and exposition of them. Kōsai, for example, advocated a single *nembutsu* doctrine (*ichinengi*): that one and only one *nembutsu* assures birth in Pure Land, since in that *nembutsu* the faith of the believer becomes one with the wisdom of the Buddha. Any *nembutsu* over and above that is extraneous.[23] Ryūkan, on the other hand, is attributed with a repeated *nembutsu* doctrine (*tanengi*): that the *nembutsu* must be spoken repeatedly throughout one's life, and only after it is finally spoken on one's deathbed is birth in Pure Land assured.[24] Shōkū presented the *nembutsu* as the sole cause of birth in Pure Land and as the essence of Amida's principal vow. Other religious practices, he asserted, have no significance in the vow.[25] Chōsai, however, maintained that both the *nembutsu* and other religious practices are propounded in Amida's vows and consequently lead to birth in Pure Land.[26] Benchō, while stressing the importance of chanting the *nembutsu* regularly, admitted that other religious practices can also contribute to birth in Pure Land.[27] Shinran, by contrast, pointed to faith lying behind the *nembutsu* as the true cause of birth in Pure Land.[28] Ippen held that with even a single *nembutsu* one achieves immediate birth in Pure Land in this lifetime and in the very body in which one dwells.[29] In short, numerous issues divided the followers of Hōnen's teachings. The most prominent of these issues were the single versus the repeated *nembutsu*, the emphasis on faith versus the encouragement of practice, and the power of Amida versus the effort of the believer.[30] These differences eventually split the Pure Land movement into innumerable branches and factions, even as it continued to attract believers during the three centuries after Hōnen's death.

The popularization of the exclusive *nembutsu* occurred at a time when Japan was undergoing profound social and political changes. One reason that many aristocratic leaders looked upon the Pure Land movement with trepidation is that its teachings were often embraced by those who sought to undermine their authority. This authority was exerted through a system of provincial estates (*shōen*) from which aristocratic society drew its wealth. The schools of Old Buddhism were an integral part of this network of control, since they also claimed proprietorship of estates and exercised taxation rights over them. This economic and political structure began to deteriorate with the rise to power of the samurai class in the provinces and later with the struggle for autonomous villages by peasants working on estates. The founding of the Kamakura military government, or *bakufu*, in 1185 was an early landmark in this process of change. In such an environment of political and social transition, the *nembutsu* came to mean different things to different people. Aristocrats in Kyoto generally followed the traditional interpretations of the orthodox Buddhist schools, treating the *nembutsu* as an ancillary practice to other religious observances. Samurai adhered to the *nembutsu* as a refuge in the face of death in battle. Lowborn townsmen and peasants in the countryside often turned to it as a deterrent against misfortune or as a deliverance from the religious consequences of evil deeds.[31] Of the many interpretations of the *nembutsu* in circulation, those emphasizing practice or the effort of the believer were closest to the position of the traditional schools of Buddhism and were therefore more likely to be tolerated. Those which rejected practice and highlighted faith were frequently blamed for social unrest and hence became perennial targets of suppression. Among the eight *nembutsu* priests sentenced to exile in 1207, Kōsai, Shōkū, Gyōkū, and Shinran are known to have stressed faith in their teachings.

Suppression of the exclusive *nembutsu* began during Hōnen's lifetime and continued at frequent intervals throughout the next century—at least twelve documented instances between the years 1207 and 1330.[32] During these suppressions the gathering places of *nembutsu* adherents were often attacked and their leaders banished. In a 1227 incident, for example, militant priests from Mt. Hiei swept down on the grave site of Hōnen, leaving it in ruins and driving Kōsai, Ryūkan, and Kūamidabutsu into exile.[33] Generally, Mt. Hiei was the most outspoken proponent of suppression and the most aggressive agent in implementing it.[34] Nonetheless, the other major temples, as well as Kyoto's aristocratic authorities and the Kamakura *bakufu*, had a stake in quelling *nembutsu* unrest and therefore took part in suppressions at one time or another. Although the suppressions began with the exclusive *nembutsu* as their target, in later centuries the Shinshū, under the sobriquet Ikkōshū, or "Single-minded school," displaced it as the primary object of persecution.

Each suppression curbed the Pure Land movement briefly and cleansed Kyoto of its more radical elements, but in the long run Pure Land adherents learned to live with this threat and to capitalize on it where they could. For instance, they spread their teachings to remote provinces when expelled from Kyoto, and in the countryside Pure Land believers often organized themselves into tight-knit groups centered around a meeting place (*dōjō*), thereby creating a social unit to encourage individuals in their beliefs and to shore them up in times of stress.[35] On the whole, suppression made these groups cautious and defensive, and it fostered a persecution consciousness in them. When such a community became isolated, it provided fertile ground for secret doctrinal transmissions and concealed religious practices, all of which were shielded from exposure by the defense mechanisms of the community. Hence, suppression occasionally yielded the opposite effect to what was intended. Instead of eradicating heresy, it sometimes generated an environment in which deviant beliefs and practices could survive, proliferate, and diversify.

Shinran and his teachings were one product of this religious ferment of the thirteenth century. Though his teachings later emerged as the most popular form of Pure Land Buddhism, during Shinran's own lifetime they were merely one philosophy of Pure Land among many in circulation. Like other leading figures of the Pure Land movement, Shinran claimed his teachings to be true, but suffered attacks and accusations of heresy from the religious establishment because of his departure from traditional doctrine. Consequently, Shinran's own idea of orthodoxy and heresy does not represent the common view of Buddhism held by his contemporaries, but rather the private reflections of one religious dissident of the period.

CHAPTER
3

SHINRAN AND
HIS TEACHINGS

Shinran (1173-1262) stands as the indisputable starting point of Shin thought and as the universally acknowledged founder of the Shinshū school.[1] This is an honor that Shinran himself would have shunned. During the last few years of his life he was aware that his teachings had attracted a dedicated following, and he was tantalized by the prestige and influence they accorded him. At one point he even admitted "desiring to be a teacher of others for fame and profit."[2] But he made this statement not as a goal to which he seriously aspired but as a confession of his own selfish inclinations. In moments of deepest introspection he felt himself unworthy and unqualified for such a position of esteem. When actually confronted with followers claiming him as their religious master, Shinran disavowed having any disciples of his own and presented himself merely as a follower of Hōnen.[3] To this extent he eschewed the role of religious master and sectarian founder. Notwithstanding his protestations, a religious movement arose in Shinran's wake heralding him as its founder. From these beginnings the Shinshū emerged.

For all Shinran's religious importance, the historical details of his life are obscure. Late sectarian biographies are so interlaced with legend that they have little historical credibility.[4] Even the *Godenshō* ("The Biography"), the oldest and most reliable one written by Kakunyo three decades after Shinran's death, must be used with caution, since its primary objective is to portray Shinran as a manifestation of Amida Buddha, a characterization that Shinran would have decried.[5] Several historians in the late nineteenth and early twentieth centuries criticized the Shinshū's sectarian biographies for their apocryphal embellishments and began to question whether an authentic image of Shinran could ever be retrieved, since there were no references to him in nonsectarian sources of the period.[6] This controversy in the scholarly community stimulated a search for the historical Shinran. Eventually in 1921 questions about Shinran's historicity were laid to rest with the discovery of a collection of letters known as the *Eshinni shōsoku*, written by Shinran's wife, Eshinni (b.1182), and containing accounts of several episodes in his life.[7]   Since then the business of reconstructing Shinran's biography has been long and painstaking, and even today the process goes on.   Little by little new sources of information have come to light, many of which corroborate Kakunyo's original "Biography."   At present the basic sources for Shinran's life are Kakunyo's "Biography," Eshinni's letters, and Shinran's own writings.[8]

Shinran left behind a fairly extensive literary corpus comprising doctrinal treatises, commentaries, religious tracts, letters, hymns (*wasan*), and other assorted pieces.   Some of these are dated and therefore provide a chronological framework for the development of his thought.   His monumental work, the *Kyōgyōshinshō* ("Teaching, Practice, Faith, and Enlightenment"), was composed over the course of two or three decades during the middle of his life, and it survives in an original manuscript which was apparently one of Shinran's intermediate working copies.   To the extent that earlier segments of this manuscript can be distinguished from later additions, it is clear that Shinran continued to expand and deepen his ideas over this period.   Since the vast majority of Shinran's writings were done after the *Kyōgyōshinshō*, during the last fifteen years of his life, they represent an elaboration of the concepts presented there.   By using all these writings, along with Eshinni's letters and Kakunyo's "Biography," it is possible to construct a general picture of the events in Shinran's life as well as the internal thought processes that led him to his view of religious truth.

SHINRAN'S EARLY YEARS

Shinran was born in 1173.[9]   According to Kakunyo's "Biography," he was the son of a Kyoto aristocrat named Hino Arinori.[10]   Other historical materials neither confirm nor contradict this pedigree, but the Hino house clearly had close ties with Shinran's family from an early period in Shinshū history.   His youngest daughter, Kakushinni (1224–83), was married to Hino Hirotsuna (d. 1249?), and subsequent descendants of Shinran's at the Honganji temple enjoyed the nominal status of adopted son in the Hino family.[11]   Shinran himself, whether or not a scion of the Hino, did not come from humble origins.   The level of education reflected in his writings and the ownership of servants (*genin*) in his family suggest that he was a product of at least the lower aristocracy.[12]

The exact reasons for Shinran's entry into the Buddhist priesthood are not known, but Kakunyo's "Biography" states that he underwent the tonsure at the age of nine under the Tendai priest Jien, the one who later criticized Hōnen and the Pure Land movement in the *Gukanshō* ("Notes of My Foolish Views").[13]   Shinran thereupon received a thorough education in the Buddhist classics, as indicated by the diverse sources cited in his writings.   His *Kyōgyōshinshō*, for instance, draws from such formidable Buddhist sutras as the *Nehangyō* (Skt. *Mahāparinirvāṇasūtra*), or "Nirvāṇa Sutra," and the *Kegonkyō* (Skt. *Avataṃsaka-*

sūtra), or "Flower Garland Sutra," and from numerous minor works such as the *Lo-pang wen-lei* ("Selected Passages on the [Pure Land] Paradise") and the *Mappō tōmyōki* ("Record of the Lamp in [the Age of] the Dharma's Decline").[14] Shinran's precise position, once inducted into the Tendai priesthood, is noted in a letter of Eshinni's: "The master served as a *dōsō* [hall priest] at Mt. Hiei."[15] The term *dōsō* was originally thought to mean *dōshu* ("hall member or attendant"), the intermediate rank in the Enryakuji's clerical hierarchy, but more recent evidence suggests it was a specific type of priest attached to one of Mt. Hiei's Jōgyōdō, or "Halls of Constant Practice."[16] In these halls a variety of *nembutsu* ceremonies were performed, including a ninety-day *nembutsu* meditation retreat (*jōgyō zammai*) and the continual *nembutsu* chant (*fudan nembutsu*). These ceremonies were the dominant form of *nembutsu* practice at Mt. Hiei, and were incorporated into the framework of Tendai meditation and doctrine.[17] Jien, Shinran's tonsure master, had ties to at least one of these halls, the Shuryōgon'in in the Yokawa section of Mt. Hiei, and it was perhaps there that Shinran first served as a hall priest. The responsibility of hall priests in these ceremonies ranged from chorus chanting of sutras and the *nembutsu* to collecting offerings, thereby indicating a relatively low status in Mt. Hiei's scholarmonk (*gakushō*) class.[18] In this environment Shinran had ample opportunity to ponder the meaning of the *nembutsu* and to experience the rigors of Tendai monastic discipline.

Dreams and visions are known to have played a momentous role in Shinran's religious development. References to them are found in his *Kyōgyōshinshō*, in Eshinni's letters, in Kakunyo's "Biography," and in an obscure work known as the *Shinran muki* ("Record of Shinran's Dreams").[19] One version of this last work describes three dreams that made a lasting impression on Shinran: one occurring in 1191, the second in 1200, and the third in 1201. The specific details, circumstances, and impact of Shinran's dreams are described differently in various sources, but in content the dreams all consisted of a miraculous figure appearing before Shinran and conveying a message to him in verse form. The figures most often mentioned are Shōtoku Taishi (574–622), the revered promulgator of Buddhism in Japan, and Kannon, one of the Bodhisattvas associated with Amida. Shinran came to regard Shōtoku Taishi as a manifestation of Kannon, and he venerated these two as Amida's agents working in the world.[20] As a result of these dreams, Shinran embarked on a new phase in his religious career, embracing Hōnen's exclusive *nembutsu* teaching and repudiating the clerical practices of the Tendai school.

One dream that marked a turning point in Shinran's life occurred at the Rokkakudō, a hexagonal temple in Kyoto containing an image of Kannon and supposedly founded by Shōtoku Taishi. Two different accounts of this dream survive, one in Eshinni's letters and the other in the "Record of Shinran's Dreams." Eshinni's version reads:

> [Shinran] left Mt. [Hiei] to seclude himself for a hundred days in the Rokkakudō temple. There he prayed concerning his next life, and at dawn

on the ninety-fifth day he received in a revelation a message composed by Shōtoku Taishi. Immediately at dawn he left the place and, seeking a karmic link that would lead him to salvation in the next life, he went and met the master Hōnen. . . .[21]

"Record of Shinran's Dreams," by contrast, states:

The Great World-Saving Bodhisattva [Kannon] of the Rokkakudō was revealed in the form of a monk of upright appearance. Dressed in simple white clerical robes and seated on a giant white lotus, he made this pronouncement to Shinran:

If the believer, because of the fruition of karma, is driven by sexual desire,
Then I shall take on the body of a beautiful woman to be ravished by him.
Throughout his entire life I shall adorn him well,
And at death I shall lead him to birth in Pure Land.[22]

The World-Saving Bodhisattva recited this message and then made the following pronouncement: "This message is my vow. Expound it to all living beings." Based on this pronouncement, I realized that I should tell this to millions of sentient beings, and I then awoke from my dream.[23]

These two accounts differ concerning the content of Shinran's dream and his response to it. In addition, two separate dates are given for Shinran's Rokkakudō seclusion: 1201 and 1203.[24] Whether these discrepancies indicate two separate dreams, both at the Rokkakudō, or whether dates and details of a single dream have been confused is uncertain.[25] What is clear is that during this period Shinran was in a state of religious turmoil. He was distressed over his fate in the next life, and he was apparently tormented by sexual impulses. The two were connected in that abandoning his priestly celibacy would jeopardize any hope of salvation, for it would constitute a violation of the Buddhist precepts which Tendai monks were sworn to obey. The tension between the two played on Shinran in his dreams and ultimately led him to drastic action. Specifically, it caused him to forsake monastic life at Mt. Hiei, to convert to Hōnen's teachings, and eventually to marry and beget a family.

EMBRACING THE PURE LAND TEACHINGS

Near the end of the *Kyōgyōshinshō* ("Teaching, Practice, Faith, and Enlightenment") Shinran wrote:

I, the Bald-headed Fool Shinran, in the year 1201 rejected rigorous religious practices and took refuge in the principal vow. In the year 1205 I received [Hōnen's] kind permission to make a copy of [his work] *Senjakushū* ("Singled-Out Collection"). During the same year on the fourth day in the middle of the first month of summer, I had Hōnen inscribe it inside in his own handwriting with the [full] title, *Senjaku hongan nembutsushū* ("Collection [of Scriptural

Passages] on the Nembutsu of the Principle Vow Singled Out [by Amida]"),
as well as with the words, "*Namu Amida Butsu*: Among the acts leading to birth
in Pure Land, the *nembutsu* is primary," and with my clerical name Shakkū.
On the same day I was entrusted with Hōnen's portrait and was allowed to
make a copy of it.[26]

Shinran definitely saw 1201 as the turning point in his life. It was at this junc-
ture that he relinquished all prospects of achieving salvation via Tendai's
program of clerical precepts, meditation, and cultivation of knowledge. In its
place he embraced the Pure Land teachings with Amida's principal vow as their
scriptural basis. Shinran considered the clearest elucidation of these teachings
to be Hōnen's *Senjakushū* ("Singled-Out Collection"):

> The core of the true teachings (*shinshū*) and the essence of the *nembutsu* are con-
> tained in this [work]. Whoever reads it will comprehend easily. Truly this is
> a rare and superlative masterpiece, a profound and unexcelled treasure. For
> days and years thousands of people have received [Hōnen's] instruction but,
> whether close to him or distant, only a few individuals have been allowed to
> copy this. I, however, was able to transcribe this work and to copy [Hōnen's]
> portrait. This is a blessing [*toku*] of the true act, the exclusive *nembutsu*, and it
> is an indication that birth in Pure Land is assured. Because of this, I [can
> hardly] hold back tears of joy and sorrow as I record these events of the past.[27]

Just as Shinran viewed the *Senjakushū* as the quintessential summation of the
Pure Land teachings, so he regarded Hōnen as the good master (*yoki hito*) imparting Amida's message to the world.[28] Shinran found it especially gratifying
that Hōnen permitted him to make a copy of the work. This was a privilege
reserved for only a select few disciples.

The precise relationship that arose between Hōnen and Shinran is difficult to
assess because of conflicting evidence in different sources. Shinran, for his part,
revered Hōnen and followed him with unswerving allegiance. A passage in
Eshinni's letters reflects this:

> People would say all types of things about where the master [Hōnen] might
> go. They would even say that he was headed for an evil rebirth (*akudō*). When-
> ever people spoke such things, [Shinran] would reply, "I am one who believes
> that I would even go [with him], since from realm to realm and from rebirth
> to rebirth I am lost already."[29]

Shinran held out no hope for salvation apart from Hōnen's teachings. If following him meant falling into one of the hells, Shinran was willing to accept
that fate. In short, his devotion to Hōnen was complete, and his gratitude
lifelong. Hōnen's estimation of Shinran, on the other hand, is less clear. According to Kakunyo's "Biography," Shinran was one of Hōnen's premier disciples, outshining Genchi and others.[30] But this characterization is perhaps
more hagiographic than factual, for outside of Shinshū sources no such description of Shinran can be found.[31] A more accurate reflection of Shinran's stand-

ing in Hōnen's following is the collection of signatures attached to Hōnen's *Shichikajō kishōmon* ("Seven Article Pledge") of 1204. Among the 190 names listed there, Shinran's appears in eighty-seventh position, far behind Genchi's.[32] This would place Shinran in the intermediate ranks of Hōnen's following. Notwithstanding this evidence, Shinran must have been a member of Hōnen's inner circle if he was allowed to copy the *Senjakushū* ("Singled-Out Collection"). Permission to do so was not given lightly. Hence, from Hōnen's point of view Shinran was probably a trusted disciple but not his leading protégé, whereas in Shinran's eyes Hōnen was the foremost religious personage of the period.

Hōnen's influence on Shinran was far-reaching, but the actual time they spent together was only six years. The event that separated them was their banishment in 1207 to different parts of the country. Hōnen was ordered to Tosa and Shinran to Echigo.[33] From that time Shinran never saw his religious mentor again. Their exile was part of the 1207 suppression of the exclusive *nembutsu* sparked by the Anrakubō and Jūren incident. That episode discredited Hōnen's Pure Land movement and substantiated accusations of wrongdoing and heresy leveled by Mt. Hiei and the Kōfukuji temple. Hōnen, as the movement's leader, was an obvious target for punishment. Shinran must have been considered a radical element also, though the precise charge against him is not known. Some scholars suspect that he was exiled because he had taken a wife while still a priest, thereby violating the clerical precepts.[34]

Ordained priests were forbidden to marry because the attachments, desires, and responsibilities of married life were regarded as detrimental to religious advancement. Nonetheless, marriage would not ordinarily warrant such a harsh punishment as exile. There had been, after all, numerous instances in Japanese history of monks taking wives.[35] As expressed in the *Shasekishū* ("Sand and Pebbles"), a collection of Buddhist stories composed around Shinran's time, "One has rarely heard in past years of a religious man (*shōnin*) during this last age (*matsudai*) who has not taken a wife."[36] Still, the Buddhist establishment did not condone the practice, no matter how widespread it was. Therefore, priests who married were often on the fringes of Japan's religious order, or at least discrete in their relations. If Shinran made no attempt to conceal his marriage, particularly in Kyoto where the traditional schools were strongest, their religious leaders may have regarded his openness as an intentional affront or as a direct challenge to their authority. When couched in the context of the Pure Land movement, Shinran's marriage was probably interpreted as a prime example of the corrosive effects of Hōnen's teachings. Hence, Shinran's exile may have been an attempt to excise what the authorities considered the most heinous effects of Hōnen's exclusive *nembutsu*.

In 1204, when Shinran signed the *Shichikajō kishōmon* ("Seven Article Pledge"), he prefaced his signature with the word "priest" (*sō*).[37] Apparently, he still adhered to the clerical precepts at that point, and thus had not taken a wife. By contrast, he described himself in 1207 as "neither priest nor layman" (*sō ni arazu zoku ni arazu*), and he adopted the pejorative title *toku*, or "Bald-head."[38] The *Shasekishū* ("Sand and Pebbles") indicates that this term was used to refer to monks who had "broken the precepts without any sense of remorse" (*hakai muzan*).[39] Shinran no doubt assumed this ignominious sobriquet as a public acknowledgment of his own fallen state. Therefore, it is likely that Shinran married sometime between 1204 and 1207.

The details of Shinran's family life are fragmentary and difficult to piece together. There have been countless theories over whether Shinran had one wife, two, or even three; over when he got married and where; and over how many children he had and by whom.[40] What is certain about Shinran's married life is that he had at least one wife, Eshinni, and that together they had at least four children, and more likely six.[41] Four are mentioned by name in Eshinni's letters, and a fifth, the oldest son Zenran (d. 1292), is known from Shinran's letters.[42] Eshinni noted in one of her letters that their son Shinrenbō was born in 1211.[43] According to later genealogies he was Shinran's third or fourth child.[44] If one allows a year or more between the birth of each child, it is reasonable to assume that Shinran had taken a wife by the time he was sent into exile in 1207. If the woman he married then was Eshinni, the harshness of his exile in Echigo was probably tempered by the fact that she came from a family with connections in that province.[45]

According to one of Hōnen's biographies, his radical disciple Kōsai had a follower named Zenshin who propagated the controversial single *nembutsu* doctrine in Echigo province.[46] Shinran also went by the name Zenshin, identical in pronunciation but differing by one character, and for this reason some rival Pure Land schools have identified Shinran as that person.[47] It is problematic, however, to equate Shinran with Kōsai's disciple because Shinran never expressed allegiance to Kōsai and never presented himself as a proponent of the single *nembutsu* doctrine.[48] At this stage in Shinran's career he probably spent little time actually propagating the Pure Land teachings. In a list of his direct disciples compiled in the early 1300s, only one person from Echigo is mentioned.[49] Most of the others were inhabitants of Kantō, the eastern provinces of Japan. This distribution implies that the evangelistic phase of Shinran's life began only after he moved to the Kantō around 1214.[50] During the seven years he lived in Echigo, Shinran occupied himself more with study and reflection than with proselytization. In this sense his years there were a continuation of the Pure Land investigations he began under Hōnen.

The only source revealing Shinran's thinking during this formative period of his career is a pair of commentaries he composed on the "Pure Land Meditation Sutra" and the "Smaller Pure Land Sutra."[51] These are Shinran's earliest known writings. In content they consist of the text of the two sutras flanked by relevant quotations from assorted Pure Land works, some written in the margins and others on the reverse side of the paper. Though the manuscript is undated, internal evidence suggests that it was drafted prior to 1217, possibly as early as Shinran's years in Kyoto with Hōnen.[52] In the commentaries Shinran made no statements of his own. Instead, he limited himself to quoting from other works. It is clear from the contents that at this stage in his thinking Shinran was overwhelmingly influenced by Hōnen. The principal sources he cited,

Shan-tao's *Kuan ching shu* ("Commentary on the Pure Land Meditation Sutra")
and *Fa-shih tsan* ("Praises for [Pure Land] Services"), were precisely the works
that Hōnen relied on to interpret the Pure Land sutras.[53] Moreover, the central
theme of Shinran's commentaries—that is, that the spoken *nembutsu* is the single
and exclusive practice conforming to Amida's eighteenth vow—was the very
doctrine to which Hōnen dedicated his entire ministry. Faith, which subsequently became the hallmark of Shinran's teachings, was not yet a conspicuous
theme.[54] In short, Shinran did not go much beyond Shan-tao's and Hōnen's
exposition of the subject. His ideas, it seems, were still in an embryonic state.
Nevertheless, these early commentaries stand as a harbinger to his magnum
opus, the *Kyōgyōshinshō*, for most of the quotations in them were subsequently
incorporated into that work.[55]

The logical steps by which Shinran arrived at his conception of faith are traditionally described as a conversion via the three vows (*sangan tennyū*).[56] Shinran
considered his own religious development to be in three stages, corresponding
to Amida's nineteenth, twentieth, and eighteenth vows respectively. Through
a highly idiosyncratic interpretation of these vows, Shinran construed each as a
distinctly different path to Pure Land. In the nineteenth vow he singled out the
expression "performing virtuous deeds" (*shu sho kudoku*), and he took this to mean
that a person could seek birth in Pure Land by means of manifold good works
and practices (*manzen shogyō*).[57] He believed, however, that through such acts
one could not achieve birth in Amida's true Pure Land (*shinjitsu hōdo*) but only
in an expedient form of Pure Land (*hōben kedo*), which he euphemistically called
birth in the forest of twin *śāla* trees (*sōju ringe ōjō*), located on the fringes (*henji*)
of Pure Land. For that reason he described this approach as the provisional
path (*kemon*) or elemental path (*yōmon*) to Pure Land.[58]

In the twentieth vow Shinran focused on the idea of "cultivating the basis of
all virtue" (*jiki sho tokuhon*), and he interpreted this as chanting Amida's name,
for he considered the *nembutsu* to be the source of all virtue and good (*zenpon
tokuhon*).[59] Shinran regarded this stage as one step higher than the previous one,
since here virtuous deeds and good works are relinquished in favor of the *nembutsu* as the means of achieving birth in Pure Land. Consequently, he called
this approach the true path (*shinmon*). Still, Shinran did not consider this the
highest stage because in it the *nembutsu* is treated as if it were an act or creation
of the believer. Therefore, one is not yet cognizant that the power of salvation
stems from Amida rather than from the believer. For that reason, pursuit of
Pure Land via this path is called birth that is difficult to comprehend (*nanji ōjō*).
As long as believers chant the *nembutsu* without realizing that its saving power
derives from Amida's vow, they cannot be born in the true Pure Land but only
in the so-called jeweled prison (*shippō rōgoku*) or the womb palace (*taigū*) of Pure
Land.[60]

Beyond these two stages there is a third one corresponding to the "vow that
Amida singled out" (*senjaku no gan*)—namely, the eighteenth vow—and symbol-
ized by the term "faith" (*shingyō*) in that vow. Shinran considered this to be
Amida's ultimate teaching. This path is predicated totally on the power of the

Buddha (*tariki*), whereas the cause of salvation in the previous two is the believer's own effort (*jiriki*). Faith, according to Shinran, means not doubting the Buddha's wisdom or his compassionate vow to save all sentient beings. Where faith exists, so does the realization that the power of salvation lies with Amida. Hence, no calculated attempt to win salvation is needed. The *nembutsu* spoken at this stage is not a personal act but the act of Amida bestowed on the believer. It is inextricably linked to faith as the true cause of birth in Pure Land. Through faith, one is born in Amida's true Pure Land, not in the expedient realm. Because salvation occurs through his unfathomable (*fukashigi*) vow, Shinran called it birth in Pure Land that is difficult to fathom (*nanjigi ōjō*).[61]

This three-fold schema was the progression in which Shinran viewed his own conversion to Amida's principal vow and his own experience of faith. In an autobiographical passage contained in the *Kyōgyōshinshō*, he described this progression:

> Therefore, reverencing the expositions of the treatise masters and relying on the exhortations of the religious teachers, I, the Bald-headed Fool Shinran, abandoned forever the provisional path of manifold practices and good works, and separated myself once and for all from birth in the forest of twin *śāla* trees. I turned to the true path, the basis of virtue and good, and gave rise to the aspiration for birth that is difficult to comprehend. But now I have utterly abandoned the expediency of the true path, and have converted to the ocean-like vow singled out [by Amida]. I have separated myself straightway from the aspiration for birth that is difficult to comprehend, and I long to attain birth that is difficult to fathom. The "vow for attainment" is truly the reason for this.[62]

Shinran's language here is obscure and coded, as it is in many passages of the *Kyōgyōshinshō*, but his message is dramatic and profound. This statement traces Shinran's own spiritual journey from religious exertions, to the *nembutsu*, and finally to faith. Shinran first sought birth in Pure Land by means of religious practices and good works. But they constitute only a provisional path leading to an expedient realm, not to the true Pure Land. Shinran then turned to the *nembutsu*, the basis of virtue and good, thereby embarking on the true path. But without understanding Amida's eighteenth vow, this path also results in birth in the expedient realm. Finally, Shinran was awakened to the oceanlike vastness of the eighteenth vow, expansive enough to embrace even the most unworthy believer. That point marked Shinran's first moment of faith, assuring him of unfathomable birth in Amida's true Pure Land.

The exact period in Shinran's life when this inner realization took place has long been a matter of controversy. The majority of scholars claim that it occurred around 1201, when Shinran became a member of Hōnen's following. Others argue that it was later—either during his study with Hōnen; or while exiled in Echigo province; or in 1214, upon moving to the Kantō region; or in 1224, when he first drafted the *Kyōgyōshinshō*; or even as late as 1231, during an illness.[63] The last of these is an event recorded in one of Eshinni's letters. Specifically, it relates that in 1231 Shinran fell ill with a fever, and as he lay quietly in bed he recited the "Larger Pure Land Sutra" to himself over and over again. After two days of chanting, he brought to mind a similar experience he had had during his move to the Kantō region seventeen or eighteen years earlier. On that occasion he had set out to recite the three Pure Land sutras a thousand times for the benefit and salvation of all sentient beings. Before he had finished his recitations he thought to himself: if one has faith oneself and causes others to have faith (*jishin kyōninshin*), there is no truer gratitude for the Buddha's gift of salvation. Outside of the *nembutsu* of faith, nothing is necessary for birth in Pure Land. Shinran reflected deeply on human attachments, especially on personal efforts (*jiriki*) aimed at salvation. He thereupon stopped his chanting of the sutra, realizing it to be an act of vanity on his part and a presumption of his own religious power.[64]

This event clearly exemplifies Shinran's turn from personal endeavors to faith as the basis for birth in Pure Land—that is, his conversion via the three vows. It is doubtful, however, that this was the first moment in which that realization had arisen in him. The incident probably represents a deepening of such a realization, or a continuing affirmation of faith against the recurring and seductive tendency to view personal religious efforts as the source of salvation. Hence, Shinran's so-called conversion via the three vows might not refer to any specific incident in his life but rather to a gradual realization arrived at over a long period of time.[65] The religious life that Shinran envisioned from this experience did not stop at "having faith oneself" (*jishin*). It extended also to "causing others to have faith" (*kyōninshin*). The aspiration to awaken others to faith arises from one's own sense of indebtedness to Amida and from the desire to share the joys and rewards of faith with others.[66] This intimate link between one's own experience of faith and the attempt to communicate it to others was the basis for Shinran's activities as a religious teacher in the Kantō region.

Shinran moved from Echigo province to the Kantō around 1214 and lived there approximately twenty years. During this time he actively preached the Pure Land teachings throughout the area. According to Kakunyo's "Biography," Shinran settled in the village of Inada in Hitachi province and won numerous converts and followers in the vicinity. He was so successful that a local *yamabushi*, or wandering mountain priest, plotted to attack him out of envy and spite. But when he finally came face to face with Shinran his enmity evaporated, and he became one of Shinran's trusted disciples, named Myōhō-bō.[67] The geographical extent of Shinran's proselytization is unclear, but later records show that the bulk of his direct disciples lived in Hitachi and the surrounding provinces.[68] Their association with Shinran presumably began during his two decades of residency there, and they subsequently assumed the leadership of congregations devoted to his teachings. Religious groups of this type, which centered around *dōjō* or meeting places, became the predominant organizational unit of Shinshū followers. This pattern of organization may have begun even while Shinran was still living in the Kantō.

The exact content of Shinran's teachings to these followers is difficult to determine because the only surviving document written by him during this period is a copy of the *Yuishinshō* ("Notes on Faith Alone"), a short Pure Land tract composed by another disciple of Hōnen's named Seikaku (1166-1235).[69] It is likely, however, that the ideas contained in Shinran's *Kyōgyōshinshō* were very much a part of his message to Kantō believers, for there is evidence that Shinran completed an early draft of the work in 1224, while living at Inada.[70] Some scholars even maintain that the reason Shinran made the move from Echigo province to the Kantō region was to write the *Kyōgyōshinshō*, since the Buddhist sources needed for its composition were available there.[71] Whatever the reason may have been, the *Kyōgyōshinshō* began to take shape from this period and over the next two or three decades emerged as Shinran's definitive statement on Pure Land Buddhism.

THE KYŌGYŌSHINSHŌ

The *Kyōgyōshinshō* is a difficult work, but it is the most extensive exposition available of Shinran's religious thought. Its formal title is *Ken jōdo shinjitsu kyōgyōshō monrui*: "Selected Passages Revealing the True Teaching, Practice, and Enlightenment of Pure Land."[72] In structure the work is divided into six fascicles dealing in succession with the themes: Teaching (*kyō*), Practice (*gyō*), Faith (*shin*), Enlightenment (*shō*), True Buddha and Pure Land (*shinbutsudo*), and Expedient Buddha Body and Pure Land (*keshindo*). The name *Kyōgyōshinshō* is a contraction of the titles of the first four fascicles. The ideas of teaching, practice, and enlightenment were long-standing Buddhist concepts in Shinran's day, defining the essential components in the Buddhist path to salvation.[73] Shinran added to them the element of faith, which in his teachings constitutes the most important factor leading to birth in Pure Land. Because the term *faith* is left out of the formal title of the work, some scholars speculate that the fascicle on faith was originally composed as a separate piece and only later incorporated into the work.[74] Those who oppose this view argue that the idea of faith is presupposed in the concept of practice, and for that reason it is not mentioned in the full title.[75] Whatever the structural evolution of the *Kyōgyōshinshō* may have been, the chapter on faith and the one on the expedient Buddha and Pure Land are the longest sections of the work and the crux of Shinran's teachings.

In composition the *Kyōgyōshinshō* consists of a collection of quotations extracted from a wide range of Buddhist writings including sutras, commentaries, and treatises originating in India, China, Korea, and Japan. Interspersed among the quotations are brief statements and interpretations by Shinran. The work resembles Hōnen's *Senjakushū* ("Singled-Out Collection") to the extent that it marshals a variety of Buddhist sources to argue that Pure Land is the true and appropriate path to salvation in this day and age, but it is more difficult to understand than Hōnen's work, since quotations are often presented with no interpretation whatsoever or with overly terse and enigmatic comments. In many cases Shinran's statements are full of poetic symbolism. For example, the image of the ocean appears frequently, in some places used to convey the breadth and depth of Amida's vow to save all sentient beings and in other places to illustrate the vastness and profundity of human failings.[76] Understanding Shinran's intent occasionally hinges on nothing more than his punctuation of a particular quotation. Despite these complexities, the sheer bulk and diversity of topics in the *Kyōgyōshinshō*, when compared to Shinran's other writings, make it his premier work.

The date of composition of the *Kyōgyōshinshō* has also been an issue of dispute. Traditionally, the year 1224 has been given because that date appears in the last fascicle of the text.[77] Some scholars maintain, however, that most of the work was written later in Shinran's life after he had resettled in Kyoto.[78] They often point to the statement in the earliest commentary on the *Kyōgyōshinshō*, written in 1360 by Zonkaku, asserting that Shinran managed to assemble all the citations he wanted to use in the work but did not live long enough to edit (*saiji*) them properly.[79] Recent research on the so-called Bandō manuscript of the *Kyōgyōshinshō* has yielded more information about the evolution of the text. This manuscript is universally recognized as Shinran's own personal working copy.[80] Judging from the handwriting and the structure of characters, some scholars estimate that the main portion of the text was copied around 1235, approximately the time Shinran left the Kantō region to return to Kyoto.[81] That year probably does not mark the earliest draft of the *Kyōgyōshinshō* but only the period when the Bandō manuscript was done. For that reason the Bandō edition is considered an intermediate draft, and earlier versions perhaps go back to the traditional 1224 date. In the Bandō manuscript there are numerous passages rewritten and many new pages added, indicating that the text underwent at least two or three major revisions after the original copying was done. The work finally assumed tentative form around 1247 when, according to postscripts in two later editions of the *Kyōgyōshinshō*, Shinran allowed his cousin and disciple Sonren (b. 1182) to make a copy. Though this date is generally recognized as the terminus ad quem for the writing of the *Kyōgyōshinshō*, minor changes continued to be made in the Bandō manuscript for perhaps ten years after that.[82] Hence, Shinran worked on the *Kyōgyōshinshō* over a two-or-three decade period during which he refined his religious views and bolstered his assertions with citations from a wide variety of Buddhist writings.[83]

The context in which Shinran wrote the *Kyōgyōshinshō* was the continued popularization of the Pure Land teachings and the periodic suppression of them by civil and religious authorities. After Hōnen's death his followers spread his teachings to far-flung parts of the country and sought to defend them from his critics. The polemic against the exclusive *nembutsu* written by Myōe in 1212, the year of Hōnen's death, prompted a steady stream of defenses by Hōnen's disciples. Shinran's *Kyōgyōshinshō* stands out as one in that series.[84] At this early stage in the Pure Land movement the prevailing concern in these writings was to explicate the meaning of the *nembutsu* in terms of traditional Buddhist philosophy to show that the *nembutsu* is not an aberrant or heretical practice. One of the recurrent questions in these works is how the *nembutsu* is related to faith.

Shinran's *Kyōgyōshinshō* takes the decisive step of presenting faith as the central meaning of the *nembutsu*, and it draws from a variety of Buddhist sources, both Pure Land and otherwise, not used by Hōnen. Most prominently, T'an-luan's *Wang-sheng lun chu* ("Commentary on the Treatise on Birth in Pure Land")—with its emphasis on "singleness of heart" (*isshin*), interpreted by Shinran to mean faith—and the *Nehangyō* ("Nirvāṇa Sutra")—containing mainstream Mahāyāna concepts such as universal salvation, that "all sentient beings have the Buddha-nature," (*issai shujō shitsu u busshō*)—give the *Kyōgyōshinshō* an emphasis and a breadth somewhat different from Hōnen's *Senjakushū* ("Singled-Out Collection").[85] The work represents a maturing of Shinran's religious thinking and an indisputable step beyond the premises laid down by Hōnen. To that extent, Shinran's purpose in writing the *Kyōgyōshinshō* was not simply to answer the criticisms of the religious establishment against the new Pure Land teachings, but also to hammer out his own convictions and to substantiate them with passages from the Buddhist classics.[86] This combination of external events and internal reflections shaped the *Kyōgyōshinshō* into a complex patchwork of religious assertions, scriptural citations, personal testimony, and critique of opponents.

The content of the *Kyōgyōshinshō*, in its most elemental form, consists of the themes found in its six fascicles: Teaching, Practice, Faith, Enlightenment, True Buddha and Pure Land, and Expedient Buddha and Pure Land. In the first five fascicles Shinran presented what he considered to be the essential components and characteristics of true religious practice resulting in birth in Pure Land. In the sixth fascicle he outlined mistaken and false approaches to religion. The "true teaching" (*shinjitsu no kyō*), referred to in the first fascicle, is none other than the "Larger Pure Land Sutra." The preaching of this sutra was, according to Shinran, the primary purpose for Śākyamuni Buddha to appear in the world, and for that reason Shinran regarded Śākyamuni as an extension of Amida, working to lead sentient beings to salvation in Pure Land.[87] The message of the "Larger Sutra" is that Amida has established his vow out of compassion for unenlightened and lowly beings and has provided them with the "treasure of virtue" (*kudoku no hō*), an allusion to the *nembutsu*, which will deliver them into Pure Land. Shinran summed up the "Larger Sutra" by describing its essence (*shūchi*) as Amida's principal vow (*hongan*) and its embodiment (*tai*) as Amida's name (*myōgō*)—that is, the *nembutsu*.[88] These two components, the principal vow and the *nembutsu*, were each stressed to the exclusion of the other by the competing faith and practice factions of the Pure Land movement. Shinran, in his interpretation of the "true teaching," considered the two components united in the "Larger Pure Land Sutra," thereby avoiding the extremes of the factions.

The second fascicle of the *Kyōgyōshinshō* identifies "true practice" (*shinjitsu no gyō*) to be "uttering the name of the Tathāgata Amida." From the beginning this "great practice" (*daigyō*) is linked to "great faith" (*daishin*).[89] The central concern in this fascicle is to show that the *nembutsu* is the one true religious practice assuring birth in Pure Land. An explication of *Namu*, the first word in the *nembutsu*, reveals the nature and function of the practice. *Namu* means "I take refuge in" (*kimyō*), and seems to imply that the act of turning toward the Buddha is initiated by the believer. Shinran, however, interpreted "taking refuge" as the "beckoning command of the principal vow" (*hongan shōkan no chokumei*).[90] That is, the true practice of invoking Amida's name does not occur because of any calculated decision on a person's part but only because of the overwhelming magnetism of the principal vow, Amida's promise to save all sentient beings. The vow has the power to elicit the *nembutsu* from people. In that sense the *nembutsu* does not originate with the believer but with Amida, who established the principle vow. The *nembutsu*, then, is a creation of Amida's which he extends to the believer. Since it emerges from the wisdom, compassion, and power of Amida, it is an unfailing practice assuring birth in Pure Land. In order to derive this meaning from the many religious texts he quoted, Shinran often had to redefine the grammatical function of words, particularly the term *ekō* or *ese*, meaning to "transfer," "offer," or "extend" religious merit to others. This word appears in the eighteenth vow of the "Larger Sutra," as well as in countless other Pure Land texts, traditionally indicating that the believer offers up religious merit as an act of devotion to the Buddha or as an act of compassion for sentient beings. Shinran, by appending the honorific suffix *tamau* to this word, reversed the direction of merit transference, making the Buddha its source and the believer its recipient. When this grammatical change is applied to the *nembutsu*, the practice becomes Amida's gift to sentient beings, not the believer's act of devotion to Amida.[91] As true practice, the *nembutsu* is based on *tariki*, the power of the Buddha, not on *jiriki*, the effort of the believer.[92] This is what distinguishes "true practice and faith" (*shinjitsu no gyōshin*) from "expedient practice and faith" (*hōben no gyōshin*).[93]

The third fascicle of the *Kyōgyōshinshō* explores the nature and content of "true faith" (*shinjitsu no shin*). Faith's relation to practice is most clearly reflected in the statement: "True faith necessarily entails Amida's name, but Amida's name does not necessarily entail faith, [which is derived] from the power of [Amida's] vow."[94] The meaning of this statement is that true faith exists only in conjunction with the *nembutsu*, whether it is spoken or simply heard, but uttering Amida's name is not necessarily an indication of true faith. The *nembutsu* can be invoked without faith underlying it, but if it lacks true faith, the invocation of the name is not true practice but only the believer's insufficient attempt to secure salvation through personal effort. Shinran considered faith (*shingyō* or *shinjin*) to be the pivotal term in Amida's eighteenth vow, but he associated it with two other terms appearing in the vow: sincerity (*shishin*) and the desire to be born in Pure Land (*yokushō* or *ganshō*).[95] These three combined are identified as "singleness of heart" (*isshin*), and together they constitute true faith (*shinjitsu no shinjin*).[96] Hence, faith encompasses a threefold state of mind, but none of these components is the product of the believer's own effort. Like the *nembutsu*, each is bestowed on the believer by Amida Buddha.[97]

Faith is an endowment from Amida enjoyed by the believer once all willful assertion ceases. It is none other than the mind of Amida implanted in the believer. Thus, various dimensions of Amida's own nature become manifest in the believer—such as, the vow to attain Buddhahood (*gansabusshin*), the desire to save all sentient beings (*doshujōshin*), the aspiration for complete enlightenment (*daibodaishin*), and the experience of great compassion (*daijihishin*).[98] These aspects of Amida, which emerge out of his infinite light and wisdom (*muryō kōmyō e*) and which comprise faith, become internalized in the believer. To highlight this transforming effect of faith, Shinran equated the true believer with Maitreya, the next Buddha (*bendō Miroku*).[99] Where faith exists, Buddhahood is imminent and truly assured (*shōjō*). There is no retrogression (*futaiten*) from it, for faith is an indestructible state of mind (*kongōshin*).[100] Because Amida rather than the believer is the wellspring of faith and because Amida has promised to "embrace all and forsake none" (*sesshu fusha*), there is no one excluded from this gift.[101] This applies particularly to sentient beings least worthy of it, those difficult to save (*nange*) because they are diseased with wrongdoings which are difficult to cure (*nanji*). Relying on Amida's vow and taking refuge in the oceanlike vastness of faith assures even them of birth in Amida's Pure Land.[102]

The fourth fascicle of the *Kyōgyōshinshō* describes enlightenment or, literally, "true confirmation" (*shinjitsu no shō*), which is the end result of true teaching, practice, and faith. When endowed with the *nembutsu* and faith, even sentient beings filled with evil inclinations (*bonnō jōju no bonbu*) are included in the ranks of those truly assured of enlightenment (*shōjōju*). With this assurance they will proceed without fail to Nirvāṇa (*metsudo*), eternal bliss (*jōraku*), utmost quiescence (*hikkyō jakumetsu*), unconditioned Dharma-body (*mui hosshin*), Dharma-nature (*hosshō*), and thusness (*shinnyo*)—all allusions to complete enlightenment and Buddhahood.[103] Like true teaching, practice, and faith, enlightenment is not the result of one's own undertakings, but is a blessing bestowed on one through Amida's great compassion (*daihi ekō no riyaku*).[104] Teaching, practice, and faith are blessings that propel one toward Pure Land (*ōsō ekō*); enlightenment, on the other hand, is a blessing that returns one from Pure Land (*gensō ekō*).[105] That is, once one achieves enlightenment in Pure Land, one is empowered to return to the world of Saṃsāra to assist other sentient beings along the same path.[106] This selfless and compassionate dimension of enlightenment places Shinran's concept of salvation squarely in the Bodhisattva tradition of Mahāyāna Buddhism. It depicts enlightenment not as benefiting oneself alone but as benefiting others at the same time (*jiri rita*).[107] Shinran differed from earlier Pure Land thinkers in that he considered this return to the world to be the working of Amida, just as true teaching, practice, and faith are. The power that delivers one into Pure Land to be enlightened is the same power that takes one back into the world to aid others. Amida is the source of both.[108]

The last two fascicles of the *Kyōgyōshinshō* deal with the true (*shin*) and the expedient (*hōben*) aspects of Amida and his Pure Land. In their true form Amida and his Pure Land are infinite, as indicated by the infinite light (*kōmyō muryō*) and infinite life (*jumyō muryō*) mentioned in Amida's twelfth and thirteenth vows.[109] Shinran's conclusion from this is that they are identical with the absolute, described variously in Buddhism as emptiness (*kokū*), complete Nirvāṇa (*dainehan*), Buddha-nature (*busshō*), the unconditioned (*mui*), the immeasurable (*fukashōryō*), and the inconceivable (*fukashigi*).[110] Sentient beings, while living in this world, cannot fathom the true nature of Amida and his Pure Land, for their vision is still obscured by attachments and evil inclinations (*bonnō*).[111] Only after they are born in Pure Land will they see with unobstructed clarity that "the Pure Land is the unconditioned realm of Nirvāṇa" (*gokuraku wa mui nehan no kai nari*).[112]

This depiction of Amida and Pure Land as an ineffable absolute is not the primary one found in the Pure Land scriptures. More common are descriptions of Amida's physical form and of Pure Land's structural layout. Shinran regarded these as the expedient Buddha body and Pure Land (*hōben keshindo*). They are also the fruit (*shūhō*) of Amida's vow to save sentient beings, but they are not their true nature.[113] This expedient Pure Land includes lower levels (*gebon*), fringe areas (*henji*), castles of doubt (*gijō*), womb palaces (*taigū*), jeweled prisons (*shippō rōgoku*), and unopened lotus buds (*ketai*), all where sentient beings of inferior religious standing are born until they are ready to enter the host of Bodhisattvas in Pure Land.[114] Shinran believed this hierarchical Pure Land to be the only one that adherents lacking true faith could envision, and he considered it the form of Pure Land into which they would be born until faith arises in them. Only then would the true nature of Amida and Pure Land become apparent. Shinran linked the expedient Buddha body and Pure Land specifically to Amida's nineteenth and twentieth vows, whereby sentient beings seek birth in Pure Land through their own efforts, either by "performing virtuous deeds" (*shu sho kudoku*) or by "cultivating the basis of all virtue" (*jiki sho tokuhon*)—that is, chanting the *nembutsu*.[115] Though the three Pure Land sutras seem to present diverse paths to salvation, Shinran was convinced that the inner meaning of the three is the same: that faith is the cause of birth in Amida's Pure Land.[116]

Another important issue addressed in the final fascicle of the *Kyōgyōshinshō* is the age of *mappō*, the decline of the Buddhist teachings. Shinran, like his Pure Land predecessors, conceived of Buddhist history in three stages: 1) the period of the true Dharma (*shōbō*), corresponding to the first five hundred years after Śākyamuni Buddha's death; 2) the period of the imitated Dharma (*zōhō*), lasting for the next thousand years; and 3) the period of the decline of the Dharma (*mappō*), extending another ten thousand years. By Shinran's own reckoning, 1224 was the 683rd year of *mappō*.[117] In ancient times, during the age of the true Dharma, Buddhist adherents could follow Śākyamuni's teachings and achieve enlightenment through them. During the imitated Dharma, they continued the traditional practices—ethical precepts, meditation, and cultivation of wisdom—but were no longer able to attain enlightenment. During the present period of the Dharma's decline, they are not even able to adhere to the practices, much less reach enlightenment. *Mappō* is the time when evils flourish and when the world is afflicted with five corruptions (*gojoku*)—corruption of events of the age (*kō*), corruption of heretical views (*ken*), corruption of evil inclinations (*bonnō*), corruption of the capacities of sentient beings (*shujō*), and corruption of their life span (*myō*).[118] Even the Buddhist order of priests and nuns is infected with these trends: religious practices wane, strife abounds, precepts are violated, and the distinction between clergy and laity breaks down. At this point priests exist in title and appearance only, but not in spiritual content.[119] Shinran looked upon this decline as an unavoidable consequence of *mappō*, and he therefore preached single-hearted devotion to the Pure Land teachings rather than a return to clerical strictness. Echoing Tao-ch'o, Shinran advocated Pure Land as the teaching (*kyō*) best suited for the religious capacities (*ki*) of sentient beings during these degenerate times (*ji*).[120]

At the end of the *Kyōgyōshinshō* Shinran discussed beliefs and practices that lie outside the Buddhist tradition. Specifically, he was concerned with: veneration of spirits (*kami*), ghosts (*ki*) and demons (*ma*); preoccupation with auspicious days (*kichiryōnichi*); belief in beneficial constellations (*shōshū*); practice of divination (*senso*); supplication of good fortune (*shōkotsu fukuyu*); casting of curses (*jusho*); and other acts aimed at personal advantage through supernatural powers.[121] Though Shinran acknowledged the existence of spirits and the popularity of magical practices, he saw no place for them in Pure Land's path to salvation, since they all pale next to the supereminence of Amida Buddha. For the true believer, there is no reason to reverence any deity but Amida and no need to embrace any practice but the *nembutsu*. Shinran's basic position concerning non-Buddhist practices is that they all lie in the realm of false (*gi*) religion.[122]

The *Kyōgyōshinshō*, though built around citations from traditional Buddhist writings, is a radical religious document. Many of its ideas go against the grain of the Buddhist orthodoxy of Shinran's day. The most striking example is its emphasis on the evil person as the primary object of Amida's vow. Shinran made this point by inserting a long quotation from the *Nehangyō* ("Nirvāṇa Sutra") near the end of the fascicle on faith. This passage tells the story of the villainous King Ajātaśatru (*Ajase*), who murdered his own father to ascend the throne. The message of the story is that wicked people such as Ajātaśatru are within the embrace of the Amida's compassion. The Buddha is constantly active in the world precisely for the sake of those overwhelmed by evil inclinations (*gusoku bonnō*). The reason they can be born in Pure Land is that the faith they are endowed with does not originate from their own store of merit but is extended to them by Amida (*mukon no shin o eshimetamaeri*).[123] This idea, which was at odds with prevailing Buddhist sentiment, was clearly a part of Shinran's thinking when he drafted the Bandō edition of the *Kyōgyōshinshō* around 1235. Additions to the manuscript over the course of the next decade or two indicate that he did not back away from this view. If anything, he asserted it all the more firmly, for the passage on Ajātaśatru was vastly expanded during later revisions of the *Kyōgyōshinshō* and eventually emerged as the longest quotation in the entire work.[124] This pattern of composition suggests that the most distinctive and radical components of Shinran's religious philosophy were in place by the time he left the Kantō region in the early 1230s. His remaining years spent in Kyoto were given to explicating and elaborating these core convictions.

SHINRAN'S RETURN TO KYOTO

Shinran lived the last three decades of his life in Kyoto. This was an intellectually vibrant time for him during which the vast majority of his writings were composed. Unfortunately, the details of Shinran's move to Kyoto and his daily activities there are as fragmentary as those of his earlier years. Neither the exact date nor the reason for his departure from the Kantō region are known. Estimates are that Shinran returned to Kyoto sometime between 1230 and 1237, most likely in 1234 or 1235.[125] Theories about why he left are manifold, but the most plausible explanation is that he departed because of religious suppression.[126] In 1235 the Kamakura *bakufu*, or military government, promulgated a ban on radical *nembutsu* priests in the city of Kamakura. To the extent that this was enforced in the surrounding area as well, it could have easily impinged on Shinran and his following. As a prominent advocate of the exclusive *nembutsu*, Shinran would have been a controversial figure and hence a likely target for punishment. Rather than become embroiled in this upheaval, Shinran apparently withdrew from the comfortable religious community he had fostered in the Kantō region and returned to his long-abandoned birthplace Kyoto.[127]

Until the twentieth century the prevailing view was that Shinran returned to Kyoto without his wife and family.[128] Eshinni's letters attest that from 1156 she was living separately in Echigo province with three of their children.[129] This fact has prompted some scholars to speculate that Shinran left the Kantō because of family turmoil caused by his marriage to another woman, the mysterious "Imagozen no haha," who is mentioned in a letter written presumably near the end of Shinran's life in which he asked his followers in Hitachi province to look after her.[130] This theory has not received widespread support for lack of corroborating evidence. In fact, it is more plausible to think that Eshinni accompanied Shinran to Kyoto and only later moved to Echigo. Her letters express a warmth and devotion to Shinran that an estranged wife might not feel, and they reveal a familiarity with people and events in Kyoto that someone who had not been there for decades would not have.[131] Eshinni owned property in Echigo, no doubt inherited from her family which had long-standing ties there.[132] In her old age she returned to Echigo along with three of their children, probably to look after her inheritance. This did not leave Shinran alone in Kyoto. Their youngest daughter Kakushinni was married to a member of the Hino family there, and after being widowed she remained in Kyoto with Shinran.[133] In addition, Shinran's oldest son, Zenran, lived in Kyoto at least part of the time, for Zenran's own son Nyoshin (1235-1300) is said to have grown up receiving instruction from Shinran.[134]

Shinran's economic circumstances while living in Kyoto have also been a matter of debate. The only clear means of support he had were the gifts (*kokorozashi*) he received from his followers in the Kantō region.[135] Kakunyo's "Biography" states that Shinran moved from place to place in Kyoto, so he evidently had no fixed residence. He stayed for a while in the southwest quadrant of the city at Gojō Nishi no Tōin, and later was taken in by his younger brother Zenbōbō Jin'u, who lived in the eastern part of the city at Oshikōji no Minami, Made no Kōji Higashi. This last place was the location of Shinran's death.[136] For a long time it was thought that Shinran lived in such dire straits that he was forced to sell his daughter Kakushinni into servitude. This assumption was based on the mistaken identification of Kakushinni as the person referred to as "Iya onna" in a letter of transfer of ownership written by Shinran in 1243.[137] With the discovery of Eshinni's letters, it became apparent that Kakushinni did not go by the name "Iya onna," who was probably a servant, or *genin*, owned by Shinran.[138] This conclusion has cast a different light on Shinran's economic situation. He may not have been in a position to keep a servant, and therefore was forced to sell her, but the mere possession of one put him in a totally different economic stratum from people who had to sell their children into servitude. Furthermore, the gifts that Shinran received from his Kantō followers were sometimes of considerable magnitude. The largest one was twenty *kanmon*, which at that time could buy enough rice to feed twenty people for a year.[139] These details suggest that Shinran's life in Kyoto was far from austere, though not lavish. This conclusion is borne out by the surviving portraits of Shinran. One entitled the Anjō no Miei ("Anjō Portrait"), dated 1255, shows him dressed in flowing black robes, seated in front of a glowing charcoal brazier, with catskin slippers and a fur-adorned walking stick laid to the side.[140] This is not the appearance of someone near destitution.

During his stay in Kyoto Shinran maintained contact with his followers in the Kantō. The majority of his surviving letters are addressed to believers there.[141] Followers who had the means sometimes made the long journey to Kyoto to see Shinran personally. One disciple named Renni (d. 1278) even came to live with Shinran to look after his daily needs.[142] The communications between Shinran and his followers were devoted primarily to spiritual concerns. He attempted to answer their religious questions and to interpret the meaning of faith for them in concrete and familiar terms.

Kakunyo's "Biography" records one visit which exemplifies this pastoral side of Shinran. The believer, a commoner named Heitarō of Hitachi province, was required to make a visit to Kumano Shrine in an official capacity to pay respects to the Shinto *kami* there. Knowing that believers of Amida's vow have no need to worship *kami*, he came to Shinran seeking advice. Shinran affirmed Heitarō's convictions saying that single-minded and exclusive devotion (*ikkō sennen*) to Amida is the essence of the Pure Land teachings. But he added that Amida takes on various manifestations (*suijaku*) in order to lead sentient beings to his oceanlike vow and that the *kami* at Kumano is one of those manifestations. Hence, there is no reason to scorn or denigrate the *kami*. Nevertheless, the believer endowed with faith need not go through the purification ritual usually required in visiting a shrine. Heitarō followed Shinran's advice, paying his respects at Kumano Shrine without observing the typical Shinto practice of purification.[143] This episode is not recorded in other early Shinshū sources. Moreover, the element of Shinto-Buddhist syncretism (*honji suijaku*) contained in it is foreign to Shinran's thought. That part, therefore, may be dismissed as an interpolation by the author Kakunyo. What does ring true is the advice Shinran gave concerning shrines and purification. Though his attitude seems conciliatory on the surface, his recommendations were fairly radical, for one of the recurrent complaints registered against *nembutsu* adherents was that they ignored Shinto purification rituals and thereby defiled Shinto shrines.[144] Shinran evidently condoned such actions. This story reveals some of the perplexities that Shinran's followers faced and some of the ways in which his teachings deviated from established norms.

The last fifteen years of Shinran's life were spent trying to ameliorate a crisis among his followers in the Kantō region. This was an especially traumatic experience for Shinran. He was already advanced in years, and amid the turmoil he was forced to disown his oldest son, Zenran, to prevent further conflict and polarization. The disturbance arose because of the appearance of radical *nembutsu* proponents among Shinran's followers. Those advocating licensed evil—that is, indulgence in wrongdoing because birth in Pure Land seems assured—dominated certain congregations and began to stigmatize Shinran's following.[145] Though his teachings differed profoundly from the prevailing Buddhism of the period, Shinran was in no way a proponent of licensed evil. He attempted to communicate his views in letters to Kantō followers and in conversations with those who visited him in Kyoto. It was difficult, however, to right the problem at such a distance. In the end Shinran dispatched Zenran to the area to act in his behalf.[146]

Zenran's handling of the situation was overly zealous and dictatorial. He enlisted the assistance of civil authorities—local lords (*ryōke*), constables (*jitō*), and overseers (*myōshu*)—in confronting licensed evil advocates.[147] He also began to claim that Shinran had imparted secret teachings at night to him alone, and he used this claim to elicit allegiance from Kantō followers.[148] Zenran's ploy was to create a religious community submissive to his authority and dependent on his religious pronouncements. This kind of master-follower dependence, commonly known as taking refuge in one's master (*chishiki kimyō*) or relying on the good master (*zenjishiki danomi*), was denounced in later Shinshū doctrine. The implication of this relationship was that the master embodies the Buddha's principles and holds the key to salvation; therefore, the believer should not look to the Buddha directly but should seek salvation in the master.[149] Reverence for one's religious teacher was deeply ingrained in the Buddhist tradition in Japan, so it was not unusual for this relationship to take root in Shinran's following as well. Zenran encouraged this kind of dependence, urging believers to "trust what he said and to leave the propagation of the *nembutsu* to other people of superior power (*kyōen*)."[150] Shinran himself, during this period, was seen as an object of veneration by many of his followers—supposedly as a manifestation of the Bodhisattva Kannon, or even Amida Buddha.[151] But Shinran never accepted aggrandizement of this type. Instead, he presented himself on the same level as other *nembutsu* adherents and following the same path to salvation as fellow believers (*dōgyō*). Shinran's openness and egalitarian spirit are seen in a passage attributed to him in the *Tannishō* ("Notes Lamenting Deviations") which describes a visit to Kyoto of a number of followers seeking perhaps the secret teachings that Zenran claimed to possess:

> Here you have come crossing the borders of more than ten provinces, unconcerned about [any risk to] your own lives. And what is it you wish to ask? Solely about the path leading to birth in Pure Land. But you are gravely mistaken if you presume that I know of any path to Pure Land outside of the *nembutsu* or that I am aware of other scriptures [indicating one]. If that is what you desire, there are many learned priests in Nara and on Mt. Hiei; you should go and ask them what is required for birth in Pure Land. As for me, Shinran, I have received and put my faith in the words of the good man [Hōnen]: "Simply utter the *nembutsu* and you will be saved by Amida." Apart from this, I have nothing else to point out.
>
> Is the *nembutsu* truly the key to birth in Pure Land? Or is it an act that will lead me to hell? Frankly, I do not know. But even if I have been deceived by Hōnen so that the *nembutsu* leads me to hell, I have no regrets. The reason is this. If I were capable of achieving Buddhahood by exerting myself in other religious practices and yet said the *nembutsu* and fell into hell, then there would be reason to regret being deceived. But since all other practices are beyond my reach, hell is where I am bound to reside anyway. If, however, the vow of Amida is true, then the teachings of Śākyamuni cannot be false. And if the Buddha's teachings are true, then the interpretations of Shan-tao cannot be false. And if Shan-tao's interpretations are true, then how can Hōnen's words be lies? And if Hōnen's words are true, then how can the things I say be in vain?
>
> This, in short, is my humble faith. Over and above this, it is up to each of you individually to take up the *nembutsu* in faith or to reject it.[152]

Here Shinran's words are simple and straightforward, without pretension or condescension. He repudiated the role of religious master and the perpetuation of secret teachings, both of which are found in Japan's Tendai and Shingon schools. This statement not only undercut Zenran's designs but also gave Shinran's following an openness and egalitarianism that distinguished it from the hierarchical structure of the orthodox Buddhist schools.

The furor caused by Zenran's activities in the Kantō culminated in his disownment by Shinran in 1256.[153] Only by doing so could Shinran convince his followers of his determination to rectify Zenran's false claims. This action caused Shinran untold grief and disappointment, for he assumed undoubtedly that Zenran understood the meaning of faith and would work with his followers in that spirit. In the end Zenran's example demonstrates how elusive Shinran's concept of faith is. It is virtually impossible to make a hard and fast correlation between outward conduct and inward faith. Zenran lived with Shinran for years and apparently gave every indication that he comprehended the meaning of Amida's vow. In the Kantō, however, his disparagement of the eighteenth vow and his high-handedness with Shinran's followers revealed that, despite his years of religious devotion, he had not yet grasped Shinran's message.[154] Not even Shinran could perceive this beforehand. The upshot is that external piety is no proof of faith. But neither is wrongdoing a sure sign of exclusion from faith. Hence, linking faith to action, good or bad, has been a vexing problem in Shinran's following from its inception.

SHINRAN'S LAST YEARS

The majority of Shinran's writings were composed from the early 1250's when the Kantō crisis began to 1262 when he died. These works were obviously a response to the quandaries that his Kantō followers faced and to the turmoil created by Zenran. Most were written in Japanese rather than Chinese, so that ordinary believers without extensive education could comprehend them.[155] Shinran's writings during this period span a variety of genre including letters, hymns (wasan), Chinese verse, doctrinal outlines, religious tracts, commentaries, copies of other people's compositions, and excerpts from sacred texts. Many of the themes in the Kyōgyōshinshō ("Teaching, Practice, Faith, and Enlightenment") reappear in these works, but are emphasized or explicated in slightly different ways. In that sense these later writings are an extension of Shinran's teachings in the Kyōgyōshinshō and a deepening of his thought.[156]

If there is one thing that draws together Shinran's diverse writings from this period, it is their idealization of faith. In the wake of the Kantō upheaval, Shinran was moved to articulate how rare and precious an endowment of faith is. Though it is totally a gift from Amida, individuals in whom faith arises are extremely few. Not even his own son Zenran could be counted in that number. Those who are blessed with it are as exalted as the Buddhas (shobutsu tōdō), for they no longer pursue salvation through their own contrivances (hakarai), but rather reside in a state of naturalness (jinen) and Dharma-nature (hōni). These themes, which are hinted at in the Kyōgyōshinshō, emerge in full force in Shinran's later works.

The idea that faith makes a person equal to the Buddhas (shobutsu tōdō) became a prominent point in Shinran's writings between 1255 and 1257.[157] The seeds for this concept were already present in quotations cited in the Kyōgyōshinshō describing the Pure Land believer as the same as Maitreya (bendō Miroku) and as equal to the Tathāgatas (sho nyorai tō).[158] Shinran's logic in making this statement was that the person who experiences faith resides in a state where enlightenment in Pure Land is truly assured (shōjōju). This is none other than the stage of nonretrogression (futaiten or ayuiotchi) achieved by the highest Bodhisattvas. At this point there is no falling back from enlightenment; it is imminent and fully assured. Maitreya, the next Buddha that will appear in this world system, is also at that stage. Hence, believers endowed with faith are said to be "the same as Maitreya." But Maitreya, though still a Bodhisattva, is already referred to as a Buddha because he is at the threshold of Buddhahood. By the same token, those who have faith are poised for enlightenment and therefore, like Maitreya, are "equal to the Tathāgatas."[159] The implication of this assertion is that there is no fall from faith. Once faith emerges in a person it is an indestructible state of mind (*kongōshin*).[160] A corollary to this is that the true believer need not wait for the moment of death to experience this assurance. This idea went against the long-standing Pure Land practice of deathbed *nembutsu* ceremonies, wherein correct thoughts during a person's last moments were seen as crucial to birth in Pure Land. Consequently, the dying believer would look into the western direction and envision Amida coming to deliver the person into Pure Land. In Shinran's view death is not the moment confirming one's salvation; rather, the first instant of faith is.[161]

By equating the person of faith to the Buddhas, Shinran ran the risk of encouraging licensed evil adherents to think that their actions were enlightened. Shinran's disciples in the Kantō region were obviously distressed by this possibility and sought clarification of his teaching. That is the reason many of Shinran's letters during this period dealt with this concept.[162] His followers were willing to accept the idea that Pure Land believers are equivalent to Maitreya, but they were reluctant to go beyond that and equate them to fully enlightened Buddhas.[163] Shinran stood by his statement because he felt that only such exalted terms could communicate the magnitude and profundity of faith. His point was not that faith is the same as enlightenment, but rather that faith is the assurance of enlightenment.[164] Those who construed the two to be the same and who used this reasoning to justify indulgent behavior, Shinran confronted in a different way. He asserted that their willful manipulation of religious ideas is nothing more than a human contrivance (*hakarai*) standing in diametric opposition to faith. That is, the self-serving ends behind their claim to faith are precisely what excludes licensed evil adherents from the circle of faith and from its assurance of enlightenment.[165]

Shinran's most important statement concerning contrivance is a paradoxical phrase that appears numerous times in his later writings: "Not having definition is to be the definition" (*gi naki o gi to su*).[166] Shinran claimed to have inherited this idea from Hōnen.[167] Indeed, the words are found in one writing attributed to Hōnen, though in a significantly different context, for Hōnen used it specifically in reference to the *nembutsu*:

> Matters of faith (*anjin*) and practice (*kigyō*) in the Pure Land school: Not to have definition is to be the definition and not to have form (*yō*) is to be the form. What is insignificant is [actually] profound. If people simply say *Namu Amida Butsu*, then they are sure to attain birth in Pure Land, even if they have committed the ten evil acts and the five damning offenses (*jūaku gogyaku*), and even if they are sentient beings in the period of the extinction of the three [Buddhist] treasures (*sanbō metsujin*), and even if they have not had a single good thought in their entire life. Śākyamuni and Amida bear witness to this.[168]

Here Hōnen used the expression "Not having definition is to be the definition" to explain the nature of the *nembutsu*. There is no set form that the *nembutsu* must take in order for it to be efficacious. It need not conform to the rituals, doctrines, or meditative practices used in the established schools of Old Buddhism; rather, it can be invoked by anyone in any circumstance. Thus, the true form and definition of the *nembutsu* is that it has no specified form or definition. Hōnen thereby sought to free the *nembutsu* for practice in any situation.[169]

Shinran, by contrast, interpreted the expression "Not having definition is to be the definition" in terms of faith. He applied it to the believer's state of mind instead of to outward practice. Perhaps no example reflects better the difference between Hōnen and Shinran than this. In Shinran's view the defining characteristic of the true believer is that no act of defining is committed. Any conscious attempt to stipulate one's own path to salvation or to define one's preferences represents an intrusion into Amida's grand design (*onhakarai*) embodied in his eighteenth vow. To put forward one's own definition of things is an act of self-effort (*jiriki*) and human contrivance (*hakarai*). Not to assert one's own definition is the state in which the person of true faith relies totally on other-power (*tariki*), the power of the Buddha. Shinran summed up these ideas in the following passage:

> In having faith in Amida's principal vow, "Not having definition is to be the definition." So spoke the great master [Hōnen]. It is said likewise that, as long as there is definition, it is not other-power (*tariki*) but rather self-effort (*jiriki*). What we call other-power is the inconceivability of the Buddha's wisdom—that is, ordinary beings (*bonbu*) who are overwhelmed by evil inclinations (*bonnō gusoku*) attain enlightenment, unsurpassed awakening, by the design (*onhakarai*) of the Buddha and the Buddha alone. It is by no means through the contrivance (*hakarai*) of the believer. Hence, it is said, "Not having definition is to be the definition." The word "definition" refers to a person's contrivance, or self-effort. As for other-power, then, not having definition is to be the definition.[170]

Through this cryptic expression and tortuous logic, Shinran sought to express the simple conviction that total submission to Amida and reliance on his vow is the essence of faith.

One last theme that dominated Shinran's later writings is the concept of *jinen hōni*, or naturalness and Dharma-nature. These two are traditional Buddhist terms indicating the intrinsic characteristic or the natural functioning of a thing in the world. *Jinen* denotes nature, or the nature of things in and of themselves. *Hōni* refers to the fact that each thing has certain features which are inherent in the thing itself—such as the hotness of fire or the wetness of water.[171] Shinran took these terms and, with an idiosyncratic etymological analysis, applied them to the state of faith in which Amida's vow exerts its power. In doing so he employed some of the other concepts described above:

On *Jinen hōni*

> With regard to naturalness (*jinen*), the *ji* means "of itself" (*onozukara*), without any contrivance (*hakarai*) of the believer. *Nen* is a word meaning "caused to be so" (*shikarashimu*). "Caused to be so" refers to the vow of the Tathāgata, not to the contrivance of the believer. Hence, it is Dharma-nature (*hōni*). With regard to Dharma-nature, since it refers to the vow of the Tathāgata, Dharma-nature means "caused to be so." Dharma-nature, because it refers to this vow, means "caused to be so, based on the virtue of this Dharma," since it is without any contrivance of the believer whatsoever. From the beginning there is altogether no contrivance of human beings [in it]. For that reason, we should realize that not having definition is to be its definition.[172]

By interpreting naturalness (*jinen*) and Dharma-nature (*hōni*) in terms of Amida's vow, which is devoid of any human contrivance or definition, Shinran infused these concepts with a Pure Land meaning. The believer embraced by Amida resides in perfect accord with this vow. It is a state of naturalness and Dharma-nature, intrinsic to itself and definable only in terms of itself. This naturalness arises not because of any effort exerted by the person but because the believer is "caused to be so" by virtue of the power of Amida's vow. This is a sublime and inexplicable condition linking the person of faith to the formlessness of unsurpassed Buddhahood.[173] In this way Shinran idealized the true believer and elevated faith to the rare and precious status of being equal to the Buddhas. Themes such as these were an overriding concern in Shinran's writings during the twilight years of his life in Kyoto.

Shinran's essay on *jinen hōni* is one of the last dated pieces in his literary corpus.[174] Two writings which some scholars believe postdate it are the two letters concerning the mysterious woman, "Imagozen no haha." One is addressed to Shinran's followers in the province of Hitachi, imploring them to look after the needs of "Imagozen no haha," since she had no one else to depend on.[175] The other one is addressed to "Imagozen no haha" herself, urging her to present the first letter to the Hitachi followers.[176] These letters have the air of a last will and testament. Moreover, the faltering handwriting in them suggests that Shinran may have written them in failing health, perhaps near the end of his life. If these two letters were indeed a deathbed testament, their month-and-day dating indicates they were written only two and a half weeks before Shinran's death.[177]

Concerning the identity of "Imagozen no haha," one scholar has proposed that she was not the shadowy later wife attributed to Shinran but rather his youngest daughter, Kakushinni.[178] This theory has met with tentative acceptance, since it conforms to most of the known facts about Shinran's later life.[179] Kakushinni was the only child of Shinran's living in Kyoto with him. She was married to Hino Hirotsuna in the early 1240s, but after his death around 1249 she and her two children probably turned to Shinran for support. Shinran, unlike his wife Eshinni, had no property of his own, but he did receive generous gifts from his followers in the Kantō region. These were sufficient to provide for himself and Kakushinni as well. As his death approached, Shinran may have been troubled over Kakushinni's fate. He had nothing of worth to leave her, and so he called upon his followers in Hitachi province, where Kakushinni had been born, to care for her needs. If this is in fact the significance of the "Imagozen no haha" letter, then it established an abiding link between Kakushinni and the Kantō following which was borne out in later events. This link, initiated in Shinran's dying wishes, led in an indirect way to the rise of the Honganji temple decades later, for at Kakushinni's behest the Kantō followers constructed at his grave site a memorial chapel which evolved into the temple.

Shinran's death occurred on 1262.11.28. The account of his passing in Kakunyo's "Biography" reads as follows:

> During the last part of the middle month of winter in 1262, the master fell into ill health somewhat. From that point on, he did not talk about worldly matters, but expounded solely on the depth of his indebtedness to the Buddha. In voice he did not speak of other things, but intently and unceasingly uttered the [Buddha's] name. In this way at noon on the twenty-eighth day of the same month, he finally breathed his last *nembutsu*, lying on his right side facing west with his head in the northern direction. At that time, he was an elderly ninety years old in full. The hermitage [where he died] was in the eastern section of the capital, at Oshikōji no Minami, Made no Kōji Higashi. Therefore, they traveled the road to a distant [part of town] east of the river, and held the cremation at the Enninji temple, south of Torinobe in the western foothills of the Higashiyama section of the capital. His ashes were gathered up and interred at Ōtani north of Torinobe in the same foothills. The disciples who were present at his death, as well as young and old who had received his instruction, each reflected on the past when he was still living and lamented the present after his passing. None were able to hold back their tears of affection.[180]

So ended the life of one of Japan's most creative religious thinkers. Shinran's teachings are a prime example of the profound impact that interior and subjective experiences can have on a body of religious thought. Filtered through Shinran's experiences and through his idiosyncratic logic, Pure Land Buddhism took on shades of meaning that it never had before. The unique philosophy that resulted was virtually ignored by aristocratic society during Shinran's lifetime. Nonetheless, his ideas managed to survive among his rural followers in the Kantō region and his descendants in Kyoto. Those teachings, comprising a curious combination of radical religious reform and self-effacing introspection, were Shinran's true legacy to later generations, and they became the backbone of Shin Buddhism's orthodoxy.

CHAPTER
4

LICENSED EVIL

The historical context in which Shinran's teachings began to spread was the Pure Land movement of the Kamakura period. This movement was often branded as heretical by the eight orthodox schools of Old Buddhism. Their unanimous condemnation, however, should not be taken as an indication of unity or agreement within the movement itself. On the contrary, the diversity of interpretation and practice in the Pure Land movement created almost as much tension among its adherents as between the entire movement and the existing Buddhist schools. Pure Land adherents sometimes railed against each other, leveling charges of heresy within their own ranks. Hence, heresy was an accusation wielded not only by the Buddhist establishment but also by Pure Land proponents. Shinran was caught up in these intramural controversies, and in that context formulated his own views of heresy. These views in no way represented the prevailing idea of heresy in his times but rather his own personal understanding of religious falsehood.

Shin sectarian scholars generally list the following as the religious controversies from which the "heresies" of Shinran's period arose: 1) whether a single *nembutsu* is the key to birth in Pure Land (*ichinengi*) or whether many *nembutsu* are required (*tanengi*); 2) whether the *nembutsu* should be performed in a meditative state (*munengi*) or outside meditation (*unengi*); 3) whether salvation results from Amida's wondrous vow (*seigan fushigi*) or from the wondrous *nembutsu* (*myōgō fushigi*); and 4) whether faith gives a person license to commit evil deeds (*zōaku muge*) or whether good deeds are required (*kenzen shōjin*).[1] Of these, the problem of licensed evil was the most notorious heresy. People inspired by this notion felt at liberty to indulge in any capricious act or to gratify any desire that might arise. Licensed evil therefore typifies the doctrinal extreme to which the Pure Land teachings could be carried, and it threatened at times to stigmatize Pure Land as a subversive doctrine undermining the ethical norms of society. Though the various controversies listed here are frequently explicated as discrete doctrinal issues, historically they were interrelated, for they arose out of a common religious milieu, and many drew on common religious assumptions. The single *nembutsu* doctrine, for example, was sometimes linked to licensed evil as a corollary, whereas the encouragement of good deeds was often advanced as a corrective to licensed evil. Consequently, the internal controversies of the Pure Land movement should be seen as a single tissue of religious debate rather than as separate and independent questions of heresy.

THE ORIGIN AND MEANING OF LICENSED EVIL

The idea of licensed evil existed under a variety of names, and encompassed a number of different beliefs and practices. The most common expression used for it was *zōaku muge*, "committing evil without obstruction." Other terms referring to it were "self-indulgence without remorse" (*hōitsu muzan*) and "flaunting Amida's vow" (*hongan bokori*).[2] All these expressions denote offensive or even malicious conduct stemming from the presumption that one is guaranteed birth in Pure Land. Such conduct could range from simple haughtiness to violent behavior, but in each case the assurance of birth in Pure Land, or at least the presumed assurance, is touted as canceling out the karmic consequences of evil deeds and as giving people liberty to do whatever they please. Shinran, Hōnen, and the traditional schools of Buddhism were united in their opposition to licensed evil, but they differed over what kinds of acts constitute licensed evil and what makes them heretical.

The origins of licensed evil are obscure, but it is likely that the Tachikawa branch of Shingon Buddhism had some influence on its formation. Tachikawa Shingon was an underground esoteric cult which secretly advocated erotic practices and physical indulgences to achieve the Shingon religious ideal. Its teachings are summed up in the following way by Shōjō (1215-68), one of its thirteenth-century adherents:

> Sexual union (*nyobon*) is the ultimate for achieving Buddhahood in this very body (*sokushin jōbutsu*), the essence of the Shingon teachings. If people entertain the idea of denying themselves sexual union, then they distance themselves from the path to Buddhahood. Eating meat is founded on the expedient teachings of the Bodhisattvas, who thereby establish their own enlightenment and aid all sentient beings. If people dislike eating meat, then they lose their way in the path leading out of Saṃsāra. Consequently, do not question what is pure and what is impure, and do not reject sexual union or meat eating. Every element in this world is pure and can lead straightway to Buddhahood in this very body.[3]

The Tachikawa teachings, despite constant suppression, spread to diverse regions of Japan during the thirteenth century. Tachikawa adherents are known to have inhabited the Kantō provinces, Kyoto, the Hokuriku seaboard, and the island of Kyūshū—all areas where Pure Land followers were active.[4] Though it is difficult to substantiate specific instances of contact between the two, a number of unorthodox interpretations of Pure Land concepts, which hint at Tachikawa influences, are recorded in certain Pure Land works. The *Nembutsu myōgishū* ("Collection on the Significance of [Amida's] Name in [the Form of] the Nembutsu"), written by Hōnen's disciple Benchō, contains one suggestive passage describing *ichinengi*, or the single *nembutsu* doctrine, in one of its myriad forms:

> It is fine and respectable to say that there is only *ichinen*, or a single *nembutsu*, to the *nembutsu*. The reason is that the character *nen* is made up of strokes which separately may be read "the heart of two people" (*hito futari ga kokoro*), and the character *ichi* is read "one." [Together they mean "the one heart of two people."] Therefore, we call it the single *nembutsu* when a man and a woman come together, and there is a pleasantness of heart between the two, and they say *Namu Amida Butsu* at the same time in a single voice. Hence, someone alone should have one other person. By realizing that without this kind of single *nembutsu* practice there will be no birth in Pure Land, that person can go on to constitute a couple with the other, in which each person has the other.[5]

This statement does not overtly advance sexual practices, but it was probably interpreted in that vein. Improper conduct between men and women was frequently cited as a wrongdoing resulting from the licensed evil doctrine. The Pure Land movement as a whole sustained criticism for this type of impropriety, as evidenced by Jien's denunciations in the *Gukanshō* ("Notes of My Foolish Views"). The execution of Anrakubō and Jūren recorded there reflects the extent to which their spending the night in the company of ladies-in-waiting of the imperial court offended social sensibilities. Defined in terms of the general mores of society, offenses of this type ranged from improper etiquette between men and women to illicit sexual relations. In terms of the conduct of Buddhist priests, they included unchastity and marriage.

HŌNEN, THE SINGLE NEMBUTSU DOCTRINE, AND CLERICAL PRECEPTS

Hōnen was fully aware of the indulgent behavior caused by licensed evil among Pure Land followers, and he sought to curb these excesses and thereby to allay the criticism of civil and religious authorities. In the fourth item of his *Shichikajō kishōmon* ("Seven Article Pledge") he specifically associated licensed evil with the violation of the clerical precepts. There he admonished his disciples not to present the Pure Land path as devoid of clerical precepts; not to encourage sexual indulgence, liquor, and meat eating, all of which constitute violations of the precepts; not to belittle others adhering to the precepts as people of indiscriminate practices; and not to teach that relying on Amida's principal vow gives one no reason to fear committing evil.[6] In the Pure Land movement of Hōnen's day repudiation of the clerical precepts was a burgeoning trend which threatened to undermine the authority of the traditional Buddhist schools. Hence, one form of licensed evil that came under strong attack was violation of the precepts without remorse (*hakai muzan*).[7]

The licensed evil heresy was also linked in Hōnen's time to the single *nembu-*

tsu doctrine (*ichinengi*). Among Hōnen's disciples Kōsai was the leading proponent of this doctrine. His teaching may be succinctly described as follows:

> A person who has faith in Amida's vow says the *nembutsu* once. But to say it 50,000 times is of no benefit. It is to have no faith in the *nembutsu*.[8]

In contrast to this, the so-called repeated *nembutsu* doctrine (*tanengi*), which was commonly attributed to Ryūkan, maintained:

> The practice of the *nembutsu* is recommended from the first moment that aspiration for enlightenment arises in one until one is born in Pure Land, so that there will be no retrogression. The reason is that the last *nembutsu* at the end of one's life is what truly launches one onto Amida's vow.[9]

The issue at stake in these two doctrines extends far beyond a simple dispute over the number of *nembutsu* required for birth in Pure Land. In essence the two represent the so-called faith and practice extremes of the Pure Land teachings, and they suggest considerably different paradigms of religious behavior. The single *nembutsu* extreme reduces religion to faith and faith alone, and construes any religious practice over and above that to be a sign of no faith. Wrongdoings are encouraged, since good deeds and clerical precepts are characterized as an attempt to save oneself and hence an indication of one's lack of faith in the Buddha's ability to do so. The single *nembutsu* doctrine thereby constitutes a conceptual basis for licensed evil. The repeated *nembutsu* extreme, on the other hand, portrays salvation as a reward to be earned through the regular practice of the *nembutsu*. As such, the onus of achieving birth in Pure Land falls squarely on the believer. Any moment of remissness in practicing the *nembutsu* could result in the loss of salvation, should death overtake the believer in that instant. When pressed to its logical end, this emphasis on the *nembutsu* as a personal endeavor to secure birth in Pure Land suggests that good deeds, pious practices, and even the clerical precepts may also be important criteria for salvation (*kenzen shōjin*). Together, these two extremes represent mutually antagonistic interpretations of Pure Land thought that divided the Pure Land movement in the thirteenth century. The single *nembutsu* doctrine emphasized faith to the exclusion of practice, and the repeated *nembutsu* doctrine advocated practice to the neglect of faith.[10]

Hōnen, during his later years, was particularly distressed by the dissemination of the single *nembutsu* doctrine among his followers. In 1209, to check the spread of this doctrine in the Hokuriku region where many of Kōsai's disciples were active, Hōnen issued a statement entitled *Ichinengi chōji kishōmon* ("Pledge to Prohibit the Single Nembutsu Doctrine"), in which he denounced the teaching and urged people not to forsake the regular practice of the *nembutsu*:

> These days there are many ignorant and misguided people among the adherents of the *nembutsu* path. They still do not understand what is upheld and

what is rejected in this one teaching of ours, nor do they comprehend the name of even a single dharma. Inwardly they have no aspiration for enlightenment, and outwardly they seek only benefit for themselves. Because of this, they capriciously fabricate falsehoods and mislead people. They blindly adhere to this as a scheme for making a living, without reflecting at all on the consequences of such wrongdoings in their next life. Brazenly, they spread the false teaching of the single *nembutsu*, and they are unrepentant of their error of having no religious practice. Also, they have established a new "no *nembutsu*" doctrine, whereby they give up even the slightest practice, the single utterance of the *nembutsu*. Even though it is a minute source of good, they cut off all traces of good in themselves. Even though their wrongdoings are grave already, they add strength unto strength to the wrongdoings within themselves. To experience the momentary pleasures which the five senses crave, they show no fear of deeds that will lead them for endless kalpas through the three benighted realms. They teach others, saying: "People who trust in Amida's vow need not abandon the five damning offenses. They can do anything according to their heart's own desires. They need not don priestly robes, but may wear ordinary attire. They need not forsake meat eating or sexual relations, but may consume deer or fowl as they wish."

The great master Kōbō (774–835), in explicating the term "ignorant sheeplike mentality" (*ishō teiyō shin*), said: "It is to think of food and sex only, and therefore it is like being a sheep." Do these people, who are blinded by their addiction to the pleasures, not belong to this group? Of the ten levels of mentality, this is the [lowest] one leading to the three benighted realms. Who could not have pity on them? They not only obstruct other teachings but also lose the practice of the *nembutsu*. They advocate acts of indolence and remorselessness, and the doctrine that they set forth is for people to abandon the clerical precepts and to return to lay life. In this country there have been no heresies (*gedō*) previously, so this must be the fabrication of demons. It wreaks havoc on the Buddhist teachings, and it throws society into confusion. To abide by these instructions is an act of utter ignorance. Even without studying the scriptures, how could any person who aspires to wisdom put faith in such things? In the *Kuan-nien fa-men* ("Methods in [Pure Land] Meditation") by the master Shan-tao it says: "Simply adhere to the precepts deeply and practice the *nembutsu*." In the *Ch'ün-i lun* ("A Treatise [Dispelling] Myriad Doubts [on Pure Land]") the meditation master Huai-kan (ca. 7th cent.), who was a disciple of Shan-tao's and an adept of meditation, explained: "Those who long for Tuṣita heaven (*tosotsu*) should not denigrate adherents of the western Pure Land, and those who delight in being born in the western Pure Land should not denigrate deeds leading to Tuṣita heaven. Both should undertake practices and study in accordance with their own inclinations and relying on their own sensibilities."

If Pure Land adherents intend to obey the teachings, they should follow in the footsteps of the masters, fervently uphold the precepts, not commit manifold wrongdoings, not obstruct other teachings, and not belittle other practices. Overall, they should cultivate a reverential attitude toward the Buddhist teachings, perform the *nembutsu* 30,000 or 60,000 times a day, and look forward to Pure Land with its five gates and nine levels. . . .[11]

Hōnen's letter is an explicit denunciation of the single *nembutsu* doctrine, licensed evil, and violation of the clerical precepts. He condemned these as heresies devised by demons. To counter such teachings, Hōnen encouraged not only frequent and extended chanting of the *nembutsu* but also adherence to the clerical precepts and the performance of good deeds. On the surface, it would appear that Hōnen was an advocate of the repeated *nembutsu* doctrine and the necessity of good deeds (*kenzen shōjin*). What distinguishes him from adherents of those doctrines is that Hōnen saw these acts not as requirements for salvation but simply as beneficial in their own way when coupled with the *nembutsu*. He recommended them to show that the Pure Land ideal is perfectly compatible with conventional Buddhist practices.

Hōnen's *Ichinengi chōji kishōmon* ("Pledge Prohibiting the Single Nembutsu Doctrine"), as well as his *Shichikajō kishōmon* ("Seven Article Pledge"), specifically associates the idea of licensed evil with violation of the clerical precepts. This is one of the most pronounced differences between Hōnen and Shinran. In Shinran's writings licensed evil is never interpreted in that way. By Hōnen's time precept violation had become a widespread phenomenon. There existed a class of priests, often itinerant monks or recluses, who acknowledged no set of clerical precepts and who maintained ties to no particular religious order.[12] Though these priests devoted their lives to religious concerns, they broke with the schools of Old Buddhism by disavowing the precepts. Some openly took wives and reared families. Many of these priests were attracted to Hōnen's teachings because he preached the *nembutsu* as a practice that could lead even those who violate the precepts to salvation in Amida's Pure Land (*hakai nembutsu ōjō*).[13] Hōnen did so not to encourage clergy to repudiate the precepts but to demonstrate the efficacy of the *nembutsu* as an unfailing religious practice for people in any situation. Hōnen himself upheld the precepts scrupulously, and he administered them unhesitatingly to anyone who sought to receive them. He did not interpret the *nembutsu* as supplanting the precepts or as giving a person freedom to disobey them. The *nembutsu* may extend across the lay-clergy distinction, but it does not undermine that distinction. Hence, Hōnen maintained, "If a person is not called a holy man (*hijiri*), he may take a wife. If he does not take a wife, he may be a holy man."[14] This affirmation of the lay-clergy distinction is one point where Hōnen's and Shinran's teachings diverge dramatically.

Shinran lived a life in clear violation of the clerical precepts. He styled himself on the semilegendary monk Kyōshin (d. 866), who broke the precepts by marrying but who dedicated his life to the *nembutsu*.[15] Shinran often described himself as neither priest nor layman (*sō ni arazu zoku ni arazu*), and to reflect his repudiation of the lay-clergy division he adopted the pen name "Shinran, the Bald-headed Fool" (*Gutoku Shinran*).[16] In concrete terms this meant that Shinran retained some vestiges of the priesthood—shaving his head, propagating the Buddhist teachings, and, if early portraits of him are accurate, donning clerical robes. But he also assumed the attributes of a layman—taking a wife and begetting a family. Shinran's marriage represented an irreconcilable break with the Buddhist establishment and a clear-cut rejection of the lay-clergy distinction. Ultimately, the practice of priests' marrying, which was passed down in the Shinshū, became the dominant feature separating it from other schools of Buddhism and stigmatizing the Shinshū in the eyes of many Buddhists. Though Shinran's personal example was unambiguous, he did not flaunt his apostasy by actively campaigning against the clerical precepts. He simply accepted the decline of the precepts as an inevitable event in the degenerate age of *mappō*, and he relinquished their role in his own career in favor of total reliance on Amida's vow. For this reason, the violation of the clerical precepts is never equated in Shinran's writings with licensed evil.

Compared to Hōnen, Shinran placed far greater emphasis on faith than on practice, just as the single *nembutsu* proponents did. Because of this, Shinran's teachings were occasionally identified as a heretical interpretation of Pure Land thought, not only by the traditional Buddhist schools but also by rival Pure Land proponents. For example, the Chinzei branch of Pure Land Buddhism has long characterized Shinran as one of Kōsai's disciples and as an adherent of the single *nembutsu* doctrine, replete with its licensed evil tendencies. It even suggests that Hōnen's letters denouncing the spread of the single *nembutsu* doctrine in the Hokuriku region were directed against Shinran and his teachings.[17] Although this portrayal of Shinran is questionable, his teachings always remained suspect to other Pure Land schools as long as those schools interpreted violation of the clerical precepts as one form of licensed evil. Apart from their incriminations, Shinran had his own views of heresy and his own arguments against licensed evil.[18]

SHINRAN'S ARGUMENTS AGAINST LICENSED EVIL

Of all the Pure Land advocates who denounced licensed evil, Shinran, it would seem, was in the least tenable position to do so. The reason is that he idealized the evil person as the primary object of Amida's vow to save sentient beings (*akunin shōki*). In the *Tannishō* ("Notes Lamenting Deviations") he is quoted as saying:

> We who are overwhelmed by evil inclinations (*bonnō gusoku*) are unable to extricate ourselves from [this world of] Saṃsāra by any religious practice of our own. Out of compassion for us, [Amida] has established his vow. The primary intention behind it is for the evil person to achieve Buddhahood (*akunin jōbutsu*). Hence, the evil person who relies on Amida's power (*tariki*) embodies, more than anyone else, the true cause of birth in Pure Land (*ōjō shōin*).[19]

Shinran saw evil as a pervasive feature in the degenerate age of *mappō*, and he sensed it in himself first and foremost, even while living in a state of faith and in the assurance of salvation in Pure Land. Shinran focused on the personal realization of evil in oneself as the condition in which one can best comprehend the power of Amida's vow and can truly experience faith. As long as people are preoccupied with their own attempts to accomplish good, they cannot fully understand their need for Amida's aid. Only when they sense the overwhelming burden of their own wrongdoings and inadequacies do they come to rely on Amida completely. To communicate this message, Shinran is sometimes cited as saying, "Even the good person can be born in Pure Land. How much more so the evil person!"[20] The subtlety of Shinran's thinking often eluded his followers, for they frequently took his idealization of the evil person as an exhortation to commit evil. To arrive at this conclusion they reversed his logic, interpreting faith as the freedom to commit evil rather than evil as the impetus for faith to arise. Hence, Shinran's followers were particularly prone to the notion of licensed evil, and under its influence some advocated wrongdoings as a sign of faith.

According to Shinran's letters, the idea of licensed evil, as it circulated among his followers, was typified by the following exhortations:

> Evil should be committed just as one pleases.[21]

> Because evil is the common state of all unenlightened beings and because evil is their nature, people should delight in those things which should not be thought, and should do those things which should not be done, and should say those things which should not be said.[22]

These statements indicate that the concept of licensed evil current among his followers was little more than an indulgence of evil inclinations (*bonnō*), whether mental, verbal, or physical. Shinran perceived a basic incompatibility between an attitude of this type and the life of faith:

> Crazed by inclinations of covetousness, people give rise to desires. Crazed by inclinations of hatred, people seek to thwart karmic retribution for despising things which they should not. Deluded by inclinations of ignorance, people give rise to things which should not even be thought. Those, however, who intentionally commit acts which should not be done or think thoughts which should not be thought, claiming that they are permissible because of the Buddha's blessed vow, have no sense of renunciation toward this world, nor do they truly realize their own state of evil. For this reason they do not have any genuine aspiration for the *nembutsu* or for the Buddha's vow. Hence, in their state of mind it will be difficult for them to be born in Pure Land in their next life, even if they say the *nembutsu*.[23]

Renunciation of this world (*ensei*), mentioned here, undergirds the desire to be born in Pure Land (*yokushō* or *ganshō*). Without perceiving this world as tainted and entrapping, no desire for birth in Pure Land arises, and without that there is no context for faith to emerge. Shinran denounced licensed evil as devoid of this sense of renunciation and thus incompatible with faith. Far from exemplifying the evil person as the primary object of Amida's vow, licensed evil obstructs people from realizing the evil in their own lives. That is, reveling in this tainted world and indulging in any caprice blinds one to the bonds of evil and to the need to rely on Amida.

Shinran's critique of licensed evil was directed ultimately against the state of mind undergirding licensed evil, rather than against evil acts per se. If it were against evil acts themselves, his teachings would be no different from licensed evil's opposite, the encouragement of good deeds (*kenzen shōjin*). Shinran recognized evil as a prevalent phenomenon in the age of *mappō*, and he acknowledged its presence in his own life. Much of this he saw as the eruption of evil inclinations (*bonnō*) or as the karmic fruition of acts perpetrated in past lives (*shukugō*). Hence, when a person commits a wrongdoing, it is often a manifestation of karmic proclivities built up over many lifetimes. According to Shinran's teachings, evil acts themselves constitute no obstruction to Amida's vow. On the contrary, Amida has promulgated his vow precisely to save those who are shackled by their wrongdoing. Nonetheless, a person may not use evil inclinations as an excuse for willfully committing misdeeds:

> It is admirable to believe that Amida's vow is for the person overwhelmed by evil inclinations. But to encourage falsehoods intentionally in one's heart, or in word or deed, simply because the vow is for the evil person, is not what we call the Pure Land teachings. Consequently, people are not to be told such things.[24]

> Because people are crazed by evil inclinations, they do things which should not be done, say things which should not be said, and think things which should not be thought, without even realizing it. But if one is dishonest with other people, doing things which one should not do and saying things which one should not say, because one thinks they are no obstruction to birth in Pure Land, then it is not a case of being crazed by evil inclinations. One is intentionally doing what should not be done, and for that reason these things should never happen in the first place.[25]

A key word in these two passages is "intentionally" (*kotosara ni* and *wazato*), indicating an element of intentionality in licensed evil. Shinran admitted that actions are dominated by karmic influences, but he did not interpret evil inclinations as a form of absolute fatalism. To cling to these inclinations as a pretext for committing wrongdoings is nothing more than a self-deception and a deception of others, since one's intentions can also be the cause of misdeeds. As long as intentionality is at work in a person, there is contrivance (*hakarai*), and that contrivance not only fuels the fires of evil inclinations but also separates the person from Amida's salvation. Once contrivance ends, faith arises. With faith, birth in Pure Land is assured, even though evil inclinations may persist in one's life. Those inclinations are lamented, and they make one aspire all the more to birth in Pure Land, but they do not stand in the way of salvation. What sets the person of faith apart from the adherents of licensed evil is this crucial change of heart that occurs with faith:

> When people come to have faith in the Buddha deep in their heart, they genuinely renounce this life, they lament their transmigration in Saṃsāra, they have deep faith in Amida's vow, and they delight in saying Amida Buddha. If

these people truly desire not to commit the evil deeds that they may be inclined to do, it is an indication of their renunciation of this world.[26]

Faith, as a transformed state of mind, militates against the human intention that underlies licensed evil, and it deprecates all wrongdoings, even those resulting from the residual karmic tendencies in the person saved by Amida's vow.

In order to convey this message to his followers, many of whom were illiterate peasants, Shinran sometimes used analogies that would be familiar to them. In one letter he likened licensed evil to drunkenness and poison in order to communicate that wrongdoings are not the logical outcome of faith. Encouraging people to do evil because Amida's vow guarantees salvation is like plying them with liquor or urging poison on them just when they are finally overcoming the stupor of those substances:

> Originally, you were intoxicated on the liquor of unenlightenment and you delighted in drinking the three poisons: desire, hatred, and ignorance. Since you first learned of the Buddha's vow, however, the intoxication of unenlightenment has gradually worn off a bit. You delight less and less in the three poisons, and you have come to desire constantly Amida Buddha's antidote. How lamentable it is that, with the intoxication not quite worn off and the poisons not quite faded, you are urged on to further intoxication and further poisoning! I feel it is altogether a pity that people tell you: "You may do whatever you please, for people are overwhelmed with evil inclinations. You may, according to your heart's desires, do those things which in body should not be done, say those things which in word should not be said, and think those things which in mind should not be thought." It is like pressing people with more liquor before they have sobered, or encouraging them to take more poison before the other has worn off. "We have the antidote, so enjoy the poison!" Such things, I feel, must never be spoken.[27]

With this analogy Shinran sought to convey that the purpose of Amida's vow is not to free people so they can commit whatever wrongdoing they please but to free them from the cycle of wrongdoings into which they are locked. That is the meaning of Shinran's idealization of the evil person.

LICENSED EVIL AND SHINRAN'S FOLLOWERS

In Shinran's letters the denunciation of licensed evil is often abstract and doctrine laden, but the problem itself was immediate and historical, erupting during the last ten or fifteen years of his life. In that period many of his followers in the Kantō region were thrown into confusion by the persuasions of licensed evil advocates. Congregations swayed by this doctrine are known to have existed at Kashima, Namekata, and Ōgun, all in the province of Hitachi.[28] At that time Shinran was not in a position to deal with the problem effectively, since he was eighty years old and living in Kyoto, some distance from the scene. He dispatched letters to his followers denouncing licensed evil, and he eventually sent his oldest son, Zenran, to the area to try to quell the unrest. The problem, however, grew so critical that local lords (*ryōke*), constables (*jitō*), and overseers (*myōshu*) instituted repressive measures against his followers, and government officials summoned some of Shinran's disciples to Kamakura for interrogation.[29]

The Kantō turmoil of the 1250s was not the first time Shinran had confronted licensed evil adherents. Earlier, perhaps during the two decades he resided in the Kantō, a licensed evil proponent by the name of Zenshōbō had attached himself to Shinran's following. After doing so he continued to hold fast to the notion of licensed evil, and Shinran eventually distanced himself from him.[30] In the 1230s Shinran left the Kantō to return to Kyoto. At that time most of his disciples remained behind to propagate his Pure Land teachings and to win more converts to the *nembutsu*. They maintained contact with Shinran through letters and occasional visits to Kyoto. Over the course of the next twenty years these disciples attracted thousands of believers to the *nembutsu*, many from the peasant class but also some from samurai and merchant backgrounds.[31] These believers were organized into informal congregations centered around meeting places, or *dōjō*, under the leadership and instruction of Shinran's disciples. *Dōjō* of this type were scattered around the Kantō region, primarily in the provinces of Hitachi, Shimotsuke, Musashi, and Shimōsa. Licensed evil took root in some of these groups, and in the 1250s it emerged as a major controversy among believers.

Shinran realized that licensed evil, when carried to an extreme, could even be used to rationalize violent crimes. In one of his letters he pointed out these implications to his followers: "If people can do whatever they please simply because they are unenlightened beings, then should they commit robbery, or murder others, or whatever?"[32] Actually Shinran's followers were not involved in misdeeds of this magnitude. The types of wrongdoings attributed to licensed evil proponents were disloyalty to parents, repudiation of religious teachers, disparagement of fellow believers, distortion of the teachings, gambling, and drunkenness.[33] They were also accused of denigrating various Buddhas and Bodhisattvas and of ridiculing *kami*, the deities of Shinto.[34] These activities reflect rebelliousness among Shinran's followers, disregard for authority, capriciousness of conduct, indolence toward responsibilities, self-indulgence of desires, and irreverence toward tradition, all in the name of faith realized through the *nembutsu*.

One conspicuous form of licensed evil that irritated the authorities was the denigration of the Buddhas, Bodhisattvas, and Shinto *kami* revered by mainstream religious groups.[35] Respect for them was part and parcel of the concept of piety advanced by the orthodox Buddhist schools and upheld by the political establishment. Consequently, derision of these figures by *nembutsu* adherents was a symbolic act of defiance against civil and religious authority, provoking repressive measures. There are elements in Shinran's teachings which in some ways lent themselves to such inclinations. Specifically, Shinran believed that all forms of Buddhism outside of the true Pure Land teachings are merely provisional (*ke*) and should be superseded. Devotion to the true teachings, when carried to its logical end, entails the rejection of all Buddhas and Bodhisattvas besides Amida. This is intimated in a passage in the *Ichinen tanen mon'i* ("Notes on the Single and the Repeated Nembutsu"):

> "Single-mindedly" (*ikkō*) means not to change to any beneficial religious practice other [than the *nembutsu*] and not to concentrate on any Buddha other [than Amida]. . . . "Exclusively" (*mohara*) means not to have any intention (*kokoro*) to change to other beneficial religious practices or to different Buddhas.[36]

Shinran did not dispute the existence of other Buddhas or Bodhisattvas, but considered reverencing them to be superfluous for the true believer.

His attitude toward Shinto was even more strident. In one of his *wasan* hymns Shinran lamented:

> How deplorable it is that both priests and lay people
> Observe auspicious times and lucky days.
> They worship the *kami* of heaven and earth,
> And perform divination and Shinto ceremonies (*saishi*).[37]

Shinran tended to relegate worship of Shinto *kami* to a vast array of beliefs and practices aimed at worldly benefits and averting calamity. Others included propitiation of ghosts and evil spirits; divination of good and evil; belief in auspicious days, times, and directions; and observance of taboos (*monoimi*), in the form of seclusion or abstinence to avoid misfortune.[38] These elements, Shinto and otherwise, had long been integrated into the established forms of religiosity that the eight schools of Old Buddhism upheld. Worldly concerns were so melded with the transcendent goals of Buddhism that in the popular consciousness they all merged into a seamless tissue of religious sensibilities. Shinran, however, went against the grain of this worldview by singling out certain elements for acceptance and others for rejection. Reverence for the Shinto *kami* fell into the latter group, which he classified as "falsehoods, teachings lying outside [the pale of Buddhism]" (*gekyō jagi*).[39] The harshness of his language reveals that in his own mind such practices were tantamount to heresy.

Despite these sentiments, Shinran by no means encouraged followers to denigrate other Buddhas, Bodhisattvas, or *kami*. On the contrary, he saw such behavior as offensive and certainly not the product of faith. In a letter addressed to all followers in the Kantō, which scholars date 1254 or 1255,[40] Shinran admonished:

> To scorn Buddhas and Bodhisattvas and to denigrate Shinto *kami* and spirits is something that should never be. Over countless rebirths and lifetimes, by means of the aid of innumerable and unlimited Buddhas and Bodhisattvas, people have undertaken all types of beneficial religious practices. Nonetheless, these people have not escaped this world of Saṃsāra through any efforts of their own, and so Buddhas and Bodhisattvas have urged them forward over

many kalpas of lifetimes. Because of their urging, these people have now encountered Amida's vow, which is extremely difficult to encounter. But not realizing their indebtedness for this, they speak ill of Buddhas and Bodhisattvas. Surely it is that they do not realize their profound indebtedness to them.

The *kami* of heaven and earth watch over people who have a profound faith in the Buddhist teachings, accompanying them as if they took the form of their shadow. Therefore, if people have faith in the *nembutsu*, they should never entertain thoughts of disclaiming the *kami* of heaven and earth. If the *kami* are not to be discarded, then how much less should they speak ill of or look down on Buddhas and Bodhisattvas. If people speak ill of Buddhas and Bodhisattvas, then they are individuals who utter Amida's name without having faith in the *nembutsu*.

In short, it is only to be expected that lords, constables, and overseers in the area, speaking falsehoods and inclined toward error, should now take measures to suppress the *nembutsu* aimed at *nembutsu* followers. Among the sayings of the Tathāgata Śākyamuni, it is said that someone who reviles those practicing the *nembutsu* is a person without sight or a person without hearing. Master Shantao accurately interpreted these words, saying:

> In this age when the five corruptions abound,
> Doubt and revilement are widespread.
> Priests and lay people alike are filled with abhorrence,
> And have lost their ability to hear.
> When they see people adhering to religious practices,
> They are filled with poisonous hatred.
> On some pretext they work havoc upon them,
> And endeavor to vent their hostilities.

This is a common occurrence in our world. Local lords, constables, and overseers of the area seem to be those who would obstruct the *nembutsu*.

Nonetheless, you should not say things against them. Rather, people who practice the *nembutsu* should have compassion and feel pity for those who would pose obstructions, and they should say the *nembutsu* fervently hoping that Amida will save even those posing these obstructions. This has been taught to us by our [illustrious] predecessors. You should reflect on it well. . . . [41]

This passage is particularly revealing, for it indicates Shinran's attitude not only toward followers denigrating Buddhas and *kami* but also toward the authorities who sought to suppress the *nembutsu*.

It is clear that Shinran opposed the denigration of Buddhas and *kami* by his followers. But it was not because he encouraged believers to integrate the vast pantheon of Buddhist and Shinto deities into their spiritual practices. Rather, he simply sought to deny that faith gives a person license to malign them. Shinran acknowledged the existence of these deities, and he even ascribed a minor role to them in Amida's grand scheme to deliver all living beings into Pure Land. That is, they aid and protect people during the countless lifetimes of their sojourn toward Amida's teachings, so the believer's natural response to them should be a sense of indebtedness. But ultimately Shinran viewed these deities as subordinate to Amida and overshadowed by his promise of salvation to all sentient beings. That is why Shinran lamented that people often become fixated on these Buddhas and *kami* without comprehending the message of Amida's vow. Moreover, Shinran looked upon worship of them, without reference to this message, as provisional or even false religion. For that reason, he urged people to turn to Amida single-mindedly. Faith in Amida is the ultimate religious state freeing a person from any need to worship or supplicate other Buddhas or *kami*, but it by no means inspires a person to vilify them.[42] On the contrary, a person who adheres to the *nembutsu* in a spirit of faith responds to them naturally with a sense of gratitude. Gratitude, not only to Amida but also to other Buddhas, Bodhisattvas, and *kami*, and even to one's religious teacher and fellow believers, is in Shinran's estimation one way in which faith might manifest itself in a person. Vindictiveness and derision, by contrast, are never an expression of faith.

Shinran's attitude toward the civil authorities, as reflected in this letter, was one of ambivalence. He acknowledged that their actions against people who gratuitously commit wrongdoings in the name of licensed evil were only to be expected. But he felt it a grave injustice that they suppressed true followers of the *nembutsu* alongside licensed evil adherents, without distinguishing between the two. From the point of view of the authorities, it was probably difficult to differentiate Shinran's true followers from licensed evil adherents, since both rejected the traditional forms of religion in favor of undivided devotion to the *nembutsu*. Perhaps the only *nembutsu* advocates exempted from suppressive measures were those who preached the necessity of good deeds (*kenzen shōjin*) over and above the *nembutsu*.[43] In Shinran's eyes the encouragement of good deeds was no truer a path to Pure Land than licensed evil was. Hence, Shinran alluded to the local lords, constables, and overseers who could not see this as persons without sight and persons without hearing.[44]

Shinran bore a sense of unjust persecution at the hands of civil authorities dating back to his banishment to Echigo in 1207. He felt profoundly wronged then by both the political and the religious establishment, which, according to his account in the *Kyōgyōshinshō* ("Teaching, Practice, Faith, and Enlightenment"), were blind to the true teachings of Buddhism:

> As I privately ponder things, I realize that practice and enlightenment via the teachings of the path of religious exertion have passed away forever, whereas enlightenment via the true teachings of Pure Land has now begun to flourish. The priests of the Buddhist temples, however, are so lost in darkness concerning the true teachings that they do not realize what the true and the provisional gateways are. The Confucian counselors in the capital are so bewildered over practices that they cannot distinguish what the right and the heretical paths (*jashō no dōro*) are. For this reason, the scholar-monks of the Kōfukuji temple petitioned the retired emperor Gotoba and the reigning emperor Tsuchimikado (1195–1231) during the early spring of the year 1207. The emperor above and his ministers below turned their backs on the Buddhist teachings and went against justice. They gave vent to anger and were consumed with resentment. Because of this, the great master Hōnen, who heralded the true teachings

(*shinshū*), and a number of his disciples were punished without demonstration of their crimes. Some were arbitrarily sentenced to death. Others were driven from the priesthood, given lay names, and exiled. I was one of them.[45]

Shinran's indignation toward the authorities expressed in this passage indicates how much he regarded their actions as detrimental to Buddhism. From Shinran's letter it is apparent that he perceived the civil authorities in the Kantō as obstructors of the *nembutsu*, and because of that he may have considered them karmically destined to punishment in the next life, just as licensed evil adherents were.[46] In short, both of them verged on the heretical. Nonetheless, he was more distressed over licensed evil as a heresy, for he considered it a "worm inside the body of the lion" (*shishi no shinchū no mushi*), undermining the true teachings of the *nembutsu* more by distortions from within than did the political authorities' attacks from without.[47]

SHINRAN'S VIEW OF ORTHODOXY AND HERESY

The pivotal concept in Shinran's mind for defining orthodoxy and heresy was faith. According to him, faith is the sine qua non in the path to salvation and, as the example of licensed evil shows, it is the element violated in the act of heresy. Shinran's writings do not present orthodoxy and heresy in any systematic or institutional way, for his ultimate intention was not to establish his own school of religious thought but to communicate to his fellow sentient beings the need for faith. In this light Shinran's teachings represent an expression of his own religious vision and personal commitment rather than a call for a new sectarian body. As concepts, Shinshū orthodoxy and heresy emerged in full-fledged form only later, after the heirs of Shinran's thought fleshed out his teachings and adapted them for institutional use.

Shinran's idea of heresy, to the extent that he articulated one, was a departure from the dominant concept of his day. The worship of Shinto *kami*, for example, was an accepted form of religious piety in the prevailing eight schools of Buddhism, and yet Shinran looked upon it as a deviation from religious truth. By contrast, repudiation of the clerical precepts was a typical example of licensed evil, cited not only by the eight schools but also by Hōnen, and yet Shinran never alluded to it in his own denunciations of licensed evil. These differences reflect what a radical reinterpretation Shinran's view of heresy was. His criterion for determining the correctness of any particular belief or practice was the presence of faith, and what went against or obstructed faith constituted heresy.

Shinran's view of orthodoxy was likewise contingent on the concept of faith. He saw faith as the central theme of the Pure Land teachings and as the highest religious state that a person could achieve. Shinran's notion of an orthodox religious tradition consisted of the teachings of the so-called seven Pure Land patriarchs: Nāgārjuna, Vasubandhu, T'an-luan, Tao-ch'o, Shan-tao, Genshin, and Hōnen.[48] Shinran saw faith as the ultimate message of their teachings, though that interpretation represents more Shinran's own subjective reading of their works than the actual content of what they said. Shinran looked upon them as the source of doctrinal orthodoxy, and he viewed himself as merely an heir or, at most, a humble transmitter of their Pure Land teachings. Within fifty years of Shinran's death, this focus would shift from the seven patriarchs to Shinran himself as the true visionary of Pure Land thought and to his writings as the repository of Shin orthodoxy.

Shinran's emphasis on faith as the basis for defining heresy and orthodoxy was, in the end, fraught with hazards. The reason is that faith, in the final analysis, is an internal state of mind or a private religious condition. Its connection to externalized forms, such as ethical behavior or even statements of doctrine, is often elusive and hard to define. Thus, it is difficult to establish public and objective criteria for certifying faith's presence in any particular individual. All religions are confronted with this problem to the extent that religious experience is private and personal; but Shinran's idea of faith is particularly problematic, since he saw the evil person as the prime candidate for faith and the principal object of Amida's vow. Tsuda Sōkichi has described the tenuousness between the inward sense of salvation and one's outward expression of it in the following way:

> It is not clear what the precise relationship is between the assurance of birth in Pure Land and one's everyday life after one has received that assurance. Until birth in Pure Land—that is, until death—one continues to live the life of an unenlightened being. If that is so, then it would seem that ordinary life and the assurance of birth in Pure Land exist alongside one another, but with no apparent connection to each other. The actions of an unenlightened being include wrongdoings, but since such actions are the result of past karma, they are altogether separate from birth in Pure Land. We can come to no other conclusion if we take Shinran's teachings to be this. If this is the case, Amida's salvation has no bearing whatsoever on one's present life; moreover, a person's present life is an independent existence with no relation to that salvation. This seems right, considering that salvation consists of birth in Pure Land, which occurs at death. Hence, it would seem that Shinran has not defined what meaning there is in the present life, or what is to govern it.[49]

Tsuda's summation of Shinran's thought is not totally accurate, in that Shinran did acknowledge that faith can be manifested in one's everyday life, though he did not delineate specific external forms which are incontrovertible evidence of faith. Nonetheless, Tsuda's description highlights the disjunction that seems to exist between one's inner life of faith, with its assurance of birth in Pure Land, and one's outer life of words and deeds. The tie between these two has been the central question in the emergence of the Shinshū, resulting in its formulation of ceremony, doctrine, ethics, and sectarian organization. In this sense, all Shinshū history can be construed to be an attempt to explicate the meaning of faith as manifested in thought and action.

CHAPTER
5

THE EARLY SHINSHŪ

Between the thirteenth and the fifteenth centuries, the Shinshū blossomed from an obscure band of Pure Land adherents into one of the largest and most powerful schools of Buddhism in Japan. Its success resulted from a variety of factors, both external and internal. First of all, the Shinshū gained a foothold among the lower classes in the countryside. As this rural population began to organize into autonomous villages, Shinshū congregations emerged as rallying points for village society, since they provided a meeting place for communities, a reason for assembling, and a religious network linking villages to one another. Hence, Shinshū growth proceeded hand in hand with the decline of the provincial estate system and the development of semiautonomous villages in Japan. Secondly, Buddhist evangelists, Pure Land and otherwise, crisscrossed the country in perhaps the most extensive dissemination of religion in Japanese history. The Shinshū eventually profited from this efflorescence of religious activity by absorbing many of these converts into its own fold. Thirdly, Shinran's descendants, particularly Kakunyo, Zonkaku, and Rennyo skillfully fashioned a sectarian doctrine from his teachings and formulated methods and devices for communicating this message to the population at large. These innovations eventually consolidated most Shinshū followers under the religious authority of the Honganji temple, especially during Rennyo's ministry, and drew thousands of believers from other schools of Buddhism. Amid this process of sectarian formation, the concepts of orthodoxy and heresy functioned as useful tools in the hands of Honganji leaders as they strove for Shinshū domination.

OVERVIEW OF SHINSHŪ DEVELOPMENT

From the time of Shinran's death in 1262, orthodoxy and heresy began to take on new significance in the Shinshū, over and above the meaning that Shinran had given them. The metamorphosis of these concepts paralleled the emergence of the Shinshū as a formal school of Buddhism. This change occurred over a long period as the Shinshū evolved from a few scattered congregations into a nationwide religious organization. During this time the Shinshū formulated its own sectarian dogma, standardized its own forms of worship, and generated its own system of religious authority. Throughout this process, the concepts of orthodoxy and heresy were frequently invoked to help define the identity of the Shinshū, both doctrinally and institutionally, and to distinguish it from other religious groups.

Shinran did not envision himself as the founder of a religious school, nor was he particularly concerned with the organizational aspects of sectarian development. In his writings he used the word *shinshū* to mean the "true teachings" or "true message," not to designate a school of Buddhism.[1] If Shinran conceived of himself as belonging to any religious school, it was to the Jōdoshū or Pure Land school revolving around Hōnen, his teacher. Hōnen had sown the seeds of a sectarian organization by endorsing the idea of a Pure Land school, comparing it to the Kegon, Tendai, and other established schools and grounding it with a traditional master and disciple lineage (*shishi sōjō*).[2] Shinran, as one of Hōnen's disciples, was heir to this Pure Land school, but like a number of Hōnen's other followers he did not couch it in institutional forms.[3] Rather, he perceived it solely in doctrinal terms, as the corpus of true teachings inherited from Hōnen. Though his own understanding of Pure Land Buddhism differed in crucial ways from Hōnen's, Shinran was convinced that what he preached was identical to Hōnen's thought, and for that reason he gave Hōnen total credit for it and claimed none for himself.[4] Shinran idealized Hōnen in the role of master, but did not in turn adopt the role for himself. He denied having even a single disciple, and instead placed himself on an equal footing with his followers, describing them as companions (*dōbō*) or as fellow believers (*dōgyō*).[5] In short, Shinran had little interest in institutional matters, such as the founding of temples or the establishment of a legitimate lineage from Hōnen through himself to his disciples. Only in subsequent generations did the architects of the Shinshū add this organizational dimension to Shinran's thought.

Shinran left no instructions on the formation of a sectarian order after his death, so his followers were forced to shape the Shinshū as best they could from his teachings. Unfortunately, Shinran's religious views were difficult to institutionalize, since they differed profoundly from the concept of religion of his day. Consequently, discrepancies arose among his followers over what form the Shinshū should take. Some envisioned a rigid hierarchical organization, similar to existing schools of Buddhism, while others preferred an unstructured community of believers, much like Shinran's following during his own lifetime. In the decades after Shinran's death, different congregations followed separate paths of development, and as a result a variety of organizational structures and doctrinal interpretations evolved. As these groups attracted more and more believers, they gradually came into conflict with one another and with other schools of Buddhism. Competition among them led to controversy over teachings and practices, and ultimately resulted in accusations of heresy. These accusations arose primarily from the doctrinal and organizational differences that divided these groups.

One point of contention among them was the integration into the Shinshū of beliefs and practices from other schools of Buddhism. This occurred because some Shinshū proponents sought to imitate other religious groups, and therefore incorporated elements from them into the Shinshū. Since many Shinshū believers were illiterate and since few copies of Shinran's writings were in circulation, it was easy for preachers to present concepts and practices of other schools as Shinran's teachings. Another reason for the absorption of extraneous elements was that the Shinshū always existed in a multisectarian society. With the influx of converts from other religious groups, Shinshū communities inevitably assimilated beliefs and customs from them. These external elements, whether intentionally incorporated or inadvertently absorbed, became the subject of criticism in works on heresy composed by major Shinshū figures, particularly the leaders of the Honganji temple.

Like other centers of Shinshū activity, the Honganji arose by adapting Shinran's ideals to organizational realities. The way in which it did so is reflected in the works of Kakunyo, Zonkaku, and Rennyo, the three most prominent figures in early Honganji history. They added an institutional dimension to the concept of heresy that was lacking in Shinran's understanding of the word. That is, they invoked the idea of heresy to indicate deviation from Honganji authority, to criticize other schools, to defend Shin teachings from denunciations, and to expand the Honganji's sphere of influence. Their use of the notion of heresy suggests that during this period the Honganji was struggling for survival in an atmosphere of intense religious competition. Accusations of heresy became one means for the Honganji to assert its religious authority against other schools of Buddhism and against rival branches of the Shinshū. Notwithstanding its institutional motives, the Honganji's doctrinal understanding of heresy was much closer to Shinran's than were the interpretations of other Shinshū factions. The reason is that, compared to other Shinshū groups, the Honganji preserved a fairly accurate version of Shinran's teachings at a time when the assimilation of external beliefs and practices was greatest.

THE SHINSHŪ DŌJŌ

When Shinran died in 1262, the preponderance of his followers were located in eastern Japan, primarily the Kantō region. The exact size of Shinran's following during his lifetime is not known, but estimates range from "several thousand" to 100,000.[6] From Shinran's letters and from an early list of his followers entitled the *Shinran Shōnin monryo kyōmyōchō* ("Register of Master Shinran's Disciples"), a total of seventy-four direct disciples can be identified.[7] Of them, more than fifty inhabited the four Kantō provinces of Hitachi, Shimotsuke, Shimōsa, and Musashi. Others resided as far away as Mutsu province in the northeast and Kyoto in the west.[8] During the first half century after Shinran's death, four communities emerged as major centers of Shinshū activity: in the Kantō region, Takada, Yokosone, and Kashima; and farther northeast, Ōami. From the fourteenth century on, the Shinshū spread primarily in a westward direction, along the Hokuriku seaboard in northern Japan, across the provinces lying between Kantō and Kyoto, throughout the region surrounding Kyoto, and from there into western Japan. By the time of Rennyo's death in 1499, Shinshū followers in the Hokuriku area and around Kyoto far outnumbered those in the Kantō, thereby supplanting them as the regional bulwark of Shinshū strength.

During this period the *dōjō*, or meeting place, emerged as the basic unit of religious organization in the Shinshū. According to Kakunyo:

> Among all the disciples to whom Shinran personally imparted his teachings long ago, there were none who established temples. He suggested that they construct a *dōjō* simply by altering an ordinary dwelling place slightly, perhaps by extending its roof.[9]

Dōjō of this type were not unique to the Shinshū, but were prevalent throughout the Pure Land movement. The local congregation affiliated with the *dōjō* became known as *nembutsu* members (*nembutsushu*) or as religious companions (*monto*). In the formative years of the Shinshū, *nembutsu* members met once a month for worship services, usually on the twenty-fifth to commemorate the day Hōnen had died. After Shinran's death, most congregations changed to the twenty-eighth of each month, in memory of Shinran's death day.[10] The centerpiece of worship in the Shinshū *dōjō* was usually a large inscription of Amida's name (*myōgō honzon*) hung over a simple altar. This kind of religious object was an innovation of Shinran's. Up to that time the center of Buddhist worship had been artistic images of the Buddha, usually carved or painted. Such icons were available primarily to the upper classes, who had the wealth to commission artists to execute religious works of art. Shinran's creation of the Amida inscription supplied the ordinary believer with a simple and accessible object of reverence for use in worship, thereby freeing religious objects from the artistic domain controlled by aristocratic society.[11] The actual content of *dōjō* worship varied from place to place, but was dominated by *nembutsu* chanting. In addition, simple sermons, the recitation of scriptures, and the singing of hymns such as Shinran's *wasan* also became common features.[12] All these components—the *dōjō*, the religious inscription, and the elements of worship—provided lowborn believers with a ready outlet for their religious inclinations and with a degree of participation in religion denied them under Japan's traditional system of temples. This fuller religious life, centering around the *dōjō*, was the reason for its popularity among peasants, and was the key to Shinshū growth during the fourteenth and fifteenth centuries.

Unlike Hōnen, who defined rules of conduct for his disciples in his *Shichikajō kishōmon* ("Seven Article Pledge"), Shinran left behind no instructions outside of a few random remarks in his letters. Nonetheless, he unconsciously set an example in his own actions which his followers naturally tried to emulate. As a result, later Shinshū groups formulated congregational rules to act as guidelines for the behavior of their members. Three such sets of rules have survived in manuscript form, thus preserving a picture of the ethical ideal advanced by the early Shinshū *dōjō*.[13] The oldest set, dated 1285, reads as follows:

Regulations

Among adherents of the single-minded and exclusive *nembutsu*, the following items are prohibited:

1. As followers of the exclusive practice, do not denigrate other Buddhas or Bodhisattvas, or people of other persuasions and practices.
2. Do not indulge in arguments with people of other persuasions and practices.
3. Do not be slack in your respect for rulers and parents.
4. Do not denigrate the *kami* just because you say the *nembutsu*.
5. Do not enter the *dōjō* laughing or whispering or with an air of haughtiness.
6. Do not give your teacher a bad reputation by preaching heresies (*jagi*) and by wrongly calling them the single-minded and exclusive teaching.
7. Do not punish disciples, simply because you are the teacher, without establishing what is right and wrong.
8. Do not denigrate your religious teacher or your fellow believers.
9. Whenever there are falsehoods spoken between fellow believers who appeal to you for judgment, listen to what is right and wrong on both sides, and show them what is correct and what is not.
10. On the day of *nembutsu* worship when you meet for services, do not do such things as eat fish or fowl.
11. Men and women should not sit together when they perform the *nembutsu*, since it will be a disruption.
12. Do not act as a merchant of horses or human beings, for it is known to be disreputable.
13. In selling something, do not lie and charge even a single *mon* of money in excess, and, if you do, return the difference.
14. Do not indulge in illicit sexual relations with another person's wife, and do not slander others by saying that they do.
15. As *nembutsu* adherents, when you drink liquor, do not get drunk and lose your senses.
16. As *nembutsu* adherents, do not steal or gamble.
17. Do not do such things as envy those who are superior or belittle those who are inferior.

The items listed above are prohibited. Abide by these seventeen correct regulations. Adherents of the *nembutsu*, the exclusive and single practice, should admonish each other in them. [If people violate them,] then even if they are called fellow believers or religious companions, you should expel them from the congregation, and you should not sit with them or join them. In witness to the aforesaid regulations.

   1285.8.13

Zen'en
(signature)[14]

The content of these congregational rules corresponds to the conventional morality of the period. Though Shinran never laid down any such injunctions, they reflect more or less Shinran's own behavior during his lifetime. A number of these regulations were derived perhaps from items in Hōnen's *Shichikajō kishōmon* ("Seven Article Pledge") and in the Kōfukuji temple's nine accusations against Hōnen's Pure Land movement.[15] Obviously, Shinshū congregations were concerned about their image in the eyes of society at large. They sought to defend themselves against charges of licensed evil by maintaining upright behavior among their members. By common consensus they used the threat of expulsion and ostracism to enforce mutual adherence to these regulations. Unfortunately, to the extent that they equated obedience to these rules with the religious state of faith, they deviated from Shinran's teachings. For that reason, the author of the *Tannishō* ("Notes Lamenting Deviations") denounced the practice of posting rules in the *dōjō* as a misguided attempt to make good works a requirement for salvation (*kenzen shōjin*).[16] Nevertheless, congregational rules, whether mistaken for the essence of Shinran's teachings or simply implemented as a pragmatic measure to maintain order and stability in the religious community, became an increasingly prominent feature in Shinshū circles.

Dōjō, as they proliferated during the fourteenth and fifteenth centuries, had a revolutionary impact on Buddhism in Japan. Compared to the traditional temple, the *dōjō* had a distinctly lay air. Zonkaku described its members in the following way:

> Today most adherents of the exclusive practice live the life of a lay person. Hence, some have a wife and children and are attached to the pleasures of the senses, while others serve overlords and bear weapons. Some till the soil, wielding plows and hoes, while others make their living as merchants, supporting themselves morning and evening.[17]

The diversity and secularity of this constituency stood in sharp contrast to that of the traditional temple, which was made up of priests ostensibly committed to full-time religious pursuits. Implicit in the temple system of the Buddhist establishment was the assumption that priests, as religious specialists, require their own locus of activity, and as specialists they are superior to lay believers in religious advancement.

Another important difference between the two institutions was that the *dōjō* operated collectively, while temples functioned according to a hierarchical order of priests. In many *dōjō* decisions were made by the group as a whole, meeting in plenary session to discuss issues.[18] This system of consensus was the reason that congregations, exerting the power of ostracism, could command adherence to congregational rules. In fiscal matters as well responsibility fell equitably to all *dōjō* members. Contributions for *dōjō* maintenance and upkeep were voluntary at first, but later they became an obligation of membership. This practice of relying on contributions for support was common throughout the Shinshū, and distinguished it from the traditional temples, which drew their wealth from their endowment of provincial estates. Consequently, the Shinshū did not slide into financial ruin, as the traditional temples did, when the estate system began to collapse in the fifteenth and sixteenth centuries.[19]

The *dōjō* was, in short, a private religious association operated and supported by its members, whereas the traditional temple was a public institution, integrated into the political and economic structure of the period.[20] For that reason, some scholars have categorized traditional temples as the embodiment of state Buddhism (*ritsuryō Bukkyō*), functioning in cooperation with civil authorities, and the *dōjō* as a form of antiestablishment Buddhism (*han ritsuryō Bukkyō*), pursuing its own religious ends apart from civil authority.[21] Though the Shinshū derived its grass-roots strength from the *dōjō*, it eventually produced its own temples as well, which helped reduce the friction that existed between traditional religion and the antiestablishment leanings of rural congregations. Since Shinran is also characterized as a champion of antiestablishment Buddhism, the founding of formal Shinshū temples in some sense went against his inclinations. Nevertheless, certain scholars maintain that, to the extent that rural peasants always made up the rank and file of Shinshū membership, it was difficult for Shinshū temples to adopt the same role in society that traditional temples did, that of upholding state Buddhism, since Shinshū leaders were constantly accountable to their peasant constituencies.[22]

THE TANNISHŌ

The most important document revealing the religious life and beliefs of the early Shinshū *dōjō* is a short religious tract called the *Tannishō* ("Notes Lamenting Deviations").[23] It was written in an attempt to preserve Shinran's ideas from distortion and to rectify a number of misconceptions circulating among his followers. The work consists of two parts: the first is a collection of ten sayings attributed to Shinran, and the second is a critique of eight misinterpretations of his teachings. In addition there is a brief explanation and personal testimony added by the author at the beginning of the work, in the middle between the two sections, and at the end.[24] The *Tannishō*'s historical value lies in the vivid picture it paints of the Shinshū in this embryonic stage. Over and above that, the work presents a powerful spiritual message which has made the *Tannishō* one of the Shinshū's most popular religious texts in the twentieth century.

For all its historical and religious importance, the *Tannishō*'s origins are shrouded in mystery. The earliest surviving copy is a manuscript made by Rennyo around 1479, almost two centuries after its presumed date of composition.[25] No references to the work exist prior to that time, and only about a dozen copies of it can be traced back to the late Muromachi period (1336-1573).[26] One reason for the *Tannishō*'s obscurity may be its radical religious contents. Rennyo intimated at this in the postscript to his copy: "This text is one of the important scriptures in our school, but it is not to be revealed capriciously to persons lacking karmic preparation for it."[27] Rennyo was obviously moved by the convictions expressed in the *Tannishō*, but he felt they could also be misinterpreted and misused. For that reason he recommended it only to believers sufficiently mature in faith. Others, he thought, would get the wrong impression. Such protective sentiments, if in fact they surrounded the *Tannishō's* early history, have concealed its origins so thoroughly that only long and involved investigations have managed to uncover them.

The key to discovering the *Tannishō's* beginnings is its authorship. The prevailing opinion during the Tokugawa period (1600–1867) was that Kakunyo composed the work. The reason is that several passages in the *Tannishō* resemble sections in Kakunyo's *Kudenshō* ("Notes of Oral Transmissions").[28] But Kakunyo was born eight years after Shinran's death, whereas the author of the *Tannishō* apparently received religious instruction from Shinran directly, as indicated in the preface to the work.[29] Other passages in the *Tannishō* suggest that the author also lived a considerable distance from the capital, more than ten provinces away.[30] One disciple named Yuienbō, who lived in the Kantō region, is mentioned twice in the text.[31] This evidence has led scholars to speculate that Yuienbō was the author of the *Tannishō*.[32]

What little is known of Yuienbō reveals the circumstances of the *Tannishō's* composition. Yuienbō was one of Shinran's direct disciples living at Kawada in the province of Hitachi. In 1288 he traveled to Kyoto and discussed religious matters with Kakunyo. Early Shinshū sources praise him for his understanding of Shinran's teachings and for his ability to communicate them to others.[33] As one of Shinran's last surviving disciples, he was active in Kantō circles at the end of the thirteenth century and in all likelihood headed a *dōjō* there.[34] With the expansion of the Kantō following, Yuienbō probably became distressed over misinterpretations of Shinran's ideas. In an effort to preserve his teachings for the next generation, Yuienbō wrote this short piece during his twilight years. This apparently was the course of events leading to the *Tannishō's* composition.[35]

The first half of the *Tannishō* presents Shinran's teachings in an extremely succinct and powerful form. The ten passages there are today among the most quoted sayings attributed to Shinran. Some of the sayings can be found in Shinran's own writings; others are recorded in additional Shinshū sources; and still others are unique to the *Tannishō*.[36] Because some passages cannot be found elsewhere, the *Tannishō* is an invaluable source revealing dimensions of Shinran's thought not highlighted in other writings. The themes which stand out most clearly are: 1) that the evil person is the primary object of Amida's vow; 2) that the *nembutsu* is not an individual's own manipulable act; and 3) that there is no reason for *nembutsu* believers to vie for disciples or to claim credit in leading others to Pure Land.

The most important theme in the *Tannishō* is that the evil person is the primary object of Amida's vow (*akunin shōki*). Had it not been for the *Tannishō*, this idea may have never risen to prominence in Shin Buddhism, for it is heavily embedded in Shinran's own writings. The third paragraph of the *Tannishō* presents this idea in its most lucid and engaging form:

> Even the good person can be born in Pure Land. How much more so the evil person! But what ordinary people usually say is: "Even the evil person can be born in Pure Land. How much more so the good person!" At first

glance this expression seems to make sense, but it [actually] goes against the other-power (*tariki*) of the principal vow. The reason is that people who perform good deeds through their own efforts (*jiriki sazen*) lack a sense (*kokoro*) of relying exclusively on the other-power [of the Buddha]. Therefore, it is not Amida's principal vow [at work in them]. But if we overturn this sense of self-effort and rely on other-power, then we will attain birth in the true Pure Land. We who are overwhelmed by evil inclinations (*bonnō gusoku*) are unable to extricate ourselves from [this world of] Saṃsāra by any religious practice of our own. Out of compassion for us, [Amida] has established his vow. The primary intention behind it is for the evil person to achieve Buddhahood (*akunin jōbutsu*). Hence, the evil person who relies on Amida's power (*tariki*) embodies, more than anyone else, the true cause of birth in Pure Land (*ōjō no shōin*). For that reason it is said, "Even the good person can be born in Pure Land. How much more so the evil person!"[37]

Shinran's point here is that only when people realize that they are unable to free themselves of the woes of this world through their own efforts do they come to rely on Amida's power totally. Those who recognize their evil propensities are more inclined to do this because they have no illusions about their own worth or about the type of rebirth they deserve. They are therefore in a position to respond to Amida's vow fully. The implication of this is that reliance on the power of the Buddha is tantamount to realizing how wrongdoing dominates one's life. Faith is none other than trust in Amida which arises when one perceives the evil that pervades oneself. Among Shinran's teachings, this particular one was the most liable to misrepresentation, especially by licensed evil proponents. To declare that the evil person is the primary object of Amida's vow could easily provoke indulgent or presumptuous behavior. And yet the author of the *Tannishō* gave this idea the greatest emphasis, even while seeking to correct misinterpretations of it. He saw it as Shinran's crowning statement.

The second noteworthy theme in the *Tannishō* concerns the *nembutsu*. Several passages make clear that the true *nembutsu* is not something to be manipulated for one's own benefit. It operates outside the tissue of human intentions and endeavors. Shinran is quoted as saying, "For the believer, the *nembutsu* is neither a practice (*higyō*) nor a virtuous act (*hizen*)."[38] This statement goes against an earlier Pure Land view that the *nembutsu* is an act of inexhaustible virtue and the religious practice par excellence. Throughout most of the Pure Land movement people were encouraged to chant the *nembutsu* for multifarious purposes and benefits. Shinran rejected this position, claiming that if the *nembutsu* is spoken with ulterior motives in mind it stems from one's own effort rather than from the power of the Buddha. When done so, it may contain some degree of personal virtue, depending on the piety invested in it by the believer. But this *nembutsu* is not the one that results in birth in the true Pure Land, since it still involves attachment to one's own actions. The true *nembutsu* is a creation of Amida's imparted to all people and intoned by them in total abandonment of their own designs (*hakarai*). In that respect it is endowed with the other-power of the Buddha instead of the self-effort of the believer.[39] The extent to which

Shinran stressed this point is seen in his repudiation of the *nembutsu* spoken in behalf of his deceased parents:

> I, Shinran, have never uttered a single *nembutsu* out of filial devotion to my father and mother. The reason is that all sentient beings have been my parents or siblings in one lifetime or another. During my next life I will achieve Buddhahood [in Pure Land] and will come to the aid of each of them. Were it [simply a matter of] the virtue I could muster through my own power, I might be able to aid my father and mother by extending my *nembutsu* to them. But if only I abandon my own efforts and achieve enlightenment posthaste, I will be able to assist all those with whom I share a karmic bond, through miraculous powers and skillful means, no matter what karmic sufferings they are immersed in within [Saṃsāra's] six realms and four types of rebirth.[40]

Shinran in this way repudiated the petty goals of human beings and their manipulation of the *nembutsu*. In doing so, he entrusted himself to Amida's broader vision with its ultimate deliverance of all. Shinran described this alternative as the single path without obstruction (*muge no ichidō*).[41]

The third theme of importance in the *Tannishō* is Shinran's disavowal of disciples. He is quoted as saying,

> It is a preposterous thing that adherents of the exclusive *nembutsu* argue over who is my disciple and who is another person's disciple. As for me, Shinran, I do not have a single disciple (*deshi hitori mo motazu*).[42]

This statement stands in sharp contrast to the tradition of master-disciple lineages that always pervaded Japanese Buddhism. Lineages were the standard means of transmitting religious teachings from one generation to another, and often the truth of what one professed was measured by who one's teacher was. Schools of Buddhism were organized around these religious transmissions and made them the basis of induction into the clergy. Because of the importance of lineages, disciples looked to their masters with veneration and revered the religious objects and texts which they bestowed upon them. To abandon one's master was generally considered a betrayal of trust, obliging one to return all religious objects to that master.[43] Shinran, by disclaiming disciples, set himself apart from this long-standing Buddhist pattern. This does not mean that he rejected his own teacher Hōnen. On the contrary, he felt a lifelong indebtedness to Hōnen, and he believed it natural for *nembutsu* adherents to respond to their religious mentors with gratitude. But he did not mistake the importance of the teacher for the essence of the teaching. That is, Shinran emphasized the primacy of Amida's message over religious lineages. Ultimately, Amida is the magnetic force drawing a person to his vow. The particular teacher communicating this message is merely the agent. In Shinran's words,

> If it were my design that caused people to utter the *nembutsu*, then they might be [described as] my disciples. But it is utterly absurd to use the term disciple to refer to those who have spoken the *nembutsu* solely entrusting themselves to

Amida's urging. If karma binds them [to a teacher], then they will be together. If karma separates them, then they will be separated. But it is incomprehensible to say, "If they turn their back on their teacher and follow another person, they will not be born in Pure Land, even if they perform the *nembutsu.*" How can anyone claim to take back, as if it were a personal possession, the faith which the Tathāgata has imparted? In no way can this be so. If people are in accord with the principle of naturalness (*jinen*), then they will realize their indebtedness to the Buddha, as well as their indebtedness to their teacher.[44]

Shinran acknowledged the believer's indebtedness to a religious teacher, but considered that relationship secondary to Amida's teachings. This view had far-reaching implications for the development of the school. The traditional master-disciple lineage, when adopted for sectarian use in the Shinshū, had to be subordinated to the primary religious concern, the personal encounter with Amida's vow. This would have important ramifications later as the Honganji developed its concept of temple headship based on religious and hereditary lineage from Shinran.

The second half of the *Tannishō* is predicated on the themes appearing in the first half. That is, Shinran's sayings set the tone for the critique of eight specific items which, according to the author, deviate from Shinran's thought.[45] The eight consist of beliefs and practices that were circulating among Shinran's followers. In criticizing them the author of the *Tannishō* seldom used the standard Buddhist terminology for heresy. Only three times do words of that type appear: the terms "aberrant doctrine" (*igi*), "wrong view" (*jaken*), and "wrong attachment" (*jashū*).[46] Instead, the prevailing tone of his criticisms is one of lament and reaffirmation of faith, as reflected in the opening paragraph of the *Tannishō*:

> As I privately turn over my own humble thoughts and reflect a bit on past and present, I [cannot help but] lament deviations from the true faith taught us by our late master. . . . By no means should we corrupt the significance of [Amida's] other-power with the insights of our own wrong views. Therefore, with the words of our now-departed master, Shinran, still reverberating in my ears, I record here a little [of what he said]. Truly I do this to dispel the doubts of fellow believers.[47]

As this opening statement suggests, the *Tannishō* is not so much an ecclesiastical pronouncement against heresy as a personal testimony. The author's words function less as a diatribe on heresy than as a call to faith. The eight paragraphs in the second half of the work, which outline various deviations, are aimed ultimately at nurturing the faith of those prone to misunderstanding.

The eight items listed in the *Tannishō*'s second half are:

1. Some people upset illiterate cohorts (*tomogara*) who say the *nembutsu* by asking them whether they say it with faith in the wondrous vow (*seigan fushigi*) or with faith in the wondrous name (*myōgō fushigi*). They thereby confuse

people's minds (*kokoro*) by dividing [Amida's] wonder into two without stating clearly any reasons (*shisai*).

2. Cohorts who do not read or study the sutras and commentaries are not assured of birth in Pure Land.

3. One will not achieve birth in Pure Land if one flaunts the principal vow (*hongan bokori*) thinking there is no reason to fear evil because of the wonder of Amida's principal vow.

4. One should have faith that profound [karmic] evil leading to eight billion kalpas [of rebirth] is eliminated with a single *nembutsu*.

5. With this body overwhelmed by evil inclinations (*bonnō gusoku*) a person already achieves enlightenment.

6. When believers with faith spontaneously (*jinen ni*) fall into anger, or commit an evil deed, or become argumentative with companions and fellow believers, they must without fail undergo conversion again (*eshin*).

7. People who achieve birth on the fringes of Pure Land will eventually fall into the hells.

8. According to the magnitude of one's donation in behalf of Buddhism, one will become a greater or a lesser Buddha.[48]

All these propositions are presented as flawed interpretations of Shinran's teachings, and one by one arguments are given to refute each. This section of the *Tannishō* constitutes one of the earliest statements of religious truth and falsehood from the Shinshū point of view—or, in short, a list of Shinshū "heresies." The surprising thing about this list is that licensed evil, the most controversial Pure Land heresy up to that time, is not included. On the contrary, most of the items either overtly or implicitly advance licensed evil's opposite: the attempt to make good works and virtuous behavior a part of salvation (*kenzen shōjin*). The conspicuous absence of licensed evil suggests that the author of the *Tannishō* was more alarmed by the beliefs and practices which Shinshū congregations were appropriating from more conventional religious groups. The emulation of mainstream Buddhism, he feared, had just as corrosive an effect on Shinran's teachings as licensed evil.

The most extensive assault on this trend is found in the *Tannishō*'s critique of the third item among the eight. The proposition denounced there is that people will not attain salvation if they are arrogant about their faith in Amida's vow and show no aversion to evil. The *Tannishō* argues that much of the evil in people's lives is the karmic fruition of past acts (*shukugō*). Even in the person of faith, flaunting Amida's vow (*gan ni hokorite*) may be the result of these unfortunate karmic tendencies.[49] Though evil is not the intention of the person, it is apt to arise if evil inclinations from the past are embedded in one's psychic make-up.[50] Such wrongdoings should not be viewed as obstructions to Amida's vow, nor should they prompt one to advocate good works as a requirement for birth in Pure Land. To do so would be to substitute conventional Buddhist morality for Shinran's ideas—that is, to advocate good deeds and to discourage wrongdoing. Licensed evil was, of course, a formidable problem in the Pure Land movement of the thirteenth century, and many Pure Land proponents sought to rectify the problem by making upright conduct a criterion for salvation. They hoped thereby to cast themselves in a favorable light to outside observers. Salvation by good deeds, however, was precisely the form of religion that Shinran opposed throughout his career. His teachings stress that one's own efforts are not what qualify one for birth in Pure Land. Only the intervention of the Buddha can accomplish that. This is the idea expressed most emphatically in the first saying of Shinran's cited in the *Tannishō*:

> In Amida's principal vow there is no distinction between young and old or good and evil persons. We should realize that faith alone is necessary. His vow therefore is aimed at saving the sentient being who is steeped in wrongdoings and blazing with evil inclinations. Consequently, if one has faith in the principal vow, no other good is necessary, since there is nothing so good that it can surpass the *nembutsu*. Nor should one fear evil, since there is nothing so evil that it can obstruct Amida's principal vow.[51]

This dissociation of faith from acts of righteousness, as well as the *Tannishō*'s emphasis on the evil person as the primary object of Amida's vow, stands in diametric opposition to the encouragement of good deeds for salvation (*kenzen shōjin*). For that reason, to demand virtuous behavior for birth in Pure Land is deemed a deviation from Shinran's thought. This is not to say that the *Tannishō* condones licensed evil. On the contrary, the work cites Shinran's own words on the subject: "Simply because there is an antidote does not mean one should savor the poison."[52] Nonetheless, to demand good works for salvation is equally misguided.

The type of virtuous action and conventional behavior included in the call for good works is indicated by the second and eighth items in the *Tannishō*'s list: reading sacred texts and making offerings to the clergy. These were common religious activities promoted by Japan's eight schools of Buddhism. Recitation and study of the scriptures were a means of cultivating wisdom and building up religious merit leading to enlightenment. Such religious practices gave educated believers an advantage over illiterate and lowly ones, who were ill-equipped to do anything more than invoke the Buddha's name. Almsgiving and offerings were likewise formal acts of piety and merit. They were the primary means for lay believers to participate in established religion and for the ordained clergy to receive its material needs. The *Tannishō* makes it clear that these traditional practices are not a part of the path that Shinran propounded. That is, they are not the easy practices (*igyō*) of the Pure Land path but rather the difficult practices (*nangyō*) of Buddhism's path of religious exertion (*shōdōmon*). Shinran advocated instead the efficacy of faith alone, which arises from the *nembutsu* created by Amida. That path is accessible to all, even to the poor, the lowly, and the ignorant. Hence, religious learning and donations to the clergy are ultimately inconsequential to one's fate in Pure Land.[53]

The tendency to stress conventional religious practice and personal effort was expressed in Pure Land idioms as well, as indicated by the fourth and sixth items in the list. There believers are urged to say the *nembutsu* or to reestablish their faith each time they commit a misdeed.[54] The idea that invoking the *nembutsu* cancels out evil karma was derived from the "Pure Land Meditation Sutra," and it pervaded both the traditional schools of Buddhism and various branches of the Pure Land movement.[55] Shinran repudiated this interpretation by calling the *nembutsu* "neither a religious practice (*higyō*) nor a virtuous act (*hizen*)."[56] That is, salvation is not a matter of reciting the *nembutsu* each time one does something wrong. By the same token, faith is not a state that must be renewed whenever one commits an offense. From the first moment that faith arises, birth in Pure Land is irreversibly assured, no matter what wrongdoings infect one's life.

Both the fourth and the sixth propositions reveal a deep-seated fear that wrongdoings can somehow obstruct Amida's vow. That kind of fear reinforces the tendency to rely on one's own efforts to shun evil and cultivate good (*dan'aku shuzen*). But if salvation were dependent on chanting the *nembutsu* or undergoing a renewal of faith each time a misdeed is done, death could overtake one unexpectedly and deprive one of salvation. The person of true faith undergoes conversion only once. In that moment the individual realizes that personal efforts—whether physical, verbal, or mental—are in vain, and as a result succumbs to wholehearted reliance on Amida's vow. From that point birth in Pure Land is assured because faith, the true cause of salvation, is enduring. It does not have to be reestablished each time an unfortunate act is committed. Such acts, though regrettable, will continue, but over and above them the inner state of faith remains. It is an utterly unpremeditated state (*wa ga hakarawazaru*), and it manifests itself in a sense of indebtedness to Amida (*Mida no goon*). Whenever the *nembutsu* is spoken in this state, it is not an attempt to dispel evil karma but rather an expression of indebtedness to the Buddha and gratitude for his virtue.[57] This understanding of faith and the *nembutsu* articulated by Shinran set him apart from most other Pure Land thinkers and certainly from the mainstream schools of Buddhism.

Additional items in the *Tannishō* suggest that Shinran's teachings were being reshaped to fit the doctrines of other Buddhist schools. Specifically, the fifth item—that one achieves enlightenment while still overwhelmed by evil inclinations—had origins in the Shingon doctrine of achieving Buddhahood in this very body (*sokushin jōbutsu*);[58] and the seventh item—that people born on the fringes of Pure Land will eventually fall into the hells—may have been influenced by Nichiren's assertion that the *nembutsu* will lead people to the hell of incessant suffering (*nembutsu muken jigoku*).[59] The *Tannishō* refutes both of these propositions by invoking Pure Land concepts and by citing passages from Shinran's writings.[60] The inclusion of the Shingon tenet in the *Tannishō*'s list of aberrant doctrines (*igi*) has one curious ramification. To the extent that this idea derived from the Shingon concept of achieving Buddhahood in this very body (*sokushin jōbutsu*), the *Tannishō* brands a long-standing principle of orthodox Buddhism as a deviation of faith, and hence as heresy. This was, in a sense, the first step in the Shinshū's protracted attempt to make Shinran's teachings the standard for orthodoxy and to measure all other ideas, including the doctrines of the eight schools of Old Buddhism, against them.

The controversies that most affected Shinran's following were not those absorbed from other schools but rather those originating from within the Pure Land movement itself. The faith-versus-practice controversy, which polarized the movement even in Hōnen's day, is the issue at stake in the first item in the *Tannishō*'s list. As it is debated there, the question takes the form of whether Amida's wondrous vow (*seigan fushigi*) or his wondrous name (*myōgō fushigi*) is the active element in one's faith.[61] Those who advocated faith without practice idealized Amida's vow as the cornerstone of salvation, whereas those obsessed with practice championed Amida's name, the chanting of the *nembutsu*, as the crucial element.[62] This dispute clearly pervaded the early Shinshū, and disquieted ordinary believers, whose faith was not based on such doctrinal hairsplitting. When they uttered the *nembutsu*, they saw no discrepancy between the power of Amida's vow and that of his name, for they sensed no conflict between the two. The *Tannishō* upholds their unsophisticated faith as the correct understanding of the two. Amida's name, in the form of the *nembutsu*, is the practice established by his principal vow; therefore, to dissociate one from the other is an act of human contrivance that does violence to Amida's original intent.[63] This doctrinal issue is ultimately related to the controversy over licensed evil and good works, which respectively represent the extremes to which the wondrous vow and wondrous name concepts could be carried. The *Tannishō*'s solution is to reject any dichotomization of the vow and the name, and to see the two as inextricably tied to one another. When that is done, the licensed evil and good works extremes are both avoided.

The eight items listed in the *Tannishō*'s second half provide a graphic image of early religious trends in the Shinshū, especially as it evolved around the *dōjō*. They exemplify the problems adherents faced and the mistakes they made in translating Shinran's thought into articles of belief and practice. Some of the items derived from concepts erroneously absorbed into the Shinshū from the traditional schools of Buddhism. Others reflect beliefs adopted from divergent Pure Land groups. Still others constitute completely new ideas read into Shinran's teachings. The *Tannishō* attempts to show that in each case Shinran's principle of faith, outlined in the first half of the work, is violated.

As indicated earlier, the surprising thing about the *Tannishō* is that licensed evil is not named as one of the items. Admittedly, the *Tannishō* mentions it in its discussion of the third item, but the central concern there is not licensed evil per se but rather its opposite, the requirement of good works for salvation (*kenzen shōjin*).[64] The tension between these two, as well as the controversy over Amida's wondrous vow and wondrous name, reveals that the faith-versus-practice issue that afflicted Hōnen's Pure Land following was alive in Shinshū circles as well. During Shinran's lifetime the faith faction advocating licensed evil was the more ominous extreme, for it threatened to lure his believers into religious misconduct and indulgent behavior. By the time the *Tannishō* was written, the situation had apparently changed. The practice faction demanding rigorous discipline and morality held the upper hand and sought to adapt Shinran's teachings to conventional religious values. The eight items listed in the *Tannishō* all bear that stamp. They present in one fashion or another the traditional Buddhist view that personal effort is necessary for salvation. Shinran explicitly rejected this idea in favor of total reliance on Amida. The author of the *Tannishō* recognized this trend and in his own way tried to reverse it. He opposed the attempt to mold the Shinshū in the image of orthodox Buddhism, especially where it sacrificed the content of Shinran's teachings. His efforts were only the first volley in a perennial campaign to keep alive the spirit of Shinran's vision amid the experimentation of organizational development.

CHAPTER
6

KAKUNYO AND THE CREATION
OF THE HONGANJI TEMPLE

Formal temples first came into existence in the Shinshū more than fifty years
after Shinran's death. The emergence of temples marked a new stage in Shinshū
development, when institutional concerns came to bear on the ideas of orthodoxy
and heresy as much as doctrinal concerns did. The most prominent temples to
appear were the Honganji, the Senjuji, the Bukkōji, the Kinshokuji, and the
temples associated with the Sanmonto communities along the Hokuriku seaboard. Of these the Senjuji grew out of a congregation in the Kantō region at
a place known as Takada, which had been a Shinshū stronghold even during
Shinran's lifetime.[1] Its pattern of development, from informal chapel into
temple, became a common occurrence in later Shinshū history, but during this
period only a few congregations actually made the transition from *dōjō* to formal temple.[2] The Bukkōji, by contrast, was established as a temple from its
inception. It rose to fame rapidly as hundreds of *dōjō* in the surrounding regions
came under its religious influence.[3] The Honganji, on the other hand, was unique in its transformation to temple status. It began as a memorial chapel at
Shinran's grave site, a natural pilgrimage spot for Shinshū believers, and
emerged in temple form under the initiative and leadership of Kakunyo.[4]

THE HONGANJI

The Honganji's ascent to Shinshū authority resulted from a combination of
two factors: its dedication to Shinran's teachings and its accommodation with
the prevailing political and religious forces. If Shinran's teachings were the vertical thread giving the Honganji continuity from one generation to the next, its
accommodation with other religious and social groups was the horizontal tie
giving it cohesion and acceptability at any particular moment in its history.
Thus, the leaders of the Honganji, including Kakunyo and Rennyo, operated
on two levels. On the one hand, they presented Shinran's teachings as the true

message of Buddhism, superseding those of other schools; on the other, they maintained cordial relations with powerful personages and influential temples of the traditional eight schools in an effort to solicit their favor and assistance. Though these two levels often seemed incongruous or even at odds with one another, the expediency and pragmatism of the second was perhaps the only way that the ideals and convictions of the first survived. Hence, there emerged in Shinshū history a number of seeming anomalies. First of all, Shinran never established a temple, and yet it was a temple, the Honganji, that became the foremost defender of his teachings. Shinran also denied having any disciples, and yet the Honganji's leaders claimed a religious and hereditary lineage going back to Shinran as the basis for their religious authority. Second, Shinran repudiated the doctrines and practices of the traditional schools, and yet most heads of the Honganji received their education in the traditional Buddhist temples, and many even underwent ordination there in their youth, before returning to the Honganji in adulthood. Third, Shinran's teaching of salvation through faith found its most enthusiastic following among Japan's peasant class, and yet the leaders of the Honganji moved comfortably among aristocrats, samurai, and powerful religious figures, and depended equally on their good services for the Honganji's survival and success.

Though the Honganji was not the dominating institution in the Shinshū before Rennyo's time, its importance in defining the identity of the school, the content of its doctrines, and the direction of its development was enormous. During Shinran's lifetime there was little to distinguish the Shinshū from the Pure Land movement as a whole. Shinran himself recognized no such differences and many of his followers inherited the same viewpoint. In keeping with Shinran's example, some looked upon Hōnen, not Shinran, as the "good master" establishing Amida's message of salvation in the world. Hence, after Shinran's death a number of *dōjō* continued to hold monthly *nembutsu* services on the twenty-fifth of the month, Hōnen's death day, instead of changing to Shinran's, the twenty-eighth.[5] This abiding reverence for Hōnen is also evident in the 1301 request from Dōshin, a member of the Nagai branch of the Kashima congregation in the Kantō region, for Kakunyo to compose a biography of Hōnen.[6] The establishment of the Honganji resulted from an attempt to focus Shinshū devotion on Shinran, rather than Hōnen, and to imbue the Shinshū with an identity of its own, separate from the broader Pure Land movement.

This process of sectarian definition began in 1277, when Kakushinni, Shinran's youngest daughter, bequeathed his grave site to all Shinshū followers as a memorial to Shinran, subsequently known as the Ōtani memorial (*Ōtani byōdō*).[7] Kakunyo, Kakushinni's grandson, further enhanced veneration of Shinran by instituting regular memorial services, the Hōonkō, in 1294 on the thirty-third anniversary of Shinran's death.[8] Nine years later Yuizen (b. 1266), Kakushinni's youngest son, won public recognition for the Shinshū by persuading the Kamakura military government to exempt Shinshū followers from a suppression directed against itinerant *nembutsu* monks, probably those belonging to the Jishū school, or at least to one of its branches, the Ikkōshū.[9] All these events worked together to give the Shinshū a distinct sectarian identity, to aggrandize Shinran in the minds of Shinshū believers, and to heighten the prestige of the Ōtani memorial within Shinshū circles.[10]

KAKUNYO

The role of Kakunyo (1270–1351) at this stage in Shinshū history was monumental.[11] Early in his career he formulated a vision of Honganji domination, and thereafter directed all of his efforts toward realizing that goal. His greatest accomplishments were: to raise Shinran to the status of founding father of the Shinshū; to transform the Ōtani memorial into a formal temple, the Honganji; and to establish a religious lineage for the Honganji based on heredity. Despite Kakunyo's talents and endeavors, his life was marked with frequent disappointments and only partial success. No doubt Kakunyo's own domineering personality and his undaunted aspirations for Honganji ascendancy were part of the reason. Though his hopes were grounded in a sincere commitment to Shinran's teachings, his tenacious and often headstrong adherence to them eventually led to a break with his oldest son, Zonkaku, himself a prodigious disseminator of Pure Land Buddhism, and to the alienation of many Shinshū congregations. As a result, Kakunyo's vision of Shinshū unity under Honganji leadership had to wait until Rennyo's time to reach fulfillment.

Kakunyo spent his youth in diverse scholarly and religious pursuits, but ultimately returned to Shinran's teachings as the cornerstone of his religious views. From the age of five, Kakunyo was sent by his father, Kakue (1239?–1307), to study with various learned priests both in Kyoto and in Nara. Under these teachers Kakunyo received a classical education in Buddhist doctrine including Tendai, Kusha, Hossō, and Sanron philosophy. He also read the non-Buddhist classics (*geten*) and became accomplished in poetry composition, an aristocratic pastime that Kakunyo continued throughout his life. In 1286, at the age of seventeen, he underwent ordination as a Buddhist priest. During the following two years, Kakunyo came into contact with Nyoshin (1235–1300), Zenran's son, who headed the Shinshū congregation at Ōami, and with Yuienbō, the reputed author of the *Tannishō* ("Notes Lamenting Deviations"). These encounters sparked Kakunyo's interest in Pure Land, and so, when he traveled to the eastern provinces with his father in 1290, Kakunyo sought out Nyoshin's instruction on Shinran's teachings. These lessons made a lasting impression on him, for from that time Kakunyo turned his attention exclusively to Pure Land thought. Upon his return to Kyoto he took up study with Anichibō Shōkū, a priest of the Seizan branch of the Jōdoshū school.[12] In later years Kakunyo looked back reverentially to Nyoshin as his own religious master who imparted Shinran's teachings to him.[13]

Kakunyo's awakening to Shinran's teachings inspired him to compose the text of a memorial service to Shinran entitled the *Hōonkō shiki* ("Liturgy of Gratitude") in 1294 and to write a biography of him known as the *Godenshō* ("The Biography") in the following year. The memorial service, called the Hōonkō, has become the foremost annual ceremony in the Shinshū. During Kakunyo's time it was performed once a month out of personal devotion to Shinran.[14] The liturgy to the service consists of three parts. The first is a eulogy to Shinran for introducing Buddhism's true teachings into the world and for propagating them with compassion to all people; the second lauds him for preaching the *nembutsu* in absolute accord with Amida's intent, thereby perfecting Hōnen's teachings and surpassing the flawed interpretations of other *nembutsu* proponents, and for skillfully communicating the *nembutsu* so that good and evil persons alike could comprehend its meaning; and the third praises Shinran for continuing to extend his teachings throughout the world, even after his death, through the writings he left behind and through the evangelistic efforts of his followers.[15]

Near the end of the Hōonkō liturgy Kakunyo included a passage aggrandizing Shinran in a way that went far beyond simple adulation of the man:

> When we think deeply about his guidance (*kedō*) of people in commonplace life (*heizei*) and when we reflect quietly on his benefit to them even in the present, we realize that our master, the founder of our school, was no ordinary person but was the transformation of a transcendent being. Some have called him the manifestation of Amida Buddha, and have also described him as a reincarnation of the master T'an-luan. These people have all received these messages in a dream, or have seen these signs in a vision.[16]

In his biography of Shinran, Kakunyo reiterated essentially the same point in the following way:

> In addition [Shinran] said: " . . . The great master [Hōnen] is the incarnation of the Bodhisattva Seishi, and [Shōtoku] Taishi is the manifestation of the Bodhisattva Kannon . . . . "
>
> At the third hour of the night on 1256.2.9, the priest Renni had a dream in which Shōtoku Taishi was worshipping the master Shinran with these words: "Reverence to the great compassionate Amida Buddha, who is reborn here to spread his sublime teachings, so that people in this evil world and during this evil age with its five corruptions may be assured of salvation, which is none other than absolute enlightenment."[17]

Kakunyo's idealization of Shinran as the incarnation of Amida Buddha cast him in a sacred aura that Shinran himself would have denied. Admittedly, it was common for believers to equate great religious personages with deities. For example, Shinran identified Shōtoku Taishi with the Bodhisattva Kannon and Hōnen with the Bodhisattva Seishi and even with Amida Buddha.[18] Nonetheless, Shinran conceived of himself as a humble beneficiary of their teachings, not as their religious superior coming into the world to perfect what they had expounded. Kakunyo's characterization of him in that very light, as a manifestation of Amida, helped stimulate a personality cult in the Shinshū centering around Shinran. There was already a tendency in this direction, as evidenced by the dream of Shinran's disciple Renni, which Kakunyo regarded as auspicious enough to include in the *Godenshō* ("The Biography"). The net effect of recording such a dream was to deify Shinran above Hōnen and Shōtoku Taishi, both of whom enjoyed widespread devotion in the Shinshū; and as veneration of Shinran increased, the Ōtani memorial, which was built around his grave site, grew in prestige and importance in the eyes of Shinshū adherents.

Kakunyo's apotheosis of Shinran was only the first step in his lifelong endeavor to advance Shinran's teachings and to make the Ōtani memorial the seat of ecclesiastical authority for the Shinshū. The next step was for Kakunyo himself to assume formal leadership of the Ōtani memorial and to wield the power of the position in pursuit of these ends. Unfortunately, headship of Ōtani was not easily obtained, and, once it was, its prerogatives were considerably attenuated. The reason is that, on the basis of Kakushinni's will, the Kantō congregations were granted proprietary rights over Ōtani, though her descendants were allowed to look after the memorial, subject to Kantō approval.[19] The Kantō followers, after all, bore the expense of constructing the original hexagonal chapel there that enshrined an image of Shinran (*goeidō*), and thereafter they provided funds to maintain the facilities and to keep Kakushinni's descendants in residence.[20] In 1283, the year of Kakushinni's death, she named her oldest son, Kakue, to become overseer of the grave site (*ohaka no gosata*), and the Kantō following assented to his appointment.[21] In 1302 Kakue designated Kakunyo to be caretaker (*gorusu*), and reaffirmed his decision in 1306, the year before Kakue's death.[22] His choice was not immediately ratified by the Kantō community because Yuizen, Kakue's younger half brother, also sought the position. In 1306 Yuizen cavalierly seized the Ōtani chapel, evicted Kakue, and began litigating for property rights. The ensuing struggle eventually resulted in Yuizen's ouster.[23] At that point the Kantō followers provisionally sent Shimotsuma Shōzen (d. 1313), grandson of Shinran's trusted disciple Renni, to oversee the memorial. Kakunyo, in the meantime, toured the Kantō congregations, petitioning their support and submitting to them a written entreaty in which he promised, among other things, not to go against their wishes, not to look upon the Ōtani chapel as his personal property, and not to belittle the Kantō followers as peasants and commoners (*denpu yajin*).[24] Persuaded that Kakunyo would not usurp the rights of the Kantō congregations, as Yuizen had, they finally consented to his appointment in 1310. Kakunyo thus assumed the post from a position of weakness, not strength.[25]

Once confirmed in office, Kakunyo set about elevating the status of the Ōtani memorial and consolidating the authority of his position. The tack he chose was to transform the memorial into a formal Buddhist temple. Although many Kantō adherents regarded Kakunyo with suspicion because of his aristocratic affectations, he had a few allies among their leaders—most notably, Kenchi and Hōchi. In collaboration with Hōchi, Kakunyo decided on a temple name for the Ōtani memorial: Senjuji, meaning "Temple of the Exclusive Practice."

Hōchi in 1312 presented Kakunyo with a temple plaque inscribed with that name to install over the chapel. Mt. Hiei's militant priests, however, protested that the word Senjuji dignified the exclusive *nembutsu*, which was a proscribed religious teaching. Rather than incur the wrath of Mt. Hiei, Kakunyo gave up the name, and Hōchi carried his plaque back to the Kantō region, where Senjuji was later adopted as the temple name for the Takada chapel.[26] Sometime during the next nine years Kakunyo fixed upon Honganji, meaning "Temple of the Principal Vow," as the name for the Ōtani memorial. The earliest known instance of the word is in a letter written by Kakunyo in 1321 to Jikyō (d. 1340) of the Myōkōin temple soliciting him to intercede before the Kamakura government in behalf of Shinshū adherents who were being suppressed alongside members of the Ikkōshū, a branch linked to the Jishū school. In this letter the line containing the word Honganji reads: "The humble petition of the followers of the master Shinran of the Honganji (*Honganji Shinran Shōnin*)."[27] Kakunyo's coupling of Shinran's name to the Honganji gave the impression that the temple was not merely Shinran's grave site but also his creation. Kakunyo sought to nourish this impression, for if he could establish a special tie between the Honganji and Shinran, he could claim the Honganji to be Shinran's legitimate authority among Shinshū followers. Hence, in subsequent works Kakunyo sometimes referred to Shinran simply as the master of the Honganji (*Honganji no Shōnin*).[28]

With the adoption of this temple name and with Kakunyo's inclusion of it in successive documents and writings, the Ōtani memorial quickly won recognition as a formal Buddhist temple. The earliest indication of this was a 1333 decree by the imperial prince Morinaga Shinnō (1308–35) designating the Honganji as a center of prayer (*gokitōjo*).[29] Notwithstanding the Honganji's transformation into a temple, the Kantō followers continued to look upon it first and foremost as a memorial to Shinran. Therefore, after the Honganji was reconstructed in 1338 Senkū (d. 1343) of Takada prevented Kakunyo from moving the image of Shinran to one corner of the temple and making a statue of Amida Buddha the centerpiece of worship, as one might expect in a Pure Land temple.[30] Such disputes reflect the gulf that began to develop between the Kantō congregations and the Honganji, once Kakunyo had raised it to temple standing.

While Kakunyo was working for Honganji recognition, he was also redefining his own position within the Honganji. This was done by means of a gradual modification of the terminology for the position. Kakushinni originally described the role as overseer of the grave site (*ohaka no gosata*). Kakue, in turn, referred to it primarily as caretaker (*gorusu*). Kakunyo expanded the term to the "office of caretaker" (*rusushiki*), implying more authority and prerogatives than the previous two expressions. What Kakunyo actually intended by this word is spelled out in his letter of bequest dated 1339.11.28, in which he equated it with the "office of head" (*bettōshiki*), an expression commonly used for the head administrator of a major Buddhist temple.[31] With this change in terminology Kakunyo sought to concentrate Honganji authority in the hands of the so-called caretaker, thereby undercutting the influence that the Kantō congregations derived from his grandmother's original will. His ability to do so was greatly enhanced by a judgment handed down in 1334 by the Shōren'in, a Tendai temple which exercised legal jurisdiction over the land on which the Honganji was situated. The judgment upheld Kakunyo's right to deny the Honganji caretakership to his oldest son, Zonkaku, even though the Kantō congregations favored him.[32] This decision in effect guaranteed control of the Honganji to its titular caretaker and foreshadowed its independence from the Kantō community.

Kakunyo further attempted to bolster his position within the Shinshū by grounding it in a master-disciple lineage going back to Shinran. Kakunyo's hereditary descent from Kakushinni qualified him to become caretaker of the Ōtani memorial, but it did not endow him with doctrinal authority in matters of Shinran's teachings. Kakunyo therefore laid claim to that authority by virtue of the instruction he received in his youth from Nyoshin. In the postscript to his *Kudenshō* ("Notes of Oral Transmissions") Kakunyo depicted Nyoshin as his personal religious master and as the figure linking him to Shinran in an orthodox religious lineage:

> At this time in the last part of the second month of winter in the year 1331, during the seven days and nights of services in gratitude and praise of our master and founder, Shinran of the Honganji, I have dictated the passages above and have had them written down. They are in essence the true teachings on Amida's power, as I have received them, and they are what our master and founder personally realized, as conveyed to me on that occasion when my predecessor and master, Nyoshin, explained orally and in face-to-face transmission (*menju kuketsu*) singleness of heart, the exclusive practice, and the uniquely established vow.[33]

In the postscript to the *Gaijashō* ("Notes Rectifying Heresy"), composed six years later, Kakunyo elaborated on this religious lineage, describing it as "a transmission (*denji*) spanning three generations (*sandai*): Kurodani [Hōnen], Honganji [Shinran], and Ōami [Nyoshin]."[34] Kakunyo clearly bore a sense of gratitude to Nyoshin for elucidating Shinran's teachings to him. Nonetheless, his aggrandizement of Nyoshin as the spiritual heir of Hōnen and Shinran reveals how contrived his justification of his own religious authority was, for Nyoshin's actual importance in Shinshū history was far less than the role Kakunyo ascribed to him.[35] What Kakunyo no doubt saw in Nyoshin was a crucial person-to-person link bridging the eight-year gap between Shinran's death in 1262 and his own birth in 1270. In Japanese society, where the right of primogeniture was strong, Kakunyo could claim Nyoshin to be Shinran's legitimate heir, since he was the son of Shinran's oldest son, Zenran.[36] Nyoshin's historical significance, however, does not lie in his descent from Shinran nor in his mastery of Shinran's teachings but only in the myth that Kakunyo built around him.

Kakunyo's description of his face-to-face association with Nyoshin echoes the master-disciple relationships of the traditional schools of Buddhism, on which doctrinal transmission and religious authority were based. Although Shinran himself disavowed the position of religious master, the lineage that Kakunyo claimed through Nyoshin in effect cast Shinran in that very role. Through this lineage Kakunyo invested himself with doctrinal authority and effectively united it with his hereditary right of Honganji caretakership, thereby making the office not only administrative but also ecclesiastical. Hence, under Kakunyo's influence the Honganji evolved a unique system of temple leadership whereby the head priest inherited his religious authority by birthright rather than by ascent through priestly ranks, as occurred in other Buddhist temples. This pattern of hereditary leadership subsequently became a common characteristic of temples in the Shinshū, distinguishing it from other schools of Buddhism.

ZONKAKU

Kakunyo left a lasting mark on the Shinshū with the conventions he established at the Honganji, but he also shaped the course of its history simply by denying the Honganji headship to Zonkaku (1290–1373), his oldest son.[37] Zonkaku was a warm and compassionate minister to ordinary Shinshū believers, contrasting sharply Kakunyo's aloof and unyielding personality. But he had a considerably different philosophy of Pure Land from Kakunyo's, and under his guidance the Honganji might have taken a radically different course. Like Kakunyo, Zonkaku received his early training in the established Buddhist temples of Kyoto and Nara, and he underwent traditional ordination by receiving the clerical precepts. Kakunyo, however, turned his attention to Shinran's teachings exclusively once he reached adulthood. Zonkaku, by contrast, maintained close relationships with the mainstream Buddhist schools and with other Pure Land groups, and he tended to couch Shinran's ideas in the context of the broader Pure Land movement. Ultimately, Kakunyo's concerns were directed inwardly toward the definition of Shinshū thought and the consolidation of Shinshū organization. Zonkaku's, on the other hand, were directed outwardly toward the unity of all Pure Land believers and the furtherance of the Pure Land teachings in general.

Kakunyo formally broke ties with Zonkaku in 1322. Thereafter he never looked upon Zonkaku as his successor, even though there were brief reconciliations between the two from 1338 to 1341 and again in 1350, shortly before Kakunyo's death. Kakunyo's disillusionment with him occurred over a twelve-year period following Zonkaku's return to Ōtani in 1310, after years of training in esoteric Buddhism (*mikkyō*) and in the teachings of various branches of the Pure Land school.[38] Zonkaku traveled with Kakunyo to numerous Shinshū communities—to Ōmachi in Echizen province, to the Kantō region, to Owari province, to Mikawa province, and to Iida in Shinano province—and he apparently won the admiration of many Shinshū followers, for in 1314 Kakunyo temporarily stepped down and passed nominal control of the Ōtani memorial to Zonkaku.[39] From that time the relationship between the two began to deteriorate.

In 1320 Kakunyo had Zonkaku give religious instruction to Ryōgen (1295–1336), who was to found the Bukkōji temple four years later. At first Kakunyo treated Ryōgen as a potential ally and disciple, but when he realized that Ryōgen, with Zonkaku's assistance, posed a threat to his own religious authority, he broke with Ryōgen and in 1322 disowned Zonkaku.[40] This act forced Zonkaku into a close association with Ryōgen and the Bukkōji temple, and it caused a strain between Kakunyo and many Shinshū communities partial to Zonkaku. Despite repeated attempts by provincial congregations to bring about a reconciliation between the two, Kakunyo was adamant in his rejection of Zonkaku. Even during the brief reconciliations that occurred, Kakunyo distrusted him and was determined to prevent him from becoming Honganji head.[41] As a result, many Shinshū congregations withheld their support from the Honganji. For example, the Kashima congregation in the Kantō region refused to make pilgrimages to the Ōtani memorial for several years after Zonkaku's disownment.[42] This ill will caused the Honganji financial difficulties during subsequent decades, since it depended on contributions from rural followers, and it also propelled the Honganji on a separate course of development from other Shinshū groups.

Underlying Kakunyo's disownment of Zonkaku were irreconcilable differences over the significance and the content of the Shin teachings. Zonkaku summed up his views in a statement made in his *Rokuyōshō* ("Notes of Essentials on the Six [Fascicles]"), the first commentary ever written on Shinran's *Kyōgyōshinshō* ("Teaching, Practice, Faith, and Enlightenment"): "When the term Shinshū is used, it means the Pure Land school."[43] In other words, Zonkaku did not consider the Shin teachings an independent body of thought as Kakunyo did, but instead looked upon them as one part of Pure Land Buddhism, which encompassed all of Hōnen's disciples and followers. Consequently, in 1347 when Jikū (d. 1351), of the Shinshū temple Kinshokuji, asked Zonkaku's advice on where to receive religious instruction, Zonkaku did not send him to a Shinshū master but recommended the An'yōji temple, of the Jōdoshū school's Seizan branch, where Zonkaku and earlier Kakunyo had studied under Anichibō Shōkū.[44] Zonkaku's own teachings drew heavily from the doctrines of other Pure Land branches, particularly their advocacy of *nembutsu* chanting. According to Zonkaku's *Jōdo shin'yōshō* ("Notes on the True Essentials of Pure Land"), "The act by which birth in Pure Land is assured is the utterance of the Buddha's name. By uttering the name one is certain to be born there."[45] This presentation of the *nembutsu* as an external act differed in emphasis from Kakunyo's interpretation—that is, that faith is the true cause of birth in Pure Land. Of the two, Kakunyo's teaching more accurately reflects Shinran's own idealization of faith as the meaning behind the *nembutsu* and as the key to salvation. For that reason Kakunyo criticized the *nembutsu* taught by Zonkaku, and in a letter written in 1339 he even denounced Zonkaku as "a heretic against the Buddhist teachings" (*Buppō ni fusu no gedō*).[46]

The estrangement of Zonkaku from Kakunyo is commonly regarded as one of the great tragedies in Shinshū history. Both men were dedicated evangelists, capable together of raising the Honganji to national prominence. There was little possibility, however, of resolving the personal differences that existed between them. Each in his own way left a mark on Shinshū history, but Kakunyo ultimately prevailed in shaping the Honganji according to his own vision of the Shinshū. That is, he made the Honganji a citadel of Shinran's teachings and linked its religious authority to hereditary descent from Shinran. He also won recognition for the Honganji as a formal temple, and gradually wrested control of it from the Shinshū congregations in the Kantō region. He failed, however, to unify Shinshū believers under his leadership; on the contrary, he alienated many of them with his determination to elevate the Honganji above them. As a result the Honganji proceeded along a somewhat separate road of development from other Shinshū communities for more than a century after Kakunyo's death, and only in Rennyo's time reconverged with them to form one of Japan's largest schools of Buddhism.

HERESIES WITHIN AND WITHOUT

The religious doctrines of Kakunyo and Zonkaku are contained in the numerous treatises that they composed, including two short works dealing with the issue of heresy in the Shinshū. Zonkaku's work on this topic was composed first, in 1324, and was named *Haja kenshōshō* ("Notes Assailing Heresy and Revealing Truth").[47] Kakunyo's, entitled *Gaijashō* ("Notes Rectifying Heresy"), was written more than a decade later in 1337.[48] In structure the two works bear a strong resemblance to each other. Both address what they regard as aberrant beliefs, practices, and assertions of their day. Each takes up specific items one by one and attempts to show where they go wrong and what the correct understanding would be from the true believer's point of view. In laying out their arguments they give a picture not only of the variety of beliefs circulating in and around the early Shinshū but also of an emergent Shinshū orthodoxy.

Traditionally Kakunyo's *Gaijashō* has been characterized as a critique of wrong beliefs inside the Shinshū, and Zonkaku's *Haja kenshōshō* as one against those outside.[49] In many ways this generalization holds true. The *Gaijashō* is concerned primarily with rectifying dubious concepts and practices adopted specifically by Shinshū followers. Nonetheless, criticisms are directed against other Pure Land groups as well, and in one place Ippen of the Jishū school and his successor are singled out by name.[50] The *Haja kenshōshō*, on the other hand, is first and foremost an attempt to defend the Shinshū against criticism from outside and to explain the rationale for Pure Land ideas. Certain passages, however, describe religious notions that were apparently current among Shinshū adherents, which Zonkaku also sought to refute.[51] Hence, each of the works addresses issues both inside and outside the Shinshū, though Kakunyo's concentrates on those within and Zonkaku's on those without.

One important similarity between the two is that they do not hesitate to invoke the concept of heresy to criticize their opponents. The term *ja*, meaning "wrong" or "heretical," appears in the title of both works, and other words indicating heresy can be found throughout the texts.[52] The way these expressions are used represents a distinct shift from their usage in Shinran's writings and the *Tannishō* ("Notes Lamenting Deviations"). The tone of those works is one of lamenting deviations (*tanni*) more than rectifying heresy (*gaija*).[53] Hence, the terminology for heresy found in them is seldom directed against specific individuals or groups. It is used more in the abstract, to take issue with certain points of doctrine or certain concepts of practice. Kakunyo and Zonkaku, by contrast, wielded these terms to criticize their opponents, and thereby brought the idea of heresy down to a mundane plane. They sought to defend the true teachings not only by righting wrong interpretations but also by assailing their adversaries. Hence, their works have a polemical tone which is far less pronounced in Shinran's writings and the *Tannishō*.

Zonkaku's *Haja kenshōshō*, written in 1324, is a graphic reminder that the Pure Land movement was still under attack from the established schools of Buddhism more than a century after Shinran originally suffered banishment from Kyoto. The majority of the work is a defense of Pure Land beliefs against the attacks of outsiders. Zonkaku wrote the *Haja kenshōshō* at the behest of Ryōgen of the Bukkōji temple and apparently in response to charges of heresy lodged with civil authorities against the Pure Land movement.[54] In it Zonkaku identified the following groups as responsible for these accusations: "monks of the rigorous religious path from the mountain temple" (*sanji shōdō no shosō*)—obviously a reference to antagonistic priests on Mt. Hiei—as well as "mountain ascetics" (*sanga* or *yamabushi*), "shamans" (*fujo* or *miko*), and "*yin-yang* teachers" (*onmyōshi*).[55] The groups mentioned here indicate that animosity toward the Pure Land movement existed not only within Mt. Hiei's militant factions but also among popularizers of miraculous powers, spirit-worship, charms, divination, and other folk beliefs and practices. The religious worldview of this latter group was no doubt threatened by Shinran's rejection of folk beliefs in favor of exclusive devotion to Amida. Zonkaku was a good representative to argue the case for the Pure Land teachings. He laid out their tenets in a rational and sober fashion, couching them in the traditional idea that all Buddhas, Bodhisattvas, and *kami* work together to bring sentient beings to salvation. Without the *nembutsu*, he argued, the lowly and ignorant would have no religious recourse, since the demands of clerical life are beyond their capability. Therefore, while conscientiously fulfilling their daily responsibilities—that is, peasants tilling their fields and vassals carrying out their official duties—ordinary believers can hope for salvation because of their faith in the *nembutsu*. In this way Zonkaku depicted Pure Land followers as law-abiding subjects upholding time-honored Buddhist principles, and he accused his opponents of fabricating lies against them.[56]

The *Haja kenshōshō* contains the following seventeen propositions, which Zonkaku sought to rebut:

1. The single-minded and exclusive *nembutsu* is not a Buddhist teaching, but rather a heretical (*gedō*) teaching; therefore, it should be suppressed (*chōji*).

2. It is not right for people to call the Mahāyāna [teachings] of the Hokke (i.e., Tendai), Shingon, and other [schools] indiscriminate practices (zōgyō).

3. The *nembutsu* is not found in Tendai, Hossō, or the other eight schools; to establish a school by the name of Pure Land (*Jōdoshū*) is to take liberties.

4. Because the *nembutsu* is a Hīnayāna teaching, it is not a practice that leads to true liberation (*shinjitsu shutsuri*).

5. The *nembutsu* is a teaching that has an unfortunate effect on this world (*seken*); therefore, it should be suppressed.

6. People should be dissuaded (*kanke*) from the idea that upholding the practices of the clerical precepts is not the practice of the Buddhist teachings and should be suppressed.

7. The *Amidakyō* ("Smaller Pure Land Sutra") as well as the [*Wang-sheng*] *li-tsan* [*chieh*] ("Verses of Worship and Praise on Birth in Pure Land") are the teachings of heretics (*gedō*), and [chanting them] is an act leading to one of the hells; the *wasan* [hymns] used in our tradition are the act leading to birth in Pure Land.

8. [*Nembutsu* adherents] denigrate the illustrious *kami* (*shinmei*).

9. Not to shun defilements and not to observe auspicious and inauspicious days is the height of non-[Buddhist] teachings.

10. [*Nembutsu* adherents] destroy the Buddhist teachings (*Buppō*) and obliterate civil law (*ōbō*).

11. It is heresy (*jaken*) in the extreme for *nembutsu* adherents not to guide their deceased through [Saṃsāra's] paths.

12. [*Nembutsu* adherents] present impurities before the Buddhist altar: meat from various animals of mountain, field, and river.

13. [*Nembutsu* adherents] attach different names to fish and fowl and consume them in the *dōjō* during *nembutsu* ceremonies.

14. After *nembutsu* ceremonies and in front of the Buddhist altar, they offer their wives to each other without any concern about who is one's own and who is another's and without any sense of propriety about parent and child.

15. It is an act of heresy (*jahō*) that adherents of the single-minded and exclusive practice present money to their religious teachers and call it lamp donation (*tōmyō*).

16. If the *nembutsu* is the act that leads to birth in Pure Land, then one can achieve birth by oneself simply by intoning it. There is absolutely no need to come into contact with a religious teacher or to establish a master-disciple lineage (*shishi sōjō*).

17. When people practice the *nembutsu*, they should perform it as their own practice, aspiring to be born in Pure Land; but it is not right for them in their unenlightened state to convert other people.[57]

Zonkaku took up these propositions one at a time and laid out a Pure Land defense for each. Some of the accusations he denied outright. Others he admitted but with justification. In each case he attempted to present the Pure Land movement in the best possible light, as a body of sincere believers being harassed by acrimonious rivals.

Some of the charges found in this list reveal the extent to which Mt. Hiei and other religious opponents were willing to slander the Pure Land movement.

Assertions that the *nembutsu* is not a Buddhist teaching or that it is a Hīnayāna practice were patently false. Zonkaku, who was well versed in the Buddhist classics, could easily cite scriptures to refute their claims, and he pointed to the great Tendai, Sanron, Hossō, and Ritsu masters of China, who all recognized Pure Land as a branch of Mahāyāna Buddhism.[58] Accusations of improprieties in their *dōjō*—meat eating and sexual misconduct—were also answered adroitly. Zonkaku did not deny that Pure Land adherents eat meat or that they are attached to the physical pleasures which lead them to marry and beget families, but he argued that there is no reason for them to indulge in these activities in any contrived fashion such as within the *dōjō*, since meat eating and sex were not forbidden to them in ordinary life.[59] In this way he dissociated the Pure Land faithful from more extreme religious elements, such as licensed evil proponents or Shingon's Tachikawa cult, while at the same time upholding their lay style of life.

Several of the items in the list are not disputed per se, but are shown to be consistent with long-standing Buddhist traditions. One example is the establishment of Pure Land as an independent school of Buddhism. The Pure Land movement was frequently censured for this action, but Zonkaku defended it adeptly. He argued that only by historical happenstance did eight schools come into existence in Japan. In China, by contrast, Buddhism was never limited to these eight. Moreover, in Japan other schools such as the Buddha-mind (*busshin*) or Zen school arrived after the eight were established, and yet this school was recognized as legitimate. Hence, there should be no contradiction in accepting the Pure Land school as well.[60] Zonkaku also defended the practice of presenting monetary offerings to religious teachers and of maintaining master-disciple lineages within Pure Land groups. Offerings, he claimed, were a part of the venerable tradition of almsgiving; thus, far from being an offense, they were a Buddhist virtue.[61] As for establishing religious lineages, he pointed out that all other forms of Buddhism maintain them. Furthermore, the teacher-follower relationship is of special importance in Pure Land circles, since most believers are unable to read the scriptures and therefore depend on their teacher to reveal the religious path to them. Lineages, he argued, are a natural extension of a sense of indebtedness to one's teacher and are an attempt to keep the Pure Land teachings alive from one generation to the next.[62]

A few of the items contained in Zonkaku's work describe practices that Pure Land believers rejected, but which Zonkaku maintained they were justified in rejecting. Two of them are the observance of auspicious and inauspicious days and the communication with deceased relatives to guide them along Saṃsāra's treacherous paths. Both of these practices were part of the auguristic worldview which Pure Land believers in general and Shinran in particular tended to spurn.[63] Zonkaku pointed out that neither of these has any basis in Buddhist scripture and that the *Nehangyō* ("Nirvāṇa Sutra") explicitly states that observing auspicious and inauspicious days lies outside the Buddhist teachings.[64] He was quick to add, however, that Pure Land believers willingly accommodate themselves to the customs and responsibilities of society—Shinto services (*shin-*

ji), civil duties (*kuyaku*), local laws (*tokoro no hō*), traditional ceremonies (*tsune no shiki*)—but that there is no reason to include the observance of auspicious and inauspicious days among them.[65]

Perhaps the most daring passage in the *Haja kenshōshō* is a section criticizing the militant clergy of Mt. Hiei, who constantly threatened and tormented members of the Pure Land movement. In it Zonkaku suggested that they, not Pure Land believers, were the ones guilty of heresy:

> Adherents of the single-minded and exclusive practice uphold the principles of these teachings; they do not slander other practices, nor do they ridicule the various schools. Nonetheless, those monks seem in form to embody the Buddhist teachings and practices, but at heart they are no different from people who renounce the Buddhist doctrine of causation (*hatsumu inga*). Hence, they devastate the chapels of *nembutsu* followers in place after place, and in each case with every occasion they deceive (*atō*) the adherents of the Pure Land path. They call paintings and sculptures of Amida heretical images, and they trample them under foot. They declare the sacred writings of Shinshū doctrine to be heretical teachings, and they spit on them and destroy them. In addition they seize and deprive us of dozens of texts, including the three major Pure Land sutras as well as the expositions of the five patriarchs. Though these are by no means great treasures in the world, is this offense not tantamount to the crime of robbery? On these occasions the monks in question marshal strongmen and ruffians (*ninzei akuto*) and sweep down on the homes of *nembutsu* adherents. What is the crime of these adherents? What stolen goods do we possess? Is our offense the practice of the Buddhist teachings, and our stolen goods the single practice of the *nembutsu*? Theirs is an act of utter abomination (*gongo dōdan*). As for their appearance, over clerical robes, which are the banner of [Buddhist] emancipation (*gedatsu dōsō*), they impiously don the armor of self-indulgence (*hōitsu*); and because their heads are shaved and tonsured, they presumptuously wear the helmet of heresy (*jaken*). They cross themselves with bows and arrows and hold up battle swords; their outfitting is alarming to behold. Their voices pierce the ears, shrieking to high heaven and suffusing the deep earth. Overall their power resounds throughout a thousand world systems, and they nearly outstrip the *asura*'s legions.[66]

This description reflects the fear which Mt. Hiei's militant priests inspired in the hearts of their opponents. They were notorious in Kyoto for their strong-arm tactics, and they terrorized not only Pure Land adherents but also other religious, political, and economic rivals. Hence, Zonkaku's protests had a number of potential sympathizers, including perhaps the civil authorities. The dubious reputation of these monks made it possible for Zonkaku to intimate that they, rather than Pure Land believers, were the true authors of heresy. This in itself was a fairly radical assertion, considering that Mt. Hiei was still the bastion of orthodox Buddhism.

Except for these few words of protest, most of Zonkaku's statements are apologetic and conciliatory in tone. He sought to portray Pure Land believers as honest and obedient members of society promoting a religious good for themselves and for others. Consequently, he argued that denigrating the Shinto *kami* or violating the laws of the land is abhorrent to Pure Land beliefs, even though radical *nembutsu* adherents had long been implicated in such activities.[67] Zonkaku's attitude toward the Shinto *kami* was clearly at variance with Shinran's. Zonkaku perpetuated the prevailing concepts of Shinto-Buddhist syncretism of the period, construing the *kami* to be manifestations (*suijaku*) of Buddhas and Bodhisattvas.[68] This was a theme that Kakunyo emphasized also.[69] Shinran never presented the *kami* in such a syncretistic fashion. The most he would say is that the *kami* act as guardians or protectors to those who have faith in the *nembutsu*.[70] Hence, there was a distinct modification of Shinran's teachings on this point in an attempt to attenuate conflict with mainstream religious sentiments.

While Zonkaku defended the Pure Land movement against its outside critics, he also repudiated any narrowness within the movement itself. For example, he denounced the notion that singing Shinran's *wasan* hymns is the only way to achieve birth in Pure Land.[71] This criticism was directed no doubt at the Sanmonto congregations of the Shinshū, who made the hymns a crucial component of their religious practice and who rejected the use of the *Amidakyō* ("Smaller Pure Land Sutra") and the *Wang-sheng li-tsan chieh* ("Verses of Worship and Praise on Birth in Pure Land").[72] Overall the *Haja kenshōshō*, like Zonkaku's other writings, is broadly Pure Land in outlook rather than distinctly Shinshū. Its cornerstone of doctrine is that the exclusive *nembutsu* is the true cause of birth in Pure Land,[73] an idea championed by Hōnen and inherited by all Pure Land factions. Hence, Zonkaku's work should be seen first and foremost as an apology for the Pure Land movement in its widest possible context rather than as a uniquely Shinshū defense.

Kakunyo's *Gaijashō* ("Notes Rectifying Heresy"), by contrast, is a work aimed specifically at defining correct beliefs and practices within the Shinshū. If the *Haja kenshōshō* is apologetic in nature, the *Gaijashō* is clearly polemical—that is, it takes the offensive in assailing its opponents. Kakunyo had a distinct vision of how Shinran's teachings were to be manifested in one's religious life, and he sought to actualize that vision through the establishment of the Honganji. But the Shinshū extended far beyond the Honganji's sphere of influence, and inevitably a variety of interpretations and practices arose. The *Gaijashō* addresses those which Kakunyo considered contrary to Shinran's ideal. Like the *Tannishō* ("Notes Lamenting Deviations") it is a valuable source revealing divergent trends within the early Shinshū.

In format Kakunyo's work resembles Zonkaku's. It presents a list of items and criticizes them one by one. The twenty items contained in the *Gaijashō*, all of them heresies in Kakunyo's eyes, read as follows:

1. [It is wrong] to corrupt the lineage (*ichiryū*) of our founder, based on your own present views, with something called salvation registers (*myōchō*).
2. It is wrong likewise to assert your own views with something called portrait lineages (*ekeizu*).
3. You should not cherish the guise of religious renunciants (*tonsei*), or delight

in appearing different, or don the skirtless clerical robe (*mo nashi goromo*), or use the black clerical mantle (*kokugesa*).

4. It is wrong to call [yourself] disciple (*deshi*) while slandering or criticizing fellow believers and peers out of your own inordinate claims.

5. When rousing fellow believers, it is wrong to pour freezing water over them in cold weather or to burn them with moxa in hot weather.

6. Whenever there is disagreement (*mujun*) between believer and religious master (*chishiki*) concerning words spoken between them, it is wrong to seize the religious texts and objects of worship [which the master has bestowed on the believer] for veneration.

7. On the lower outside cover of religious texts and on objects of worship where your name is inscribed as religious aspirant (*ganshu*), you should not write the name of the person you claim as religious master.

8. It is wrong to argue and to make distinctions over who is your own fellow believer (*dōgyō*) and who is another person's fellow believer.

9. If believers who practice the *nembutsu* become followers of a religious master, it is wrong to make them write out an agreement (*kishōmon*) that says they will accept punishment (*bachi*) or to set up a list of numerous rules (*sūkajō*) and have them sign it.

10. It is wrong to adopt a Buddhist name (*hōmyō*) as if you were a cleric (*shukke*) while retaining the appearance of a layman (*ubasoku*) or a laywoman (*ubai*).

11. It is wrong to establish the two equinox seasons (*higan*) as periods for *nembutsu* retreats (*nembutsu shugyō*).

12. [It is wrong] to occupy separate meeting places standing eave to eave and divided only by a fence, and to call them *dōjō*.

13. Among cohorts who call themselves disciples of our founder and master it is unacceptable—whether moving, standing still, sitting, or lying down— to use the word "profiting" (*tokubun*) with regard to the two Dharmas, that of the world and that of world abandonment (*se shusse no nihō*).

14. It is wrong to say the *nembutsu* intentionally imitating the accented pronunciation of the rural provinces, when your voice is not actually accented.

15. It is wrong to focus on the words "single-minded and exclusive" (*ikkō senju*) without turning your attention to the fact that one achieves birth in Pure Land through the wonder of the Buddha's wisdom (*Butchi no fushigi*).

16. It is wrong for cohorts who call themselves adherents of this tradition, when they assemble to express gratitude and thanks for our founder and patriarchs (*soshi sendoku*), to decide by common consensus to emphasize services for the dead (*motsugo sōrei*) without turning their attention to faith which leads to birth in Pure Land.

17. Likewise it is wrong for people who call themselves followers of our founder to renounce the Buddhist doctrine of causation (*inga hatsumu*).

18. Among people who call themselves adherents of the master of the Honganji, it is wrong to worship their religious teacher (*chishiki*), to liken [the teacher] to Amida Tathāgata, or to consider the structure in which the teacher dwells to be the true Pure Land [generated] by [Amida's] unique vows (*betsugan*).

19. It is wrong to try to construe the self-effort (*jiriki*) thoughts and deeds of ordinary beings as the fully actualized embodiment of the Buddha's wisdom.

20. It is an inauspicious matter for an insignificant follower to describe the chapel (*sōdō*) he has set up as the main center (*honjo*) and for him to discourage people throughout the provinces from going to worship at the Honganji, the grave site of our master.[74]

The items mentioned here, though occasionally obscure or framed in opaque language, suggest great diversity and experimentation in the Shinshū during its initial period of institutional development. These items bear on various facets of Shinshū doctrine and practice. Some are clearly deviations from Shinran's teachings. Others differ more with Kakunyo's own interpretation. Kakunyo's criticism of each represents an attempt to extrapolate from the Shinshū principles inherited from Shinran in order to define a correct religious stance for his own day. In this respect the *Gaijashō* is as much an early postulation of Shinshū orthodoxy as a critique of heresy.

A few passages in the *Gaijashō* deal with crucial doctrinal matters. Kakunyo's central objective in them was to uphold the primacy of faith over practice. One example is the item contrasting the "single-minded and exclusive" with the "wonder of the Buddha's wisdom." In it Kakunyo aimed at reaffirming Shinran's original claim that the *nembutsu*—that is, the single-minded and exclusive practice—is predicated on faith—namely, reliance on Amida in his boundless wisdom. To stress the *nembutsu* at the expense of faith is to lapse into the presumption that one's own effort (*jiriki*) is the key to birth in Pure Land.[75] At work in this issue is the perennial debate over faith versus practice. Kakunyo unambiguously came down on the side of faith, apparently in opposition to renewed and burgeoning advocacy of practice in Shinshū circles. Kakunyo's formulaic response to this problem was that faith is the primary cause of birth in Pure Land (*ōjō jōdo no shōin*), whereas religious acts or practices are the expression of one's gratitude to the Buddha (*Butsuon hōsha*).[76] This doctrinal axiom subsequently became a cornerstone of Shinshū thought and perhaps the most frequently cited summation of Shinran's teachings. Kakunyo wielded it to argue not only against one-sided emphasis on the *nembutsu* but also against the need to hold special religious retreats for practicing the *nembutsu* during the two equinox seasons.[77] Retreats of this type were common in other Pure Land branches. Nonetheless, Kakunyo considered them inappropriate for Shinshū believers, since their tradition pivoted around faith rather than practice.

Several additional passages in the *Gaijashō* describe religious affectations which Shinshū adherents adopted from other Buddhist groups or, in some cases, evolved on their own. These practices reflect an attempt to pattern the Shinshū after long-standing Buddhist customs. For instance, the donning of black clerical robes, the usage of Buddhist clerical names by lay believers, and the preoccupation with religious services for the dead all suggest that Shinshū congregations were seeking to model themselves on the Buddhist establishment.[78] Also, the formulation of special ways of chanting the *nembutsu*, using regional accents and intonations, may indicate the development of a primitive liturgy by certain *dōjō*.[79] Kakunyo criticized these practices as inconsistent with Shinran's ideal, wherein the cleric has no precedence over the lay person and whereby the way of saying the *nembutsu* is left open to individual believers. From its inception the Shinshū developed a strong lay orientation in its congregations, and Kakunyo attempted through these criticisms to preserve that ideal. He was suspicious of the tendency to emulate temple Buddhism, and hence championed the *dōjō* as the correct organization for Pure Land believers.[80] He envisioned the *dōjō* not as an insular clique vying with other religious factions for members but as an open meeting place set up for the convenience of believers in a certain area. Kakunyo therefore denounced the internecine haggling and the fragmentation that occurred in many Shinshū congregations, such as the establishment of competing *dōjō* standing side by side.[81]

The most widespread cause of factional division was the domination of Pure Land groups by particular religious teachers. Many of the items in the *Gaijashō* concern methods teachers employed to organize, consolidate, and regiment their followers. They include salvation registers (*myōchō*) and portrait lineages (*ekeizu*), used to indicate who had been accepted as a legitimate member of the group; bestowing sacred objects and religious texts on a follower, which were to be confiscated if the follower later abandoned the teacher; requiring followers to sign written agreements or lists of rules to acknowledge their submission to the teacher; and subjecting members to physical austerities such as dousing them with freezing water in winter or burning them with moxa in summer.[82] Without a doubt there was rivalry and enmity between religious factions, so that the followers of one teacher were constantly maligning those of another and distinguishing their own cohorts from those belonging to other cliques.[83] This excessive concern over one's religious teacher led to an obsession with religious lineages and to the practice of inscribing the name of one's teacher on religious objects and texts.[84] In some cases it even resulted in the adoration of the religious master as an embodiment of Amida Buddha.[85] Kakunyo regarded all these practices as contrary to Shinran's example and to the principles of the Shinshū tradition.

Kakunyo's criticisms in the *Gaijashō* were not made in the abstract. They were leveled against specific teachers and congregations that he considered divisive to the Shinshū and deviating from Shinran's teachings. Though few names are mentioned, the particular items listed in the *Gaijashō* can be traced to various rivals of the Honganji. For instance, salvation registers and portrait lineages were popular proselytization devices of Ryōgen and the Bukkōji temple. The bestowing of sacred objects and texts, which had to be returned if a follower apostatized, developed not only in the Bukkōji tradition but also at the Kinshokuji temple. The use of skirtless clerical robes and black clerical mantles was a feature of the Jishū school. And veneration of one's religious teacher was believed to exist in the Sanmonto congregations.[86] Kakunyo objected to these practices not only because he viewed them as deviations from the Shinran's teachings but also because they subverted his own religious goals. The last item in the *Gaijashō*'s list best reflects Kakunyo's personal interest in the matter. He lamented the decline of the Honganji to the chapel of an insignificant follower (*shigoku mattei*)—probably referring to Ryōgen and the Bukkōji temple.[87] Kakunyo's criticisms therefore had behind them a very concrete concern, the success of the Honganji.

The arguments that Kakunyo presented in his work are not simply emotional and self-serving diatribes. They are soundly reasoned, and substantiated with citations from Shinran's writings and from the Pure Land classics. It would seem, then, that his criticisms were well founded. The problem is whether Kakunyo himself was guilty of some of the same offenses that he accused his competitors of. For example, he opposed the transformation of *dōjō* into formal Buddhist temples, and yet he raised Shinran's grave site to temple status. He assailed the religious lineages of others, and yet he based his own authority on religious and hereditary descent from Shinran. He denounced his rivals for deifying their religious teachers, and yet he portrayed Shinran as a manifestation of Amida. It would appear that Kakunyo did not judge himself with the same measuring stick that he applied to others.

Notwithstanding Kakunyo's dual standards, he veered less in these directions than others did. Furthermore, he was more faithful to Shinran's original principles and to his concept of a religious community than were other Shinshū figures of his period. Hence, if there is a defense to be made for Kakunyo's actions, it is that they were far less extreme than those of his rivals. While others wholeheartedly embraced clerical airs, Kakunyo sought to preserve the lay flavor of the Shinshū. While others venerated their religious master as Amida, he ascribed that status only to Shinran, without claiming it for himself as Honganji head. While others aggrandized their teacher as the final religious authority, he made the teachings primary and the teacher their agent.[88] Most importantly, while others imported an admixture of Pure Land thought into the Shinshū, he held firm to Shinran's basic message of salvation through faith. His adoration of Shinran and his founding of the Honganji both stemmed from devotion to that message. Without it the Honganji lacked any reason for existence, since its purpose was to preserve and promote the experience of faith in believers. And without that experience there would be no sense of gratitude for Shinran's teachings, and hence no impetus to hold him in reverence. Therefore, only as long as the teachings were paramount did Shinran as "founder" and the Honganji as "head temple" have meaning. It was upon this kind of reasoning, an inner logic of faith, that Kakunyo justified his actions.

The writings of Kakunyo and Zonkaku, though different in aim and outlook, served two important functions in early Shinshū history. Zonkaku's acted as a bridge to other Pure Land groups at a time when outside suppression was still a constant threat. Kakunyo's, on the other hand, upheld the integrity of Shinran's teachings in the face of misrepresentation and compromise. Together they helped sustain Shinshū believers in their external ties to society at large and in their internal convictions as an emergent sectarian group. Of the two, Kakunyo's writings represent an attempt to build an institutional body around Shinran's ideas. They make judgments as to which practices and beliefs are compatible with Shinran's teachings and which are not. To this extent

Kakunyo, more than Zonkaku, was the architect of Shinshū orthodoxy. In doctrinal content his conception of orthodoxy was faithful to Shinran's ideal; but in institutional form—specifically, in the establishment of the Honganji—it was a new creation. Though Kakunyo's vision of orthodoxy never became the dominant view during his own lifetime, it was inherited by Rennyo and prevailed as a result of his initiatives.

CHAPTER

7

THE SHINSHŪ AND
RIVAL SCHOOLS OF BUDDHISM

The fourteenth and fifteenth centuries were a time of religious expansion in Japan when the teachings of Kamakura's Buddhist innovators attracted a national following, thereby giving rise to new schools of Buddhism. The Shinshū, championing Shinran's teachings, was only one among these. At first these new schools were decentralized, existing only as regional pockets of religious influence with at most loose ties to other communities claiming the same religious heritage. These groups emerged because certain temples or religious centers were able to rally followers into their fold and could persuade, or sometimes pressure, other congregations to submit to their religious authority. Nonetheless, such groups were never static. There was a constant ebb and flow of believers and congregations from one to another. The decline of one famed temple often signaled the rise of some other, or perhaps the emergence of a new Buddhist movement capitalizing on the atrophy of the old. This was, in short, a period of intense religious rivalry, when prodigious followings could be gained or lost in the space of a few generations. Such ferment eventually resulted in the formation of new Buddhist schools dedicated to the teachings of the Kamakura founders. The Honganji was one of many temples to pass through the fire of this competitive religious environment, eventually drawing a majority of Shinshū congregations under its leadership and attracting countless followers from other religious groups.

THE BUDDHIST ESTABLISHMENT

The eight schools of Old Buddhism were the eventual losers in this process of religious expansion, for the new Buddhist movements—Pure Land, Zen, and Nichiren—far outstripped them in number of converts. Nevertheless, the old schools did not bow to the newcomers easily or quickly. At first they reacted harshly toward them, condemning them as heretical and seeking to suppress them.[1] Subsequently they initiated a revival within their own ranks and propagated popular Buddhist devotions to compete with the new schools on their own terms.[2] In the end they resigned themselves to coexistence with the new movements and, where feasible, established informal relationships with them. Throughout this period the traditional temples maintained their reputation as the repositories of Buddhist learning and hence as the seat of orthodoxy. Moreover, they enjoyed the economic support of the provincial estate system. Estates submitted yearly remittances (*nengu*) to them in the form of rice, produce, crafted goods, and sometimes cash, and they provided manpower for temple projects. As long as this estate system lasted, the old schools managed to hold their own against the expanding new schools. But with the demise of estates in the sixteenth century the traditional temples were cut off from their economic means of support and were quickly overshadowed by their younger competitors.

The Honganji, though a product of the New Buddhism of the Kamakura period, established some valuable ties with older temples that were often crucial to its existence. The most important one was with the Shōren'in, the influential Tendai temple in Kyoto, which claimed absentee proprietorship rights to the land on which the Honganji stood. Based on this relationship the Shōren'in frequently litigated in behalf of the Honganji before civil and religious authorities. The closeness between the two temples is reflected in the fact that, until the nineteenth century, successive head priests of the Honganji underwent tonsure at the Shōren'in, nominally because Shinran had done so as a child.[3] Besides the Shōren'in, several other traditional temples, such as the Ichijōin and the Daijōin, both subtemples of the Kōfukuji temple in Nara, established a rapport with the Honganji and provided religious training for its leaders.[4] Since the Honganji was located in Kyoto, it had ample opportunity to interact not only with traditional temples but also with aristocratic families, who were equally valuable as allies. The Hino family in particular played a prominent role in Honganji history. Each generation of Shinran's descendants at the Honganji was generally accorded the status of adopted son (*yūshi*) by the Hino family.[5] These ties to traditional temples and to Kyoto aristocrats sheltered the Honganji from political antagonisms and blunted the perennial attacks of its most persistent adversary, the militant monks of Mt. Hiei (*sanmon no taishu*).

Until late in Rennyo's ministry, the militant priests of Mt. Hiei were an ever-present menace to Shinshū groups in Kyoto and the surrounding area. They launched major attacks against the two leading Shinshū temples in Kyoto—the Honganji and the Bukkōji—in 1338, 1352, and 1465. The Honganji was spared in 1352 because of the intercession of the Shōren'in, but in 1465 it was burned to the ground.[6] The politics of Mt. Hiei during this period were complicated by the fragmentation of the clergy into numerous factions. The group that gained control over the office of head priest (*zasu*) was a clique consisting of several aristocratic temples in Kyoto, including the Shōren'in.[7] Hence, the Shōren'in had clout in Mt. Hiei affairs during the Shinshū's earliest period of development, but as the office of head priest at Mt. Hiei degenerated into a figurehead position the Shōren'in became less effective in mitigating the attacks of factions hostile to the Shinshū. It is unclear exactly what group on Mt. Hiei was most antagonistic to the Shinshū, since few primary sources survived the destruction of the Hiei temple complex by Oda Nobunaga (1534–82) in 1571. Whoever these militant monks were, they apparently found Shinshū congregations as much a social and economic threat as a religious one, for many of their attacks were directed against Shinshū groups in nearby Ōmi province where Mt. Hiei controlled vast estates and economic enterprises. The Honganji therefore had a precarious existence in Mt. Hiei's shadow until well into Rennyo's ministry. Its fate was often tied to the vicissitudes of power and politics in the traditional temples of Kyoto.

THE NICHIREN SCHOOL

The Shinshū's first and foremost challengers in the provinces were the other new schools of Buddhism. The Zen school had minimal impact on Shinshū affairs until around Rennyo's time,[8] but the Nichiren school proved to be an acrimonious opponent from the beginning. Its hostility toward the Pure Land tradition dated back to the time of Nichiren (1222–82), who launched diatribes against Hōnen's *nembutsu* teaching. As early as 1255, Nichiren denounced the *nembutsu* as a pernicious practice leading people to the lowest level of hell (*nembutsu muken jigoku*).[9] During his lifetime Nichiren and his followers resided primarily in the Kantō region, and there they came into conflict with a variety of Pure Land groups, some adhering to Ryūkan's interpretation, some to Chōsai's, some to Benchō's, and possibly some to Shinran's.[10] After Nichiren's death in 1282 his disciples spread his teachings in a westward direction, forming congregations in Kyoto in the early 1300s and from there extending farther into such provinces as Bizen and Bitchū.[11] These followers inherited Nichiren's antipathy for the Pure Land teachings, thereby generating friction between themselves and Shinshū proponents. Both Kakunyo and Zonkaku composed treatises defending the *nembutsu* against the criticisms of the Nichiren school.[12] The specific event that prompted Zonkaku to write his defense is described in the following passage from his biography:

> In the third month [of 1338, Zonkaku] debated the Hokke [Nichiren] school before the provincial governor (*shugo*) of Bingo province. Because his disciples requested him to do this, he set aside his hesitations, but he changed his name and appeared in the debate under the pseudonym Goichi. The Hokke school was defeated, and as a result our side has flourished all the more. On this occasion he composed his treatise the *Ketchishō* ("Notes on the Establishment of Wisdom").[13]

This entry indicates that the Shinshū's encounters with the Nichiren school were not limited to pale literary volleys. Sometimes confrontation was face-to-face, as in this debate, which inspired Zonkaku to compose his rebuttals to Nichiren's attacks. One by-product of such encounters was that Kakunyo and Zonkaku attempted to present the Pure Land teachings as harmonious in ultimate intent with the "Lotus Sutra," the central text of the Nichiren school. Their arguments may have given the Shinshū greater acceptance in society at large, but in the process they glossed over Shinran's idealization of the Pure Land path above other Buddhist paths.[14]

THE CHINZEI BRANCH OF THE JŌDOSHŪ SCHOOL

Although ties with the Nichiren school were clearly antagonistic, the Shinshū's relationship with the various branches of the Jōdoshū school was more ambivalent and complex. The Shinshū shared a common Pure Land tradition with them, but disagreed over specific doctrines and methods. Among the many groups tracing their lineage back to Hōnen, the one that differed most sharply from the Shinshū was the Chinzei branch, which straightforwardly presented itself as Hōnen's original school.

The de facto founder of the Chinzei branch was Hōnen's disciple Benchō (1162–1238), who laid down the rudiments of its doctrine. Benchō focused on religious practice, embodied primarily in the *nembutsu*, as the ultimate message of the Pure Land teachings, in contrast to the Shinshū's emphasis on faith. According to Benchō's *Matsudai nembutsu jushuin* ("Personal Seal [Attesting] to the Transmission of the Nembutsu in the Latter Days"), chanting the *nembutsu* is the true practice leading to birth in Pure Land (*kushō shōgyō*), but it is augmented by four other practices: recitation of scripture (*dokuju*), meditation (*kanzatsu*), worship (*raihai*), and praises and offerings (*sandan kuyō*). Inwardly, three states of mind (*sanshin*) undergird the believer's practice of the *nembutsu*: a sincere mind (*shijōshin*), a mind of profound faith (*jinshin*), and a mind offering up personal religious merit in aspiration for birth in Pure Land (*ekō hotsugan shin*). The important thing, however, is for the *nembutsu* to be practiced outwardly, particularly in three specific contexts: in daily routine (*jinjō gyōgi*), in special religious retreats (*betsuji gyōgi*), and in a deathbed ceremony (*rinjū gyōgi*).[15] These various components of practice, all traceable to Shan-tao's *Kuan ching shu* ("Commentary on the Pure Land Meditation Sutra") and Genshin's *Ōjōyōshū* ("Collection [of Scriptural Passages] on the Essentials for Birth in Pure Land"), encompass the three spheres of human activity (*sangō*)—the physical, the verbal, and the mental (*shinkui*)—thereby engaging the whole person in the religious endeavor.[16] They indicate how crucial the idea of religious practice was to Benchō's teachings and to Chinzei doctrine in general.

Benchō wrote his *Matsudai nembutsu jushuin* ("Personal Seal [Attesting] to the Transmission of the Nembutsu in the Latter Days") in the form of a religious transmission to his closest disciples, and he personally presented an inscribed copy to each of them, bearing testimony to the correctness of their teachings and the authenticity of their lineage from Hōnen.[17] Benchō himself limited his ministry to the southern island of Kyūshū, but his chief disciple, Ryōchū (1199–1287), spread the Chinzei teachings to other parts of Japan, particularly to the city of Kamakura and the surrounding Kantō region.[18] He inherited Benchō's strong sense of religious lineage, and he instilled it in his own disciples by bestowing on them copies of Benchō's *Matsudai nembutsu jushuin*, to which he appended a postscript declaring it to be a religious "transmission spanning three generations" (*sandai sōjō*):[19] from Hōnen, to Benchō, to Ryōchū. In his interpretation of the *nembutsu* Ryōchū stressed the *nembutsu*'s efficacy in eliminating any evil karma that obstructs one from birth in Pure Land. The greater a person's evil, the more that person must practice the *nembutsu* to root it out.[20] He also asserted that even practices unrelated to the *nembutsu* (*zōgyō*), which Hōnen himself had set aside, can lead a person to Pure Land if the believer has the capacity to undertake them.[21] In this way Ryōchū defined religious practice more broadly than his two predecessors had, and thereby gave the Chinzei branch a more rigorous religious air. This emphasis on practice, especially as a means of eradicating evil karma, stood in diametric opposition to Shinran's interpretation of the *nembutsu* as a gift from Amida and as a response of gratitude to Amida.

After Ryōchū's death his disciples divided the Chinzei into six subbranches, three in the Kantō region and three in Kyoto, but they all upheld Ryōchū's concept of religious practice and stressed concerted effort on the part of the believer. The Chinzei branch's seventh patriarch, Shōgei (1341–1420), even couched the Pure Land teachings in categories used by the Zen school in an attempt to refute criticisms of Pure Land by Zen masters.[22] He also endorsed Shinto-Buddhist syncretism and declared that, since the Shinto *kami* are protectors of *nembutsu* adherents and are ultimately manifestations of Amida Buddha, to say the *nembutsu* before the *kami* is not an impious act but rather an acceptable form of worship.[23] Shōgei's great contribution, however, was to systematize Benchō's and Ryōchū's concept of doctrinal transmission and precept ordination, thereby laying the groundwork for clerical lineages and sectarian organization.[24] Because of Shōgei's doctrinal and organizational creativity, his subbranch, the Shirahata lineage centering around Kamakura, eventually emerged as the dominant strand of the Chinzei branch, drawing the other subbranches into its sphere and extending its influence into various provinces under the patronage of samurai converts.

Perhaps the most important event in the Chinzei branch's rise to prominence was its appropriation of the Chion'in, the temple in Kyoto that evolved from Hōnen's grave site. Hōnen's disciple Genchi, who originally presided over the grave site chapel, had no formal connection with the Chinzei branch. The Chinzei's earliest link to the Chion'in was through the temple's eighth head priest, Nyoichi (1262–1321), sometimes referred to as Nyokū, who was an important follower of Ryōchū's disciple Ryōkū (d. 1297). Nyoichi's successor at the Chion'in, Shunjō (1255–1335), sought to project this Chinzei connection back in time by recording in his monumental biography of Hōnen a meeting between Genchi's follower Shin'e (1205–81) and Ryōchū. The biography states that they joined their two lineages together because no doctrinal differences existed between them.[25] With this passage Shunjō in effect legitimized the tie between the Chinzei branch and the Chion'in temple. Kyoto, however, was always a stronghold of the Seizan branch of the Jōdoshū school, and most of the early head priests of the Chion'in were linked more to the Seizan tradition than to the Chinzei.[26] Only in 1450 did the Chinzei branch gain undisputed control over the Chion'in temple when Keijiku (1403-59), a disciple of Shōgei's successor Shōsō (1366-1440), was named the twenty-first head priest there, thanks to the backing of the emperor Gohanazono (1419-70).[27] From that time the Chion'in temple remained in the Chinzei branch's hands, thereby adding the prestige and aura of Hōnen's grave site to the branch and reinforcing its claim to be the true heir of Hōnen's Jōdoshū school.

The Chinzei's rise to power at the Chion'in temple during the fifteenth century would have provided ample opportunity for contact, or perhaps conflict, with the Shinshū if warfare in the capital had not intervened.[28] The Chion'in was located only a few minutes from the Honganji, and prior to Keijiku's time there was frequent association between the two temples. The twelfth head priest of the Chion'in, Seia (d. 1374), even oversaw Kakunyo's funeral arrangements.[29] Nevertheless, little interaction occurred once the Chinzei came to dominate the Chion'in because political upheavals in Kyoto cut short the occasion for contact. With the outbreak of the Ōnin war in 1467, the Chion'in was relocated in the province of Ōmi and remained there for more than fifteen years.[30] The Honganji, for its part, was destroyed by Mt. Hiei's militant priests in 1465, sending Rennyo fleeing into the provinces where he eventually built up his following.[31] After that the most momentous encounter between the Chion'in and the Honganji came almost 150 years later, when the great unifier of Japan, Tokugawa Ieyasu (1542-1616), expropriated the land on which the original Ōtani memorial stood and donated it to the Chion'in to expand its facilities.[32] Under Tokugawa patronage the Chinzei eventually emerged as the largest and most influential branch of the Jōdoshū school. Its teachings, however, always stood at the opposite end of the doctrinal spectrum from those of the Shinshū.

THE SEIZAN BRANCH OF THE JŌDOSHŪ SCHOOL

Unlike the Chinzei, the Seizan branch of the Jōdoshū school was always centered in Kyoto. Until the fifteenth and sixteenth centuries, when the Chinzei overshadowed it, there was constant intermingling between the Seizan branch and the Shinshū, especially during the Honganji's early development. The most notable points of contact were the religious instruction that Kakunyo and Zonkaku received from the Seizan priest Anichibō Shōkū of the An'yōji temple; the introduction of Seizan terminology and ideas into Shinshū doctrine; and the Shinshū's appropriation of the *Anjin ketsujōshō* ("Notes on the Firm [Abode] of Faith"), an obscure Pure Land text probably written by a Seizan priest. These points indicate that the relationship between the Seizan branch and the Shinshū was cordial during the fourteenth and fifteenth centuries and that Shinshū doctrinal developments occurred in part under the influence of Seizan concepts.

The Seizan branch was established by Shōku (1177–1247),[33] one of the disciples that Hōnen selected to assist him in the composition of his magnum opus, *Senjakushū* ("Singled-Out Collection"). Shōku inherited Hōnen's *nembutsu* as the pivotal concept of his teachings, but in contrast to Benchō of the Chinzei branch he denied that the *nembutsu* is a form of religious practice. Instead, Shōku interpreted it to be an act of Amida uniting the believer with the Buddha. Faith, commonly designated by the term *anjin* in Shōku's writings, is the active element leading the believer to the *nembutsu*. In order for faith to arise, the believer must first repudiate the path of religious practices (*gyōmon*) and embark upon the path where Pure Land is cognized (*kanmon*). From there the believer enters the path of Amida's boundless vow (*guganmon*) and upon hearing the vow realizes that everything necessary for salvation has already been accomplished by Amida when he attained Buddhahood ten kalpas ago.[34] In the way Amida framed the principal vow, his own enlightenment is inextricably united with the salvation of the believer, so that one is not possible without the other occurring also. Hence, if Amida's Buddhahood cannot be disputed, then the salvation of the believer cannot be doubted either. This very absence of doubt is none other than faith, and the *nembutsu* of faith is tantamount to the coalescence of believer and Buddha.[35]

Of the six characters used to write the *nembutsu*, the first two, *Namu*, indicate the believer's reliance on the Buddha, whereas the remaining four, *Amida Butsu*, symbolize the Buddha's salvation of the believer. When all six are brought together in a single utterance of faith, the *nembutsu* constitutes the inseparability of the Buddha and the believer. Hence, the believer, who is limited in religious capacity, and the Buddha, who is grounded in absolute truth, become one substance (*kihō ittai*).[36] To that extent, the believer's *nembutsu* is not a personal religious practice aimed at acquiring birth in Pure Land; rather, it is Amida's act of ten kalpas ago, achieving both salvation for the believer and Buddhahood for himself. From the moment that faith arises in the believer and the *nembutsu* is uttered, birth in Pure Land becomes an immediate reality (*sokuben ōjō*), for there is no longer any division between believer and Buddha.[37] When a person is united with the Buddha in this way, all actions—whether physical, verbal, or mental (*shinkui*)—are expressions of the *nembutsu* and represent the power of the Buddha transmuted in the person. Consequently, religious acts in the so-called three spheres of human activity (*sangō*) are rejected if originating in the effort of the believer, but are reaffirmed if stemming from the Buddha's power. In his daily conduct Shōku, like Benchō, lived a life of constant religious activity—*nembutsu* chanting, recitation of scriptures, adherence to clerical precepts, religious retreats, temple lectures, and so forth—but he viewed those practices as the workings of Amida in him, not as his own attempt to attain birth in Pure Land.[38]

The Seizan branch, like the Chinzei, was divided into six subbranches after

Shōkū's death, four of them established by Shōkū's direct disciples and the other two by Seizan priests of subsequent generations. All these subbranches were centered in Kyoto and propagated their teachings primarily to Kyoto's aristocracy. Since Shōkū's writings were somewhat recondite, usually taking the form of question-and-answer commentaries on Shan-tao's *Kuan ching shu* ("Commentary on the Pure Land Meditation Sutra"), his brand of Pure Land thought appealed largely to educated believers of the imperial and aristocratic strata. Emperor Gosaga (1220-72), for instance, was a supporter of the Seikoku and the Saga subbranches; emperor Gofukakusa (1243-1304) a patron of the Tōzan and the Fukakusa subbranches; emperor Godaigo (1288-1339) a convert of the Honzan subbranch; and emperor Gokomatsu (1377-1433) an adherent of the Rokkaku subbranch.[39] Of these, the one that exerted the strongest influence on Kakunyo and Zonkaku was the Tōzan, which flourished in eastern Kyoto for a century and a half after Shōkū's death. Both Kakunyo and Zonkaku studied at the An'yōji, a Tōzan temple, under the Seizan priest Anichibō Shōkū. Little is known of him except that he derived his religious lineage from both the Tōzan and the Fukakusa subbranches. Kakunyo and Zonkaku received instruction from him in Shan-tao's *Kuan ching shu* and in other Pure Land works.[40] It is not surprising then that Seizan terminology appears in their writings—for example, the expression *kihō ittai*, indicating that the believer and the Buddha are of one substance.[41] The use of such terms eventually paved the way for the absorption of a Seizan text, the *Anjin ketsujōshō* ("Notes on the Firm [Abode] of Faith"), into the Shinshū.

The *Anjin ketsujōshō* might have passed into oblivion if it had not been for the Shinshū, for it was never a major treatise in the Seizan tradition.[42] Although Kakunyo himself did not refer to the work in his writings, it is likely that he was familiar with it because the work was circulating during his lifetime, and a surviving manuscript of the text dated 1346 was reputedly made by his disciple Jōsen (d. 1352).[43] Zonkaku, for his part, quoted passages directly from the text, though he did not mention the text by name.[44] In content the *Anjin ketsujōshō* centers on the concept of *kihō ittai*: the inseparability of believer and Buddha, and the simultaneity of the Buddha's enlightenment and the believer's birth in Pure Land. It points to the *nembutsu* as the crystallization of both the Buddhahood of Amida and the salvation of the believer, since the requirements for both are fulfilled in it. Hence, salvation for the believer is not a matter of personal endeavor, but simply of comprehending (*ryōge*) or taking refuge in (*kimyō*) the fact that salvation has already been accomplished. When this happens, the believer's thoughts, words, and deeds (*shinkui*) become extensions of the *nembutsu*, indistinguishable from those of the Buddha.[45]

Kakunyo and Zonkaku included the idea of *kihō ittai* in their teachings, but they did not make it a crucial theme there, nor did they always interpret it the same way that the *Anjin ketsujōshō* did.[46] Nonetheless, its appearance in their writings provided an important doctrinal stepping-stone for Rennyo's popularization of the text a century later and for his incorporation of its concepts into Shinshū thought.[47] From that time the work became so integrated into

Shinshū literature that it was taken for a Shinshū composition, frequently attributed to Kakunyo.[48] Notwithstanding the Shinshū's early appropriation of the *Anjin ketsujōshō*, present-day scholars agree that it was originally produced by the Jōdoshū's Seizan branch.[49] Despite its origins, Seizan terminology assumed an increasingly conspicuous place in Shinshū teachings beginning in Kakunyo's period and proceeding through Rennyo's, just at a time when the Seizan branch itself fell under the shadow of the Chinzei branch's ascendancy.

THE JISHŪ SCHOOL

Seizan doctrine influenced not only the Shinshū's foremost thinkers but also Ippen (1239–89), the founder of the Jishū school. Ippen can be considered an heir of Shōkū's teachings because he was an important follower of Shōkū's disciple Shōtatsu. Nonetheless, Ippen's religious concerns ranged far beyond Seizan doctrine, and he is generally ranked alongside Hōnen and Shinran as a Buddhist innovator of the first order.[50] Consequently, his following, the Jishū, is regarded not as a subbranch of the Seizan tradition but as an independent school of Kamakura Buddhism. The Shinshū's early relationship with the Jishū was uncomfortably close, since both were major proponents of the Pure Land teachings in the provinces and were often mistaken for each other during early suppressions of the *nembutsu*. The Jishū, of all the schools of Kamakura Buddhism, was probably the Shinshū's most tenacious rival for converts in the countryside. As a result, certain branches of the Shinshū, principally the branch under the Bukkōji temple, adopted Jishū methods of proselytization in order to compete with it head on. The Bukkōji was fairly successful in meeting the Jishū challenge, but Rennyo was the one who eventually succeeded in winning over countless Jishū followers to the Shinshū.

Ippen's doctrinal starting point was essentially the same as the Seizan branch's—that is, both regarded the *nembutsu* as the union of believer and Buddha through which birth in Pure Land becomes an immediate reality.[51] But Shōkū, the founder of the Seizan branch, couched this conviction in scriptural studies and in standard clerical practices at Kyoto's aristocratic temples, whereas Ippen took up the life of a wandering holy man (*hijiri*), distributing *nembutsu* amulets (*fusan*) to everyone he met in his travels. He considered the simple act of accepting an amulet sufficient in establishing a karmic link (*kechien*) between the giver and the receiver. Through this act the recipient is assured of birth in Pure Land, whether or not faith is professed in the *nembutsu*.[52] Thus, Ippen detached the *nembutsu* from faith and interpreted it instead in terms of birth in Pure Land and union with the Buddha. In the single moment when one *nembutsu* is uttered, this union occurs. Even though it is chanted repeatedly throughout one's life, it still constitutes a single timeless instant of coalescence with the Buddha.[53] This interpretation stood behind Ippen's ceaseless practice and propagation of the *nembutsu* and his distribution of thousands of *nembutsu* amulets over the course of his sixteen-year career of religious itinerancy (*yugyō*).

In conjunction with the *nembutsu*, Ippen adopted a number of other religious practices that were prevalent in the popular Buddhism of his day. The first was the worship of Shinto *kami*, especially those identified as manifestations of Amida Buddha or as guardians of his teachings. Ippen's advocacy of Shinto devotions was more in line with prevailing religious attitudes of his day, and stood in contrast to the anti-Shinto leaning of some Pure Land groups.[54] The second was an ecstatic form of dancing called *yuyaku nembutsu*, performed to the engrossing rhythm of *nembutsu* chanting and signifying the joy (*kangi*) of the *nembutsu* at work in the body.[55] The third was the practice of recording in a register the *amigō*, or the adopted "Amida name," of deceased *nembutsu* followers. This record was called the *Ōgo no kakochō*, ("Register of the Past"), and it was patterned after the solicitation registers (*kanjinchō*) compiled by itinerant priests of the period.[56] Ippen brought together all these elements—the *nembutsu*, amulets, itinerancy, Shinto-Buddhist devotions, ecstatic dancing, and registers of believers—into a highly successful religious movement that attracted adherents in all walks of life. Ippen referred to these adherents as *jishū*, or "timely members," thereby giving the school its name.[57]

The formation of the Jishū began in Ippen's later years, when a large following coalesced around him. Among his converts Ippen distinguished between clerical adherents (*dōjishū*) and lay adherents (*zokujishū*), in effect laying the groundwork for a Jishū priesthood.[58] Clerical members included both men and women who, like Ippen, took up the homeless life to propagate the *nembutsu*. During Ippen's time they made up his entourage as he traveled from place to place. Though they were not ordained into the regular precepts of the Buddhist clergy, their austerities and their religious commitment set them apart from ordinary Jishū adherents. Ippen prescribed a life of simplicity for them and stipulated only twelve items that they were allowed to own, mostly articles of clothing worn by itinerant monks.[59] He also formulated a set of eighteen vows that they were obliged to live by.[60] Together these rules and practices gave Ippen's companions a clerical air that was not characteristic of his lay followers. Lay adherents continued to live in society, but counted themselves among Ippen's converts because of the *nembutsu* amulet received from him assuring them of birth in Pure Land and inspiring them to practice the *nembutsu*. Lay believers, in turn, offered the hospitality of their homes to Ippen and his companions as they traveled throughout Japan, and supported their evangelistic activities with contributions.[61] The *nembutsu* amulet was a particularly ingenious method of popularizing the *nembutsu*, for it gave believers a tangible object, a palpable religious symbol, on which they could focus their convictions and devotions. Along with the subsequent establishment of meeting places, or *dōjō*, it was largely responsible for the success of the Jishū school in attracting converts.

Following Ippen's death, his chief disciple Shinkyō (1237–1319) began to fashion a religious organization out of the movement that Ippen left behind. At first Shinkyō emulated Ippen by leading his band of followers around Japan disseminating *nembutsu* amulets, but in 1305, after sixteen years of religious itinerancy, he settled down in the Kantō region and established a *dōjō*. This and other *dōjō* founded either by Ippen's disciples or by other charismatic leaders quickly became the backbone of the Jishū organization and, like Shinshū *dōjō*, drew an enthusiastic response from rural converts. This shift from evangelistic itinerancy to established congregations changed the complexion of the Jishū school, making it less a spontaneous religious movement but giving it more institutional stability and permanence. Different *dōjō* emerged as major centers of activity, thereby engendering separate branches of the Jishū school, but the most influential one was Shinkyō's *dōjō*, which later evolved into the Shōjōkōji temple in the town of Fujisawa.[62] Shinkyō and his successors concentrated religious authority in the hands of the *dōjō* priest by preaching complete reliance on one's religious master (*chishiki kimyō*), since the master was thought to be the person through whom the ordinary believer establishes a karmic link to Pure Land. The *dōjō* leader, in short, became the believer's guide to salvation, and only through submission and obedience to that person could birth in Pure Land be realized.[63] The head priest of the Shōjōkōji temple was by extension the religious master of all Jishū adherents, and therefore assumed the position of Amida's representative in matters of salvation.[64] He granted individual priests the authority to distribute *nembutsu* amulets, and he controlled the Jishū register of believers born in Pure Land. A person's name could easily be entered into the register upon conversion, but it could also be stricken from the record simply by appending the words "Not born in Pure Land" (*fuōjō*), a notation that occasionally appears in the Jishū's "Register of the Past."[65] In essence the head priest exercised the right to bestow and to withdraw salvation, and through it he commanded the allegiance of subordinate *dōjō* priests and members.

Jishū leaders exerted these ecclesiastical prerogatives to gain large followings in Sagami, Musashi, and Kai provinces in eastern Japan; in Ōmi province east of Kyoto; and in Echizen, Kaga, and Echigo provinces along the Hokuriku seaboard. By the early fifteenth century the Jishū school boasted as many as 2000 *dōjō* in its organization.[66] The Shinshū, when confronted with this burgeoning religious movement, reacted in various ways. Kakunyo, on the one hand, denounced the Jishū school in his *Gaijashō* ("Notes Rectifying Heresy") for the sharp distinction it made between lay and clerical adherents through its use of clerical robes.[67] On the other hand, Ryōgen, who founded the Shinshū's Bukkōji temple, emulated the Jishū by establishing salvation registers (*myōchō*) and portrait lineages (*ekeizu*), patterned after the Jishū's "Register of the Past."[68] These actions, though important in Shinshū history, posed minimal threat to the Jishū during its fourteenth-century expansion into the provinces. A century later, however, Rennyo proselytized actively among Jishū believers and apparently succeeded in drawing many into the Shinshū, as reflected in the drastic decrease in the number of members in Jishū registers during this period.[69] This was precisely the time when the Honganji enjoyed substantial increases in its membership.

THE IKKŌSHŪ

Unlike the other religious groups described above, the Ikkōshū was an obscure band of Pure Land proponents whose history is known today only in the most fragmentary form. The Shinshū itself was identified by the name Ikkōshū from the fifteenth century on, and as a result few people realize that there was a distinctly different group by that name earlier. Its founder, Ikkō Shunjō (1239–87), was a disciple of Ryōchū of the Jōdoshū school's Chinzei branch. Nonetheless, his method of proselytization was extremely close to Ippen's in that he advocated religious itinerancy and ecstatic *nembutsu* dancing, and he also addressed his followers as *jishū* or "timely members."[70] For that reason, the Ikkōshū came to be identified as a branch of the Jishū school. There were, however, substantive differences between the two as well. Specifically, the Ikkōshū looked upon Shinto *kami* with disdain, and its adherents sometimes behaved in a scandalous manner. A late thirteenth-century work, the *Tengu sōshi* ("Book of Goblins"), describes the group:

> Those calling themselves the Ikkōshū revile people who adhere to any Buddha other than Amida, and they turn their back on anyone who goes to worship Shinto *kami* . . . . They generally wear roughly woven garments (*umaginu*) that have no skirting (*mo*) attached to the robe. When they perform the *nembutsu*, they dance shaking their head and swinging their shoulders like wild horses. The commotion they make is no different from that of monkeys in the mountains. They do not keep their private parts covered, neither male nor female. They eat with their fingers, and they are attracted to all types of improprieties.[71]

This kind of disreputable behavior was precisely what civil and religious leaders feared most from the spread of the *nembutsu* movement among the common people. Though Ikkō's successor Raichia (1252–1325) established rules of conduct to curb the excesses of Ikkōshū followers, he did not succeed in mending the group's reputation completely.[72] Consequently, the Ikkōshū became a perennial target of government suppression.

From early in its history the Shinshū was frequently mistaken for the Ikkōshū. Instances of this confusion date back to the beginning of the 1300s when Kakunyo and his uncle Yuizen petitioned civil and religious authorities not to suppress Shinshū believers alongside members of the Ikkōshū.[73] More than a hundred years later, Rennyo was waging a similar campaign to divest the Shinshū of this mistaken identity. In his letters he argued that the Ikkōshū derived its tradition from the Jishū and traced its lineage back to Ippen and Ikkō. Hence, the name should not be used to refer to the Shinshū.[74] Rennyo failed, however, to dissociate the Shinshū from this group, possibly because some of his converts were coming from Ikkōshū ranks. Many may have carried the name with them into the Shinshū. The absorption of Ikkōshū believers can only be conjectured at this point, extrapolated from Rennyo's letters. If true, it is consistent with the pattern of Rennyo's early proselytization efforts, which centered on areas of Ikkōshū strength—especially Ōmi province and the Hokuriku seaboard.[75]

Rennyo may have derived not only converts from the Ikkōshū but also doctrinal concepts—specifically, the idea of "relying on Amida to please save me" (*tasuke tamae to tanomu*). This is an issue previously unexamined by scholars of Shinshū history and doctrine.[76] In Shinshū literature Rennyo's letters were the earliest instance in which phrases of this type appeared. They are not found in Shinran's, Kakunyo's, or Zonkaku's writings, though such expressions may have been circulating at the popular level during their lifetime. The supplication, "Buddha, please save me" (*Butsu tasuke tamae*), for example, does appear in Japan's tale literature of the early 1100s.[77] From Rennyo's time the idea of "relying on Amida to please save me" evolved into a major doctrinal theme in the Shinshū. Sectarian scholars have tended to ascribe the origins of this doctrine to various branches of the Jōdoshū school.[78] Expressions like "please save me" (*tasuke tamae*), however, are not nearly as prevalent in Jōdoshū sources as in the letters of Raichia, Ikkō's chief disciple.[79] Rennyo was apparently familiar with Raichia's writings, for one passage in them is reproduced almost verbatim in Rennyo's letters.[80] If the letters attributed to Raichia do in fact date back to the thirteenth century, when he lived, then it seems clear that they influenced Rennyo in his adoption of the idea of "relying on Amida to please save me."[81] In all likelihood Ikkōshū adherents of Raichia's tradition popularized this expression in the Hokuriku region, and Rennyo merely incorporated it into his own teachings. He infused the phrase with a Shinshū meaning, and thereby made it a device for absorbing Ikkōshū believers into the Shinshū.

Ultimately, the influx of Ikkōshū members into the Shinshū was so great that the name Ikkōshū itself became synonymous with Shinshū. Despite Rennyo's protests against its use, the name emerged as the most common form of address for the Shinshū after Rennyo's time, and only in the nineteenth century was the government finally persuaded to use the title Jōdo Shinshū instead of Ikkōshū to refer to the school.[82]

CHAPTER
8
SHINSHŪ FACTIONS

The Shinshū, like other schools of Kamakura Buddhism, emerged as a full-bodied religious organization only after a long period of development. Between the time of its founding in the 1200s and its rise to national stature three centuries later, the school existed merely as a collection of semiautonomous regional branches with loose ties to one another based on their common lineage to Shinran. The major institutions that presided over these branches were the Bukkōji temple in Kyoto, the Kinshokuji temple in Ōmi province, the Senjuji temple at Takada in the Kantō region, the Sanmonto temples in Echizen province, and of course the Honganji in Kyoto. All of them arose as religious centers in the 1300s and gradually expanded their influence by propagating their teachings both in surrounding areas and in distant regions. Networks of congregations evolved under them, some loosely structured and others rigid and hierarchical. At one time or another each branch had a charismatic leader who was largely responsible for its doctrinal themes, its methods of proselytization, and its sectarian organization. Relations between the branches were sometimes cordial, but at other times strained. Kakunyo's ambitions, for example, generated considerable friction between the Honganji and other groups. Collectively, the various branches carried Shinshū teachings to diverse parts of Japan, but there was little coordination in disseminating them and little agreement in interpreting them. Nonetheless, their efforts gave the Shinshū a broad geographical base from which Rennyo later endeavored to unify the school under Honganji leadership.

THE BUKKŌJI BRANCH

Until Rennyo's time, the most successful branch of the Shinshū was the Bukkōji. In a passage dated 1413 from the records of the Honpukuji temple in Ōmi province, the Honganji and the Bukkōji are compared in the following way:

> These days people are hardly ever seen going to worship at the Ōtani chapel [i.e., Honganji], whereas at the Bukkōji temple in Shibutani, with its salvation

registers and portrait lineages, people are as dense as clouds or fog. This is altogether astonishing to behold.[1]

This account indicates that by the early fifteenth century the Bukkōji had displaced the Honganji as the most popular pilgrimage site in Kyoto for Shinshū believers and that the reason for its popularity was the use of salvation registers and portrait lineages. The Bukkōji's rise to fame during this period was almost meteoric, for it had only been in existence about ninety years.

The Bukkōji's founder, Ryōgen (1295–1336), was a native of the Kantō region, but he moved to the Kyoto area around 1320. His purpose was "to build a small chapel on the outskirts of Yamashina [east of Kyoto] in Yamashiro province and there to enshrine an image of Amida Buddha along with one of Shōtoku Taishi."[2] Ryōgen was a disciple of the Shinshū master Myōkō (1286–1353) of Amanawa in Kamakura, and so upon his arrival in Kyoto he sought the assistance of Kakunyo at the Honganji. Kakunyo presented him with a name for his new temple, Kōshōji, and he instructed Zonkaku to give Ryōgen religious training and copies of religious texts. Ryōgen developed an immediate rapport with Zonkaku, but over the next few years Kakunyo gradually became disgruntled with both of them. By the time Ryōgen finally opened the Kōshōji temple in 1324, Kakunyo had cut off ties with him and had disinherited Zonkaku. Hence, Ryōgen's temple arose in the shadow of Kakunyo's enmity. Nonetheless, Ryōgen was an energetic evangelist, and by enlisting Zonkaku's support he capitalized on the prestige and popularity that Zonkaku enjoyed among Shinshū congregations. During the first year of the temple's existence, Zonkaku presided over its autumn equinox memorial services (*higan*), and he composed four short homiletic manuals for Ryōgen to use: *Jōdo shin'yōshō* ("Notes on the True Essentials of Pure Land"), *Shojin hongaishū* ("Collection on the Original Intent of the [Shinto] Kami"), *Jimyōshō* ("Notes on Holding Fast to the Name"), and *Nyonin ōjō kikigaki* ("Recorded Sayings on the Birth of Women in Pure Land").[3] By 1329 the Kōshōji temple was so successful that it gave up its location outside Kyoto and moved into the city. Ryōgen built his new temple at Shibutani, very near the Honganji, and Zonkaku selected a new name for it, Bukkōji, or "Temple of the Buddha's Light," to replace the one Kakunyo had originally bestowed. Ryōgen parlayed the Bukkōji into a hub of religious activity, and he spread its fame and influence through preaching tours in the provinces. During one such tour in 1336, Ryōgen fell victim to highway bandits and was murdered.[4] With his passing his son Genran (1318–47) succeeded to the headship of the Bukkōji temple, but he too died young, only eleven years later. Nonetheless, the temple continued to flourish primarily because of the *nembutsu* inscriptions, salvation registers, and portrait lineages that it distributed from the time of its founding by Ryōgen. The salvation registers and portrait lineages were, of course, singled out for criticism in Kakunyo's *Gaijashō* ("Notes Rectifying Heresy").[5]

One common object of worship popularized by the Bukkōji temple was the *kōmyō honzon*, or sacred light inscription. This usually took the form of a calligraphic wall hanging of the *nembutsu* written in one of its alternate pronunciations: *Namu Fukashigi Kō Nyorai*, "I take refuge in the Tathāgata of Wondrous Light." In *kōmyō honzon* these words are inscribed in the center of the hanging, and from them rays of light are shown radiating outward toward pictures of Pure Land personages. The figures depicted most frequently are Kannon, Seishi, Nāgārjuna, Vasubandhu, T'an-luan, Tao-ch'o, Shan-tao, Huai-kan, Shao-k'ang, Shōtoku Taishi, Genshin, Hōnen, Seikaku, Shinran, and his disciples, often including Ryōgen. Inscriptions of the *nembutsu* can be traced back to Shinran himself, though his were much simpler, and most of them used different readings of the *nembutsu*. Some scholars speculate that the rays of light and the inclusion of Pure Land figures may have derived from the *Sesshu Fusha Mandara* ("Mandala of Those Embraced and Never Forsaken") popular in Hōnen's time, but it is difficult to verify a link between the two. Whatever the origins of sacred light inscriptions, they rapidly became one of the typical objects of worship in Shinshū congregations, and they were particularly prevalent in *dōjō* belonging to the Bukkōji branch.[6]

Another religious object that became the trademark of the Bukkōji temple was the *myōchō*, or salvation register. Only in the last few decades has one example of a salvation register come to light revealing much about their format and use.[7] This document, originally dated 1343, indicates that salvation registers were based on the idea of lineage but functioned primarily as registers of membership. They fulfilled precisely the same purpose as the "Register of the Past" (*kakochō*) of the Jishū school and were apparently inspired by the Jishū example.[8] The opening paragraph of this recently discovered salvation register discloses what it means to have one's name included in the roll:

> We have fervently carried on a single lineage from the time of the esteemed patriarch of Japan, master Hōnen, and we have preserved the traditions of his one school. For that reason believers of like conviction have been listed in this register of names *(myōchō)*. We regard admission into the register to be the first moment of faith *(ichinen hokki)*, and we consider inclusion in this lineage to be our karmic link to the Pure Land of the one Buddha. Hence, to have one's name entered into the register is to assume a karmic link to that Pure Land. We respectfully beseech the Tathāgata Amida, lord of salvation *(keshu)* in the western paradise, and we humbly implore past generations of masters *(sendoku)* in our lineage to have pity on us and receive us, and to acknowledge and attest [our salvation].[9]

This opening passage is followed by a list of 132 names. The first is that of a Buddhist priest, Ryōninbō, through whom the people in this register traced their religious lineage. Next come the names of the *dōjō* priest (*bōzu*), Ryōshinbō, and his wife, Enshinbō, who is euphemistically called *dōjō* caretaker (*bōmori*). After them 129 members are listed, 70 male and 59 female, and beside their names their village or resident estate (*shōen*) is frequently noted.[10]

This salvation register suggests several things about early Shinshū *dōjō*, especially those belonging to the Bukkōji branch. First of all, it shows that the *dōjō* head was often married and that his wife lived and worked alongside him in the *dōjō*, meriting almost as much status as he did.[11] Secondly, it reveals that the congregation was divided fairly evenly between men and women and that, based on the types of names given, they all came from peasant occupations such as farming, fishing, crafts, and hunting. None of the people listed seems to have been a samurai. It is also clear from the residences mentioned that the members lived over a broad geographical area covering seven estates and more than a dozen villages.[12] This might imply that the *dōjō* priest Ryōshinbō, named at the head of this register, served a number of congregations at various locations. Therefore, the adherents in this list may have comprised several different *dōjō*, all under the leadership of a single traveling priest. Finally, the opening paragraph of the register indicates that inclusion of one's name therein was considered tantamount to salvation. Like *nembutsu* amulets and the "Register of the Past" of the Jishū school, the salvation register gave ordinary believers a tangible form of assurance that they would be born in Pure Land. The net effect of this kind of religious document was to concentrate congregational authority in the hands of the *dōjō* priest, since he was the person who controlled the register. This priestly power caused *dōjō* in the Bukkōji branch to revolve first and foremost around the clergy, in contrast to other Shinshū congregations, where believers were theoretically equal in religious status and responsibility.[13]

Ekeizu, or portrait lineages, were another proselytization device used to great advantage by the Bukkōji temple. The earliest ones date back to Ryōgen's time and were probably drafted under his supervision.[14] In construction the portrait lineage is a scroll consisting of a prefatory statement and a series of portraits connected by red lines to indicate a transmission of teachings. The introductory passage, identical in most surviving examples, names five successive masters linking Shinran to Ryōgen: Shinbutsu, Genkai, Ryōkai, Seikai, and Myōkō.[15] The purpose of the *ekeizu* was to extend this lineage from Ryōgen to the people depicted in the portraits. They were the ones who, according to the preface, "established the *dōjō*, set up religious images in them, promoted karmic links leading to Pure Land, and spread the *nembutsu*."[16] As members of this lineage, they were expected not to go against its tradition and not to foment discord among believers. If they did, they were required to return scriptures and objects of worship—including no doubt the portrait lineage—to their master, thereby separating themselves from the lineage.[17] In early *ekeizu* the first portrait is that of Ryōgen, and from him lines extend to subsequent figures, each identified by name. The number of portraits varies from sixteen to thirty-four in the portrait lineages surviving today.[18] Most of the people illustrated in them are clergy, typically dressed in clerical robes, though a few are lay believers wearing secular garb. Men generally outnumber women. Moreover, the portraits of women are frequently displayed beneath their husband's. In a few instances children are also depicted.[19] The individuals selected for inclusion represent the leadership level of *dōjō* organization. They included not only priests and their wives but also powerful members and benefactors of the *dōjō*. In their hands the portrait lineages functioned as a testimonial document certifying the authenticity of their lineage and the truth of their teachings.

The portrait lineage had a dual impact on *dōjō* priests belonging to the Bukkōji branch. First, it heightened their status before their congregations by presenting them as direct or indirect disciples of Ryōgen, and hence as recipients of Shinran's teachings. *Dōjō* priests often used lineage portraits as homiletic devices demonstrating the venerated figures of their religious heritage, and as a result *ekeizu* themselves became objects of worship in some groups.[20] Such practices placed the *dōjō* leader on a pedestal before other believers and, combined with his control of the salvation register, imbued him with special religious authority. Secondly, the portrait lineage made the *dōjō* priest dependent on the Bukkōji temple, since the Bukkōji issued it and could just as easily recall it. The temple's domineering attitude toward affiliated *dōjō* is reflected in a document attributed to Ryōgen, whereby he sought to merge his following with that of Myōkō, his teacher:

> If there are any people who turn their back on this agreement, then they are no longer followers of Myōkō [and by extension of Ryōgen]. May they immediately suffer the punishment (*shōbatsu*) of the two world-honored Buddhas, Śākyamuni and Amida, as well as of Shōtoku Taishi, Hōnen, Shinran, and all the other patriarchs and masters of our lineage; and may they forever forfeit the great benefits of birth in Pure Land.[21]

Ryōgen in effect commanded total obedience of his followers, upon pain of eternal punishment by Buddhas and patriarchs. Fear of such retribution, as well as the Bukkōji's emphasis on religious lineage, brought *dōjō* priests to heel under the temple's leadership. As a result, a strongly hierarchical relationship arose between the Bukkōji temple and its regional *dōjō*. At each level of its organization authority lay with the group leader. *Dōjō* members looked to the local priest for guidance, and priests in turn looked to the Bukkōji temple. In short, the Bukkōji branch took on some of the characteristics of the Jishū school, especially its view of the religious master as the arbiter of salvation. Like the Jishū, it made submission to one's religious master a cardinal principle of membership.[22]

Between the time of Ryōgen and Rennyo the Bukkōji built up a large following in the provinces along Kyoto's southern flank as well as in western Japan. Ryōgen's last preaching tour, for example, carried him into Tōtōmi, Mikawa, Owari, Ise, and Iga provinces.[23] Kyōen, a follower of Ryōgen's teacher Myōkō, founded a major temple in the western province of Bingo and subsequently extended his influence into Bitchū and Bizen provinces as well.[24] From there successive generations of Shinshū adherents organized religious groups first in the province of Aki and later in Izumo, Iwami, and Nagato farther west.[25] Since Ryōgen and Myōkō joined their followings together, all of these congregations eventually fell under the purview of the Bukkōji temple.

During Rennyo's time the Bukkōji lost most of its members to the Honganji. This shift occurred around 1481, when Kyōgo (d. 1490), who was in line to be the fourteenth head priest of the Bukkōji temple, became Rennyo's protégé. Bukkōji sources depict Kyōgo's acquiescence to Honganji authority as a betrayal of his own tradition.[26] More likely, he acted out of expediency, seeking a kindred spirit and ally in Rennyo against the rampaging priests of Mt. Hiei.[27] Whatever the reason, Rennyo welcomed him enthusiastically and granted him a new clerical name, Renkyō, containing a character from his own name. Kyōgō proceeded to set up a temple called the Kōshōji, the name Kakunyo had originally bestowed on the Bukkōji, and he attracted several thousand local congregations (*sūsen matsuji*) from Bukkōji affiliation.[28] This defection decimated the Bukkōji's ranks, but it gave the Honganji a far broader constituency than it ever had before. From that time the Kōshōji became one of the influential temples in the Honganji's religious organization, and whenever the Honganji moved to a new location the Kōshōji always followed suit, rebuilding next door to the Honganji as one of its cadet temples.[29]

THE KINSHOKUJI BRANCH

Like the Bukkōji, the Kinshokuji temple grew up on the periphery of the Honganji and likewise benefited from the personal involvement of Zonkaku. In fact Zonkaku was instrumental in elevating the Kinshokuji to distinction within Shinshū circles, and his youngest son, Kōgon (1334–1419), eventually became head priest there. Compared to the Bukkōji, the Kinshokuji temple was never as bitter a rival of the Honganji, but their relations were not always cordial either. Generally, the Kinshokuji was less a threat to Honganji authority, for it did not achieve the dazzling success that the Bukkōji did. Nevertheless, it won a respectable following in central Japan. And it was at odds with the Honganji to the extent that it shared some of the Bukkōji's attitudes toward adherents.

The Kinshokuji temple was located in Ōmi province, just to the east of Kyoto, and its de facto founder was the priest Jikū (d. 1351).[30] Under his leadership the temple became active as a Pure Land center, and it probably adopted the name Kinshokuji about the mid-1300s.[31] Jikū and his older brother Gutotsu (d. 1352), who also played an important role in the formation of the temple, supposedly derived their religious lineage from Shinran's disciple Shōshin of the Yokosone congregation in the Kantō region.[32] There is some indication, however, that Jikū's early ties were with the Jōdoshū school rather than the Shinshū and that only through Zonkaku's influence did he join the Shinshū tradition.[33] Whatever his affiliations may have been, it was Zonkaku's association with Jikū and Gutotsu that led the Kinshokuji to prominence in the Shinshū.

The most immediate link between Zonkaku and these two was through marriage. This is especially noteworthy because marriage became an important mechanism for cementing ties between Shinshū congregations. Such practices were out of the question for other schools of Buddhism, since clergy were expected to remain celibate. Zonkaku's wife, Nau, was apparently a relative of Gutotsu's, perhaps his daughter.[34] It is not surprising, then, that Zonkaku and his family took up temporary residence at Uryūzu, where Gutotsu lived, directly after his disownment in 1322.[35] Gutotsu, though constantly supportive of

Zonkaku, also remained on friendly terms with Kakunyo. He gave refuge to Kakunyo when he was forced to flee Kyoto in 1336 because of warfare; he was instrumental in bringing about a reconciliation between Kakunyo and Zonkaku in 1338; and in the same year he accompanied Kakunyo on a tour of congregations in Yamato province.[36] Kakunyo's association with Jikū, who was the actual head priest of the Kinshokuji temple, was not as congenial. In 1349, when Kakunyo's wife died, Jikū traveled to the Honganji to express his condolences but was turned away by Kakunyo.[37] Hence, of the two brothers Gutotsu was the more influential in Zonkaku's life. He acted not only as a supportive in-law but also as an important mediator to Kakunyo. Jikū, however, was Zonkaku's direct link to the Kinshokuji temple itself.

It is not clear when the relationship between Zonkaku and Jikū began. The first reference to Jikū in Zonkaku's biography is dated 1347, when Jikū sought Zonkaku's advice on studying the teachings of the school.[38] That date, however, is decidedly late. Clearly their association began much earlier, for Jikū looked to Zonkaku as his foremost spiritual ally. On his deathbed in 1351, just a few months after Kakunyo's own death, Jikū expressed the desire that Zonkaku succeed him as head priest of the Kinshokuji temple. Gutotsu, hoping to fulfill Jikū's dying wishes, implored him to accept the position. But Zonkaku hesitated because of his own advanced age. In his place he recommended his youngest son, Kōgon.[39] With Kōgon's ascent to the headship of the Kinshokuji, an enduring bond was established between the temple and Zonkaku, and under Kōgon's direction the Kinshokuji emerged as an influential temple in the Shinshū.

Kōgon, who took the name Jikan after succeeding Jikū, was an able person to occupy this position. Like his father, he received a traditional education in the Buddhist classics, studying at the Tōdaiji temple in Nara and the Shōren'in temple in Kyoto. The extent to which he excelled in this area is indicated by the fact that he was named in 1358 to the honorary clerical rank of *gon shō sōzu* ("Assistant Lower Prelate"), typically bestowed on eminent Buddhist priests.[40] From the time of Kōgon's investiture at the temple, Zonkaku was constantly involved in Kinshokuji activities. Many objects of worship distributed by the temple were inscribed by Zonkaku, and they came to be valued as sacred possessions in local Shinshū congregations.[41] Zonkaku's trust and affection for Kōgon is reflected in the fact that in 1362 he passed on to Kōgon his personal copy of the *Rokuyōshō* ("Notes of Essentials on the Six [Fascicles]"), Zonkaku's seminal commentary on Shinran's *Kyōgyōshinshō* ("Teaching, Practice, Faith, and Enlightenment").[42] By the same token, evidence of Kōgon's devotion to his father is found in his composition of Zonkaku's biography—entitled *Zonkaku ichigoki* ("Record of the Life of Zonkaku")—written perhaps while Zonkaku himself recounted the events of his life.[43] All these occurrences testify to the closeness that existed between the two and to Zonkaku's personal concern for the success of the Kinshokuji temple. It was no doubt consoling to Zonkaku that, though he had been deprived of leadership at the Honganji, his hereditary lineage would be preserved through Kōgon at the Kinshokuji.

Under Kōgon the Kinshokuji branch gradually amassed a devoted following in the Shinshū. Its primary means of establishing ties with local congregations was by bestowing sacred objects of worship. By the fourteenth century a variety of such objects were circulating in the Shinshū, ranging from simple inscriptions of the *nembutsu* to the more elaborate sacred light inscriptions (*kōmyō honzon*) and graphic representations of Amida Buddha.[44] Virtually all the major Shinshū temples distributed objects of worship to affiliated *dōjō*. There are several known examples of religious objects traceable to the Kinshokuji temple which have inscriptions in Zonkaku's own hand. The most revealing one, reflecting both Zonkaku's attitude and the policies of the Kinshokuji, reads: "If by any chance the adherent should apostatize, then this should be returned to the main temple."[45] This inscription indicates that the Kinshokuji and Zonkaku himself subscribed to the view that a temple or a religious teacher has the prerogative to reclaim religious objects from followers who abandon the teachings. This right of confiscation dated back to several early Shinshū groups and was instituted at the Bukkōji temple as well.

Kakunyo denounced this practice in the *Gaijashō* ("Notes Rectifying Heresy"), arguing that the same issue had come up in Shinran's lifetime and that Shinran had allowed former followers to keep the religious objects they had received. His reasoning was that the objects might fall into different hands and thereby lead others to the Pure Land teachings, even if the original recipient no longer derived meaning from them.[46] This dispute reflects a fundamental difference between Zonkaku and Kakunyo, and by extension between the Kinshokuji and Honganji branches. The Kinshokuji sought to concentrate authority in the hands of a religious head, primarily through the control of objects of worship and sacred texts.[47] The Honganji, while bestowing such objects, claimed their true purpose to be the spread of the teachings rather than the binding of believers to a religious authority.[48] It would be naive to say that the Honganji disregarded such allegiances, but there were subtle distinctions between what it demanded of its affiliated *dōjō* and what the Kinshokuji and Bukkōji branches demanded. The requirement that followers return all religious objects to the temple if they changed affiliation is the most striking example of their differences.

From Zonkaku's time the Kinshokuji branch was successful in drawing Shinshū believers into its fold. Like the Bukkōji, it was particularly active in the provinces along Kyoto's southeastern perimeter. Zonkaku made frequent preaching tours in the area, and one major Shinshū center at Yoshino had ties with the Kinshokuji even before Kōgon assumed office.[49] Kōgon and his descendants, the hereditary head priests of the Kinshokuji temple, gradually built up a strong following in the provinces of Ōmi, Iga, Yamato, and Ise.

By Rennyo's time the Kinshokuji was an important branch of the Shinshū in its own right. In 1493, however, a dispute arose between its head priest and many of its adherents. Forty major congregations in Iga, Yamato, and Ise provinces followed Shōe (d. 1559), son of the head priest, in breaking ties with the Kinshokuji temple and in casting their lot with Rennyo's Honganji. Shōe formalized this alliance by marrying Rennyo's daughter Myōshō (1477–1500), and after she passed away in 1500 he married her sister, Myōyū (1487–1512). From that time the fortunes of the Kinshokuji branch declined rapidly, but its numbers were not lost to the Shinshū. As in the case of the Bukkōji branch, the great beneficiary amid this upheaval was the Honganji. Virtually all the Kinshokuji's followers ended up with Honganji affiliation.[50] Nonetheless, it survives today as the so-called Kibe branch of the Shinshū, with about 250 associated temples.

THE SENJUJI BRANCH

In many ways the Senjuji temple had the most legitimate claim to being the oldest of the major Shinshū temples. Though the name Senjuji did not come into use until the late 1300s,[51] the congregation itself existed from Shinran's time. This group was originally organized around a local chapel known simply as the Nyoraidō, or Tathāgata Hall, located at Takada in the Kantō region. Tradition has it that Shinran himself built the chapel in 1225 and enshrined an Amida triad there which came from the Zenkōji, a famous temple in Shinano province.[52]

Little is known of the early congregation apart from the personalities of its first two leaders, Shinbutsu (1209–58) and Kenchi (1226–1310). Both were direct disciples of Shinran. Shinbutsu, to whom three of Shinran's surviving letters are addressed,[53] was a tireless proponent of the *nembutsu* who traveled throughout the Kantō region and its surrounding provinces spreading Shinran's teachings.[54] He, rather than Shinran, may have been the true founder of the Nyoraidō chapel at Takada, or at least the person who brought it into Shinshū circles.[55] Kenchi, who was one of the few Kantō disciples present at Shinran's death, was also a prodigious disseminator of the *nembutsu*. He was responsible for transmitting the Shinshū teachings to the province of Mikawa, midway between the Kantō region and Kyoto, where a vibrant following developed even during Shinran's lifetime.[56] Together these two exemplify the missionary zeal which emerged among Kantō believers to spread Shinran's teachings to other parts of Japan. It is therefore not surprising that out of the major branches of the Shinshū that arose after Shinran's death two, the Bukkōji and Sanmonto branches, traced their lineages back to Shinbutsu, Kenchi, and the Takada congregation rather than to Kakunyo and the Honganji.

The Takada congregation was perhaps the most influential group in shaping the directions of the Shinshū during the first half century after Shinran. It not only carried his teachings to diverse regions of the country but also supported the Ōtani temple built at his grave site. Kenchi oversaw the construction of the original hexagonal chapel there and later raised funds to restore it after Yuizen left it in ruins in 1309.[57] His successor at Takada, Senkū (d. 1343), was instrumental in having a new building assembled at Ōtani after the original one was destroyed by warfare in 1336.[58] The Takada community was in fact the most important ally of Kakue and Kakunyo in their succession dispute against

Yuizen, who for his part received the support of the other important Shinshū community in the Kantō region, the Yokosone congregation.[59] Hence, strong ties were forged between Takada and the Honganji which lasted through the first half of the fourteenth century. It was Kakunyo's efforts to elevate the Honganji above other Shinshū groups that eventually strained these ties.

The Nyoraidō chapel at Takada took on the characteristics of a formal Buddhist temple only gradually. From the beginning it may have been substantially larger than a typical wayside chapel. One *nembutsu* inscription that Shinran presented to the chapel is approximately six feet long and, when mounted, would occupy a space over eight feet high. If this was displayed at the original Nyoraidō, it would mean that even during Shinran's lifetime the building was considerably larger than the ordinary Shinshū *dōjō*. Moreover, if the chapel possessed an Amida triad from the Zenkōji—and the Senjuji temple today does own one such triad—that alone could have made it a popular place of worship.[60] In short, the Nyoraidō had some of the makings of a Buddhist temple even before it took on formal temple status.

The transformation of the Takada congregation into a temple probably began under Senkū, perhaps in reaction to Kakunyo's attempt to do the same with Shinran's grave site. Senkū looked upon the Honganji strictly as a memorial chapel to Shinran, and hence he, as well as his successors at Takada, Jōsen (1317-69) and Junshō (1331-90), opposed the installation of an Amida image there, as was found at the Nyoraidō chapel.[61] Moreover, the establishment of a memorial to Shinbutsu in 1311 gave Takada some of the appeal that the Honganji possessed as a pilgrimage spot, without detracting from the chapel's basic function as a place of worship to Amida.[62] The Wada congregation in Mikawa province, for instance, made pilgrimages eastward to Takada just as frequently as westward to the Honganji.[63] Thus, criticism in Kakunyo's *Gaijashō* ("Notes Rectifying Heresy") of chapels (*sōdō*) set up as if they were main centers (*honjo*) which "discourage people throughout the provinces from going to worship at the Honganji, the grave site of our master," may have been directed as much against the Takada chapel as against the Bukkōji temple.[64] All this bespeaks the emergence of Takada as a major center of Shinshū activity long before the temple name Senjuji was formally adopted.

Throughout the fourteenth century the prevailing religious concerns of Takada were fairly faithful to Shinran's own beliefs. Its enshrinement of the Amida triad from the Zenkōji mirrored Shinran's own reverence for the Zenkōji Buddha.[65] Its popularization of images of Shōtoku Taishi arose out of Shinran's veneration of him as the promulgator of Buddhism in Japan.[66] Its sustained effort to spread the Pure Land message to other regions derived from Shinran's conviction that one should "have faith oneself and cause others to have faith" (*jishin kyōninshin*).[67] In the leaders of the Takada congregation, all this took the form of the *hijiri*, or itinerant priest, ideal.[68] Kenchi is the best example of this ideal, traveling widely in the provinces and attracting converts to Shinran's teachings. Later Takada leaders such as Jōjun (1389-1457) styled themselves on Kenchi, if in no other respect than making pilgrimages to worship centers of Shōtoku Taishi.[69] The *hijiri* spirit was consonant with the entire Pure Land tradition, and it resulted in the early success of the Takada community in winning converts. But as the fourteenth century wore on, it was gradually outstripped by other religious groups such as the Bukkōji branch, the Jishū school, and the Chinzei branch of the Jōdoshū school.

The title Senjuji was originally proposed as the temple name for the Honganji in 1312, but was rejected because of protests from opponents on Mt. Hiei.[70] The name apparently circulated widely in the Shinshū, for other early temples also bore it.[71] The Takada congregation, for its part, adopted this title rather late. The first known instance of its use in reference to Takada is in a document dated 1465.[72] Prior to that time the term *Amidaji* was occasionally used, appearing as early as 1315. It was not so much a temple name as an identification of the type of chapel at Takada: "a temple to Amida." Hence, the word Nyoraidō continued to be used for the chapel alongside it and can be found in writings as late as 1373.[73] This belated adoption of a formal temple name was in many ways consonant with Shinran's *dōjō* ideal. He regarded the informal congregation as more conducive to religious life than the formal temple. But for all intents and purposes the Senjuji existed as a temple, in all but name, from the mid-1300s.

The Senjuji branch had its greatest impact on the Shinshū during the first half of the fourteenth century. By the end of the century its influence had waned and other branches of the school superseded it. It is likely that the Senjuji branch would have suffered mass defections to the Honganji, just as the Bukkōji and the Kinshokuji did, if it had not been for its tenth head priest Shin'e (1434–1512), one of Rennyo's contemporaries. Though overshadowed by Rennyo's astounding achievements, Shin'e succeeded in building up a following loyal to the Senjuji and in preserving it as the second largest branch of the Shinshū. For his efforts Shin'e, like Rennyo, is remembered as the restorer (*chūkō*) of his branch of the school.[74]

Shin'e, who apparently had aristocratic roots, was not born into the Senjuji temple but came to it during his youth.[75] He became the disciple of Jōken (1416–64), the Senjuji's head priest, and also studied at nearby Jōdoshū and Tendai temples. At the age of twenty-five Shin'e took upon himself the task of reviving the fortunes of the Senjuji branch, which had fallen from prominence during the preceding century. He set out on a preaching tour that included the region around Kyoto, the Hokuriku seaboard, and the province of Ise, and within two years won numerous converts in these areas.[76] Part of the reason for Shin'e's success was the religious objects he popularized. One of them was a funeral mantle called a *nogesa*, inscribed with the *nembutsu* and with sayings from the "Larger Pure Land Sutra." This simple religious article was well received by peasant believers who had neither the means nor the status to merit a traditional Buddhist funeral. To this day such mantles are used in Senjuji funerals.[77] Another innovation of Shin'e's was the idea of direct followers (*jikisanshu*). The typical *dōjō* was related to a head temple through several layers of organization such as regional temples, branch temples, and *dōjō* priests.

Shin'e sought to establish a direct link between *dōjō* and the head temple by becoming the nominal leader of individual congregations.[78] This system was particularly successful in Ise province, where religious organization was relatively undeveloped, but less so in Mikawa and Echizen provinces, where regional religious leaders had already consolidated their authority.[79] For that reason Ise became one of the strongholds of the Senjuji branch from Shin'e's time.

Shin'e was active in some of the same regions that Rennyo of the Honganji was. During their early ministry the two were on good terms, and Shin'e even visited Rennyo at the Honganji. It is said that there was no difference of opinion between them and that they agreed not to lure members from each other's branch of the Shinshū.[80] Sometime in the 1460s discord arose. Senjuji sources claim that Rennyo broke their agreement and began drawing temples away from the Senjuji branch in the provinces of Mikawa and Kaga.[81] What divided the two, more likely, was their relationship with Mt. Hiei.

During this period militant priests on Mt. Hiei became more and more belligerent toward Shinshū groups in Ōmi and other nearby provinces, which they called the Mugekōshu ("Unobstructed Light Adherents"). This name derives from the *nembutsu* inscriptions which they venerated, containing the words "Tathāgata of Unobstructed Light" (*Mugekō Nyorai*) for Amida. Mt. Hiei accused the Mugekōshu of heresy, and associated them specifically with the Honganji. This was the justification for Mt. Hiei's attack on the Honganji in 1465.[82] During the course of events Shin'e sought to dissociate himself from the Mugekōshu. In 1465 he convinced religious authorities at Mt. Hiei to recognize the Senjuji as separate from the Mugekōshu and as the main temple of the Shinshū (*ikkō senju nembutsu dōjō no honji*) preserving Shinran's teachings against distortion.[83] Shin'e thereby took his stand against what he regarded as the licensed evil tendencies of Shinshū groups, and he no doubt saw himself as a defender of the faith against heresy. But in doing so he aligned himself with the Buddhist establishment against Rennyo and the Honganji. In the short run this action protected Shin'e and the Senjuji branch from Mt. Hiei's enmity, but in the long run Shin'e's ministry proved less appealing than Rennyo's to peasant believers in the provinces.[84]

Shin'e may not have been as successful an evangelist as Rennyo was, but he did manage to preserve the Senjuji as an independent branch of the Shinshū, primarily through the establishment of a major temple in the town of Isshinden in Ise province. This location gave the Senjuji branch a strong religious base in central Japan, and more importantly it provided a new site for the Senjuji temple itself, where it stands today. According to tradition Shin'e was responsible for moving the Senjuji from Takada to Isshinden. This was supposedly done through the beneficence of several wealthy patrons whom he had converted during his preaching tours there.[85] Certainly Shin'e chose Isshinden as his center of activity after he assumed the office of head priest in 1464, and clearly Isshinden became the subsequent location of the Senjuji temple, but doubts have arisen in recent years whether Shin'e was the one who took the momentous step of relocating the head temple there.

What is clear is that Shin'e established a major temple at Isshinden, though it probably represented an outpost of the Senjuji rather than a new site for it. There is no evidence in sources prior to the seventeenth century that Shin'e attempted to relocate the head temple per se.[86] Furthermore, during most of the sixteenth century the temple at Isshinden went by the name Muryōjuji rather than adopting Takada's formal name of Senjuji.[87] The first instance in which Senjuji was officially used for the Isshinden temple dates from the 1590s.[88] Therefore, it is more likely that the temple at Isshinden only gradually appropriated the name and function of the Senjuji, not that Shin'e deliberately transferred the temple to Isshinden.[89]

The Senjuji's survival against the vaunted ambitions of the Honganji was dependent in part on its establishing a convincing claim to Shinran's religious heritage. The Honganji had succeeded in doing so under Kakunyo by exalting the hereditary office of caretaker (*rusushiki*) of Shinran's grave site chapel. The Senjuji, for its part, laid claim to the so-called status of Shinran (*Shinran'i*) and based the authority of its head priest on it. Implicit in this claim was the idea that only one person was heir to Shinran's true oral teachings (*yuiju ichinin kuketsu*) and that that person alone could assume the status of Shinran. Shinbutsu was the first to receive these teachings, but because he died before Shinran they were subsequently bestowed on Kenchi and then Senkū. From these two the status was passed down from one generation to the next through the head priests of the Senjuji temple.[90] The historicity of such episodes in Shinran's life is highly suspect, since no record of them can be found outside of late Senjuji sources. Nonetheless, the legend became an essential component of the Senjuji's claim to special religious authority.

This claim has the unmistakable quality of the so-called secret teachings (*hiji bōmon*) which proliferated in the Shinshū from Zenran's time on.[91] The basic assumption in them is that Shinran secretly transmitted a sublime and mystical teaching which gives the recipient religious authority over other believers. Secret teachings became a common guise used by fringe groups in the Shinshū to hide and preserve concepts and practices that had no basis in the tradition. The discovery in 1911 of a set of ten letters of secret transmissions (*hiden*) confirmed the existence of secret teachings in the Senjuji branch. The secret teachings preserved in them include such concepts as achieving Buddhahood in this very body (*sokushin jōbutsu*) and attaining birth in Pure Land within this very body (*sokushin ōjō*), ideas which Shinran supposedly communicated in private but which cannot be found in his writings.[92] The claim in these letters is that they are the transmissions Shin'e passed on to his disciple Shinchi (1504–85). Consequently, scholars have identified Shin'e as a pivotal figure in promoting secret teachings in the Senjuji branch. Some have even speculated that the practice of preserving secret teachings originated in Senjuji circles and subsequently spread to the Sanmonto branch as well.[93] But recent discoveries reveal these letters to be forgeries of the seventeenth century fabricated during a succession dispute, thereby exonerating Shin'e of secret teachings.[94] It would seem, therefore, that secret teachings came into prominence rather late in the Senjuji branch. The Sanmonto temples, by contrast, incorporated secret teachings from the fourteenth and fifteenth centuries on and used them to bolster their own claims to religious authority. Perhaps the Senjuji temple took its inspiration from the Sanmonto example when it formulated its concept of the status of Shinran.[95] If so, it reflects the desperate measures to which the Senjuji was driven in its attempt to legitimize itself against the rising domination of the Honganji.

THE SANMONTO BRANCH

The Sanmonto branch of the Shinshū differs from the others in that no single temple acted as its focal point, but rather five temples shaped its history: the Senjuji at Ōmachi, the Shōjōji at Yokogoshi, the Jōshōji at Sabae, the Senshōji at Nakano, and the Gōshōji at Yamamoto. Of these, all except the Senjuji survive today, each of which constitutes a small but separate branch of the Shinshū. The history of these temples is complex, for there was never a clear-cut hierarchy or unity among them. In some respects their shifting alliances, their occasional name changes, and their independent religious activities reflect more accurately the random evolution of the early Shinshū than does the orderly growth of other branches. The Sanmonto temples each followed a somewhat different path of development, allied sometimes with one another and sometimes with such temples as the Bukkōji or even the Honganji. If there is anything that bound them together, it was their geographical proximity to each other in the province of Echizen on the Hokuriku seaboard, their popularization of secret teachings (*hiji bōmon*), and, except for the Gōshōji, their historical descent from the priest Nyodō (1253–1340).

Nyodō was the first Shinshū proselytizer to establish a lasting following in the Hokuriku region. He came out of the Wada congregation in Mikawa province, which traced its religious lineage back to Shinbutsu and the Senjuji branch. Around 1290 Nyodō made his way across the mountains of central Japan and founded a *dōjō* at Ōmachi in Echizen province. This rapidly grew into the foremost Shinshū temple along the Hokuriku seaboard and soon took on the name Senjuji, long before the Takada temple claimed the name for itself. Subsequently, Nyodō's disciples Dōshō (ca. 1345) and Nyokaku (1250–1311) began other Shinshū congregations at nearby Yokogoshi and Sabae, which evolved into the temples Shōjōji and Jōshōji, respectively. Together the three came to be known as the Sanmonto, or the "three congregations."[96] Two later occurrences expanded the number of temples active in the vicinity of the Sanmonto. One was the division of the Senjuji temple into two factions at the beginning of the 1400s. The seceding faction, headed by Nyodō's grandson Jōichi (1364–1438), built a new temple at Nakano called the Senshōji. Later, when the Senjuji died out at Ōmachi, the Senshōji temple was left as the only heir of Nyodō's lineage.[97] The other occurrence was the relocation of the Gōshōji temple from Kyoto to Yamamoto in Echizen province. The Gōshōji was founded by

Kakunyo's close disciple Jōsen (d. 1352) at Izumoji in Kyoto, but after its destruction by warfare sometime during the fifteenth century the temple was moved to Echizen province with the assistance of the Shōjōji temple there.[98] This series of events brought together five energetic temples within the boundaries of a single province. From there the Shinshū teachings spread along the Hokuriku seaboard, making it a Shinshū stronghold long before Rennyo's time.

The earliest description of the Sanmonto congregations is contained in a polemical work entitled the *Guanki* ("Record of Foolishness and Darkness") written by a Tendai priest living in Echizen province during the early 1300s. The purpose of this work was to denounce the religious practices of the Shinshū and other new Kamakura movements from the perspective of Tendai orthodoxy. Its specific criticism of the Sanmonto temples reads:

> At the present time lay men and women of the single-minded *nembutsu* (*ikkō nembutsu*) gather to sing the *wasan* hymns composed by the exile named Gutoku Zenshin [Shinran] and to chant the *nembutsu* at length in unison. In the "Larger Pure Land Sutra," where it describes the characteristics of the three classes [of sentient beings] born in Pure Land, there is the phrase, "The single-minded and exclusive Amida *nembutsu*" (*ikkō sennen Muryōju Butsu*). They take this to be the central message [of the sutra]. Pointing out the appearance of the key phrase "single-minded *nembutsu*," they refuse to recite the "Smaller Pure Land Sutra," nor will they perform [Pure Land] praise-singing at the six designated times of day (*rokuji raisan*). Rather, when men and women do their religious practices, they exert themselves, chanting the six character [formula of Amida's] name, and they sing in unison the *wasan* hymns of [Shinran]. They are not admonished against such impurities as meat eating, nor do they concern themselves with clerical mantle (*kesa*), robes, rosary, or full attire. Even if they put on a robe, they do not drape the clerical mantle across it, and they wear it over their silk narrow-sleeve gown of various colors. They do not set up monuments (*sotoba*) to offer up religious merit (*tsuizen*) to the dead, and they teach that one should not observe such things as prohibitions or taboos. This is folly.[99]

The Tendai priest who wrote this, referred to cryptically as the Hermit of Mt. Ko (*Kosan inshi*), considered the behavior of the Sanmonto adherents scandalous because they disregarded the beliefs and customs advanced by the Tendai tradition: reciting scripture, abstaining from eating meat, performing religious ceremonies with proper dress and decorum, offering up merit to deceased relatives, heeding social and religious prohibitions, and so forth. He even faulted them for not reciting the "Smaller Pure Land Sutra" and not singing the Pure Land praises six times a day (*rokuji raisan*), practices widespread in the Pure Land movement. In short, he found Sanmonto adherents religiously negligent, even of practices of their own unorthodox movement, and perhaps, by extension, guilty of licensed evil. The only two practices that he confirmed in the Sanmonto congregations were *nembutsu* chanting—which was universal among Pure Land believers—and singing *wasan* hymns—written by Shinran precisely for that purpose. Though their ways may have been heretical to an orthodox

Tendai priest, they did not deviate substantively from Shinran's image of the believer's practice. The description in this diatribe is a fairly representative picture of what early Shinshū religious life was like. What is most noteworthy is that *hiji bōmon*, or secret teachings, for which later Shinshū writers condemned Nyodō and the Sanmonto, are not mentioned at all.[100]

Of the writings attributed to Nyodō, the only one nowadays judged to be authentic is his rebuttal to this polemic, entitled *Guanki hensatsu* ("Reply to Record of Foolishness and Darkness").[101] What appears in it is not an explanation based on secret teachings or hidden transmissions but a straightforward presentation of Pure Land beliefs as a justification of practice. The prevailing idea in the work is:

> The layman, even as layman, can attain birth in Pure Land if he chants [the *nembutsu*]; the woman, even as woman, will be ushered into Pure Land (*raikō*) if she chants [the *nembutsu*]. Since no distinction whatsoever is made in it as to the purity or impurity of one's body, it is the practice [to be followed] whenever one is walking, standing, sitting, or lying.[102]

Over and above this basic message, there are many complex arguments revealing interpolations of doctrine from the Seizan branch of the Jōdoshū school and even a defense of the Jishū school's dancing *nembutsu* (*yuyaku nembutsu*).[103] But there is little in the work that can be identified as secret teachings or as egregious deviations from Shinran's ideas. Hence, it is unlikely that Nyodō was the author of the Sanmonto's notorious secret teachings. In fact, fourteenth-century historical works indicate that Nyodō was on good terms with the Honganji—receiving instruction on the *Kyōgyōshinshō* ("Teaching, Practice, Faith, and Enlightenment") when Kakunyo and Zonkaku visited Echizen province in 1311, traveling to Kyoto to study with Kakunyo, and even attending Kakunyo's funeral.[104]

The absence of secret teachings in Nyodō's writings does not discount their presence among his contemporaries. Kakunyo's *Gaijashō* ("Notes Rectifying Heresy"), written in 1337, confirms the existence of secret teachings among Shinshū believers:

> Among people who call themselves adherents of the master of the Honganji, it is wrong to worship their religious teacher (*chishiki*), to liken [the teacher] to Amida Tathāgata, or to consider the structure in which the teacher dwells to be the true Pure Land [generated] by [Amida's] unique vows (*betsugan*) . . . . People mix the term "middle-of-the-night teachings" (*yonaka no hōmon*) with descriptions of this kind. They cite the expression "the open and the concealed" (*kenshō onmitsu*) which appears in the master's treatise, the *Kyōgyōshinshō* ("Teaching, Practice, Faith, and Enlightenment"). Concerning the term "concealed," they say that he interpreted it to mean that one should not make public this one principle. Is this not an outrageous misstatement?[105]

Traditionally, this passage has been taken as a critique of the Sanmonto congregations,[106] though there is no explicit statement in Kakunyo's work singling them out. The description shows, nonetheless, that secret teachings were circulating in Kakunyo's time and that they took the form of "middle-of-the-night teachings," reminiscent of the secret transmission that Zenran claimed he alone received from Shinran at night.[107] Specifically in this case, secret teachings were used to construe a religious teacher to be the manifestation of Amida and the agent to whom ordinary members of a congregation should look for salvation.

Though Nyodō himself may not have been a proponent of "middle-of-the-night teachings," it is certain that secret teachings became a common component of the Sanmonto tradition subsequent to his time. The fact that two of the Sanmonto temples eventually included Zenran in their religious lineages attests to the importance they placed on secret teachings.[108] It is unclear when exactly these teachings became prominent in the Sanmonto branch. The *Hogo no uragaki* ("Scribblings on Discarded Paper"), a historical work written by Rennyo's grandson Kensei (1499–1570), accuses Nyodō himself of devising them.[109] More likely, they date from around the time of Jōichi, Nyodō's grandson, since relations with the Honganji became strained from that period.[110] By Rennyo's day, however, the Sanmonto congregations were rife with secret teachings.

What Rennyo encountered when he proselytized in Echizen and nearby provinces was a great diversification of secret teachings. Not only were they used to giving *dōjō* leaders domination over members, but in some cases they also became the justification for arrogant religious behavior by followers. This type of behavior stemmed from the belief that not only religious teachers but also their followers can achieve enlightenment in this world and thus attain the status of a Buddha. Shinran's own statement that the true believer is "equal to the Buddhas" (*shobutsu tōdō*) could easily be misinterpreted in this light.[111] The implication derived from it would be that whenever people bow down before an image of the Buddha they are really bowing to themselves, since Buddhahood lies within. In its most extreme form, it would mean that there is no need to worship any Buddha outside of oneself.[112] This kind of thinking proliferated in Sanmonto circles and eventually branded them as the Sanmonto "no-worship" adherents (*Sanmonto ogamazu no shu*).[113] When Rennyo made his way into the Hokuriku region during the fifteenth century, they became one of several iconoclastic groups that he attempted to reform in his campaign against heresy.

THE HONGANJI BRANCH

Between the time of Kakunyo and Rennyo the Honganji was an influential branch of the Shinshū but by no means the leading branch. It did its share of proselytizing in the provinces and thereby gained valuable allies there, but its greater contribution was in preserving Shinran's teachings and making them accessible to those who sought instruction. Formally, there were four head priests of the Honganji during this period: Zennyo (1333–89), Shakunyo (1350–93), Gyōnyo (1376–1440), and Zonnyo (1396–1457). They, together with

Zonkaku and his brother Jūkaku (1295–1360), laid the foundations for the Honganji that Rennyo would inherit.

After Kakunyo's death Honganji leaders carried on his ideal of raising the temple to eminence in the Shinshū, but they were generally more diplomatic in their relations with various Shinshū groups than Kakunyo had been. Zonkaku was the epitome of diplomacy. He maintained warm ties with the Bukkōji and Kinshokuji temples, he traveled widely ministering to congregations in the provinces, he made copies of scriptures and *nembutsu* inscriptions to bestow on believers, and he composed short religious tracts (*dangihon*) to explain doctrine to them.[114] Though Zonkaku never became head priest of the Honganji, he left his mark on it in all of these ways as well as in serving as mentor to his nephew Zennyo, Kakunyo's successor. No one at the Honganji until Rennyo approached Zonkaku's level of activity, though each head priest in his own way contributed to the tradition.

Over the course of this period the Honganji underwent lasting structural and institutional changes. One was the enshrinement of an image of Amida Buddha in the memorial hall to Shinran. This occurred around the end of Zennyo's tenure or at the beginning of Shakunyo's. The installation of an Amida image had first been attempted under Kakunyo, but was abandoned when the Takada congregation opposed it. Once installed, the image gave the Honganji the air of a true Buddhist temple rather than simply a memorial to Shinran, and by the time of Zonnyo's headship an entirely separate hall was built for it.[115] The other major change was the appointment of the Shimotsuma family to act as administrators at the Honganji. The Shimotsuma were descendants of Shinran's disciple Renni. During the Yuizen crisis of 1306–9 the Kantō congregations sent Shimotsuma Shōzen to oversee the memorial chapel while Kakunyo sought confirmation in the position of caretaker (*gorusu*). From that time the Shimotsuma remained in Kyoto and became allied with the Honganji. Under Shakunyo they were given the responsibility of opening and closing the worship hall, and they eventually took charge of day-to-day operations and finances as well. This made the Shimotsuma a powerful agent in Honganji affairs. But at the same time it allowed the head priest to concern himself less with the mundane duties of the temple.[116]

Though the Honganji's success could not compare with the Bukkōji's, it did make modest gains in winning adherents. Perhaps its most significant achievement was the establishment in 1390 of a major temple named the Zuisenji at the town of Inami in Etchū province. Shakunyo accomplished this during the last few years of his life after early retirement from Honganji headship.[117] The Zuisenji became the Honganji's first outpost in the Hokuriku region, and from there a network of temples and *dōjō* evolved in Echizen, Kaga, and Noto provinces, as well as in the province of Ōmi east of Kyoto along the route leading into the Hokuriku. The founding of the Chōshōji temple in Echizen province by Shakunyo's son Ton'en (d. 1447) was a watershed, for it brought the Honganji into direct competition with the Sanmonto temples in the region.[118] During this time one practice that came into common usage was for the head priest of the Honganji to send relatives to occupy positions of authority in these outly-ing temples.[119] This strategy was later used to great advantage by Rennyo.

While some branches of the Shinshū employed new proselytization devices to attract followers, the Honganji relied primarily on the traditional religious ob-jects popularized by Shinran and Kakunyo. The most important of these was the *nembutsu* inscription. From Kakunyo's time the ten-character version of the inscription, which reads *Kimyō Jin Jippō Mugekō Nyorai*, "I take refuge in the Tathāgata of Unobstructed Light Suffusing the Ten Directions," became stand-ard.[120] This remained popular until Rennyo's ministry, when he reverted to the six-character formula, *Namu Amida Butsu*, "I take refuge in the Buddha Amida."[121] *Nembutsu* inscriptions were the central object of worship displayed in temples and *dōjō*. By providing them the Honganji established a religious bond between itself and affiliated congregations. In addition it supplied copies of scriptures and pictorial biographies of Shinran.[122] They were often used as source books for religious instruction and for explaining the origins of the Shinshū. All these were the Honganji's answer to the salvation registers and portrait lineages popularized by the Bukkōji branch. Both temples provided believers with tangible objects to help sustain belief and practice, but the Hon-ganji did so without the strictures that the Bukkōji placed on its objects.

The Honganji's foremost contribution was to keep alive Shinran's teachings at a time when Shinshū groups were steadily absorbing external beliefs. The *Kyōgyōshinshō* ("Teaching, Practice, Faith, and Enlightenment"), Shinran's most complex work, was rewritten in Japanese grammar by Zennyo in 1360, there-by making it accessible to people who could not read the original Chinese.[123] Zonkaku wrote the first commentary on the work in the same year, entitled the *Rokuyōshō* ("Notes of Essentials on the Six [Fascicles]"), which became a valu-able study guide during subsequent generations. Also, the Honganji began to distribute copies of the *Kyōgyōshinshō* to closely allied temples. These gave fol-lowers more exposure to the work than they ever had before. Shinran's simpler writings also attracted attention. Jūkaku drew together Shinran's most impor-tant letters and compiled them in 1333 under the title *Mattōshō* ("Notes on the Lamp in the [Age of the Dharma's] Decline"). They became a rich and exten-sively circulated source of Shinran's ideas framed in everyday language. Other writings that had widespread appeal were Shinran's three collections of hymns: *Jōdo wasan* ("Hymns on Pure Land"), *Kōsō wasan* ("Hymns on the Patriarchs"), and *Shōzōmatsu wasan* ("Hymns on the True, the Imitated, and the Declining [Dharma]"). The singing of these was common in the Sanmonto branch and apparently spread throughout the Shinshū as a popular form of worship. Hence, copies of the *wasan* hymns came to be prized possessions in many congrega-tions.[124]

The Honganji's typical method of spreading Shinran's teachings was to dis-tribute copies of religious texts. This practice had multiple benefits. One was to strengthen the Honganji's bonds with temples and congregations, while car-rying Shinran's words to remote areas. Another was to distinguish the Hon-ganji as a seat of learning in the Shinshū tradition. Such a reputation was justified to the extent that all its head priests received formal training in the Buddhist classics and were well versed in Shinran's writings. The Honganji's location in Kyoto undoubtedly added to its prestige, since Kyoto was the center of culture and erudition in Japan. The high level of learning there made the Honganji more sophisticated than rural temples, and attracted Shinshū priests from the countryside for religious instruction.[125] Such personal contacts inevitably became one way for the Honganji to foster allies in the provinces.

Most of the trends that characterize the Honganji's development in this period found full expression during the lifetime of Zonnyo (1396–1457), the seventh head priest. He distributed scriptures extensively to Shinshū congregations and took in disciples for instruction in the Pure Land teachings. Moreover, under his direction an independent Amida hall was built at the Honganji, and congregations affiliated with the branch increased in number in Kaga, Echizen, and Ōmi provinces.[126] The Honganji did not become wealthy or dominant during Zonnyo's headship, but precedents were set that would have lasting influence on its history. What is most important is that his son, Rennyo, received valuable lessons from him in religious leadership. By the time of Zonnyo's death in 1457 the Honganji branch stood poised for expansion with Rennyo at its helm.[127]

CHAPTER
9

RENNYO AND THE
CONSOLIDATION OF THE SHINSHŪ

Rennyo (1415–1499), more than anyone else, brought the Shinshū into the highest ranks of Japanese Buddhism.[1] During his tenure as eighth head priest of the Honganji, the temple emerged as the premier institution of the school, and the Shinshū itself burgeoned into one of Japan's largest and most powerful schools of Buddhism. This was the period when the new schools of Kamakura Buddhism finally came into their own and when the scattered followers of Shinran's teachings were forged together into a massive religious organization. Rennyo is often credited with the consolidation of the school, and he is revered as the restorer (*chūkō shōnin*) of the Honganji. This, needless to say, was not a single-handed accomplishment on his part, for many of the elements necessary for the Shinshū's emergence were already in place when Rennyo arrived on the scene. Nonetheless, Rennyo was indisputably one of those rare individuals who had the energy and vision to seize the moment. He propagated Shinran's teachings tirelessly, he recast them in an idiom attuned to ordinary believers, and he united Shinshū followers under Honganji authority. Rennyo's rendering of Shinran's ideas, contained in his *Ofumi*, or "pastoral letters," eventually emerged as the most lucid statement of the school's tenets.[2] Without him it is questionable whether Shinran's religious message would have ever become the widespread and enduring creed that it has.

The sundry writings existing today by or about Rennyo reveal him to be a complex and multifaceted figure. In his pastoral letters he comes across as a dedicated evangelist propounding Shin teachings with intense conviction and personal humility. In the biographical collections of sayings compiled by his followers and descendants a generation or two after his death he is presented as a commanding and charismatic leader inspiring veneration by later Shinshū adherents.[3] In the research of social historians of the twentieth century he is depicted as a wily politician fraternizing with religious and secular powers alike and wielding his influence with ordinary believers to achieve his organizational ends.[4] These images suggest that Rennyo operated at several different levels in his endeavors. He was first of all a religious teacher holding Shinran's ideals to be the highest truth. Secondly, he was an awe-inspiring sectarian organizer seeking to make the Honganji the supreme authority of the Shinshū. Finally, he was a man of social and political sensibilities who attempted to win acceptance and recognition for his following in the broader historical context. All these concerns converged in Rennyo to make his words and deeds a curious combination of religious exhortation and social expediency. The ideal of belief and practice that he advocated ultimately emerged as the paradigm of Shin orthodoxy.[5]

RENNYO'S TIMES

Rennyo lived in a time when upheaval and turmoil, partly real and partly imagined, pervaded the popular consciousness. His most active period of proselytization occurred during the Ōnin War, which began in 1467 plunging Japan into the so-called Warring States (*Sengoku*) period (1467–1568). Warfare ravaged the capital and eventually debilitated the political and economic structure of the country, creating a century of social instability and excruciating change. Though this is occasionally regarded as the dark age of Japanese history, it actually held great potential for creative minds. The ordinary strictures and conventions of society were not as rigidly enforced, so there was greater latitude for innovation and experimentation. Hence, the economy expanded, the arts flourished, and new social and political systems arose.[6] In the area of religion there was also considerable potential. Buddhist preachers traveled the provinces offering their prescriptions for salvation and attracting believers into their fold. The schools of New Buddhism from the Kamakura period were the most successful in this enterprise, and Rennyo was perhaps the best.[7] But this does not mean that he achieved his goals without challenges, setbacks, or uncertainties. On the contrary, Rennyo experienced numerous hardships and on several occasions was forced to flee for his life. Moreover, the opportunities for proselytization and innovation which worked in his favor also benefited his religious rivals. Consequently, Rennyo had to come to terms with other forms of Buddhism and confront the claims of Shinshū competitors, many of whom he considered heretical, before he could succeed.[8]

The pervading ambience of the Warring States period was one of a world in chaos. In the wake of the Ōnin War the prevailing political and religious institutions declined, and whatever sense of stability or security there had been waned. The traditional authorities no longer held sway, but new ones had not yet clearly emerged. In this context Buddhism's age-old doctrine of impermanence rang especially true, and it became a common theme in Rennyo's message to his followers, as described in one of his pastoral letters:

> Upon reflection we can see that human existence is but an illusory delight, [passing away] like a flash of lightning or a dewdrop at dawn. Even if we are

ensconced in luxury and splendor and do just as we please, [such comforts] will last a mere fifty years, or one hundred at the most. Were the winds of impermanence to sweep down and call us at this instant, what sickness would it be that leads us to naught? At the moment of death not one thing, neither family nor fortune, to which we have clung in the past can accompany us. Thus, at the end of death's mountain road we come alone to the great river of the three benighted realms (sanzu). Because of this the only thing we should long for deeply is the life hereafter (goshō). And the thing we should rely on is Amida Tathāgata. And the thing we should know is that the establishment of faith will lead us to the Pure Land of bliss.[9]

Rennyo did not express these feelings out of sentimental abstraction. During his lifetime four wives and seven children preceded him to the grave.[10] His was an age of uncertainty, when the only thing that seemed sure to him was Amida and his promise of salvation. He therefore spoke with a sense of urgency.

Rennyo himself was deeply affected by the sufferings and insecurities of his world. From the time of his birth in 1415 he was confronted with tragedy and hardship. His mother was apparently a servant girl at the Honganji who conceived Rennyo out of wedlock when his father, Zonnyo, was only eighteen years old. Six years after his birth she was sent away, as Zonnyo was betrothed to someone befitting his standing. This separation grieved Rennyo, and numerous times throughout his life he sought to locate his mother, but to no avail.[11] Not only did he never see her again, but he also suffered the disdain of his stepmother, Nyoen. Rennyo's childhood and youth were further complicated by the relative poverty of the Honganji. The temple itself was modest in scale, with the Amida hall measuring only about eighteen feet (sangen) in length and the memorial hall to Shinran about thirty feet (goken).[12] In the worst of times Rennyo was reduced to one meal or less a day, he had no hot water to wash in, and he was forced to study by moonlight for lack of lamp oil. Even after he was grown and married there were periods of hardship. He is said to have washed out the soiled baby garments of his children by himself and to have sent out six of his oldest children for rearing in other situations.[13] All these events bespeak the financial difficulties that the Honganji underwent and the humbling experiences that Rennyo endured prior to his tenure as head priest.

Even Rennyo's ascent to the headship of the Honganji did not come without trial and tribulation. Rennyo seemed the natural choice to succeed Zonnyo as head priest, since he was the oldest son and had assisted his father in temple duties for years. These included making copies of religious texts for distribution to affiliated congregations and accompanying Zonnyo on evangelistic tours of the provinces.[14] But in 1457 when Zonnyo died, Nyoen maneuvered to have her own son Ōgen (1433–1503) named head priest though he was just twenty-four years old at the time, eighteen years Rennyo's junior. Rennyo managed to claim the office only because Zonnyo's younger brother Nyojō (1412–60), who was head priest of the powerful Zuisenji and Honseiji temples in the Hokuriku region, spoke up in his behalf.[15] Hence, Rennyo assumed the position under a cloud of controversy rather than as a unanimous choice. Once confirmed as head priest, however, he quickly proved himself to be an able leader.

Rennyo's first area of proselytization was the province of Ōmi to the east of Kyoto. This was a region where the Bukkōji and Kinshokuji branches were strong, but the Honganji had strategic allies in the towns of Kanegamori and Katada on the eastern and western shores of Lake Biwa. The Katada congregation was headed by Hōjū (d. 1479), one of Rennyo's staunchest supporters in the region. These communities were involved in shipping, crafts, and trade, and represented a different social stratum from the peasant converts that Rennyo would attract later. Their wealth helped shield the Honganji against attacks and suppression during his early ministry.[16] Rennyo established ties with these groups through the traditional means of bestowing religious texts and *nembutsu* inscriptions on them, as well as by preaching appearances before their congregations. Receiving scriptures or objects of worship was, of course, tantamount to affiliating with the Honganji branch. In addition to the standard scriptures distributed by the Honganji, Rennyo composed a brief commentary on Shinran's *Shōshinge* ("Verses on True Faith"), a long hymn contained in his *Kyōgyōshinshō* ("Teaching, Practice, Faith, and Enlightenment").[17] This work foreshadowed Rennyo's adoption of the hymn as a devotional text. In 1460 a copy of it was given to Dōsai (1399–1488), head of the Kanegamori congregation, who originally requested the commentary. The congregation was also the recipient of Rennyo's first pastoral letter, dated 1461.[18] At this stage, however, pastoral letters were not a major component in Rennyo's ministry. Only seven of them were written over the ten-year period prior to his departure for the Hokuriku region in 1471.[19] Instead, *nembutsu* inscriptions were the most common religious objects distributed by Rennyo. Ten of them presented to various congregations in Ōmi province during the years 1459 to 1464 survive today.[20] Also, temples in Mikawa province, which was traditionally the Senjuji branch's sphere of influence, began accepting Rennyo's inscriptions, thereby indicating inroads among adherents in that area as well.[21] The version of the *nembutsu* used in these inscriptions was the ten-character formula popularized by Kakunyo: *Kimyō Jin Jippō Mugekō Nyorai*, meaning "I take refuge in the Tathāgata of Unobstructed Light Suffusing the Ten Directions." Hence, Rennyo's followers in Ōmi and surrounding provinces were dubbed the Mugekōshu, or Unobstructed Light Adherents, especially by the monks of Mt. Hiei.

Rennyo's success in the provinces near Kyoto provoked his opponents on Mt. Hiei to move against him. At the beginning of 1465 warrior priests swept down on the Honganji and destroyed the temple complex. A dozen or so Shinshū adherents had come from Ōmi province to stand guard, but they were no match for the assailants.[22] The reasons given for the assault were the often repeated charges leveled against the Pure Land movement: assembling bands, destroying scriptures and Buddhist images, denigrating the Shinto *kami*, indulging in outrageous behavior, committing wrongdoings, and so forth.[23] But the more immediate concern of Mt. Hiei may have been the economic ramifications of Shinshū expansion. Mt. Hiei claimed proprietorship over numerous estates and monopolies in Ōmi province, and was no doubt threatened by the Honganji's burgeoning organization in its territory. Peace with the militant monks was finally bought after the congregations at Katada and in Mikawa province raised an "offering" to present to the attackers and after the Honganji agreed to become a branch temple (*matsuji*) of Mt. Hiei and to pay the requisite temple dues each year.[24]

The 1465 attack is sometimes seen as the Honganji's darkest hour. It confirmed in the minds of Shinshū adherents the cruelty and impermanence of the times. During the attack Rennyo and the revered image of Shinran from the Honganji's memorial hall narrowly escaped destruction. For the next four years Rennyo carried it with him as he moved from place to place, primarily in the province of Ōmi. Eventually the image was placed in the care of the Miidera temple, Mt. Hiei's archrival located just to its east in the town of Ōtsu. A chapel was built for it called the Chikamatsu Bōsha, and it remained at Ōtsu attracting Shinshū pilgrims for over ten years, until 1480 when it was moved to a new Honganji in the Kyoto suburb of Yamashina.[25] Rennyo, for his part, was forced to live a peripatetic life until the construction of the Yamashina Honganji. During his travels he took shelter where he could with affiliated congregations. Still, he was not insulated from Mt. Hiei's wrath because the warrior monks made repeated forays into Ōmi province striking at the so-called Mugekōshu heretics.[26] This was the period when the Ashikaga military government, based in Kyoto, became embroiled in the Ōnin War, thereby reducing the possibility that civil authorities would temper Mt. Hiei's impetuosity. This series of events was a source of great anxiety to Rennyo, for just as the Honganji was coming to be recognized as the seat of Shinran's tradition the resentment of Mt. Hiei had reduced it to ashes.

Despite the instability of the times, or perhaps because of it, Rennyo continued to win converts and allies, not only in Ōmi province but also in Mikawa and in areas south of Kyoto such as Settsu province and Yoshino.[27] In 1469 he even made a second visit to the Kantō region in eastern Japan, possibly to remove himself from hostilities in the vicinity of the capital. In contrast to his earlier visit there with his father, Rennyo found many Shinshū congregations hospitable and open to his teachings, even though the Kantō was dominated by his rival, the Senjuji branch of the Shinshū.[28] His welcome there suggests that Rennyo was well on his way to becoming a religious personage of national stature. Nonetheless, he did not feel secure with his base of support in the Kyoto area because of the constant threat of attack. Once, when asked to rebuild the Honganji at Katada in Ōmi province, Rennyo pointed in the direction of Mt. Hiei and said, "That is too close."[29] Therefore, in 1471 Rennyo decided to withdraw from the region and to reestablish himself far from Mt. Hiei's influence. This move was the most consequential decision of Rennyo's career, for the experience brought his own religious thinking to maturity and catapulted him into the ranks of Japan's foremost religious figures.

THE HOKURIKU CAMPAIGN

The site Rennyo chose for his new center of activity was the hamlet of Yoshizaki in Echizen province on the Hokuriku seaboard. When Rennyo first moved there Yoshizaki was a desolate spot infested with wild animals, but it was scenically pleasing and conveniently located on the coastal road along the Japan Sea.[30] By 1473 the place was a thriving religious center. Pilgrims by the thousands flocked to hear Rennyo from nearby Kaga, Etchū, Noto, and Echigo provinces, as well as from the far-flung provinces of Shinano, Dewa, and Mutsu. One to two hundred buildings, mostly *taya* or travelers' lodges operated by Shinshū priests, lined the route.[31] In short, a virtual city sprang up where only wilderness existed before. What drew them to Yoshizaki was Rennyo himself.

The excitement that Rennyo inspired is well illustrated by an experience he had at the Zuisenji temple in 1473. Rennyo had planned to make his third trip to the Kantō region, but, when he stopped at the Zuisenji in Etchū province on the way, such massive crowds assembled that five to ten people were crushed to death each day, eventually forcing Rennyo to return to Yoshizaki.[32] It is difficult to say what prompted this outpouring of sentiment. It may have been simply the arrival of an eminent priest from the city proselytizing in this remote and backward area. Or, it may have been Rennyo's skill and ingenuity in communicating religious ideas to ordinary people. Or, it may have been that Rennyo's ministry coincided with the rise of autonomous villages in the Hokuriku, which provided a social unit for spreading his teachings. Whatever the factors were, Rennyo's presence at Yoshizaki created a mysterious and powerful chemistry that sparked an unprecedented religious awakening in the region. This period proved to be the pivotal point in Rennyo's life. When he finally returned to the Kyoto area in 1475 he commanded such widespread support in the provinces that Mt. Hiei could never pose a threat to the Honganji again.

Rennyo's success in the Hokuriku region came initially from his preaching tours. The Honganji had a network of congregations there dating back to the founding of the Zuisenji temple in 1390 by Rennyo's great-grandfather Shakunyo. In addition, the Sanmonto branch maintained a long-standing influence in the area, and Shin'e, Rennyo's counterpart in the Senjuji branch, proselytized in Echizen, Echigo, and other provinces only a decade earlier.[33] All these circumstances created a surplus of Shinshū sympathy on which Rennyo could draw.

Once his reputation was established, Rennyo began to rely more and more on pastoral letters to communicate with followers. These constitute the bulk of his literary corpus, and the majority of them were written after his move to the Hokuriku region. The pastoral letters proved to be an extremely effective means of sustaining contact with congregations, particularly after Rennyo had achieved such fame that it was difficult for him to make personal visits. The letters were framed in clear, comprehensible language so that the most lowly believer could grasp their meaning. Moreover, they were composed to be read aloud at congregational meetings so that even illiterate followers could receive Rennyo's message. As a proselytization tool, they proved to be far more successful than distributing copies of scriptures because, as Rennyo expressed it, "There are variant ways of reading scriptures and their meaning does not always come across, but there is certainly no variant way of reading my letters."[34] In short, their meaning was straightforward and unambiguous. Rennyo was particularly adept at mixing anecdote, down-to-earth imagery, religious exhortation, and pastoral concern in his letters. They functioned as the Shinshū's most important instrument for imparting Shinran's ideas to peasant believers.

Another vital aspect of Rennyo's ministry was his own humility and openness. Unlike his predecessors, who put on airs by sitting on raised platforms, Rennyo seated himself on the same level with lowborn followers.[35] He was constantly solicitous of their needs and served them sake, warmed in winter and chilled in summer, when they came to visit.[36] These gestures made Rennyo quite effective as a proselytizer during his years in the Hokuriku region.

Rennyo, like his predecessors in the Shinshū, was ever mindful of questions of heresy. His interest in the matter had two facets. One was to defend the Shinshū against accusations of heresy leveled primarily by critics at Mt. Hiei. The other and more consuming concern was to correct mistaken beliefs circulating among adherents. By confronting these two he sought to vindicate the Shinshū's position outwardly and rectify its teachings within. Rennyo was always conscious of the Shinshū's image in the public eye, and he was cautious about how and to whom its tenets were presented. But his reticence did not arise out of any doubts over Shin teachings. On the contrary, Rennyo was so convinced of the supremacy of Shinran's ideas that when he used the term "Buddhist teachings" (*Buppō*) in his letters it was not an open-ended reference to Buddhist concepts in general but rather a straightforward reference to Shin beliefs.[37] For Rennyo, true Buddhism was none other than Shinran's Buddhism.

By Rennyo's time the Shinshū had become skilled at defending itself against charges of heresy. Circumspection and tact in defense of the school generally characterized Rennyo's writings. He never launched into diatribes against his antagonists on Mt. Hiei, nor did he accuse them of falsehood or misconduct. Although he tacitly urged believers to forsake the traditional path of salvation, exhorting them to repudiate indiscriminate practices (*zōgyō*) and to rely on Amida's vow totally, Rennyo did not openly campaign against the established schools of Buddhism.[38] This is not true, however, of his response to rival forms of Pure Land Buddhism. In the minds of ordinary believers, the differences between the Shinshū and other Pure Land groups were fairly opaque. Therefore, Rennyo made a point of contrasting Shinshū concepts to other Pure Land ideas, and he specifically singled out various Pure Land schools for comparison.[39]

Rennyo spoke out both to convey Shinran's ideas accurately and to establish a distinct identity for the Shinshū. When he first traveled to the Hokuriku area in 1471 he intended to remain no longer than a year, but he found the religious views of Shinshū adherents there so mixed that he ended up staying more than four years trying to set them straight.[40] The misconceptions that he confronted derived from diverse sources. Some were absorbed from the Jishū, the Ikkōshū, and various branches of the Jōdoshū school. Others bore the influence of the traditional schools of Buddhism or even the Zen school. Still others were characteristic of rival branches of the Shinshū. And a few were straightforward misinterpretations of Shinran's ideas without identifiable origins.[41] Rennyo spent considerable time and energy in the Hokuriku challenging multifarious beliefs and practices, and he perceived his ministry there to be as much a campaign against heresy as a mission to convert new adherents.

Though Rennyo's foremost concern during his Hokuriku sojourn was to spread Shinran's teachings, he was not oblivious to the social and political events occurring around him. On the contrary, he perceived the formation of autonomous villages in the region as a boon to religious recruitment, if only they could be penetrated. Rennyo's strategy was to convert village leaders first and through them win over the remaining village members, a principle he often recited to his followers:

> There are three people whom we want to convert to the teachings. They are the priest (*bōzu*), the elder (*toshiyori*), and the headman (*otona*). If these three will lay the basis for Buddhism in their respective places, then all the people below them will conform to the teachings and Buddhism will flourish.[42]

In this passage the priest refers to the local clergy, who might belong to another school of Buddhism, the elder to the head of each family in the village, and the headman to the most powerful cultivator of the community. All three were typically upper-class peasants (*myōshu*) who dominated village affairs. Rennyo considered them crucial to the spread of the Shinshū, and he thereby linked the success of the Shinshū to the emerging village organization.

During Rennyo's years in the Hokuriku the *kō* or local congregation became the grass-roots unit of the Honganji's religious organization. This was the functional equivalent of the *dōjō* in earlier times. Once or twice a month Shinshū believers would meet as a congregation for religious discussion, exhortation, and worship. Often village leaders or priests would organize congregations by making their own home available as a *dōjō*, or meeting place. Congregations did not necessarily conform to village geography. One congregation might encompass a few villages, or one village might contain several congregations. A small congregation would consist of ten to twenty adherents, whereas a large one could include several thousand. Usually a congregation was affiliated with the Honganji through several layers of local and branch temples. An important temple might have a number of local temples under it, and each of them would have several congregations. Gifts and offerings (*kokorozashi*) made by village congregations passed up through this temple chain and were the Honganji's most important source of income.[43] Over and above its purely religious activities, the congregation in time took on social and political functions as well, becoming a center of recreation and political discussion. During Rennyo's residency in the region the number of congregations in the Shinshū began to increase dramatically.[44]

Rennyo's residence in the Hokuriku and his attraction of great crowds inevitably led to complications. The first was that his ministry alarmed and threatened the traditional temples and shrines of the region. In his early ministry Rennyo did not encourage derision of other Buddhas and *kami*, but neither did he advocate worship of them.[45] His followers, however, tended toward benign neglect at best and open disparagement at worst of the traditional religious institutions and their deities. The second problem that beset Rennyo's community stemmed from the volatile political events of the period as the Ōnin War spilled over into the Hokuriku area. The neighboring province of Kaga was engulfed in a power struggle between Togashi Masachika and Togashi Kōchiyo, brothers competing for the title of provincial governor (*shugo*). Rennyo and his movement commanded widespread allegiance in the region, and hence there was pressure on him to swing his support to one side or the other. At first Rennyo sought to remain aloof from these problems. He admonished his followers not to belittle the *kami* and the Buddhas, and for a while he attempted to keep believers from congregating at Yoshizaki lest the crowds become provocative.[46] Eventually he was forced to take more decisive action when samurai began to appear on the scene, some sympathetic to his movement and others hostile.[47]

The bulk of Rennyo's following in the Hokuriku region were peasants, but gradually low-level samurai also attached themselves to the movement. Although samurai had different political concerns from village peasants, Pure Land beliefs made it possible for them to join together with peasants to form the *Ikkō ikki* or Shinshū leagues. The ideological basis of these leagues, from a religious point of view, was that all believers possess equal standing in the eyes of Amida.[48] No distinction is made between young and old, intelligent and ignorant, rich and poor, good and evil, male and female, and so forth.[49] Not even hunters and fishermen, who support themselves by the taking of life, are excluded from the gates of Pure Land.[50] Hence, samurai and peasants alike could be included among those destined for Pure Land. Individuals who embraced the teachings were therefore united in a common religious goal, even though their worldly responsibilities and privileges separated them. In this way Pure Land beliefs helped vitiate distinctions of status and class, and thereby facilitated an alliance between low-level samurai and village peasants. These were the religious underpinnings for the Shinshū leagues that eventually sided with Togashi Masachika in 1473 in his campaign for the Kaga governorship.

The alliance between Masachika and his Shinshū supporters was short-lived. In 1488 they fell into conflict with him, surrounded his castle, and cut him off from outside reinforcements. In defeat Masachika took his own life.[51] From that time the provincial governorship in Kaga was, for all intents and purposes, dead. For the next ninety-three years administrative power rested in the hands of a political coalition of Shinshū adherents. The machinations and mobilizations of the Shinshū leagues confirmed the worst suspicions of the declining political and religious establishment. But to the extent that the Honganji had clout with these leagues, its own stock rose in political and religious circles, and the Shinshū itself came to be viewed as a formidable Buddhist power.

Rennyo's attitude toward the military ventures of his followers was always circumspect. He never encouraged them in their exploits; on the contrary, he did his best to restrain their excesses. But it would be wrong to portray him as a champion of the reigning establishment. Admittedly, Rennyo was on good terms with the military government in Kyoto, and he was beholden to various political and religious authorities for facilitating his stay in the Hokuriku region.[52] Nonetheless, he could not bring himself to side with them against Shinshū adherents. During Masachika's defeat in 1488, for example, the military government's *shōgun*, Ashikaga Yoshihisa (1465–89), ordered Rennyo to expel the Shinshū participants of Kaga province from his religious organization. Rennyo was pained to do so and finally assuaged the *shōgun*'s anger by sending reprimands to the Hokuriku temples that had mobilized members for combat, rebuking and admonishing them against further violence.[53] This was the tack that Rennyo took throughout his career. He maintained good relations where he could with the powers at hand, and he urged Shinshū believers to be upright in conduct, but he never abandoned his following, even when they rose up and commandeered entire provinces.

The precipitous events that began during Rennyo's Yoshizaki years forced him to institute *okite*, or rules of conduct, to govern his movement. These were one of the innovations resulting from Rennyo's Hokuriku experience. The rules present guidelines for behavior which all Shinshū adherents were expected to follow. To a certain extent they derived from the congregational rules used in Shinshū *dōjō* two centuries prior to Rennyo's time. Many of the items in Rennyo's rules were virtually the same as those in congregational rules, and both sets were enforced identically through the threat of expulsion from the fellowship of believers. The important difference was that Rennyo's were promulgated throughout the school, whereas congregational rules were arrived at by common consensus in individual *dōjō*. This was the first time that rules of this type were established on such a wide scale in the Shinshū. Rennyo's original list of rules was drawn up in the Hokuriku during the eleventh month of 1473:

Items To Be Prohibited Among Shinshū Adherents

1. Do not denigrate the various *kami* or the Buddhas and Bodhisattvas.
2. Never slander the various teachings or the various schools.
3. Do not attack other schools by comparing them to the practices of our own school.
4. Though taboos (*monoimi*) are not something adhered to by Buddhists, observe them scrupulously before public officials and [members of] other schools.
5. Do not proclaim the Buddhist teachings while arbitrarily adding alongside them words that have not been handed down in our school.

6. As *nembutsu* adherents, do not denigrate the provincial governor (*shugo*) or the constables (*jitō*).

7. In a state of ignorance, do not display your own ideas to other schools or proclaim the teachings of your own school without any sense of discretion.

8. If you yourself are not yet established in faith (*anjin ketsujō*), do not proclaim the teachings of faith (*shinjin*) using words you have heard from other people.

9. Do not eat fish or fowl when you meet for *nembutsu* services.

10. On the day that you assemble for *nembutsu* services, do not drink liquor and lose your senses.

11. Among *nembutsu* adherents, indulgence in gambling is prohibited.

Concerning these eleven items, you should firmly expel from your assembly any people who turn their back on these regulations. In witness to the aforesaid regulations.[54]

These rules were aimed at checking the unruly behavior of Shinshū adherents in the Hokuriku region during the 1470s. From this time, however, rules of conduct emerged as an important tool for shaping the Shinshū into a socially acceptable religious movement. Although the content of the rules changed from time to time, the idea that rules are incumbent on all believers became an accepted principle in the Shinshū from Rennyo's time.[55]

The formulation of rules of conduct marked a turning point in Rennyo's religious thinking whereby he sought to adapt the Shinshū to existing social norms. This shift is best reflected in Rennyo's attitude toward the Shinto *kami*. From about this time Rennyo took a more conciliatory attitude toward the *kami*. In his explanation of the first rule, which concerns the *kami*, he allotted to them a far more esteemed position in the Pure Land teachings than he ever had before:

First of all, in regard to the illustrious *kami* (*shinmei*), in Buddhism [the Buddha] laments that sentient beings without faith will fall hopelessly into the hells, and so in order to come to their aid in some way he temporarily assumes the form of the illustrious *kami*. He thereby establishes a tenuous bond with them, and relying on that he finally guides them to the Buddhist teachings. [The Buddha] takes on the appearance of a *kami* as an expedient means (*hōben*) for this purpose. Consequently, if among sentient beings today there are those who rely on Amida, who become established in faith, who say the *nembutsu*, and who assume the state whereby they will be born in Pure Land, then all the illustrious *kami* consider this to have been their primary intent, and so they rejoice and guard over the *nembutsu* adherent. Because of that, even if a person does not worship the *kami* separately, still while relying on the one Buddha Amida, that person has faith in them all without relying on them individually because the *kami* are encompassed in [the Buddha].[56]

With this statement Rennyo construed the *kami* to be extensions of Amida Buddha. Without disavowing his earlier stance that there is no need for Pure Land adherents to worship them, he nonetheless included the *kami* in Amida's grand scheme of salvation in a way that Shinran never did. There was ample precedent for this interpretation in Kakunyo's and Zonkaku's writings. They too drew from Japan's mainstream tradition of Shinto-Buddhist syncretism—specifically, the *honji suijaku* doctrine that *kami* are manifestations of the Buddhas working in this world to lead sentient beings to the Buddhist teachings. The net effect of this interpretation was to encourage a more tolerant attitude in Shinshū believers toward the *kami*. This in the end integrated the Shinshū better into the prevailing beliefs and customs of society.

The rules of conduct that Rennyo framed clearly performed a social function in the Shinshū, but over and above that they hint at a paradigm for religious life that Rennyo was in the process of formulating. On one level Rennyo regarded the rules simply as pragmatic measures to ensure the stability of his religious movement, but on another level he instituted them as acts of faith. Certainly they are presented in that light in his pastoral letter for the Hōonkō service of 1475, in which he referred to them as the "honored rules (*on'okite*) laid down by our master and founder," as if Shinran himself had established them.[57] Among the various items listed in the rules, some undoubtedly fall into the category of socially expedient measures, such as the observance of taboos. Rennyo willingly admitted that taboos have no basis in Buddhist doctrine, and he made no attempt to rationalize their existence as he did the Shinto *kami*. Nonetheless, he called upon his followers to observe taboos out of prudence and in deference to other religious groups.[58] On this point Rennyo even went beyond Zonkaku, who refused to endorse such practices.[59] Additional items in the rules, by contrast, seem to bear more directly on the nature and practice of faith. The admonition against proclaiming faith without having experienced it was directed against false teachers, and it encouraged believers to reflect on their own religious state. Also, the warning against publicizing one's personal religious views without discretion or forethought struck against presumptuous behavior and airs of superiority, which Rennyo considered inappropriate to faith. In short, there are elements in the rules which point to a religious ideal that he attempted to foster in his followers from this period on.

Much of Rennyo's ministry was aimed at curtailing behavior which he considered to be at variance with faith. In many of his endeavors he saw himself as waging a campaign against heresy. Beginning with his years in the Hokuriku, Rennyo gradually evolved a paradigm for the religious life of Shinshū adherents. The impetus for formulating that paradigm was the insolent attitude that certain Pure Land believers in the region exhibited. They would brag to civil authorities of their reverence for the Buddhist teachings and their attainment of faith, and thereby aggrandized themselves over their social superiors.[60] Such actions bear a striking similarity to flaunting Amida's vow (*hongan bokori*), common in Shinran's day. Rennyo denounced this type of arrogance and admonished his followers to be respectful not only of the Buddhist teachings (*Buppō*) but also of civil law (*ōbō*). The precise formula he gave for this was: "Outwardly dedicate yourself fully to the civil laws, but in your heart make the Buddhist teachings primary."[61] Rennyo went a step beyond this proposition when he instructed believers not to display their faith openly but to hide it in their hearts:

> To uphold correctly the established rules of our tradition means to act in such a way toward other schools and toward society that the contents of our school are not public for the eyes of others to see. In recent days, however, some individuals among the *nembutsu* adherents of our tradition have intentionally revealed the contents of our tradition for the eyes of others to see, and they think that by doing so it is for the fame and honor of our school and that other schools in particular will be worn down. This is a senseless notion.[62]

Rennyo was clearly sensitive to the opinions of others, and he was aware of how radical Shinran's teachings appeared to other people in society.[63] For that reason he advised discretion and prudence, not merely because it would shelter the school from outside criticism but also because humility is the mark of a person of faith. Ultimately the ideal that Rennyo advanced was for believers to present themselves simply as followers of the *nembutsu* rather than as members of this or that school.[64] He therefore developed the paradigm of the person who lives an intense religious life inwardly but who is unobtrusive and self-effacing outwardly. Rennyo considered this to be the way faith manifests itself in the believer and, though variations might occur based on the karmic differences of individuals, he promoted this paradigm of faith as the standard for the Shinshū.

RENNYO'S RELIGIOUS MESSAGE

Rennyo's paradigm of the ideal Shinshū adherent was not the only innovation of his Hokuriku ministry. Most of the elements in his doctrinal system also took shape during this period. Rennyo made his mark as a proselytizer first and foremost, but he was also a creative religious thinker in his own right. His creativity lay not so much in originating doctrine, as Shinran's did, but rather in synthesizing and popularizing it. He had a gift for translating complex ideas into lucid and cogent tenets and couching them in language that engaged the individual. Rennyo used popular terminology to explain Shin ideas, and thereby wedded Shin teachings to the idiom of his day. His greatest accomplishment was to render Shinran's doctrinal abstractions into simple religious formulas accessible to the humblest believer and to explain them in the context of daily devotional practices.

If there is one theme that resounds throughout Rennyo's writings, it is that faith is the true cause of birth in Pure Land (*shinjin shōin*) and that reciting the *nembutsu* is an expression of gratitude to Amida (*shōmyō hōon*). This succinct formulation of Shin thought has emerged as the most widely invoked doctrinal principle of the school. It had roots in Shinran's teachings and was emphasized in Kakunyo's also, but it was never stated as persistently and unambiguously as in Rennyo's writings.[65] Shinran inherited the *nembutsu* from Hōnen, but invested it with a slightly different meaning: that the efficacy of the *nembutsu* derives from faith. Thus, rote chanting of the *nembutsu* could not be the crucial act assuring salvation. Beginning with Kakunyo and culminating with Rennyo, faith was accentuated even more as the essential element for birth in Pure Land and as the true significance of Shinran's *nembutsu*. Rennyo made this point repeatedly in his letters, as exemplified by the following passage:

> If we have deep faith in the principal vow of the Tathāgata Amida, if we rely with single and undivided heart on the compassionate vow of the one Buddha Amida, and if our faith is true at the very moment that we think of him to please save us, then we will definitely be received into the salvation of the Tathāgata. Over and above this, what should we take to be the meaning of reciting the *nembutsu*? It is a response coming from one's indebtedness [to the Buddha] (*goon hōsha*), thanking him that one is saved through birth in Pure Land by the power of faith in the present. As long as we have life in us, we should say the *nembutsu* thinking of it as a response of thankfulness. It should be said by the person of faith (*shinjin*) who is established in the faith (*anjin*) of our tradition.[66]

Here faith is presented as the crux of the religious experience, without which *nembutsu* chanting would lose its meaning. Practice of the *nembutsu* is not abandoned, however, as it would be according to the single *nembutsu* doctrine. Rather, it is construed to be an outward expression of thanks arising naturally from the inward transformation of faith. Hence, the *nembutsu* arises out of faith and represents an extension of faith, but it can never be potent apart from faith. When Shinran idealized the *nembutsu*, he did so strictly in this vein.

In Rennyo's descriptions of faith there frequently appears terminology that is slightly different from Shinran's. Specifically, Rennyo used the word *anjin*, seldom seen in Shinran's writings, as often as the word *shinjin* to refer to faith. Rennyo inherited this term from Kakunyo, and his letters even quote Kakunyo's *Gaijashō* ("Notes Rectifying Heresy"), which singles out *anjin* as the crucial element resulting in birth in Pure Land.[67] Semantically, Rennyo equated *anjin* with *shinjin*, though in nuance and actual usage he seemed to recognize subtle differences between them.[68] For one thing, he frequently used the expression *tōryū no anjin* ("the faith of our tradition") to refer to the whole range of attitudes and experiences that arise in the life of the believer.[69] Rennyo also alluded to another difference of nuance when he explicated the religious significance of the word *anjin*:

> The two characters in *anjin* may be read "a mind at peace" (*yasuki kokoro*). This is its meaning. By faith (*shinjin*) alone, wherein we rely on the Tathāgata single-mindedly and with oneness of heart even though we perform no actions whatsoever, we will be born in the Pure Land of bliss. This faith (*anjin*)—how easy it is to comprehend! Pure Land—how easy it is to go there![70]

Anjin, meaning literally "a mind at peace," conveys better the sense of tranquility and assurance that emerges from faith than does *shinjin*, meaning simply "a mind of faith." Rennyo presented this richer imagery as a part of his paradigm of the Shinshū adherent. The connotations of peace and serenity imputed into the state of faith no doubt appealed to ordinary believers and helped them face the hardships and insecurities that buffeted their lives.

The prevailing doctrinal concern in most of Rennyo's letters is the inward experience of faith, but the outward practice of the *nembutsu* is also discussed at length. Not only did Rennyo recognize the *nembutsu* to be the foremost expression of gratitude to the Buddha, but he also considered it a sacred symbol embodying the meaning of salvation for the believer. According to Rennyo, the *nembutsu* is none other than the confirmation (*shishō*) that sentient beings are saved by Amida.[71] To arrive at this interpretation Rennyo borrowed from the doctrinal explanations found in the *Anjin ketsujōshō* ("Notes on the Firm [Abode] of Faith"). Though it might seem inconsistent that Rennyo campaigned against rival Pure Land teachings on the one hand and embraced this work on the other, there were clear-cut antecedents for drawing from the *Anjin ketsujōshō* in Kakunyo's and Zonkaku's writings. Rennyo is said to have read the work devotedly for over forty years and and to have worn out seven copies of it.[72] From it he derived the concept of *kihō ittai*: that the believer of limited capacity (*ki*) and the Buddha of absolute truth (*hō*) are united as one substance (*ittai*). Using this concept he explained the significance of the *nembutsu*:

> What it means for faith to be established (*shinjin ketsujō*) is for one to understand completely the significance of the six characters *Namu Amida Butsu*. The two characters *Namu* stand for sentient beings of limited capacity (*ki*) who have faith in Amida Buddha, and the four characters *Amida Butsu* signify that Amida Tathāgata of absolute truth (*hō*) saves sentient beings. Hence, the meaning is that in *Namu Amida Butsu* those of limited capacity and that of absolute truth are [united] as one substance (*kihō ittai*). Therefore, [the *nembutsu*] indicates that the three types of action (*sangō*) on the part of sentient beings and the three types of action on the part of Amida become one substance . . . .[73]

This explanation of the *nembutsu* incorporates elements of Seizan doctrine, those derived from the *Anjin ketsujōshō*.[74] The point Rennyo sought to make using Seizan concepts was that the *nembutsu* is the palpable sign of Amida's assurance of salvation. It symbolizes the unification of the saver and the saved, and it thus comprises both the reason for faith and the result of faith. Though Shinran did not propound the *kihō ittai* doctrine per se, Rennyo's adoption of it was not incongruous with Shinran's reverence of the *nembutsu* as the sacred creation of Amida by which his power is extended to sentient beings.[75] It is therefore no accident that the *nembutsu*, of all the possible ways of showing thanks, is the foremost expression of gratitude to the Buddha. The reason is that the *nembutsu* embodies both the means and the rationale for showing gratitude—because in it the believer is united with the Buddha.

One more theme which Rennyo used extensively in his teachings is that the believer should "rely on the Buddha to please save me" (*tasuke tamae to tanomu*). Rennyo was the first Shinshū thinker to utilize this concept. In his writings he equated it with the experience of faith itself. In some ways Rennyo considered this expression more revealing of what faith is than the words traditionally used for faith:

> When we speak of *shinjin* or *anjin*, uneducated people do not understand. In speaking of *shinjin* and *anjin*, they take them to be different things. All they need to know is that ordinary beings can achieve Buddhahood and that they should rely on Amida to please save them in their next life (*goshō tasuke tamae to Mida o tanome*). No matter how uneducated sentient beings may be, if they hear this they will attain faith. In our tradition there is no other teaching besides this.[76]

Rennyo's adoption of this idea was aimed at helping ordinary individuals understand the nature and content of faith. Many scholars attribute this expression to the Jōdoshū school, specifically to the Chinzei branch, since the phrase *tasuke tamae*, "please save me," is found in Hōnen's, Ryōchū's, and Shōgei's works.[77] More likely, the obscure Ikkōshū group was the major proponent and popularizer of this idea, since the letters of Raichia, the second patriarch of the Ikkōshū, use the expression repeatedly.[78] Whatever its origins, the practice of calling upon the Buddha to "please save me" was widespread among people, especially in times of distress.[79]

Early on, Rennyo objected to the use of this expression because its pleading tone seems to resonate with self-effort (*jiriki*), which is incompatible with Shinran's fundamental ideas. He even admonished followers against using the plea in his first pastoral letter saying, "Though you may chant the *nembutsu*, do not think, 'Buddha, please save me!'"[80] Nonetheless, Rennyo eventually recognized the value of this phrase as a proselytization device, and he managed to read a Shinshū meaning into it, just as he did with the Seizan doctrine of *kihō ittai*. Rennyo infused the expression with the Shinshū idea of faith, as exemplified in the following passage:

> When people understand clearly what our tradition teaches, they realize that they will be born in the Pure Land of bliss. These people will comprehend, first of all, faith which comes from [Amida's] power (*tariki no shinjin*). What is the essence of this faith that comes from [Amida's] power? It is the awareness that ordinary beings of misery such as ourselves can easily go to Pure Land. And what form does this faith coming from [Amida's] power take? Without any ado whatsoever, we simply rely (*tanomitatematsurite*) on Amida Tathāgata intently, single-mindedly, and with oneness of heart and we think "Please save me!" (*tasuke tamae*). From that very moment Amida Tathāgata unfailingly sends forth his light to embrace us, and we are enveloped in that light as long as we reside here in Saṃsāra. This is the state wherein our birth in Pure Land is assured.[81]

In this way Rennyo grafted the phrase "please save me" onto the realization of faith. His reinterpretation of the plea hinges on linking it to the experience of relying (*tanomu*) on the Buddha. It implies faith only if it arises out of reliance on Amida rather than from one's preoccupation with the act of pleading itself.

Shinshū scholars have expended great energy over the centuries trying to show a qualitative difference between Rennyo's use of this expression and the Chinzei branch's use.[82] The Chinzei considered the thought "please save me" to be the constant mental act by which one attains birth in Pure Land, just as the *nembutsu* is the constant verbal act.[83] Rennyo, by contrast, tried to purge all traces of personal effort from the idea and to associate it instead with relying on the Buddha. Only then does it reflect the Shinshū's concept that faith emerges out of Amida's power rather than from the believer's effort. To the extent that Rennyo succeeded in doing this, he introduced the Shinshū's message of faith to believers who had already internalized the plea "please save me."

All the elements that Rennyo stressed in his letters combined to make a comprehensive system of belief geared to the needs of the common people and compatible with their capacity for religious practice. Rennyo made faith the centerpiece of this system. The other religious components that he incorporated into it were to revolve around faith or to radiate from it. For example, within the experience of faith there arises a mind at peace and a reliance on the Buddha to "please save me." As a result, the believer is inspired to respond with gratitude out of indebtedness to the Buddha (*goon hōsha*). The form that this gratitude takes is the invocation of the *nembutsu*, which is no ordinary means of expressing thanks. It is none other than the creation of the Buddha bestowed on the believer and thus embodies the very reason for gratitude. In this invocation the need of the believer, symbolized by *Namu*, and the power of the Buddha, signified by *Amida Butsu*, are united as one. In this way the concepts and images adopted by Rennyo came together to form a multifaceted religious experience pivoting around faith. Rennyo considered the realization of faith to be the crowning event in a person's life, and he sought to trigger it in other people through the exhortations in his letters. In very sympathetic pastoral tones he challenged individuals to examine their present religious condition, and he thereby hoped that through self-reflection faith would arise in them.

THE NEW HONGANJI

Rennyo departed the Hokuriku region during the eighth month of 1475, after the political situation there became volatile.[84] His four years in the region marked the turning point of his career. During that period his religious thinking reached maturity, so that by the time he returned to Kyoto all the doctrinal elements in his teachings were firmly in place. The intellectual richness of this stage in Rennyo's life is reflected in the fact that, of the 221 pastoral letters known to have been written between 1461 and 1498, at least 76 were composed during this short four-year period, many of them containing the most substantive elements of his teachings.[85] Rennyo's proselytization of the Hokuriku provinces brought him fame and a huge following. He came to be recognized as one of the leading religious figures of his day, and he thereby commanded the deference of many in Kyoto who had ignored or opposed him earlier. After his return Rennyo did not rest on his laurels. He proceeded with the work of proselytization primarily in the provinces around the capital, utilizing both pastoral letters and *nembutsu* inscriptions. While amassing an ever larger following, Rennyo also laid plans for the construction of a new Honganji and for the consolidation of believers under its authority. The net effect of Rennyo's efforts was to provide the basis for a religious organization that would eclipse Japan's old schools of Buddhism. Hence, the new Honganji was more than a temple edifice. It was a new religious order replete with defined rituals, orthodox doctrine, and sectarian organization. It was the Shinshū come of age.

Upon Rennyo's return from the Hokuriku he based himself temporarily at Deguchi near present-day Osaka. From there he propagated his teachings in the provinces south of Kyoto while remaining in communication through letters with followers in Ōmi, Mikawa, and the Hokuriku provinces. His earlier ministry had drawn many converts from the Sanmonto and Senjuji branches of the Shinshū, as well as from the Jishū, the Ikkōshū, and other schools of Buddhism. His efforts at this point attracted followers more from the Bukkōji and Kinshokuji branches, which traditionally enjoyed influence in the provinces near Kyoto.[86] In addressing these groups Rennyo did not hesitate to criticize unruly conduct that would antagonize the authorities, such as disregarding the law, denigrating the *kami* and the Buddhas, disobeying constables (*jitō*) and provincial governors (*shugo*), and withholding yearly tax remittances (*nengu*).[87] He also attacked beliefs and practices that he considered at odds with the Shinshū tradition. For instance, he denounced congregational leaders who espoused secret teachings (*hiji bōmon*), especially those claiming enlightenment for themselves.[88]

Rennyo's campaign against provocative behavior and heretical teachings was an ongoing endeavor because of the constant influx of new adherents into his following. The views that they brought were sometimes contrary to Rennyo's, and prompted him to advance his own religious paradigm all the more. This increase in adherents coincided with the proliferation of Shinshū uprisings (*ikki*) in various provinces. The involvement of Rennyo's followers in these uprisings confirmed the worst suspicions of his opponents, despite Rennyo's efforts to improve the reputation of the school. Nonetheless, the sheer number of adherents and their broad geographical distribution gave adversaries pause before attacking the Shinshū. Rennyo's consolidation of these followers was not accomplished over night, but by the time the new Honganji was completed in 1483 he was near realizing that dream. The bulk of Bukkōji members, led by Kyōgō, shifted affiliation in 1481, and most Kinshokuji members followed suit in 1493, led by Shōe.[89] Combined with converts from other branches and schools, they made the Honganji one of the powerful religious institutions in Japan.

Rennyo remained at Deguchi a little over two years, but throughout that period he was preparing for the reconstruction of the Honganji. In 1478 a new site was finally chosen, and Rennyo moved into temporary lodgings there. The location was the eastern suburb of Kyoto named Yamashina.[90] The selection of this spot reflects the confidence with which Rennyo returned to Kyoto. Yamashina was within easy striking distance for Mt. Hiei's warrior monks, but neither they nor any other foe of the Shinshū dared stand in Rennyo's way at this point.[91] The construction of the Honganji at Yamashina proceeded methodically over the next five years. First, residences (*shinden*) were built for Rennyo and the other functionaries of the temple. Next, the memorial hall to Shinran was erected to house the revered image.[92] As the central building in the complex, its completion in 1480 and the transfer of Shinran's image from the Chikamatsu chapel in the town of Ōtsu marked the high point of the construction project.[93] Rennyo himself was so emotionally charged on this occasion that, according to one letter, he could not sleep all night before the first Hōonkō memorial service was conducted in the hall. He saw it as the fulfillment of a lifelong goal.[94] Finally, in 1483 the Amida hall was added to complete the temple.[95] The entire complex contained not only these buildings but also gardens, moats, bridges, walls, and huge gates. In addition, a bustling town sprang up around it to serve the hundreds of pilgrims who flocked there. This new Honganji was particularly dazzling in the context of Kyoto's battle-scarred landscape after the Ōnin War. One visitor later described it in these effusive terms: "The vastness of the temple and its inexhaustible splendors make it seem just like the [Pure] Land of the Buddha (*Butsudo*)."[96] The magnificence of the Honganji gave the Shinshū prominence and greater respectability in aristocratic Kyoto. But the strongest impression was probably made on ordinary Shinshū believers, who were unaccustomed to such opulence. When they traveled to worship at the Honganji they were overwhelmed by its grandeur. For them it was both gratifying and humbling to be associated with this massive religious edifice.

One event that came to have new meaning and importance in Rennyo's time was the Hōonkō service in memory of Shinran. It became the preeminent annual ceremony of the Honganji. Throughout the temple's history the Hōonkō was always observed scrupulously, taking place each year during the seven days leading up to the anniversary of Shinran's death, the twenty-eighth day of the eleventh month.[97] Under Rennyo, however, it evolved into a mass service to which multitudes of ordinary believers came, if they could manage the journey to Kyoto.[98] A surprising number of Rennyo's letters were written specifically to be read during the Hōonkō.[99] They reveal the service to be a rather different event from what it had been earlier. The original tenor of the Hōonkō, as a time of remembrance and thanksgiving, was retained, but superimposed over it were new elements of exhortation, admonition, confession, and even conversion. For those firmly established in the faith it became a special time for renewing religious commitments. For those outside the faith it presented a setting for introspection, airing of doubts, and conversion to the faith. As an annual weeklong event in which diverse activities could be construed as expressions of gratitude to Shinran, it provided a special occasion each year for renewal and growth, both individually and institutionally.[100]

Rennyo's transformation of the Shinshū extended far beyond his redefinition

of the Hōonkō's content and function. Another accomplishment was the refor-
mulation of devotional practices. As a result of Rennyo's efforts, Shinran's
Shōshinge ("Verses on True Faith") became the most popular and widespread
religious chant in the Shinshū. Rennyo considered the verses—which extol the
two Buddhas, Śākyamuni and Amida, and the seven patriarchs—to be an in-
structive digest of Pure Land tenets and a fitting expression of praise. He therefore recommended it as the best chant for ordinary believers to use in daily
devotions.[101] Rennyo also promoted Shinran's *wasan* hymns for devotional purposes. Unlike the *Shōshinge* verses, they had long been used in religious
ceremonies, especially by the Sanmonto branch. Rennyo gave these hymns an
expanded role in Honganji liturgy by incorporating them into the temple's
morning and evening services in place of the hymns found in Shan-tao's *Wang-
sheng li-tsan chieh* ("Verses of Worship and Praise on Birth in Pure Land").[102]

Rennyo also standardized the *nembutsu* inscription that was enshrined as the
central object of worship in *dōjō*. Up to his time several different versions of
the inscription had been in circulation, and even Rennyo vacillated among them
during his early career. But he eventually settled on the simplest formula, *Namu
Amida Butsu*, as the most meaningful and appropriate wording for the inscription. Part of his motivation in adopting this version may have been the controversy that swirled around the inscription *Kimyō Jin Jippō Mugekō Nyorai* ("I
take refuge in the Tathāgata of Unobstructed Light Suffusing the Ten Directions") that branded Shinshū followers as the Mugekōshu, or Unobstructed Light
Adherents. But also his reverence of the words *Namu Amida Butsu*, interpreted
through the *kihō ittai* doctrine, no doubt underlay his choice. During his later
years the demand for *nembutsu* inscriptions of this type was overwhelming, and
Rennyo spent long hours personally inscribing copies for various *dōjō*. This activity consumed so much of his time that Rennyo once claimed that no one in
Japan had made more *nembutsu* inscriptions than he had.[103] For the next two
centuries this version of the inscription remained the standard object of worship
in the Shinshū, treasured above even painted and sculpted images of the Buddha.[104]

Over and above the devotional conventions that he instituted, Rennyo also
oversaw the development of an extensive network of temples and congregations
under the Honganji. Generally this network took the form of a pyramid with
the Honganji on top, intermediary temples in the middle, and local congregations, or *kō*, at the bottom. The bestowing of temple names and the granting
of *nembutsu* inscriptions was the means by which the Honganji made official the
affiliation of a temple or congregation. From approximately this period large
and influential congregations in the provinces began to assume the status of
temples, and thus they sought temple names from the Honganji. The vast
majority of ordinary congregations, however, did not attempt the transition to
formal temple status until the seventeenth century.[105] *Nembutsu* inscriptions,
rather than temple names, were their endowment from the Honganji. Though
there was a perennial tendency to treat these inscriptions with awe and reverence,
Rennyo always stressed that there is no magical power attached to them. As

he put it, even if people wrap themselves in seven or eight layers of them, if those people have not realized faith, then there is still no hope of attaining Buddhahood.[106] From these groups the Honganji in turn received material support. Contributions, which gradually evolved into annual pledges (*mainen yakusoku no bun*), came from congregations at all levels. Some of these offerings were of considerable size.[107] Rennyo personally acknowledged many of the gifts in handwritten notes to the donor groups, often with a pastoral word of encouragement added at the end.[108] This system of annual contributions provided sustained economic support for the Honganji at a time when the established institutions of Old Buddhism were declining because they had lost control of the endowed lands on which they depended.

Under Rennyo the Honganji developed a network of authority that stretched throughout this expanding religious organization. In addition to the regular hierarchy of head temple, intermediary temple, and local congregation, Rennyo established a family council called the *ikkeshu*, consisting of himself, his sons, and their sons. Rennyo strategically placed his children at major temples in regions where the Shinshū enjoyed greatest strength. These temples were tied directly to the Honganji either because they were founded by it or because the appointment of Rennyo's blood descendants imbued them with special status. Examples of them are the Zuisenji temple in Etchū province, established by Rennyo's great-grandfather Shakunyo and headed by his son Renjō (1446–1504); the Shōkōji and Kōgyōji temples, both in Kaga, begun and headed by Rennyo's sons Renkō (1450–1531) and Rensei (1455–1521); the Kenshōji temple in the town of Ōtsu, originally built as the Chikamatsu chapel to house the revered image of Shinran after the Honganji was destroyed in 1465 and later headed by Rennyo's son Renjun (1464–1510); the Honshūji temple in Mikawa province, established by Rennyo during his trip to the Kantō region in 1468 and later headed by his grandson Jitsuen (d. 1555); and the Kyōgyōji temple in Settsu province, founded by Rennyo in 1476 during his stay at Deguchi and headed first by his daughter Jusonni (1453–1515) and later by his son Rengei (1484–1523). Placing family members in regional temples had been a common practice among earlier Honganji leaders, but none of them used it to the degree that Rennyo did. His twenty-seven offspring provided ample candidates to fill these positions, thereby making possible a family network extending throughout the Shinshū.

The rationale for this network was to give the Honganji direct contact with grass-roots congregations, instead of relying completely on intermediary temples. There was always concern expressed in Rennyo's letters about the liberties taken by local priests, both in doctrine and in practice.[109] Having family members present in the provinces created a check against egregious deviations from the Honganji's norm and against the exploitation of believers by domineering religious masters. The temples that Rennyo's descendants headed often commanded greater prestige than other Shinshū temples because they were seen as direct outposts of the Honganji. Hence, their existence prevented intermediary temples from monopolizing followers in a particular region and from disregarding Honganji authority. Beyond this function, the family council also acted as an advisor to the head priest of the Honganji, the ecclesiastical leader of the school. In Rennyo's letter of bequest naming his fifth son Jitsunyo (1458–1525) to be his successor at the Honganji, Rennyo specifically instructed him to seek the assistance of his brothers in leading the school.[110] The family council therefore became the de facto ruling body of the Shinshū beginning with Rennyo's retirement in 1489, and it continued to serve in that capacity for at least two generations. During the decades following Rennyo's death the council built up extraordinary powers, wielding excommunication (*hamon*) and in times of warfare even the threat of execution (*shōgai*) as a means of enforcing its will.[111] Despite the abuses that occurred, the influence of the Honganji and the number of followers joining its ranks continued to grow under the council's direction throughout the sixteenth century. In effect it institutionalized the charisma that Rennyo exerted during his own lifetime.[112]

The emergence of the Honganji as a formidable religious organization inevitably led to changes in the character of the Shinshū. For one thing, the Honganji took on the air of a formal Buddhist temple. This trend began during the tenure of Rennyo's father, Zonnyo, when the Amida hall was added to the Honganji. Rennyo heightened this image by insisting that members of the family council all dress in black clerical robes, which set them off unambiguously as a priesthood, even though he himself did not always don them.[113] Also, the burgeoning use of temple names by large and established congregations in the provinces foreshadowed the demise of the *dōjō* as the Shinshū's organizational unit and the transition to temple status of local congregations.[114]

Despite these changes, certain features of the Honganji stayed the same, thereby preserving its distinctly Shinshū character. For example, even after the construction of the sanctuary to Amida, the memorial hall to Shinran remained the center of the temple and the Hōonkō service commemorating his death continued to be its foremost religious event. Also, the Shinshū priesthood did not abandon its lay life style, notwithstanding its use of clerical attire. For instance, priests ate fish and meat, and they even served it to guests inside the Honganji.[115] This practice was forbidden in traditional Buddhist temples. Another distinguishing feature of the Shinshū priesthood was the custom of marrying and having a family. There was never any attempt in the Shinshū to institute celibacy as a precept of the clergy. Certainly Rennyo's example, marrying five times and begetting twenty-seven children, ran diametrically counter to such an ideal.

Rennyo's tenure as head priest of the Honganji formally ended in 1489 when he yielded the position to his son Jitsunyo. Nonetheless, Rennyo remained active, even at the age of seventy-five. At first he took up residence within the Honganji complex, but in 1496 he built himself a hermitage on the spot that later grew into the city of Osaka. Throughout this period Rennyo received pilgrims from the provinces, made *nembutsu* inscriptions, and continued to write his pastoral letters. During his last years Rennyo reflected on the events of his life and with some degree of satisfaction concluded:

I have restored the tradition of our master [Shinran]. I have [re]built the memorial hall [to him] and the worship hall [of the temple]. I have passed on the position of head priest [to Jitsunyo]. I have constructed the Osaka residence. And I have retired. Hence, the old saying could be applied to me, "When works are completed and fame is achieved, to withdraw oneself is the way of Heaven."[116]

With this sense of accomplishment Rennyo passed away in 1499 at the age of eighty-four. After his death his pastoral letters came to be treasured as the words of Amida and were eventually raised to the level of scriptures for the ordinary believer.[117] Many of them, such as his letter for the Hōonkō service of 1477, which describes the life and teachings of Shinran, became important texts for congregational worship displacing earlier scriptures.[118] The widespread appeal of Rennyo's letters have made them his most enduring bequest to the Shinshū. Generation after generation, they have communicated Shinran's basic message of salvation through faith to countless adherents, acting as "a mirror to ordinary beings [seeking] birth in Pure Land."[119]

RENNYO'S LEGACY

Rennyo's most obvious accomplishment during his stewardship of the Honganji was the transformation of the Shinshū from a secondary religious movement into a formidable Buddhist school in Japan. The vast number of peasants joining its ranks, during an era of struggle for autonomous control of their villages,[120] made it a power to be reckoned with both socially and politically. Throughout most of the sixteenth century the Honganji wielded authority and influence on a par with the greatest political forces of Japan.[121] Even when the temple was partitioned into Nishi Honganji and Higashi Honganji at the beginning of the seventeenth century and its followers divided into two independent branches, both remained awesome powers simply because of the enormous number of temples and adherents affiliated with each.[122] In short, the Shinshū has been one of Japan's dominant schools of Buddhism, dwarfing most of its rivals, from Rennyo's time down through the present.

With size came social acceptance and respectability. The groundwork for these too was laid by Rennyo. Prior to his time the Shinshū lingered on the margins of social acceptance. Shinran's idealization of the evil person as the primary object of Amida's salvation had long been associated with the licensed evil heresy, and Shinshū adherents themselves were repeatedly implicated in a variety of antisocial activities—from denigrating Shinto *kami* and the deities of other Buddhist schools to fomenting peasant uprisings (*ikki*). Rennyo's *okite*, or rules of conduct, helped bring structure and discipline to unrestrained Shinshū groups. In the context of the Honganji's massive new temple organization, they functioned as hallowed rules around which believers could order their lives. Though the old stereotype of Shinshū adherents as troublemakers in society did not disappear altogether,[123] by and large the Shinshū received the acceptance and approbation enjoyed by other schools of Buddhism.

Shinran's teachings contain various elements that put Shin Buddhism into conflict with the prevailing norms of Japanese society. Some of them, such as his views of Shinto *kami*, had to be tempered before the Shinshū could be tolerated. One element, however, that Rennyo and his predecessors never compromised on was the marriage of Shinshū clergy. In Hōnen's day such a breach of Buddhist tradition was regarded as licensed evil. Outside criticism, however, diminished over the years, in part because of widespread laxity in other schools of Buddhism also. It is noteworthy, for example, that among the charges listed in Mt. Hiei's letter of 1465 justifying its destruction of the Honganji, the accusation of priests' marrying is not included.[124] It seems that the Shinshū had gradually won social acceptance for its ways. This acceptance was formalized in the *Shoshū jiin hatto* ("Laws for Temples of All Schools") promulgated by the Tokugawa government in the seventeenth century. One regulation in them states that clerics are not allowed to house women in their quarters but that "exceptions should be made for those priests who customarily take a wife."[125] This proviso was added specifically to accommodate the Shinshū. Eventually all schools of Buddhism in Japan permitted the marriage of clergy, diverging from established Buddhist practices in other parts of Asia. The Shinshū's example no doubt provoked this revolutionary change.

Perhaps the least visible but most consequential achievement of Rennyo's was his synthesis of Shin doctrine. Rennyo was without question heir to Shinran's ideas, but he recast them in a popular religious idiom and wedded them to concepts derived from religious movements outside the Shin tradition. His teachings represent the culmination of a long process of doctrinal development initiated by Shinran, extended by Kakunyo and Zonkaku, and inherited by himself. In Rennyo's writings Shin teachings take on a configuration that has emerged as the doctrinal norm for the Shinshū. None of the doctrinal principles in the Shinshū's *anjin rondai* ("Points of Faith") originated after his time.[126] They are all traceable to the major Shin thinkers from Shinran to Rennyo. Hence, Rennyo's ideas stand at the terminal point in the evolution of Shin orthodoxy. Just as Rennyo's Honganji set the pattern for the Shinshū's institutional structure, likewise his teachings fixed the contours for Shin orthodoxy.

Perhaps the greatest testimony to Rennyo's impact on Shin doctrine is the short creed known as the *Ryōgemon* ("Statement of Conviction"):

> We abandon all indiscriminate religious practices and undertakings (*zōgyō zasshu*) and all mind of self-assertion (*jiriki no kokoro*), and we rely with singleness of heart on the Tathāgata Amida in that matter of utmost importance to us now—to please save us in our next lifetime.
>
> We rejoice in knowing that our birth in Pure Land is assured and our salvation established from the moment we rely [on the Buddha] with even a single *nembutsu* (*ichinen*), and that whenever we utter the Buddha's name thereafter it is an expression of gratitude and indebtedness to him.

We gratefully acknowledge that for us to hear and understand this truth we are indebted to our founder and master for appearing in the world and to successive generations of religious teachers in our tradition for their profound encouragement.

We shall henceforth abide by our established rules (*okite*) as long as we shall live.[127]

As a confessional statement the *Ryōgemon* embodies the crux of the Shin teachings: faith, gratitude, reverence for Shinran, and rules of conduct. The surprising thing about the creed is that it does not contain the word *shinjin*, or faith, even though that is the most important concept in Shinran's writings. Instead, the terminology used to convey the idea of faith is that of "relying on the Buddha to please save me." When closely examined, the *Ryōgemon*'s contents reveal it to be none other than the words of Rennyo extracted from his letters.[128] Though the creed is not used as extensively today as it has been in past centuries, its promulgation as a normative statement of belief reflects the lasting influence of Rennyo's teachings on Shin doctrine. Whenever believers recite the creed nowadays, as is done at the annual Hōonkō memorial service or during Shinshū ordination ceremonies (*tokudo*), they are borrowing Rennyo's words to express the nature of their own faith. His articulation of the content of faith has thus been preserved as a model expression of Shin orthodoxy.

AFTERWORD

SHIN BUDDHISM
An Appraisal

It is an indisputable fact that in Rennyo's wake the Shinshū emerged as a major religious power in Japan, but the significance of Shin teachings in the overall scheme of Buddhism is still a matter of debate. To a certain extent Shin Buddhism, as well as Pure Land Buddhism in general, has suffered the unenviable fate of being treated as a marginal version of Buddhism. Though it is recognized as Buddhist in affiliation, Shin is often perceived as divergent in character and content, especially when compared to other prominent traditions such as Theravāda, Tibetan Buddhism, and Zen. What stands in greatest contrast to these traditions is the exclusive devotional character of Shin and the primacy of faith. And what is the greatest transgression in the eyes of other Buddhists is Shin's repudiation of clerical celibacy and monasticism, which have been institutional cornerstones of Buddhism since its formative centuries in India. These pronounced differences are one reason that questions of orthodoxy and heresy have constantly swirled around the Shinshū. Under these circumstances a crisis of identity has preoccupied Shin Buddhists throughout much of their history. It is a crisis perpetuated not only by detractors of Shin Buddhism but also by its defenders in their perennial efforts to formulate the perfect apology for Shin beliefs and practices.

The traditional lines of defense by which Shin Buddhists have attempted to justify their ways derive primarily from the corpus of Pure Land teachings that they inherited. The centerpiece of these teachings is the sacred story of Amida Buddha and his creation of the Pure Land as the religious path for sentient beings with little hope of enlightenment otherwise. Faith and devotion stand as quintessential elements in this path, since reliance on the Buddha's power (*tariki*) obviates the need for personal religious effort (*jiriki*). Based on these principles, the aspiration for self-perfection through clerical rigors becomes superfluous, for nothing beyond ordinary lay living is required.[1] Added to this sacred story is the eschatology of *mappō*, the decline of the Buddhist teachings. According to this eschatology, the Pure Land path is the only viable religious alternative in this day and age, since the capabilities of human beings have declined so much that they are unable to put other Buddhist teachings into practice.[2] The problem with these traditional arguments is that to outsiders, who do not embrace the eschatology of *mappō* or the sacred story of Pure Land, they carry little weight. Rather than presenting objective and compelling evidence that Shin Buddhism lies within the Buddhist mainstream, they reveal the very features that separate Shin from other forms of Buddhism. In short, they indicate what is distinctive about Shin, not what is shared with all of Buddhism.

A different tack taken by certain scholars, both sectarian and otherwise, has been to argue that some of Buddhism's time-honored principles lie at the core of Shin as well. One point frequently stressed is that Amida and his Pure Land are identical with the ineffable and inconceivable reality that lies at the heart of Buddhism. That reality is sometimes referred to as complete Nirvāṇa (*dainehan*), emptiness (*kū*), Buddha-nature (*busshō*), and the unconditioned (*mui*). Accordingly, Amida is described as the Dharma-body of Dharma-nature (*hosshō hosshin*)—that is, the perfect Dharma essence. Presenting Pure Land in this light undergirds its particular religious myth with the universal principles of Buddhism, and thereby treats the differences between Shin and other forms of Buddhism as superficial.[3] It also answers critics who would portray Pure Land as nothing more than a simplistic paradise where an anthropomorphic deity offers a blissful afterlife to naive believers.

Another argument aimed at showing that the underlying values of Shin stand squarely in the Buddhist tradition centers around the theme of no-self (*muga*). Though Shin rarely uses this term in its teachings, it nevertheless advocates the abandonment of all self-effort (*jiriki*) in reliance on the power of the Buddha (*tariki*). The mind of faith coalescing in that experience includes by definition the abnegation of self.[4] Other schools of Buddhism often link no-self to the clerical life. The strenuous practices and discipline required of monks and nuns are intended to liberate them from any sense of an independent, controlling, and enduring self. Release from that view is part and parcel of Buddhism's ultimate realization. Shin, needless to say, stands in contrast to those traditions, for it rejects the clerical ideal. Instead, it advances a pragmatic selflessness largely in the form of gratitude. The person of faith looks on Amida, the world, and other people with a self-abandoning sense of indebtedness and thankfulness. These qualities, which are common to all cultures and societies, bring the rarefied experience of no-self down to the level of ordinary human interchange. Thus, Shin Buddhism is true in its own way to the doctrine of no-self, even while disavowing the clerical regimen that is traditionally associated with it.

Some arguments in Shin's behalf relate it to the principles of Mahāyāna Buddhism in particular. Mahāyāna, or the "great vehicle," is the branch of Buddhism from India that pervaded the countries of East Asia. During the course of its development it championed the idea of universal salvation: that Buddhism's highest goal of enlightenment is accessible to believers in all conditions and situations.[5] Shin in a sense carried this idea to its logical conclusion. It proclaimed the path of salvation to extend across all worldly distinctions—whether between cleric and lay person, rich and poor, man and woman, or good and evil. Since salvation is solely the work of Amida, faith is the endowment of all people. In this way Shin infused its concept of faith with a strongly Mahāyāna flavor.

One other argument based on Mahāyāna principles centers around the concept of merit transference (*ekō*). Though merit transference is sometimes given cursory treatment in summations of Mahāyāna doctrine, it is in fact the soteriological mechanism that makes possible the Bodhisattva ideal. If there were no way to offer up religious merit to others, then the efficacy of the Bodhisattva's selfless and compassionate acts would be lost. That is, others would accrue no benefit from the Bodhisattva's efforts in their behalf. Moreover, the Bodhisattva would be thwarted from attaining the wisdom of enlightenment, since the perfection of wisdom depends in part on the exercise of compassion. The sacred story of the Pure Land tradition—the account of Amida's enlightenment and his creation of the Pure Land—is predicated on this concept of merit transference. Amida's vows make his own enlightenment contingent on leading others to enlightenment via Pure Land.[6] The very stuff that Pure Land is fashioned out of is the vast store of merit that Amida makes available to others. Hence, if it were not possible for his merit to be transferred to others or to be used for their benefit, then neither they nor Amida would have any hope of enlightenment, for his vows would be devoid of the capacity to be fulfilled. The efficacy of merit transference is what gives the vows their potency.[7] This kind of argument differs from the others in that the previous ones tend to de-emphasize the sacred story of Pure Land and to highlight themes which do not stand out as conspicuously in the Pure Land tradition. That is, they begin with themes which are prominent in other forms of Buddhism and attempt to show ways in which Pure Land thought accords with them. This argument, by contrast, takes a central theme of Pure Land and reaffirms it as a pivotal, though often overlooked, component of Mahāyāna Buddhism. The virtue of this argument is that it allows Pure Land's sacred story to remain prominent, even while placing it in the mainstream of the Mahāyāna tradition.

All the arguments outlined here are doctrinal in nature. They are designed to show that conceptual continuities exist between Pure Land thought and Buddhism as a whole. Whether or not they are convincing depends in large part on the audience to whom they are addressed. Those standing within the Pure Land tradition may feel justified by such arguments, and may draw strength from them. Those standing outside the tradition may or may not be swayed by their reasoning. Some probably continue to look upon Pure Land as a deviant form of Buddhism despite its points of commonalty with mainstream ideas. Doctrinal issues aside, there is one important way of perceiving Shin Buddhism which, in my opinion, does place it squarely in Buddhism's mainstream. That is to view it in the context of lay Buddhism. Shin Buddhism is perhaps the most fully developed form of lay Buddhism in existence.

In every branch and school of Buddhism there has always been a lay constituency. It was part of Buddhism's earliest make-up in India, dating back to the historical Buddha himself. Even schools that stress clerical and monastic values, such as Theravāda and Zen, have made a place for lay adherents in their spiritual paths. In all these schools lay religiosity consists primarily of reverence for the Buddha. The Buddha, whether identified as Śākyamuni or as one of the many Mahāyāna Buddhas, is perceived as the embodiment of truth and as a wellspring of aid and comfort. Thus, lay believers look to him with trust and devotion. Though they ultimately aspire to the same liberating experience of enlightenment that the clergy strives for, lay followers are daunted by the strenuous practices undertaken by the clergy in its pursuit of that experience. Hence, they tend to feel distant from enlightenment or ill-equipped to achieve it. Instead of aspiring for enlightenment in the present, they generally nourish the hope that in a future lifetime they will be born in a state in which enlightenment is possible. For now, however, their religious life is limited to worship, devotional practices, offerings, and conventional morality. Standing behind these external acts is a religious frame of mind consisting of aspiration for enlightenment and reliance on the Buddha, the Buddhist teachings, and the Buddhist community. Needless to say, there are other dimensions of lay religiosity besides these, but the religious outlook described here is common to virtually all Buddhist schools.

Shin Buddhism is none other than one specific form of this general lay Buddhist outlook. Its specific aspects are its Buddha, Amida; its path to enlightenment, via Pure Land; its sacred story of how Amida established that path; and its practices, the *nembutsu* and otherwise. But if Shin is demythologized—that is, if its specific aspects are stripped away—then the religious sensibilities and practices remaining are not significantly different from those found in lay Buddhism throughout Asia. They are faith-oriented and devotional. Shin has not created a new form of Buddhism, but rather idealizes the lay dimension of the religion. What is unique about Shin is not the beliefs and practices it propounds but its advocacy of the lay path over the clerical one. It maintains that lay Buddhism is the only practicable form surviving today.

By and large lay Buddhism has languished in the shadow of the clerical path. It has typically been depicted as inferior to the clerical ideal or at best preparatory to it. One would follow the lay path only if one was incapable of clerical rigors, and even then one would hope all the while to be reborn as a cleric in a future lifetime. The assumption implicit in this view is that clerical practices are the true vehicle to enlightenment and that one must eventually undertake them in some lifetime or another. Lay life is thereby portrayed as a prefatory stage to the clerical path or as an ancillary path lying at Buddhism's periphery. This view of lay life is precisely what Shin Buddhism repudiates. It maintains that clerical practices are no longer a realistic option for humans and, more importantly, that the lay frame of mind—that is, the psychological dynamics of faith and reliance on the Buddha—is more conducive to enlightenment in the long run.

It would be easy to conclude that lay Buddhism is inferior if there were irrefutable evidence that clerical practices are both necessary and sufficient for enlightenment. Unfortunately, that statement cannot be made, neither as a universally accepted doctrinal tenet nor as an empirical fact. At the doctrinal level, how and why enlightenment occurs remains in part inexplicable. At the experiential level, the instances of enlightenment occurring in the world seem fewer and farther between. The Pure Land eschatology of *mappō*, it would seem, is not entirely wrong. In this context Shin offers an alternative path which has Buddhist roots as deep and enduring as the clerical path. Whether or not Shin is an attractive and compelling path depends in large part on what one's preconceived notions of Buddhism are.

This then, I believe, is the significance of Shin Buddhism. It brings to the forefront a path of Buddhism, the lay path, which has always existed but which has long been relegated to the background. It reveals elements in that path, both conceptual and psychological, which may be more efficacious in inculcating Buddhism's outlook and core values in people than the clerical ones are. And it presents a realistic path that humans can actually follow in this day and age. Far from being branded as heretical, Shin Buddhism should awaken other Buddhists to the broader dimensions of their religious heritage, and should spark a reassessment of the scope and nature of Buddhism.

Glossary of Japanese and Chinese Terms

Ajase 阿闍世
Aki 安芸
akudō 悪道
akunin jōbutsu 悪人成佛
akunin motomo ōjō no shōin nari
　　悪人もとも往生の正因なり
akunin ōjō no ki 悪人往生の機
akunin shōki 悪人正機
ama ga kodomo 尼が子供
ama nyūdō 尼入道
Amanawa 甘縄
Amida 阿弥陀
Amida Butsu 阿弥陀仏
Amidaji 阿弥陀寺
Amidakyō 阿弥陀経
Amidakyō shūchū 阿弥陀経集註
amiginu 阿弥衣
amigō 阿弥号
Anichibō Shōkū 阿日房彰空
anjin 安心
anjin ketsujō 安心決定
Anjin ketsujōshō 安心決定鈔
anjin rondai 安心論題
Anjinshō 安心鈔
Anjō no Miei 安城御影
An-lo chi 安楽集
Anrakubō (d.1207) 安楽房
An'yōji 安養寺
Asakura Toshikage (1428-81)
　　朝倉敏景
Ashikaga 足利
Ashikaga Yoshihisa (1465-89)
　　足利義尚
Ashikaga Yoshimasa (1436-90)
　　足利義政
atō 阿黨
ayuiotchi 阿惟越致
bachi 罰
bakufu 幕府
Bandō 坂東
Benchō (1162-1238) 弁長
bendō Miroku 便同弥勒
betsugan 別願
betsuge 別解
betsuji gyōgi 別時行儀
bettōshiki 別当職
Bingo 備後
bingū konbō 貧窮困乏
Bishamon 毘沙門

Bitchū 備中
Biwa 琵琶
Bizen 備前
bodai 菩提
bodaishin 菩提心
Bokieshi 慕帰絵詞
bōmori 坊守
bonbu 凡夫
Bonmōkyō 梵網経
bonnō 煩悩
bonnō gusoku 煩悩具足
bonnō jōju no bonbu 煩悩成就凡夫
bosatsukai 菩薩戒
bōzu 坊主
Bukkōji 仏光寺
Bukkōji chūkō Ryōgen Shōnin den
　　仏光寺中興了源上人伝
Buppō 仏法
Buppō ni fusu no gedō 附仏法之外道
busshin 仏心
busshō 仏性
Butchi no fushigi 仏智の不思議
Butsu tasuke tamae 仏助ケ給へ
Butsudo 仏土
Butsuon hōsha 仏恩報謝
Chih-i (538-97) 智顗
Chikamatsu 近松
Chikamatsu Bōsha 近松坊舎
ching-t'u 浄土
Chinzei 鎮西
Chinzei myōmoku mondō funjinshō
　　鎮西名目問答奮迅鈔
Chion'in 知恩院
chishiki 知識
chishiki kimyō 知識帰命
Chōgen Shunjōbō (1121-1206)
　　重源俊乗房
chōji 停止
Chokuden 勅伝
Chōsai (1184-1266) 長西
Chōsai Zenkōbō 澄西禅光房
Chōshōji 超勝寺
chūkō 中興
chūkō shōnin 中興上人
Ch'ün-i lun 群疑論
Chūtarō 中太郎
Dai Nihon koku zokusan ō Shōtoku
　　Taishi hōsan 大日本国粟散王
　　聖徳太子奉讃

daibodaishin 大菩提心
Daidai shōnin kikigaki 代々上人聞書
daigyō 大行
daihi ekō no riyaku 大悲回向之利益
Daihōdō daranikyō 大方等陀羅尼経
daijihishin 大慈悲心
Daijōin 大乗院
Daijōji 大乗寺
Daikaku (1297-1364) 大覺
dainehan 大涅槃
Dainichikyō 大日経
daishin 大信
dan'aku shuzen 断悪修善
dangihon 談義本
danjō 談場
danzengon 断善根
Deguchi 出口
denji 伝持
denpu yajin 田夫野人
deshi 弟子
deshi hitori mo motazu
    弟子一人ももたず
Dewa 出羽
dōbō 同朋
dōgyō 同行
dōjishū 道時衆
dōjō 道場
dokuju 読誦
Dōsai (1399-1488) 道西
Dōshin 導信
Dōshō (ca. 1345) 道性
dōshu 堂衆
doshujōshin 度衆生心
dōsō 堂僧
e 慧
Echigo 越後
Echigo no suke 越後介
Echizen 越前
Eigenki 栄玄記
Eiheiji 永平寺
Eison (1209-90) 叡尊
ekeizu 絵系図
ekō 回向
ekō hotsugan shin 回向発願心
endonkai 円頓戒
enja 縁者
Ennin (794-864) 円仁
Enninji 延仁寺
enri edo 厭離穢土
Enryakuji 延暦寺
ensei 厭世
Enshinbō 円心房
ese 回施
ese shitamaeri 回施したまへり

ese shitamau 回施したまふ
eshin 回心
Eshinni (b. 1182) 恵信尼
Eshinni shōsoku 恵信尼消息
Etchū 越中
Etchū no kuni Kōmyōbō e tsukawasu
    gohenji 越中国光明房へつかわす
    御返事
Fa-shih tsan 法事讃
fudan nembutsu 不断念仏
Fujisawa 藤沢
Fujiwara 藤原
fujo 巫女
Fukakusa 深草
fukashigi 不可思議
fukashōryō 不可称量
fuōjō 不往生
fusan 賦算
fusatsukai 布薩戒
futaiten 不退転
fuyōshū 附庸宗
gaija 改邪
Gaijashō 改邪鈔
Gaikemon 改悔文
gakushō 学生
gan ni hokorite 願にほこりて
Ganganshō 願々鈔
gansabusshin 願作仏心
ganshō 願生
ganshu 願主
gebon 下品
gechijō 下知状
gedatsu dōsō 解脱幢相
gedō 外道
gekyō jagi 外教邪偽
Genchi (1183-1238) 源智
Genchi (1734-94) 玄智
Gengibunshō 玄義分抄
genin 下人
Genkai 源海
Genkū 源空
Genran (1318-47) 源鸞
Genshin (942-1017) 源信
gensō ekō 還相回向
geta 足駄
geten 外典
gi (definition) 義
gi (false) 偽
gi naki o gi to su 義なきを義とす
gijō 疑城
Gobunshō 御文章
Godaigo (1288-1339) 後醍醐
Godenshō 御伝鈔
goeidō 御影堂

Gofukakusa (1243-1304) 後深草
gogyaku 五逆
Gohanazono (1419-70) 後花園
Goichi 悟一
Gojō Nishi no Tōin 五条西洞院
gojoku 五濁
goken 五間
gokitōjo 御祈禱所
Gokomatsu (1377-1433) 後小松
Gokuraku jōdo shūgi 極楽浄土宗義
gokuraku wa mui nehan no kai nari
　　極楽無為涅槃界
gon shō sōzu 權少僧都
Gonengyō no oku ni kiseru onkotoba
　　護念經の奥に記せる御詞
gonenmon 五念門
gongo dōdan 言語道断
gongu jōdo 欣求浄土
goon hōsha 御恩報謝
gorusu 御留守
Gosaga (1220-72) 後嵯峨
Goshinji 悟真寺
goshō 後生
goshō tasuke tamae to Mida o tanome
　　後生助けたまへと弥陀をたのむ
Gōshōji 毫摂寺
Goshōsokushū 御消息集
Goshōsokushū Zenshōbon
　　御消息集善性本
Gotoba (1180-1239) 後鳥羽
gōzoku 豪族
Gozokushō 御俗姓
Guanki 愚闇記
Guanki hensatsu 愚闇記返札
gudon gechi 愚鈍下智
guganmon 弘願門
Gukanshō 愚管抄
gunzoku 群賊
Gusanshingi 具三心義
gūshū 寓宗
gusoku bonnō 具足煩悩
Gutoku Shinran 愚禿親鸞
Gutoku Zenshin 愚禿善信
Gutotsu (d. 1352) 愚咄
gyakuma 逆魔
gyō 行
Gyōkū Hōhonbō 行空法本房
gyōmon 行門
Gyōnen (1240-1321) 凝然
Gyōnyo (1376-1440) 巧如
haja kenshō 破邪顕正
Haja kenshō mōshijō 破邪顕正申状
Haja kenshōgi 破邪顕正義
Haja kenshōshō 破邪顕正鈔

hakai mukai 破戒無戒
hakai muzan 破戒無慚
hakai nembutsu ōjō 破戒念仏往生
hakai ōjō 破戒往生
hakarai はからい
hamon 破門
han ritsuryō Bukkyō 反律令仏教
hangyō hanza zammai 半行半坐三昧
Hannen 範宴
Hanni 範意
hashizutsu 箸筒
hatsumu inga 撥無因果
Heike monogatari 平家物語
Heitarō 平太郎
heizei 平生
henji 辺地
hiden 秘伝
Hiei 比叡
Hieizan 比叡山
higagoto o omoi ひがごとをおもひ
higan 彼岸
Higashi Honganji 東本願寺
Higashiyama 東山
higyō 非行
hihō shōbō 誹謗正法
hiji bōmon 祕事法門
hijiri 聖
hiki 疋
hikiire 引入
hikkyō jakumetsu 畢竟寂滅
Hino 日野
Hino Arinori 日野有範
Hino Hirotsuna (d. 1249?) 日野広綱
Hino ichiryū keizu 日野一流系図
Hirohashi 広橋
Hitachi 常陸
hito futari ga kokoro 人二人が心
hitsuji 未
hizen 非善
hō 法
Hōamidabutsu 法阿弥陀仏
hōben 方便
hōben kedo 方便化土
hōben keshindo 方便化身土
hōben no gyōshin 方便行信
Hōbutsuji 報仏寺
Hōchi 法智
Hogo no uragaki 反故裏書
hōitsu 放逸
hōitsu muzan 放逸無慚
Hōjū (d. 1479) 法住
Hokekyō 法華經
Hōki 泊耆
Hokke 法華

Hokke mondō　法華問答

Hokkedō　法華堂

Hokkezammaidō　法華三昧堂

Hokuriku　北陸

hōmyō　法名

hon　本

Hōnen (1133-1212)　法然

Hōnen Shōnin denki　法然上人伝記

Hōnen Shōnin gyōjō ezu

　　法然上人行状絵図

hongan　本願

hongan bokori　本願誇り

hongan jōju no mon　本願成就文

hongan shōkan no chokumei

　　本願招喚之勅命

Honganji　本願寺

Honganji no Shōnin　本願寺の聖人

Honganji no Shōnin Shinran denne

　　本願寺の聖人親鸞伝絵

Honganji sahō no shidai

　　本願寺作法之次第

Honganji Shinran Shōnin

　　本願寺親鸞聖人

hōni　法爾

honji　本地

honji suijaku　本地垂迹

honjo　本所

honjoshiki　本所職

Honkokuji　本圀寺

Honpukuji　本福寺

Honpukuji atogaki　本福寺跡書

Honseiji　本誓寺

Honshūji　本宗寺

Honzan　本山

Hōonko　報恩講

Hōonkō shiki　報恩講式

Hōrakuji　法楽寺

hosshō　法性

hosshō hosshin　法性法身

Hossō　法相

Hsüan-i fen　玄義分

Huai-kan (ca. 7th cent.)　懐感

ianjin　異安心

Ibaragi　茨城

ichi

Ichijōin　一乗院

Ichimai kishōmon　一枚起請文

Ichimi wagō keiyaku no koto

　　一味和合契約之事

ichinen　一念

ichinen hokki　一念発起

Ichinen tanen funbetsuji

　　一念多念分別事

Ichinen tanen mon'i　一念多念文意

ichinengi　一念義

Ichinengi chōji kishōmon

　　一念義停止起請文

ichiryū　一流

idō　異道

Iga　伊賀

igaku　異学

ige　異解

igi　異義

igyō　易行

Igyōbon　易行品

Iida　飯田

ike　異計

Ikeda Mitsumasa (1609-82)　池田光政

iken　異見

ikkeshu　一家衆

ikki　一揆

ikkō　一向

Ikkō ikki　一向一揆

ikkō nembutsu　一向念仏

ikkō senju　一向専修

ikkō senju nembutsu dōjō no honji

　　一向専修念仏道場之本寺

ikkō sennen　一向専念

ikkō sennen Muryōju Butsu

　　一向専念無量寿仏

Ikkō Shunjō (1239-87)　一向俊聖

Ikkōdō　一向堂

Ikkōshū　一向衆

Ikkōshū　一向宗

Ikkyū (1394-1481)　一休

Imagozen no haha　いまごぜんのはは

Inada　稲田

Inami　井波

indō　引導

inga hatsumu　因果撥無

ingan　因願

Ippen (1239-89)　一遍

Ippen hijiri e　一遍聖絵

Ippen Shōnin goroku　一遍上人語録

Ise　伊勢

ishō teiyō shin　異生羝羊心

ishū　異執

issai shujō shitsu u busshō

　　一切衆生悉有仏性

issendai　一闡提

isshin　一心

Isshinden　一身田

ittai　一体

Iwami　石見

Iya onna　いやおむな

Iya onna yuzurijō　いやおむな譲状

Izu　伊豆

Izumo　出雲

Izumoji 出雲路
ja 邪
jadō 邪道
jafū 邪風
jagi (wrong doctrine) 邪義
jagi (wrongness and falsehood) 邪偽
jahō 邪法
jaken 邪見
jakyō 邪教
jashō no dōro 邪正道路
jashū 邪執
ji (itself) 自
ji (time) 時
Jien (1155-1225) 慈円
jiga aisei 自我愛性
Jikan (1334-1419) 慈観
jiki sho tokuhon 直諸徳本
jikisanshu 直参衆
jikkō 十劫
Jikū (d. 1351) 慈空
Jikyō (d. 1340) 慈慶
Jimyōshō 持名鈔
jinen 自然
jinen hōni 自然法爾
jinen ni 自然に
jinjō gyōgi 尋常行儀
Jinrei (1749-1817) 深励
jinshin 深信
jiri rita 自利利他
jiriki 自力
jiriki no kokoro 自力の心
jiriki sazen 自力作善
jishin 自信
jishin kyōninshin 自信教人信
Jishinbō (d. 1292) 慈信房
jishū 時衆
Jishū 時宗
jitō 地頭
Jitsuen (d. 1555) 實円
Jitsugo (1492-1583) 実悟
Jitsugo kyūki 実悟旧記
Jitsugoki 実悟記
Jitsunyo (1458-1525) 実如
Jizō 地蔵
jō 定
jōdo 浄土
Jōdo hōmon genrushō
　　浄土法門源流章
Jōdo nizō nikyō ryakuju
　　浄土二蔵二経略頌
jōdo sanbu kyō 浄土三部経
Jōdo sangyō ōjō monrui
　　浄土三経往生文類
Jōdo Shinshū 浄土真宗

Jōdo shin'yōshō 浄土真要鈔
Jōdo wasan 浄土和讃
Jōdoron 浄土論
Jōdoshū 浄土宗
jogō 助業
Kōbō (774-835) 弘法
Kōfukuji 興福寺
Kōfukuji sōjō 興福寺奏状
Kōgen (1290-1373) 光玄
Kōgon (1334-1419) 綱厳
Kōgyōji 興行寺
Kōkakubō 好覚房
Kokan Shiren (1278-1346) 虎関師錬
kokoro 心
kokorozashi 志
koku 石
kokū 虚空
kokugesa 黒袈裟
kōmyō honzon 光明本尊
kōmyō muryō 光明無量
kōmyō shingon 光明真言
Kōmyōbō 光明房
Kōmyōji 光明寺
kongōshin 金剛心
Konjaku monogatarishū 今昔物語集
konmōjō 懇望状
koromo 衣
Kōsai (1163-1247) 幸西
Kosan inshi 孤山隠士
Kosha shokan 古写書簡
kōshi 講師
Kōshōji (Bukkōji's original name)
　　興正寺
Kōshōji (Kyōen's temple) 光照寺
Kōsō wasan 高僧和讃
Kōtaishi Shōtoku hōsan
　　皇太子聖徳奉讃
kotosara ni ことさらに
Kōzanji 高山寺
Kūamidabutsu (1156-1228)
　　空阿弥陀仏
Kuan ching shu 観経疏
Kuan-nien fa-men 観念法門
Kudenshō 口伝鈔
kudoku no hō 功徳之宝
Kujō Kanezane (1149-1207) 九条兼実
Kumano 熊野
Kumano Hongū 熊野本宮
Kurodani 黒谷
Kusha 倶舎
kushō shōgyō 口称正行
kuyaku 公役
Kuzenki 空善記
kyō 教

kyōen 強縁
Kyōen 慶円
Kyōgō (d. 1490) 経豪
Kyōgyōji 教行寺
Kyōgyōshinshō 教行信証
kyōgyōshō 教行証
kyōman 憍慢
kyōninshin 教人信
Kyōshin (d. 866) 教信
Kyōto 京都
kyū Bukkyō 旧仏教
Kyūshū 九州
Lao Tzu 老子
Lo-pang wen-lei 楽邦文類
ma 麿
mainen yakusoku no bun
　毎年約束之分
manzen shogyō 万善諸行
mappō 末法
Mappō tōmyōki 末法燈明記
masse 末世
Masukata Ubō 益方有房
matsu 末
matsudai 末代
Matsudai nembutsu jushuin
　末代念仏授手印
matsuji 末寺
Mattōshō 末燈鈔
menju kuketsu 面授口訣
metsudo 滅度
Mida no goon 弥陀の御恩
Miidera 三井寺
Mikawa 三河
mikkyō 密教
miko 巫女
Miroku 弥勒
Miyoshi Tamenori 三善為教
mo 裳
mo nashi goromo 裳無衣
mohara もはら
Mo-ho chih-kuan 摩訶止観
mon 文
monoimi 物忌
Mononobe no Moriya 物部守屋
monto 門徒
Morinaga Shinnō (1308-35) 護良親王
Motochika shin o torite hongan o
　shinzuru no yō 基親取信
　信本願之様
motsugo sōrei 没後葬礼
Muchū mondō 夢中問答
muge 無碍
muge no ichidō 無碍の一道
Mugekō Nyorai 無碍光如来

Mugekōshu 無碍光衆
mui 無為
mui hosshin 無為法身
mujun 鉾楯
Mukashi monogatariki 昔物語記
mukon no shin o eshimetamaeri
　獲無根信
munengi 無念義
Muromachi 室町
muryō kōmyō e 無量光明慧
Muryōjuji 無量寿寺
Muryōjukyō 無量寿経
Muryōjukyō ubadaisha ganshōge
　無量寿経優婆提含願生偈
Musashi 武蔵
Musō Soseki (1275-1351) 夢窓疎石
Mutsu 陸奥
muzan 無慚
myō 命
myōchō 名帳
Myōe (1173-1232) 明恵
Myōe Shōnin yuikun 明恵上人遺訓
myōgō 名号
myōgō fushigi 名号不思議
myōgō honzon 名号本尊
Myōhen (1142-1224) 明遍
Myōhōbō 明法房
Myōkenji 妙顕寺
Myōkō (1286-1353) 明光
Myōkōin 妙香院
Myōshō 明性
Myōshō (1477-1500) 妙勝
myōshu 名主
Myōshū (d. 1487) 明秀
Myōyū (1487-1512) 妙祐
Myōzui (d. 1787) 妙瑞
Nagai 長井
Nagato 長門
naiin 内因
Nakano 中野
Namekata 行方
Namu 南無
Namu Amida Butsu 南無阿弥陀仏
Namu Fukashigi Kō Butsu
　南無不可思議光仏
Namu Fukashigi Kō Nyorai
　南無不可思議光如来
Namuamidabutsu (1121-1206)
　南無阿弥陀仏
nange 難化
nangyō 難行
Naniwa 難波
nanji 難治
nanji ōjō 難思往生

nanjigi ōjō 難思儀往生
Nara 奈良
Natsu ofumi 夏御文
Nau 奈有
Nehangyō 涅槃経
nembutsu 念仏
nembutsu muken jigoku 念仏無間地獄
Nembutsu muken jigokushō
　　念仏無間地獄抄
Nembutsu myōgishū 念仏名義集
nembutsu shugyō 念仏修行
nembutsushu 念仏衆
nen (caused to be so) 然
nen (contemplating, uttering the name) 念
nengu 年貢
nenju 念珠
Nichichō (1422-1500) 日朝
Nichijō (1298-1369) 日静
Nichiren (1222-82) 日蓮
Nichishin (1407-88) 日親
Nichizō (1269-1342) 日像
Ninnaji 仁和寺
Ninshō (1217-1303) 忍性
ninzei akuto 人勢悪徒
Nishi Honganji 西本願寺
Niso Raichia Shōnin shōsoku
　　二祖礼智阿上人消息
nogesa 野袈裟
nōmin 農民
Noto 能登
nyobon 女犯
Nyodō (1253-1340) 如導
Nyoen 如円
Nyoichi (1262-1321) 如一
Nyojō (1412-60) 如乗
Nyokaku (1250-1311) 如覚
Nyokō (d. 1467) 如光
Nyokū (1262-1321) 如空
Nyonin ōjō kikigaki 女人往生聞書
Nyoraidō 如来堂
Nyoshin (1235-1300) 如信
Ōami 大網
obi 帯
ōbō 王法
Oda Nobunaga (1534-82) 織田信長
Odagiri 小田切
Ofumi 御文
ōgen 応現
Ōgen (1433-1503) 応玄
Ōgo no kakochō 往古過去帳
Ōgun 奥郡
Oguro Nyobō 小黒女房
ohaka no gosata 御墓の御沙汰
ōjō jōdo no shōin 往生浄土の正因

ōjō no shōin 往生の正因
ōjō shōin 往生正因
Ōjōki 往生記
Ōjōyōshū 往生要集
Okayama-han 岡山藩
okite 掟
okushimon 抑止門
Ōmachi 大町
Ōmi 近江
onhakarai 御はからい
Ōnin 応仁
onmyōshi 陰陽師
on'okite 御掟
onozukara おのづから
Ōsaka 大阪
Oshikōji no Minami, Made no Kōji
　　Higashi 押小路南万里小路東
ōsō ekō 往相回向
Ōtani 大谷
Ōtani byōdō 大谷廟堂
Ōtani Honganji tsūki 大谷本願寺通紀
otona 長
Ōtsu 大津
Owari 尾張
Paekche (Korean) 百済
Raichia (1252-1325) 礼智阿
raihai 礼拝
raikō 来迎
Renge mengyō 蓮華面経
Rengei (1484-1523) 蓮芸
Rengo (1468-1543) 蓮悟
Renjō (1446-1504) 蓮乗
Renjun (1464-1510) 蓮淳
Renjunki 蓮淳記
Renkō (1450-1531) 蓮綱
Renkyō (d. 1490) 蓮教
Renni (d. 1278) 蓮位
Rennyo (1415-99) 蓮如
Rennyo Shōnin itokuki
　　蓮如上人遺徳記
Rensei (1455-1521) 蓮誓
rinjū gyōgi 臨終行儀
Ritsu 律
ritsuryō Bukkyō 律令仏教
Rokkaku 六角
Rokkakudō 六角堂
rokuji raisan 六時礼讃
Rokujō monryū 六条門流
Rokuyōshō 六要鈔
rusu 留守
rusushiki 留守職
Ryōchi no sadame 了智の定
Ryōchū (1199-1287) 良忠
ryōge 領解

Ryōgemon 領解文
Ryōgen (912-85) 良源
Ryōgen (1295-1336) 了源
Ryōhen (1194-1252) 良遍
ryōke 領家
Ryōkū (d. 1297) 良空
Ryōkū (1669-1733) 良空
Ryōninbō 了忍房
Ryōshinbō 了心房
Ryōshō (1788-1842) 了祥
ryōshu 領主
Ryūkan (1148-1227) 隆寛
Sabae 鯖江
Sado 佐渡
Saga 嵯峨
Sagami 相模
sagan 作願
sagō 作業
Saichō (767-822) 最澄
Saidaiji 西大寺
Saihō shinanshō 西方指南抄
Saii Zenshakubō 西意善綽房
saiji 再治
saikyo 裁許
saishi 祭祀
Saishu kyōjū ekotoba 最須敬重絵詞
saitai chikuhatsu 妻帯蓄髪
samurai 侍
san 讃
sanbō metsujin 三宝滅盡
sandai 三代
sandai denji 三代伝持
sandai sōjō 三代相承
sandan 讃嘆
sandan kuyō 讃嘆供養
sanga 山臥
sangan tennyū 三願転入
Sange gakushōshiki 山家学生式
sangen 三間
sangō 三業
Sangō wakuran 三業惑乱
sanji shōdō no shosō 山寺聖道の諸僧
San-lun hsüan-i 三論玄義
sanmon 山門
sanmon no taishu 山門の大衆
Sanmonto 三門徒
Sanmonto ogamazu no shu
　三門徒おがまずの衆
Sanron 三論
sanshin 三心
santo 山徒
Sanzengi mondō 散善義問答
sanzu 三途
se shusse no nihō 世出世の二法
Seia (d. 1374) 誓阿

seigan fushigi 誓願不思議
Seikai 誓海
Seikaku (1166-1235) 聖覚
Seikanbō (1183-1238) 勢観房
Seikoku 西谷
Seishi 勢至
Seisho 清書
Seizan 西山
seken 世間
sendoku 先徳
Sengoku 戦国
Senjaku hongan nembutsushū
　選択本願念仏集
senjaku no gan 選択の願
senjaku no gankai 選択願海
Senjakushū 選択集
senju nembutsu 専修念仏
Senjuji 専修寺
Senkū (d. 1343) 専空
Sennyūji 泉涌寺
Senshōji 専照寺
sensō 占相
seshimetamaeri せしめたまへり
sesshō kanpaku 摂政関白
sesshu fusha 摂取不捨
Sesshu Fusha Mandara
　摂取不捨曼陀羅
Settsu 摂津
Shakkū 綽空
Shakunyo (1350-93) 綽如
Shakuson nembutsu 釈尊念仏
shana 遮那
Shan-tao (613-81) 善導
Shao-k'ung 少康
Shasekishū 沙石集
shibomeru hana ni tatoete
　しぼめるはなにたとへて
Shibunritsu 四分律
Shibutani 渋谷
Shibutani rekise ryakuden
　渋谷歴世略伝
Shichijō monryū 七条門流
Shichikajō kishōmon 七箇条起請文
shichiso 七祖
shigoku mattei 至極末弟
shijōshin 至誠心
shikan 止観
shikarashimu しからしむ
Shikoku 四国
Shimōsa 下総
Shimotsuke 下野
Shimotsuma 下間
Shimotsuma Shōzen (d. 1313)
　下間性善
Shin 真

shin (faith) 信
shin (true) 真
shin Bukkyō 新仏教
shin fushin 信不信
Shinano 信濃
Shinbutsu (1209-58) 真仏
shinbutsudo 真仏土
Shinchi (1504-85) 真智
shinden 寝殿
Shin'e (1205-81) 信慧
Shin'e (1434-1512) 真慧
shingi mitei 真偽未定
Shingon 真言
shingyō 信楽
shinji 神事
shinjin 信心
shinjin kangi 信心歓喜
shinjin ketsujō 信心決定
shinjin shōin 信心正因
shinjitsu hōdo 真実報土
shinjitsu no gyō 真実行
shinjitsu no gyōshin 真実行信
shinjitsu no kyō 真実教
shinjitsu no shin 真実信
shinjitsu no shinjin 真実信心
shinjitsu no shō 真実証
shinjitsu shutsuri 真実出離
Shinjō 心定
Shinkū (1146-1228) 信空
shinkui 身口意
Shinkyō (1237-1319) 真教
shinmei 神明
shinmon 真門
shinnyo 真如
Shinobu しのぶ
Shinran (1173-1262) 親鸞
Shinran muki 親鸞夢記
Shinran Shōnin monryo kyōmyōchō
    親鸞聖人門侶交名帳
Shinran Shōnin no inaka no
    godeshitachi
    しんらん上人のい中の御でしたち
Shinran Shōnin shōtōden
    親鸞聖人正統伝
Shinran'i 親鸞位
Shinrenbō Myōshin (b. 1211)
    信蓮房明信
Shinshō (1167-1230) 真性
Shinshō (1443-95) 真盛
shinshū 真宗
Shinshū 真宗
Shinshū saikō 真宗再興
Shintō 神道
shin'yū 辛酉
shippō rōgoku 七宝牢獄

Shirahata 白籏
Shirutani 汁谷
shisai 子細
shishi no shinchū no mushi
    師子の身中の蟲
shishi sōjō 師資相承
shishin 至心
shishin ni ekō seri 至心に回向せり
shishin ni ekō seshimetamaeri
    至心に回向せしめたまへり
shishō 支証
shishu zammai 四種三昧
shitennō 四天王
shō 証
sho nyorai tō 諸如来等
shōbatsu 賞罰
shōbō 正法
shobutsu tōdō 諸佛等同
shōdō 聖道
shōdōmon 聖道門
Shōe (d. 1559) 勝恵
shōen 庄園
shōgai 生害
Shōganbō 性願房
Shōgei (1341-1420) 聖冏
shōgun 将軍
Shojin hongaishū 諸神本懐集
shōjō 正定
Shōjō (1215-68) 正定
shōjōgō 正定業
Shōjōji 証誠寺
shōjōju 正定聚
Shōjōkōji 清浄光寺
Shōkōji 松岡寺
shōkotsu fukuyu 請乞福祐
Shōkū (1177-1247) 証空
shōmon shōken 少聞少見
shōmyō 称名
shōmyō hōon 称名報恩
shōnin 上人
Shōren'in 青蓮院
Shōshin 性信
Shōshin nembutsuge 正信念仏偈
Shōshinge 正信偈
Shōshinge taii 正信偈大意
shōshū 星宿
Shoshū jiin hatto 諸宗寺院法度
Shōsō (1366-1440) 聖聡
Shōtatsu 聖達
Shōtoku Taishi (574-622) 聖徳太子
shōton 性頓
Shōzōmatsu wasan 正像末和讃
shu sho kudoku 修諸功徳
shūchi 宗致
shugo 守護

shūhō　酬報

Shūi　拾遺

Shūi kotokuden ekotoba
　　　拾遺古徳伝絵詞

Shūi shinseki goshōsoku
　　　拾遺真蹟御消息

Shūjishō　執持鈔

shujō (sentient beings)　衆生

shujō (the emperor above)　主上

shukin　手巾

shukke　出家

shukugō　宿業

Shunjō (1166-1227)　俊芿

Shunjō (1255-1335)　舜昌

Shunjōbō (1121-1206)　俊乗房

Shuryōgon'in　首楞厳院

Shūshō (1270-1351)　宗昭

Shusse gan'i　出世元意

shuto　衆徒

sō　僧

sō ni arazu zoku ni arazu　非僧非俗

sōdō　草堂

Sōjiji　総持寺

sōju ringe ōjō　雙樹林下往生

sokuben ōjō　即便往生

sokushin jōbutsu　即身成仏

sokushin ōjō　即身往生

Songō shinzō meimon　尊号真像名文

sono myōgō o kikite　聞其名号

Sonren (b. 1182)　尊蓮

soshi sendoku　祖師先徳

Sōtō　曹洞

sotoba　卒都婆

sōton　相頓

sōtongyō　相頓教

suijaku　垂迹

sūkajō　数箇条

sūsen matsuji　数千末寺

sūsennin　数千人

Tachikawa Shingon　立川真言

tadaima no shōmyō　只今の称名

tai　体

taigū　胎宮

Takada　高田

Takada no shōnin daidai no kikigaki
　　　高田ノ上人代々ノ聞書

Takashina Yasutsune (d. 1201)
　　　高階泰経

tamau　たまふ

tanengi　多念義

T'an-luan (476-542?)　曇鸞

tanni　歎異

Tannishō　歎異抄

Tannishō kōrinki　歎異抄講林記

Tannishō monki　歎異抄聞記

tanomitatematsurite
　　　たのみたてまつりて

tanomu　たのむ

Tao-ch'o (562-645)　道綽

tariki　他力

tariki no shinjin　他力の信心

Ta-sheng ch'i-hsin lun　大乗起信論

tasuke tamae　たすけたまへ

tasuke tamae to tanomu
　　　たすけたまへとたのむ

taya　他屋

Ten'andō　天安堂

Tendai　天台

Tengu sōshi　天狗草子

tennyū　転入

Tōdaiji　東大寺

Togashi Kōchiyo　富樫幸千代

Togashi Masachika (1455-88)
　　　富樫政親

tokoro no hō　ところの法

toku (bald-headed)　禿

toku (blessing)　徳

tokubun　得分

tokudo　得度

Tokugawa　徳川

Tokugawa Ieyasu (1542-1616)
　　　徳川家康

tomogara　輩

tōmyō　燈明

tonchūton　頓中頓

Ton'en (d. 1447)　頓円

tongyō　頓教

tonsei　遁世

Toribami　鳥喰

Torinobe　鳥部

tōryū no anjin　当流の安心

tōryū no shinjin　当流の信心

Tosa　土佐

toshiyori　年老

tosotsu　都卒

tōtoku ōjō　当得往生

Tōtōmi　遠江

Tōzan　東山

Tsuchimikado (1195-1231)　土御門

Tsuda Sōkichi　津田左右吉

tsuizen　追善

tsune no shiki　つねの式

ubai　優婆夷

ubasoku　優婆塞

umaginu　馬衣

unengi　有念義

Uryūzu 瓜生津
Ushū Kōgan gokyōkai
　　羽州公厳御教誡
wa ga hakarawazaru
　　わがはからはざる
Wada 和田
Wang-sheng li-tsan chieh 往生礼讃偈
Wang-sheng lun chu 往生論註
wasan 和讃
wazato わざと
yamabushi 山臥
Yamamoto 山元
Yamashina 山科
Yamashiro 山城
Yamato 大和
yasuki kokoro やすきこころ
Yasutsune (d. 1201) 泰経
yin-yang 陰陽
yō 様
yō naki o yō to su 様なきを様とす
Yokawa 横川
yoki hito よきひと
Yokogoshi 横越
Yokosone 横曽根
yokushō 欲生
yōmon 要門
yonaka no hōmon 夜中の法門
Yoshino 吉野
Yoshizaki 吉崎
yuge 遊戯
yugyō 遊行
Yuienbō 唯円房
yuiju ichinin kuketsu 唯授一人口訣
Yuiryō (1323-1400) 唯了
Yuishinshō 唯信鈔
Yuishinshō mon'i 唯信鈔文意
Yuizen (b. 1266) 唯善

yūshi 猶子
yuyaku nembutsu 踊躍念仏
Zaijarin 摧邪輪
zan 慚
zasu 坐主
Zen 禅
Zenbōbō Jin'u 善法房尋有
Zen'en 善円
Zen'en no seikin 善円の制禁
zenjishiki danomi 善知識頼み
Zenjōbō 善乗房
Zenkōji 善光寺
Zennyō (1333-89) 善如
zenpon tokuhon 善本徳本
Zenran (d. 1292) 善鸞
Zenshin 善心
Zenshōbō densetsu no kotoba
　　禅勝房伝説の詞
zōaku 造悪
zōaku muge 造悪無碍
Zōga (917-1003) 増賀
zōgyō 雑行
zōgyō zasshu 雑行雑修
zōhō 像法
zokujishū 俗時衆
zonji 存じ
Zonkaku (1290-1373) 存覚
Zonkaku hōgo 存覚法語
Zonkaku ichigoki 存覚一期記
Zonnyo (1396-1457) 存如
Zuisenji 瑞泉寺
zukin 頭巾
Zenshin (Shinran) 善信
Zenshō 善性
Zenshōbō 善証房
Zenshōbō 善勝房

Notes

1. JŌDO SHINSHŪ

1. Daisetz T. Suzuki is largely responsible for popularizing the term Shin Buddhism in the West. See for example Daisetz T. Suzuki, *Shin Buddhism* (New York: Harper and Row, 1970), and *Collected Writings on Shin Buddhism* (Kyoto: Shinshū Ōtaniha, 1973).

2. For studies in English dealing with the life and thought of these two figures, see Alfred Bloom, "The Life of Shinran Shōnin: The Journey to Self-Acceptance," *Numen* 15 (1968): 1-62, and *Shinran's Gospel of Pure Grace* (Tucson: University of Arizona Press, 1965); Stanley Weinstein, "Rennyo and the Shinshū Revival," in *Japan in the Muromachi Age*, ed. John Whitney Hall and Toyoda Takeshi (Berkeley: University of California Press, 1977), pp. 331-58; Minor Lee Rogers, "Rennyo Shōnin 1415-1499: A Transformation of Shin Buddhist Piety" (Ph.D. dissertation, Harvard University, 1972); and Ira Michael Solomon, "Rennyo and the Rise of Honganji in Muromachi Japan" (Ph.D. dissertation, Columbia University, 1972).

3. This sectarian view of the two Buddhas and the seven patriarchs is an elaboration of Shinran's *Shōshin nembutsuge*, or more simply *Shōshinge*, a long hymn contained in his seminal work, the *Kyōgyōshinshō*, in Shinshū Shōgyō Zensho Hensanjo, ed., *Shinshū shōgyō zensho*, 5 vols. (Kyoto: Kōkyō Shoin, 1940-41), 2:43-46. For an English translation, see Ryukoku Translation Center, trans., *The Shōshin Ge* (Kyoto: Ryukoku University, 1966). Hereafter *Shinshū shōgyō zensho* is cited as *SSZ*.

4. This characterization of Shinran is the central theme of the *Hōonkō shiki*, *SSZ*, 3:655-60, a memorial service to Shinran composed thirty-three years after his death.

5. Within a generation of his death, Rennyo became revered as the "reviver of the Shinshū" (*Shinshū saikō*). See the *Rennyo Shōnin itokuki*, *SSZ*, 3:869, written in 1524 by Rennyo's son Rengo (1468-1543).

6. The Honganji was actually divided into two branches, the Nishi and the Higashi, in 1602, but the head priests of both are descended from Shinran and Rennyo, and claim religious authority through that lineage. Concerning the division of the Honganji, see Murakami Senjō, *Shinshū zenshi* (Tokyo: Heigo Shuppansha, 1916), pp. 517-44.

7. This general picture of Shinshū history is evident in the first sections of the Nishi Honganji's by-laws. See Hayashima Kyōshō and Bandō Shōjun, eds., *Nihon Bukkyō kiso kōza 5, Jōdo Shinshū* (Tokyo: Yūzankaku, 1979), pp. 61-63.

8. For an outline of the fundamental principles of Pure Land Buddhism, see G.P. Malalasekera, gen. ed., *Encyclopedia of Buddhism* (Colombo: Government of Ceylon, 1964-), 1:434-63, s.v. "Amita." Also see Mircea Eliade, gen. ed., *The Encyclopedia of Religion*, 16 vols. (New York: Macmillan and Free Press, 1987), s.v. "Amitābha," "Ching-t'u," and "Pure and Impure Lands."

9. Copies of these three sutras can be found in *SSZ*, 1:1-72, but the punctuation there is based on Shinran's unique interpretation of their contents. Another standard edition of these sutras is Takakusu Junjirō and Watanabe Kaikyoku, eds., *Taishō shinshū daizōkyō*, 85 vols. (Tokyo: Taishō Issaikyō Kankōkai, 1924-32), 12:265c-79a, 340b-46b, 346b-48b. Hereafter *Taishō shinshū daizōkyō* is cited as *TD*. No reconstructed Sanskrit title of the *Kanmuryōjukyō* is given here because the prevailing scholarly view is that the bulk of this sutra was composed in central Asia and perhaps parts of it even in China. See Fujita Kōtatsu, *Genshi Jōdo shisō no kenkyū* (Tokyo: Iwanami Shoten, 1970), pp. 121-36.

Rough English translations of these three sutras are contained in *The Shinshu Seiten: The Holy Scripture of Shinshu* (Honolulu: The Honpa Hongwanji Mission of Hawaii, 1955), pp. 7-106. Also, they are found in F. Max Müller, gen. ed., *Sacred Books of the East*, 50 vols. (Oxford: Clarendon Press, 1894), vol. 49: *Buddhist Mahāyāna Texts*, pt. 2, pp. 1-107, 161-203. The translations therein of the "Larger Sutra" and the "Smaller Sutra" are from variant Sanskrit manuscripts rather than from the Chinese texts recognized by the Shinshū. The most recent translation of the "Meditation Sutra" is Ryukoku Translation Center, trans., *The Sūtra of Contemplation on the Buddha of Immeasurable Life as Expounded by Śākyamuni Buddha* (Kyoto: Ryukoku University, 1984).

10. *Muryōjukyō*, *SSZ*, 1:9. The five damning offenses (*gogyaku*) consist of either of two sets. The Hīnayāna set includes: 1) killing one's father, 2) killing one's mother, 3) killing an *arhat*, 4) shedding the blood of a Buddha, and 5) destroying the harmony of the Buddhist order. The Mahāyāna set varies from text to text, but one example is: 1) destroying a stupa, burning the sutras, or stealing the treasures of Buddhism; 2) slandering the truth of Buddhism's three vehicles or abusing the sacred treasures of Buddhism; 3) attacking a monk; 4) killing father, mother, or *arhat*, shedding the blood of a Buddha, or destroying the harmony of the Buddhist order; and 5) not believing in the principle of causation and constantly committing the ten evil acts. Slander of the true teachings (*hihō shōbō*) means to deny the existence of the Buddha and to turn one's back on his teachings. See Yamabe Shūgaku and Akanuma Chizen, *Kyōgyōshinshō kōgi*, 3 vols. (1914; rpt. Kyoto: Hōzōkan, 1967-68), 1:63. This work is a sectarian commentary on Shinran's *Kyōgyōshinshō*.

11. *Muryōjukyō*, *SSZ*, 1:24. Shinran interpreted one phrase in this vow quite differently from the way it is translated here. He attributed the act of "extending religious merit to others" to Amida, not to the believer. To make this point, Shinran added the honorific suffix *seshimetamaeri* to the word *ekō* in the vow, clearly making it Amida's action. The implication of this is that believers achieve birth in Pure Land not because of any action they perform themselves but because of the religious merit that Amida has extended to them. This view differed from the way the vow had been interpreted by all of Shinran's predecessors.

12. *Amidakyō*, *SSZ*, 1:69.

13. *Kanmuryōjukyō*, *SSZ*, 1:65.

14. For a summary of the teachings of the seven Pure Land patriarchs, presented from the Shin point of view, see Ryūkoku Daigaku, ed., *Shinshū yōron* (Kyoto: Hyakkaen, 1953), pp. 12-40. A more recent work dealing with this topic is Ishida Mizumaro, *Shinran shisō to shichikōsō* (Tokyo: Daizō Shuppansha, 1976).

15. *Igyōbon*, *SSZ*, 1:253-54, 258-61. The *Igyōbon* is the ninth chapter of Nāgārjuna's *Jūjū bibasharon* (Skt. *Daśabhūmikavibhāṣāśāstra*?), *TD*, 26:20a-122b. Many scholars question whether Nāgārjuna was the actual author of this work.

16. *Jōdoron*, *SSZ*, 1:269-71. The full name of this work is the *Muryōjukyō ubadaisha ganshōge* (Skt. *Sukhāvatīvyūhopadeśa*?), *TD*, 26:230c-33a.

17. *Wang-sheng lun chu*, *SSZ*, 1:279, 281-82, 312-13, 343-48. For an English translation of this work, see Roger Jonathan Corless, "T'an-luan's Commentary on the Pure Land Discourse: An Annotated Translation and Soteriological Analysis of the *Wang-sheng lun chu* (T. 1819)" (Ph.D. dissertation, University of Wisconsin, 1973).

18. *An-lo chi*, *SSZ*, 1:378-79, 405-12. Concerning Tao-ch'o, see David Wellington Chappell, "Tao-ch'o (562-645): A Pioneer of Chinese Pure Land Buddhism" (Ph.D. dissertation, Yale University, 1976).

19. *Kuan ching shu*, *SSZ*, 1:442-43, 537-38, 554-55. For a study of this work, see Julian Pas, "Shan-tao's Commentary on the *Amitāyur-Buddhānusmṛti-sūtra*" (Ph.D. dissertation, McMaster University, 1973).

20. *Ōjōyōshū*, *SSZ*, 1:729-74, 798-811, 854-61. For a study of this work, see Allan A. Andrews, *The Teachings Essential for Rebirth* (Tokyo: Sophia University, 1973).

21. *Senjaku hongan nembutsushū* (or more simply *Senjakushū*), in Ishii Kyōdō, ed., *Shōwa*

shinshū Hōnen Shōnin zenshū (1955; rpt. Kyoto: Heirakuji Shoten, 1974), pp. 310–13, 317–20, 347. Hereafter *Shōwa shinshū Hōnen Shōnin zenshū* is cited as *HSZ*.

22. *Kyōgyōshinshō*, *SSZ*, 2:33–34, 58–59, 62; and *Mattōshō*, *SSZ*, 2:658–61. For English translations of these works see: Ryukoku Translation Center, trans., *The Kyō Gyō Shin Shō* (Kyoto: Ryukoku University, 1966), an abridged translation; Daisetz T. Suzuki, trans., *The Kyōgyōshinshō* (Kyoto: Shinshū Ōtaniha, 1973), also an abridged translation; Ueda Yoshifumi, gen. ed., *The True Teaching, Practice, and Realization of the Pure Land Way, A Translation of Shinran's Kyōgyōshinshō*, 4 vols. (Kyoto: Hongwanji International Center, 1983–), a complete translation; and Ueda Yoshifumi, gen. ed., *Letters of Shinran, A Translation of Mattōshō* (Kyoto: Hongwanji International Center, 1978).

23. *Kudenshō*, *SSZ*, 3:28; *Ganganshō*, *SSZ*, 3:46; *Gaijashō*, *SSZ*, 3:75; and Inaba Masamaru, ed., *Rennyo Shōnin ibun* (1937; rpt. Kyoto: Hōzōkan, 1972), *Ofumi*, no. 7 (1475.3.2.), pp. 60–61; no. 40 (1473.12.12), pp. 136–37; no. 55 (1474.3.3), pp. 181–83; no. 162 (undated), p. 459; and no. 172 (undated), pp. 470–71. Hereafter *Rennyo Shōnin ibun* is cited as *RSI*. All dates mentioned in this study are given with the year according to the Western calendar and the month and day according to the East Asian calendar.

24. See for instance *Jūjikyōron* (Skt. *Daśabhūmikasūtraśāstra?*), *TD*, 26:125ab; *Ta-sheng ch'i-hsin lun*, *TD*, 32:576a; and *San-lun hsüan-i*, *TD*, 45:1a. For a discussion of the idea of assailing heresy and revealing truth, see Mochizuki Shinkō, ed., *Bukkyō daijiten*, 10 vols. (Tokyo: Sekai Seiten Kankō Kyōkai, 1960), 5:4200c–4201a, s.v. *"Haja kenshō."* Hereafter *Bukkyō daijiten* is cited as *BDJ*.

25. The earliest occurrence of the word *ianjin* that I have found is in an 1802 ecclesiastical judgment issued by the doctrinal authority (*kōshi*) of the Higashi Honganji. See the *Ushū Kōgan gokyōkai*, in Shinshū Tenseki Kankōkai, ed., *Zoku Shinshū taikei*, 24 vols., *Bekkan*, 4 vols. (1936–41; rpt. Tokyo: Kokusho Kankōkai, 1976–77), 18:95. Hereafter *Zoku Shinshū taikei* is cited as *ZST*.

26. Okamura Shusatsu, ed., *Shinshū daijiten*, 3 vols. (1936; rpt. Kyoto: Nagata Bunshōdō, 1972), 1:40–42, s.v. *"Ianjin."* Hereafter *Shinshū daijiten* is cited as *SDJ*.

27. For an overview of the history of heresy in the Shinshū, see James C. Dobbins, "The Concept of Heresy in the Jōdo Shinshū," *Transactions of the International Conference of Orientalists in Japan* 25 (1980): 33–46; and "Shinshūshi ni okeru itan ni taishite no mikata," *Shinshūgaku* 63 (Feb. 1981): 44–55.

2. HŌNEN, THE EXCLUSIVE NEMBUTSU, AND SUPPRESSION

1. For an outline of the characteristics of Kamakura Buddhism, see Stanley Weinstein, "The Concept of Reformation in Japanese Buddhism," in *Studies in Japanese Culture*, ed. Saburō Ōta (Tokyo: Japan Pen Club, 1973), 2:75–86.

2. Hōnen is also known by the name Genkū. For consistency's sake I have used only the name Hōnen in reference to him throughout this study. Modern biographical works on Hōnen include: Tamura Enchō, *Hōnen Shōnin den no kenkyū* (Kyoto: Hōzōkan, 1972); Sanda Zenshin, *Seiritsushi teki Hōnen Shōnin shoden no kenkyū* (Kyoto: Kōnenji Shuppanbu, 1966); Tamura Enchō, *Hōnen*, Jinbutsu sōsho, no. 36 (Tokyo: Yoshikawa Kōbunkan, 1959); and Ōhashi Shunnō, *Hōnen—Sono kōdō to shisō*, Nihonjin no kōdō to shisō, no. 1 (Tokyo: Hyōronsha, 1970). There were many traditional biographies of Hōnen composed during the first two centuries after his death, but the most extensive one was the *Hōnen Shōnin gyōjō ezu*, commonly called the *Chokuden*, compiled by Shunjō (1255–1335). This biography, contained in Jōdoshū Shūten Kankōkai, ed., *Jōdoshū zensho*, 20 vols. (Tokyo: Jōdoshū Shūten Kankōkai, 1908–14), 16:100–698, is closely associated with the Chinzei branch of the Jōdoshū school. (Hereafter *Jōdoshū zensho* is cited as *JZ*.) A modern edition of this biography is included in Ikawa Jōkei, *Hōnen Shōnin den zenshū* (Osaka: Hōnen Shōnin Den Zenshū Kankōkai, 1967), pp. 3–318. A somewhat dated English translation of this biography can be found in Harper Havelock Coates

and Ryugaku Ishizuka, trans., *Hōnen, The Buddhist Saint*, 5 vols. (1925; rpt. Kyoto: Society for the Publication of Sacred Books of the World, 1949).

3. Tamura Enchō, *Hōnen*, pp. 33–35.

4. Mibu Taishun, *Eizan no shinpū* (Tokyo: Chikuma Shobō, 1967), pp. 90–92. See also Ishida Mizumaro, *Bonmōkyō* (Tokyo: Daizō Shuppansha, 1971), pp. 69–263. The Bodhisattva precepts, which are derived from the *Bonmōkyō*, (Skt. *Brahmajālasūtra?*) *TD*, 24:997a–1010a, were not originally used as the standard rules of discipline regulating Buddhist monks and nuns before Saichō's time. Rather, the *Shibunritsu*, (Skt. *Dharmagupta[ka]vinaya*) *TD*, 22:567a–1014b, containing 250 vows for monks and 348 for nuns, had been the basis for ordination in China and Japan. Up to Saichō's time, the Bodhisattva precepts were usually conferred on lay members as a form of commitment to Buddhist values. Occasionally, they were also administered to monks and nuns as a means of instilling Mahāyāna ideals, but not as a substitute for the *Shibunritsu* precepts. Saichō broke with this tradition and instituted the Bodhisattva precepts at Mt. Hiei as the sole criterion for ordination into the Tendai school. Though the Bodhisattva precepts are fewer in number and less detailed than those contained in the *Shibunritsu*, discipline was by no means less rigorous at the Enryakuji than in other schools. Saichō's purpose in instituting them was to give the precepts of Tendai a Mahāyāna rather than a Hīnayāna flavor. He adapted the Bodhisattva precepts for monastic use by supplementing them with temple rules—including a complete ban on liquor and women at Mt. Hiei—to make discipline there just as austere, at least in principle, as at other major temples. For a complete study of this question, see Paul Groner, *Saichō: The Establishment of the Japanese Tendai School* (Berkeley: Berkeley Buddhist Studies Series, 1984).

5. Saichō's program of religious training at the Enryakuji is outlined in his *Sange gakushōshiki*, *TD*, 74:623c–25b. This work is summarized by Mibu Taishun, *Eizan no shinpū*, pp. 95–133. It has been translated in Paul Groner, *Saichō: The Establishment of the Japanese Tendai School*, pp. 116–23, 131–35, 138–44. For a brief description of the content of religious study at Mt. Hiei around Hōnen's time, see Kuroda Toshio, *Jisha seiryoku*, Iwanami shinsho, no. 117 (Tokyo: Iwanami Shoten, 1980), pp. 135–36.

6. *Senjakushū*, *HSZ*, p. 320.

7. Ōhashi Shunnō, *Hōnen—Sono kōdō to shisō*, pp. 56–58, 83–85.

8. Tamura Enchō, *Hōnen Shōnin den no kenkyū*, pp. 122–32.

9. *Shichikajō kishōmon*, *HSZ*, pp. 787–93.

10. Sanda Zenshin, *Seiritsushi teki Hōnen Shōnin shoden no kenkyū*, pp. 124–33; and Tamura Enchō, *Hōnen*, pp. 85–94.

11. *Senjakushū*, *HSZ*, p. 347.

12. Ibid., p. 350.

13. Sanda Zenshin, *Seiritsushi teki Hōnen Shōnin shoden no kenkyū*, pp. 189–93; and Tsuji Zennosuke, *Nihon Bukkyōshi*, 10 vols. (Tokyo: Iwanami Shoten, 1960–61), 2:318–19. The original text of the petition to Shinshō no longer exists, but the gist of it is preserved in the writings of Nichiren (1222–82). See *Shōwa teihon Nichiren Shōnin ibun*, 4 vols. (Minobu: Sōhonzan Minobu Kuonji, 1952–59), 3:2260–61.

14. *Shichikajō kishōmon*, *HSZ*, pp. 783–93.

15. *Kōfukuji sōjō*, in Kamata Shigeo and Tanaka Hisao, eds., *Kamakura kyū Bukkyō*, Nihon shisō taikei, no. 15 (Tokyo: Iwanami Shoten, 1971), pp. 31–42. Translation of these nine items previously appeared in James C. Dobbins, "From Inspiration to Institution: The Rise of Sectarian Identity in Jōdo Shinshū," *Monumenta Nipponica* 41.3 (Autumn 1986): 333. Concerning the nine, see also Tamura Enchō, *Hōnen*, pp. 158–63; Akamatsu Toshihide, *Shinran*, Jinbutsu sōsho, no. 65 (Tokyo: Yoshikawa Kōbunkan, 1961), pp. 108–109; and Ōhashi Shunnō, "Hōnen to Jōdoshū kyōdan no keisei," in *Ajia Bukkyōshi, Nihonhen*, 9 vols., eds. Nakamura Hajime, Kasahara Kazuo, and Kanaoka Shūyū (Tokyo: Kōsei Shuppansha, 1972–76), 3:114–17.

16. Tamura Enchō, *Hōnen Shōnin den no kenkyū*, pp. 162–73; and Ōhashi Shunnō, *Hōnen—Sono kōdō to shisō*, pp. 171–84.

17. Okami Masao and Akamatsu Toshihide, eds., *Gukanshō*, Nihon koten bungaku taikei, no. 86 (Tokyo: Iwanami Shoten, 1967), pp. 294–95; and Nakajima Etsuji, *Gukanshō zenchūkai* (Tokyo: Yūseidō, 1969), pp. 520–24. I have also consulted the English translation of the *Gukanshō* by Delmer M. Brown and Ishida Ichirō, *The Future and the Past* (Berkeley: University of California Press, 1979), pp.171–73, but have rendered a number of sentences in a slightly different way, following primarily the notes in the two Japanese works cited here. A brief portion of this passage was previously published in James C. Dobbins, "From Inspiration to Institution: The Rise of Sectarian Identity in Jōdo Shinshū," pp. 334–35.

18. Taga Munehaya, *Jien*, Jinbutsu sōsho, no. 15 (Tokyo: Yoshikawa Kōbunkan, 1959), pp. 188–189. Jien was not always an adversary of Hōnen and the Pure Land movement. He had associations with them while he was head priest of the Shōren'in, a Tendai temple with proprietary ties to the Ōtani hermitage where Hōnen resided. Jien also administered the tonsure to Shinran in 1181, and he took custody of Hōnen's disciples Kōsai and Shōkū during the 1207 suppression. Nonetheless, by 1219, when the *Gukanshō* was written, the Pure Land movement had so polarized the religious community that Jien was forced to take sides with the traditional Buddhist schools.

19. *Shichikajō kishōmon*, *HSZ*, pp. 787–93. Only the beginning sentence in each of the seven articles has been translated here.

20. I have borrowed the term "licensed evil" from Ueda Yoshifumi, gen. ed., *Letters of Shinran, A Translation of Mattōshō*, p. 7.

21. *Tannishō*, *SSZ*, 2:794–95. For an English translation of this work, see Ryukoku Translation Center, trans., *The Tanni Shō* (Kyoto: Ryukoku University, 1980). Briefer accounts of the 1207 suppression are found in the *Kyōgyōshinshō*, *SSZ*, 2:201–202, and in the *Kechimyaku monjū*, *SSZ*, 2:721–22.

22. *Zaijarin*, *JZ*, 8:375. See also Tanaka Hisao, *Myōe*, Jinbutsu sōsho, no. 60 (Tokyo: Yoshikawa Kōbunkan, 1961), pp. 94–98; and Ōhashi Shunnō, "Hōnen to Jōdoshū kyōdan no keisei," in *Ajia Bukkyōshi, Nihonhen*, 3:107–109. For studies of Myōe in English, see Bandō Shōjun, "Myōe's Criticism of Hōnen's Doctrine," *Eastern Buddhist* (N.S.) 7.1 (May 1971): 37–54; and George Joji Tanabe, Jr., "Myōe Shōnin (1173–1232): Tradition and Reform in Early Kamakura Buddhism" (Ph.D. dissertation, Columbia University, 1983). Aspiration for enlightenment is the indispensable first step in the traditional path of the Bodhisattva in the quest for Buddhahood. See Taya Raishun, Ōchō Enichi, and Funabashi Issai, eds., *Bukkyōgaku jiten* (Kyoto: Hōzōkan, 1974), pp. 407–408, s.v. "*Bodaishin*." Hereafter *Bukkyōgaku jiten* is cited as *BGJ*.

23. Etani Ryūkai, *Gaisetsu Jōdoshūshi* (Tokyo: Ryūbunkan, 1978), p.55.

24. Ibid., p. 57. Ishida Mitsuyuki, *Nihon Jōdokyō no kenkyū* (Kyoto: Hyakkaen, 1963), pp. 167–69, points out that, though Ryūkan is commonly attributed with the *tanengi* position (cf. Gyōnen [1240–1321], *Jōdo hōmon genrushō*, *TD*, 84:197c), there is ample evidence in his writings that he did not interpret the *nembutsu* to be efficacious because of one's own effort (*jiriki*) in chanting it but rather because of Amida's power (*tariki*). Based on this understanding, Ryūkan acknowledged even a single *nembutsu* to be sufficient for birth in Pure Land, even though he encouraged regular practice of it. In this light, it would be difficult to characterize Ryūkan as a strict proponent of the *tanengi* doctrine. See Ryūkan's *Ichinen tanen funbetsuji*, *SSZ*, 2:766–69. For an English translation of this work, see Ueda Yoshifumi, gen. ed., *Notes on Once-calling and Many-calling, A Translation of Shinran's Ichinen-tanen mon'i* (Kyoto: Hongwanji International Center, 1980).

25. Etani Ryūkai, *Gaisetsu Jōdoshūshi*, p. 60.

26. Ibid., p. 66. Chōsai based the *nembutsu* on Amida's eighteenth vow and other practices on his twentieth vow.

27. Ishida Mitsuyuki, *Nihon Jōdokyō no kenkyū*, pp. 283, 292–93.

28. Ibid., pp. 451–53.

29. Ōhashi Shunnō, *Jishū no seiritsu to tenkai* (Tokyo: Yoshikawa Kōbunkan, 1973), pp. 26-27.

30. Ishida Mitsuyuki, *Nihon Jōdokyō no kenkyū*, p. 139. Concerning the single and the repeated *nembutsu* controversy, see James C. Dobbins, "The Single and the Repeated *Nembutsu* Extremes," in *Jōdokyō no kenkyū*, ed. Ishida Mitsuyuki Hakase Koki Kinen Ronbunshū Kankōkai (Kyoto: Nagata Bunshōdō, 1982), pp. 1045-60.

31. Tamura Enchō, *Nihon Bukkyō shisōshi kenkyū, Jōdokyōhen* (Kyoto: Heirakuji Shoten, 1959), pp. 35-50.

32. Ibid., pp. 63-64, gives specific dates of these suppressions.

33. Etani Ryūkai, *Gaisetsu Jōdoshūshi*, pp. 38-39.

34. Tamura Enchō, *Nihon Bukkyō shisōshi kenkyū, Jōdokyōhen*, p. 64.

35. Inoue Toshio, "Shinshū shoha no hatten," in *Shinshūshi gaisetsu*, ed. Akamatsu Toshihide and Kasahara Kazuo (Kyoto: Heirakuji Shoten, 1963), pp. 75-76.

3. SHINRAN AND HIS TEACHINGS

1. Shinran was also known by the names Hannen, Shakkū, Zenshin, and Gutoku at different periods in his life. I have used the name Shinran in most instances for the sake of consistency within this study.

2. *Shōzōmatsu wasan, SSZ*, 2:531, v. 116.

3. *Tannishō, SSZ*, 2:773-77.

4. This is true, for example, of the *Shinran Shōnin shōtōden*, in Yūki Reimon, gen. ed., *Gendaigoyaku Shinran zenshū*, 10 vols. (Tokyo: Kōdansha, 1974), 4:225-356, composed in 1715 by Ryōkū (1669-1733). Hereafter *Gendaigoyaku Shinran zenshū* is cited as *GSZ*.

5. *Godenshō, SSZ*, 3:639-54. The complete title of this work is the *Honganji no Shōnin Shinran denne*.

6. Kitanishi Hiromu, "Shinshūshi kenkyū no ayumi," in *Shinshūshi gaisetsu*, p. 5; and Fukushima Kazuto, *Kindai Nihon no Shinran* (Kyoto: Hōzōkan, 1973), pp. 121-22, 124, 136-37, 144-45, 149.

7. *Eshinni shōsoku, SSZ*, 5:99-115.

8. A summary of the historiography on Shinran's life is found in Miyazaki Enjun, "Shinran denki ni tsuite," in *GSZ*, 4:5-26.

9. This year can be calculated from a number of Shinran's surviving manuscripts in which he recorded both the date of composition and his age. See, for example, the *Ichinen tanen mon'i, SSZ*, 2:620, containing the date 1257 and Shinran's age, eighty-five. By subtracting his age from the date and then adding one year to account for *kazoedoshi* (the traditional East Asian practice of considering a person to be one year old at birth), Shinran's year of birth comes out to be 1173.

10. *Godenshō, SSZ*, 3:639.

11. Concerning the Hino family and its relation to the Shinshū, see Yamada Bunshō, *Shinshū shikō* (1934; rpt. Kyoto: Hōzōkan, 1968), pp. 175-86; Miyazaki Enjun, *Zoku Shinran to sono montei* (Kyoto: Nagata Bunshōdō, 1961), pp. 182-83; and Inoue Toshio, *Honganji* (Tokyo: Shibundō, 1962), p. 116. At the time of Shinran's birth, the Hino family was not in the preeminent ranks of the Kyoto aristocracy, but it rose to that level in the 1300s and from that time became a powerful ally to the Honganji. See Akamatsu Toshihide, *Shinran*, pp. 2-3.

12. Ownership of *genin*, or servants, by Shinran's family is documented in a letter by Shinran contained in the *Shūi shinseki goshōsoku, SSZ*, 2:724, and in letters by his wife, *Eshinni shōsoku, SSZ*, 5:99-100.

13. *Godenshō, SSZ*, 3:639.

14. For a sampling of the many works cited in the *Kyōgyōshinshō*, see Matsuno Junkō, *Shinran—Sono shōgai to shisō no tenkai katei* (Tokyo: Sanseidō, 1959), pp. 6-11.

15. *Eshinni shōsoku, SSZ*, 5:106.

16. The three levels of priests at Mt. Hiei were the scholar-monks (*gakushō* or *shuto*), the hall members or attendants (*dōshu*), and the temple menials (*santo*). See Kageyama Haruki, *Hieizan to Kōyasan* (Tokyo: Kyōikusha, 1980), p. 88. Concerning the specialized meaning of *dōsō*, as distinguished from *dōshu*, see Yamada Bunshō, *Shinshū shikō*, pp. 189-93.

17. The *jōgyō zammai* was one of four types of meditation outlined in Chih-i's *Mo-ho chih-kuan*, *TD*, 46:11a-16b. Amida Buddha is the focal point of this meditation, and the *nembutsu* is used as a meditative chant. Among the four types of Tendai meditation, the only other one that was widely established at Mt. Hiei was the *hangyō hanza zammai*, a twenty-eight day meditative retreat using the *Daihōdō daranikyō* during the first seven days and the *Hokekyō* in the last twenty-one days. The so-called Hokkedō, or Lotus Halls, at Mt. Hiei were erected as centers of this meditation. The *fudan nembutsu*, or continual *nembutsu*-chanting ceremony, was instituted by the Tendai priest Ennin after his return from China in 847. Ennin was the founder of the first Jōgyōdō on Mt. Hiei. Concerning the Enryakuji's meditation practices and halls, see *BGJ*, p. 194, s.v. "*Shishu zammai*"; and p. 398, s.v. "*Hokkezammaidō*." See also Yamada Bunshō, *Shinshū shikō*, pp. 194-96.

18. In the tenth and eleventh centuries, the word *dōsō* also referred to low-level temple priests at the Hokkedō as well, but by Shinran's time it meant only those at the Jōgyōdō. For a summary of the scholarship on the term *dōsō*, see Matsuno Junkō, *Shinran—Sono shōgai to shisō no tenkai katei*, pp. 2-3, 16-19; and Akamatsu Toshihide, *Shinran*, pp. 31-34.

19. *Kyōgyōshinshō*, *SSZ*, 2:202; *Eshinni shōsoku*, *SSZ*, 5:104-105; and *Godenshō*, *SSZ*, 3:640. There are two versions of the *Shinran muki*. The first, listing a total of three dreams, is reproduced in Furuta Takehiko, *Shinran shisō—Sono shiryō hihan* (Tokyo: Fuzanbō, 1975), pp. 3-5. Until recently this version was considered spurious, but Furuta, pp. 3-35, has attempted to refute all previous arguments against it, thereby reasserting the authenticity of the text. Several other scholars have followed Furuta's lead in recognizing it as genuine. See, for instance, Matsuno Junkō, *Shinran—Sono kōdō to shisō*, Nihonjin no kōdō to shisō, no. 2 (Tokyo: Hyōronsha, 1971), pp. 76-79; and Tamaki Kōshirō, *Shōtoku Taishi to Shinran*, *Hitotsu no suitei no kokoromi* (Tokyo: Shōtoku Taishi Hōsankai, 1980), p. 105. The second version, reproduced in Shinran Shōnin Zenshū Kankōkai, ed., *Teihon Shinran Shōnin zenshū*, 9 vols. (Kyoto: Hōzōkan, 1969-70), vol. 4, pt. 2, pp. 201-202, mentions only one dream. (Hereafter *Teihon Shinran Shōnin zenshū* is cited as *TSSZ*.) It contains a more detailed account of the third dream than the other *Shinran muki* does. The manuscript on which this second version is based was done by Shinran's disciple Shinbutsu (1209-58), and therefore must date no later than Shinbutsu's death in 1258. This version has always been considered authentic, since its contents are corroborated by the *Godenshō*, *SSZ*, 3:640, and more recently by a fragment written in Shinran's own handwriting discovered at the Senjuji temple. Concerning the fragment, see *TSSZ*, *Bessatsu* (supplementary volume), pp. 39-42.

20. *Shōzōmatsu wasan*, *SSZ*, 2:526-29; *Kōtaishi Shōtoku hōsan*, *SSZ*, 2:532-41; *Dai Nihon koku zokusan ō Shōtoku Taishi hōsan*, *SSZ*, 4:23-42; and *Songō shinzō meimon*, *SSZ*, 2:591-92.

21. *Eshinni shōsoku*, *SSZ*, 5:104.

22. Matsuno Junkō, *Shinran—Sono kōdō to shisō*, p. 83, points out that in content this verse strongly resembles a passage in the *Kakuzenshō* and therefore may have been patterned on it.

23. *Shinran muki* (Shinbutsu's version), *TSSZ*, vol. 4, pt. 2, pp. 201-202. The same account of the dream is recorded in the *Godenshō*, *SSZ*, 3:640.

24. *Shinran muki* (Three dreams version), in Furuta Takehiko, *Shinran shisō—Sono shiryō hihan*, p. 4; and *Godenshō*, *SSZ*, 3:640.

25. Though the *Godenshō* gives the date 1203, some manuscript copies of the work also contain the sexagenary date *shin'yū*, corresponding to the year 1201. One theory concerning this discrepancy is that Kakunyo wrote the *Godenshō* thinking that the

Rokkakudō dream occurred in 1203, but later, when he read Eshinni's letters, he realized that it took place in the same year that Shinran became Hōnen's disciple. Since the *Kyōgyōshinshō*, *SSZ*, 2:202, indicates that he turned to Hōnen's teachings in the year *shin'yū*, or 1201, Kakunyo added this sexagenary date to subsequent copies of the *Godenshō*. See Akamatsu Toshihide, *Shinran*, pp. 51-56.

26. *Kyōgyōshinshō*, *SSZ*, 2:202. Shakkū was Shinran's clerical name during this period.

27. *Kyōgyōshinshō*, *SSZ*, 2:202-203.

28. *Tannishō*, *SSZ*, 2:774.

29. *Eshinni shōsoku*, *SSZ*, 5:105. Similar passages are found in the *Tannishō*, *SSZ*, 2:774, and the *Shūjishō*, *SSZ*, 3:38.

30. *Godenshō*, *SSZ*, 3:644-46. Genchi is mentioned under his alternate clerical name, Seikanbō. A similar passage is found in the *Tannishō*, *SSZ*, 2:790-91.

31. For example, Shinran is not mentioned in the *Hōnen Shōnin gyōjō ezu*, in Ikawa Jōkei, *Hōnen Shōnin den zenshū*, pp. 3-318. Nonetheless, one passage on pp. 97-98 is remarkably similar to the debate over faith found in the *Godenshō*, *SSZ*, 3:645-46. This might imply that the *Godenshō*'s account is not a fabrication. Moreover, since the *Godenshō* was written more than a decade before the *Hōnen Shōnin gyōjō ezu*, it is possible that the *Godenshō*'s version is more accurate. See Masutani Fumio, *Shinran Dōgen Nichiren* (Tokyo: Shibundō, 1956), pp. 54-56.

32. *Shichikajō kishōmon*, *HSZ*, pp. 790-93. Shinran is listed as the priest Shakkū, which was his clerical name at the time. Genchi's name appears in fifth place. One problem in using the *Shichikajō kishōmon* as an indication of Shinran's position in Hōnen's following is that his disciples signed this document on three different days. Shinran's name, though eighty-seventh in the overall list, is seventh among the sixty-one followers who signed on the second day. This may indicate that his standing was not as low as the eighty-seventh position might imply.

33. There is some speculation that Tosa and Echigo were selected because of the intercession of Hōnen's devoted lay follower, Kujō Kanezane, the former regent. Although Kanezane was not able to have Hōnen's sentence commuted, he perhaps hoped to lessen its impact by having him sent to a place where he would receive hospitable treatment. He might have done the same for Shinran, though there is no concrete evidence that he did. The Kujō family held nominal proprietorship over the two provinces, and thus could have provided good treatment there. See Matsuno Junkō, *Shinran— Sono shōgai to shisō tenkai katei*, p. 163. Kanezane died a month after Hōnen went into exile. Hōnen apparently never arrived in Tosa, though he spent his exile on the island of Shikoku. See Tamura Enchō, *Hōnen*, pp. 194-97.

34. Akamatsu Toshihide, *Shinran*, pp. 115-16.

35. Tsuji Zennosuke, *Nihon Bukkyōshi*, 2:392-95.

36. Watanabe Tsunaya, ed., *Shasekishū*, Nihon koten bungaku taikei, no. 85 (Tokyo: Iwanami Shoten, 1966), p. 480. For an abridged English translation of the *Shasekishū*, see Robert E. Morrell, *Sand and Pebbles* (Albany: State University of New York Press, 1985). The passage cited here, from the *Shūi* section of the *Shasekishū*, is not included in Morrell's translation.

37. *Shichikajō kishōmon*, *HSZ*, p. 792.

38. *Kyōgyōshinshō*, *SSZ*, 2:201-202.

39. Watanabe Tsunaya, ed., *Shasekishū*, p. 186. For a summary in English of this passage, see Robert E. Morrell, *Sand and Pebbles*, p.144.

40. For a summary of these theories, see Kikumura Norihiko and Nishina Ryū, *Shinran no tsuma Eshinni* (Tokyo: Yūzankaku, 1981), pp. 74-82.

41. Kakunyo's *Kudenshō*, *SSZ*, 3:19, states that Eshinni had a total of six children. This agrees with the *Hino ichiryū keizu*, in Kashiwabara Yūsen, Chiba Jōryū, Hiramatsu Reizō, and Mori Ryūkichi, gen. eds., *Shinshū shiryō shūsei*, 13 vols. (Kyoto: Dōbōsha, 1974-83), 7:520-21, a genealogy drawn up in 1541 by Rennyo's son Jitsugo (1492-

1583). (Hereafter *Shinshū shiryō shūsei* is cited as *SSS*.) This genealogy indicates that Shinran had another son, Hanni, by an earlier marriage to Kujō Kanezane's daughter. This attribution, however, is highly suspect. See Hattori Shisō, *Zoku Shinran nōto* (1950; rpt. Tokyo: Fukumura Shuppan, 1970), pp. 5–8; and Miyazaki Enjun, *Zoku Shinran to sono montei*, pp. 24–26.

42. *Eshinni shōsoku, SSZ*, 5:100, 102, 103, 104, 106; and *Goshōsokushū, SSZ*, 2:704, 705–706, 707–709. Zenran was also known by the name Jishinbō, but for consistency's sake I have referred to him only as Zenran in this study. There is some evidence suggesting that Eshinni was not Zenran's mother. Concerning this issue, see Akamatsu Toshihide, *Shinran*, pp. 122–24.

43. *Eshinni shōsoku, SSZ*, 5:102. Specifically, the letter states that he was born in the *hitsuji* year and that he would be fifty-three years old. Since the letter is dated 1263, the *hitsuji* year referred to here, fifty-three years prior to that, is 1211.

44. *Hino ichiryū keizu, SSS*, 7:520–21.

45. One theory is that Eshinni's father, Miyoshi Tamenori, was a minor aristocratic official in Kyoto who held the post of *Echigo no suke*. Another theory is that he was head of a powerful local family in Echigo province. Even if Eshinni was born and reared in Echigo, she may have met Shinran in Kyoto while serving as a lady-in-waiting there. See Matsuno Junkō, *Shinran—Sono shōgai to shisō no tenkai katei*, pp. 168–74.

46. *Hōnen Shōnin denki*, in Ikawa Jōkei, *Hōnen Shōnin den zenshū*, p. 430.

47. See for example the textual gloss in the *Nembutsu myōgishū, JZ*, 10:384, an important work in the Chinzei branch of the Jōdoshū school.

48. For further discussion of this problem, see James C. Dobbins, "The Single and the Repeated *Nembutsu* Extremes," in *Jōdokyō no kenkyū*, pp. 1045–60.

49. *Shinran Shōnin monryo kyōmyōchō, SSS*, 1:984.

50. Yamada Bunshō, *Shinshūshi no kenkyū* (1934; rpt. Kyoto: Hōzōkan, 1979), pp. 3–4.

51. These commentaries, commonly called the *Kanmuryōjukyō shūchū* and the *Amidakyō shūchū*, are reproduced in *TSSZ*, vol.7.

52. Ishida Mitsuyuki, *Shinran kyōgaku no kiso teki kenkyū* (Kyoto: Nagata Bunshōdō, 1970), pp. 350–51; and *TSSZ*, vol. 7, pt. 2, pp. 158–59.

53. Ishida Mitsuyuki, *Shinran kyōgaku no kiso teki kenkyū*, pp. 350, 352–53.

54. One passage in the commentaries that foreshadows Shinran's emphasis on faith is a long quotation from Shan-tao's *Wang-sheng li-tsan chieh* concerning the three states of mind (*sanshin*) leading to birth in Pure Land. *Kanmuryōjukyō shūchū, TSSZ*, vol. 7, pt. 2, pp. 44–55. In the *Kyōgyōshinshō, SSZ*, 2:59–73, he equated these three to the concept of faith.

55. Ishida Mitsuyuki, *Shinran kyōgaku no kiso teki kenkyū*, pp. 351, 356–58, sees these commentaries as a transitional step between Hōnen's *Senjakushū* and Shinran's *Kyōgyōshinshō*.

56. The expression *sangan tennyū* was not used by Shinran himself, but was coined by later Shinshū scholars. Nevertheless, the concept is based on a passage in Shinran's *Kyōgyōshinshō, SSZ*, 2:166, in which he used the term *tennyū* to refer to his conversion from the so-called provisional path (*kemon*) and true path (*shinmon*) to the absolute way, the oceanlike vow singled out by Amida (*senjaku no gankai*), namely the eighteenth vow. See *SDJ*, 1:698–701, s.v. "*Sangan tennyū*."

57. Amida's nineteenth vow in the *Muryōjukyō, SSZ*, 1:9–10, reads:

> Were I to attain Buddhahood, and yet if I were not to appear surrounded by my host before sentient beings of the ten directions at the time of their death even though they gave rise to the aspiration for enlightenment, performed virtuous deeds, and established a vow with sincerity of heart desiring to be born in my Pure Land, then I would not accept true enlightenment.

This vow is the basis for the *nembutsu* deathbed ceremony popularized in Japan from Genshin's time, whereby dying believers are to envision Amida coming to usher them into Pure Land. Shinran saw the crux of this vow not as the promise of a deathbed appearance by Amida but as an indication that "virtuous deeds" could lead to Pure Land.

58. *Kyōgyōshinshō, SSZ*, 2:153–54; and *Jōdo sangyō ōjō monrui, SSZ*, 2:554–55. According to legend, Śākyamuni passed away in a forest of twin *śāla* trees and entered Nirvāṇa without remainder. It symbolizes therefore a portal from this expedient realm into Nirvāṇa.

59. The twentieth vow in the *Muryōjukyō, SSZ*, 1:10, reads:

> Were I to attain Buddhahood, and yet if sentient beings of the ten directions were not to achieve their reward even though they heard my name, concentrated their thoughts on my Pure Land, cultivated the basis of all virtue, with sincerity of heart extended their religious merit to others, and desired to be born in my Pure Land, then I would not accept true enlightenment.

60. *Kyōgyōshinshō, SSZ*, 2:156–58; and *Jōdo sangyō ōjō monrui, SSZ*, 2:557–59.

61. *Jōdo sangyō ōjō monrui, SSZ*, 2:551–54, 557.

62. *Kyōgyōshinshō, SSZ*, 2:166. For interpretations of various terms in this passage, see Yamabe Shūgaku and Akanuma Chizen, *Kyōgyōshinshō kōgi*, 3:1403–1409. The "vow for attainment" *(kasui no chikai)* usually refers to the twentieth vow. Therefore, the last sentence is interpreted by sectarian scholars to mean that, once people understand the twentieth vow, they are inevitably led to the eighteenth vow containing Amida's ultimate promise of salvation.

63. For a summary of the different scholarly opinions on this question, see Furuta Takehiko, *Shinran shisō—Sono shiryō hihan*, pp. 88–89; and Yamabe Shūgaku and Akanuma Chizen, *Kyōgyōshinshō kōgi*, 3:1404–1406.

64. *Eshinni shōsoku, SSZ*, 5:101–102.

65. There are a number of scholars who regard Shinran's "conversion via the three vows" not as a historical event but as a religious outlook which Shinran described in temporal terms. See Furuta Takehiko, *Shinran shisō—Sono shiryō hihan*, p. 89; and Yamabe Shūgaku and Akanuma Chizen, *Kyōgyōshinshō kōgi*, 3:1405.

66. *Jishin kyōninshin* is a phrase which Shinran borrowed from Shan-tao's *Wang-sheng li-tsan chieh, SSZ*, 1:661. Shinran quoted it in his *Kyōgyōshinshō, SSZ*, 2: 77, 165. This phrase is often cited as the sectarian rationale for propagating Shin Buddhism and expanding the religious community. See Futaba Kenkō, *Shinran no kenkyū* (Kyoto: Hyakkaen, 1970), pp. 339–65.

67. *Godenshō, SSZ*, 3:649. This episode is probably grounded in historical fact, since there is a reference in one of Shinran's letters to Myōhōbō's earlier "thoughts of wrongdoing" *(higagoto o omoi)*. See *Mattōshō, SSZ*, 2:686.

68. Kasahara Kazuo, *Shinran to tōgoku nōmin* (Tokyo: Yamakawa Shuppansha, 1975), pp. 269–71.

69. *Yuishinshō, SSZ*, 2:739–56. This copy is dated 1230. For an English translation of Seikaku's *Yuishinshō* and Shinran's commentary, see Ueda Yoshifumi, gen. ed., *Notes on Essentials of Faith Alone, A Translation of Shinran's Yuishinshō mon'i* (Kyoto: Hongwanji International Center, 1979).

70. This date appears in the *Kyōgyōshinshō, SSZ*, 2:168.

71. Akamatsu Toshihide, *Shinran*, p. 154.

72. *Kyōgyōshinshō, SSZ*, 2:1.

73. Jōdoshū Daijiten Hensan Iinkai, ed., *Jōdoshū daijiten*, 4 vols. (Tokyo: Sankibō, 1974–82), 1:296, s.v. "*Kyōgyōshō.*" Hereafter *Jōdoshū daijiten* is cited as *JDJ*.

74. Yūki Reimon, "Kyōgyōshinshō Shinkan bessensetsu no yōshi," in *Kyōgyōshinshō senjutsu no kenkyū*, ed. Keika Bunka Kenkyūkai (Kyoto: Hyakkaen, 1954), pp. 80–81.

75. Ōe Junjō, "Kyōgyōshinshō Shinkan bessensetsu no hihan," in *Kyōgyōshinshō senjutsu no kenkyū*, pp. 111–12, 135–36.

76. *Kyōgyōshinshō, SSZ*, 2:41, 44, 59, 60, 62, etc.

77. *Kyōgyōshinshō, SSZ*, 2:168.

78. One of the foremost scholars rejecting the 1224 date is Miyazaki Enjun, "Shinran no tachiba to Kyōgyōshinshō no senjutsu," in *Kyōgyōshinshō senjutsu no kenkyū*, pp. 1–37.

79. *Rokuyōshō, SSZ*, 2:275. This statement implies that the *Kyōgyōshinshō*, as it stands today, is an unfinished work.

80. The Bandō manuscript is now in the archives of the Higashi Honganji. Shinran in his old age apparently gave the Bandō manuscript to his disciple Renni (d. 1278), for his name appears on the cover of two of the fascicles. From him it somehow passed to two other disciples, Shōshin and Myōshō successively. Their names are found in postscripts at the end of the second and the sixth fascicles. See Ishida Mitsuyuki, "Kyōgyōshinshō kaidai," in *Shinran*, ed. Hoshino Genpō, Ishida Mitsuyuki, and Ienaga Saburō, Nihon shisō taikei, no. 11 (Tokyo: Iwanami Shoten, 1976), pp. 581–82. Two other copies of the *Kyōgyōshinshō* were once regarded as handwritten originals by Shinran. They are the Seisho manuscript at the Nishi Honganji and the Takada manuscript of the Senjuji temple. In recent years the authenticity of these manuscripts has come into question. See *TSSZ*, vol. 1, pp. 387–99.

81. This judgment is based on the similarity of the handwriting in the main portion of the manuscript and Shinran's handwriting in a copy of the *Yuishinshō* dated 1235. Other sections of the Bandō manuscript were copied as late as the 1250s, for the handwriting in them resembles his works written in that period. See Akamatsu Toshihide, *Zoku Kamakura Bukkyō no kenkyū* (Kyoto: Heirakuji Shoten, 1966), p. 49.

82. An example of such a change is the division of the last fascicle into *hon* and *matsu* halves. Concerning this and the 1247 date, see Ishida Mitsuyuki, "Kyōgyōshinshō kaidai," in *Shinran*, Nihon shisō taikei, no. 11, p. 585.

83. For a summary of the present scholarship on the composition of the *Kyōgyōshinshō*, see Ishida Mitsuyuki, *Shinran kyōgaku no kiso teki kenkyū*, pp. 295–312.

84. Works by Hōnen's other followers written during this period include *Gusanshingi* (1216) and *Gokuraku jōdo shūgi* (1220) by Ryūkan; *Yuishinshō* (1221) by Seikaku; *Gengibunshō* (1218) by Kōsai; *Kanmon yōgishō* (1221–26) by Shōkū; and *Matsudai nembutsu jushuin* (1228) by Benchō. See Ishida Mitsuyuki, *Shinran kyōgaku no kiso teki kenkyū*, p. 304.

85. Ishida Mitsuyuki, *Shinran kyōgaku no kiso teki kenkyū*, pp. 323–24.

86. Kasahara Kazuo, *Shinran to tōgoku nōmin*, pp. 212–15.

87. *Kyōgyōshinshō, SSZ*, 2:2. See also *Jōdo wasan, SSZ*, 2:496, v. 88, where Shinran described Śākyamuni as a manifestation (*ōgen*) of Amida.

88. *Kyōgyōshinshō, SSZ*, 2:2–3.

89. Ibid., 2:5.

90. Ibid., 2:22.

91. The most prominent example of Shinran's changing of the grammatical function of words is at the beginning of the third fascicle of the *Kyōgyōshinshō, SSZ*, 2:49, in his citation of the fulfilled form of the principal vow (*hongan jōju no mon*). The phrase which is ordinarily read *shishin ni ekō seri* is changed to *shishin ni ekō seshimetamaeri*, indicating that Amida extends religious merit to the believer with a sincere heart, not that the believer extends it to Amida. Shinran used this same grammatical alteration in the second fascicle in talking about the *nembutsu*: "The Tathāgata has already established his vow and has extended (*ese shitamau*) the practice (*gyō*) to sentient beings." See *Kyōgyōshinshō, SSZ*, 2:22.

92. This point seems to be the purpose of a series of quotations in the second fascicle, *Kyōgyōshinshō, SSZ*, 2:35–38, dealing specifically with *tariki*.

93. This question is touched upon in a passage near the end of the second fascicle, *Kyōgyōshinshō*, *SSZ*, 2:42-43.

94. *Kyōgyōshinshō*, *SSZ*, 2:68.

95. The reason that two different Japanese terms are given here for faith and for desire to be born in Pure Land is that slightly different wording is used in the two versions of the eighteenth vow in the *Muryōjukyō*, *SSZ*, 1:9, 24. Shinran used these terms interchangeably, even though the word *shingyō* implies faith and joy and is equivalent to *shinjin kangi* in the fulfilled form of the vow.

96. *Kyōgyōshinshō*, *SSZ*, 2:59, 68. Shinran used the term *faith* to refer both to the overall state of mind leading to salvation—*shinjitsu no shinjin*—and to one of the three components in that state of mind—*shingyō*. The relationship between the three is that sincerity (*shishin*) is the substance (*tai*) of faith (*shingyō*), and faith is the substance of desire to be born in Pure Land (*yokushō*). Each undergirds the other or is manifested in the other, and together they make up the state of true faith. See *Kyōgyōshinshō*, *SSZ*, 2:62, 65.

97. To show that these three are all gifts of Amida, Shinran again used the expression *ese shitamaeri* in reference to each. See *Kyōgyōshinshō*, *SSZ*, 2:60, 62, 66.

98. *Kyōgyōshinshō*, *SSZ*, 2:72. Shinran linked faith to the aspiration for enlightenment perhaps to answer Myōe's criticism of Hōnen. Myōe said that Hōnen's exclusive *nembutsu* ignores the first and crucial step in the Buddhist path, the aspiration for enlightenment (*bodaishin*), and thus lacks religious efficacy. Shinran, by defining faith as the essence of the *nembutsu* and by tying it to the aspiration for enlightenment, attempted to allay this criticism.

99. *Kyōgyōshinshō*, *SSZ*, 2:79.

100. Ibid., 2:67-68, 79.

101. The assurance that Amida will "embrace all and forsake none" is found in the *Kanmuryōjukyō*, *SSZ*, 1:57.

102. *Kyōgyōshinshō*, *SSZ*, 2:97. Shinran included in this group the three types of sentient beings whom Buddhists traditionally exclude from enlightenment: 1) those who commit the five damning offenses (*gogyaku*); 2) those who slander the true teachings (*hihō shōbō*); and 3) *icchantika* (*issendai*), incorrigible heretics who have cut off the karmic base of meritorious deeds (*danzengon*). Shinran saw faith as extending particularly to these undeserving beings, thereby assuring them of enlightenment in Amida's Pure Land. See *Kyōgyōshinshō*, *SSZ*, 2:81-102.

103. *Kyōgyōshinshō*, *SSZ*, 2:103.

104. Ibid., 2:106.

105. Ibid., 2:2, 5, 48, 106-107.

106. Ibid., 2:107.

107. Ibid., 2:111-12.

108. Ibid. 2:106-107, 118-19.

109. Ibid., 2:120.

110. The quotations in the *Shinbutsudo* fascicle, particularly those from the *Nehangyō*, deal with these themes, though not specifically in reference to Amida. Shinran, by citing them here, sought to apply these themes to the true Buddha and Pure Land. See *Kyōgyōshinshō*, *SSZ*, 2:123-28.

111. *Kyōgyōshinshō*, *SSZ*, 2:140.

112. Ibid., 2:139.

113. Ibid., 2:141.

114. Ibid., 2:143-46, 151.

115. Ibid., 2:143, 144, 158.

116. Ibid., 2:147-48, 153-54. Shinran distinguished between "the open and the concealed meaning" (*kenshō onmitsu no gi*) in the *Kanmuryōjukyō* and the *Amidakyō*. He believed that their open meaning is different from the *Muryōjukyō*'s but that the concealed meaning is the same.

117. *Kyōgyōshinshō*, *SSZ*, 2:168. Shinran adopted the Chinese dating of the Buddha's death—948 B.C.—and therefore believed his own time to be more than 2000 years after Śākyamuni's, in the period of *mappō*. Concerning the Chinese dating of the Buddha's life, see Matsubara Yūzen, *Mappō tōmyōki no kenkyū* (Kyoto: Hōzōkan, 1978), pp. 35–38.

118. *Kyōgyōshinshō*, *SSZ*, 2:168. For a description of the five corruptions, see *JDJ*, 1:455–56, s.v. *"Gojoku."*

119. *Kyōgyōshinshō*, *SSZ*, 2:168–74. Shinran's views on the decline of the Dharma and the degeneration of the clergy are contained in a long quotation from the *Mappō tōmyōki*, in Tsumaki Jikiryō, ed., *Shinshū zensho*, 74 vols. (Kyoto: Zōkyō Shoin, 1913–16), 58:495–502, which is a work of obscure origins popularly attributed to Saichō. For an annotated edition of the *Mappō tōmyōki*, see Matsubara Yūzen, *Mappō tōmyōki no kenkyū*, pp. 176–94. Hereafter *Shinshū zensho* is cited as *SZ*. For an English translation of the *Mappō tōmyōki*, see Robert F. Rhodes, trans., "Saichō's Mappō Tōmyōki: The Candle of the Latter Dharma," *Eastern Buddhist* (N.S.) 13.1 (Spring 1980): 79–103.

120. *Kyōgyōshinshō*, *SSZ*, 2:167–68.

121. Ibid., 2:175–201, contains a long series of quotations concerning such beliefs and practices. Specific mention of the ones listed here is found on pp. 175, 175–77, 190, 191, and 200.

122. *Kyōgyōshinshō*, *SSZ*, 2:175.

123. Ibid., 2:81–97; see particularly pp. 81, 87, and 97.

124. Akamatsu Toshihide, *Zoku Kamakura Bukkyō no kenkyū*, pp. 61–63; and *Shinran*, pp. 201–203.

125. Miyazaki Enjun, *Shinran to sono montei* (Kyoto: Nagata Bunshōdō, 1956), pp. 76–80.

126. For a summary of the various theories concerning Shinran's departure from the Kantō, see Kitanishi Hiromu, "Shinran to sono kyōdan," in *Nihon Bukkyōshi*, 3 vols., ed. Ienaga Saburō, Akamatsu Toshihide, and Tamamuro Taijō (Kyoto: Hōzōkan, 1967), 2:104–105.

127. Kasahara Kazuo, *Shinran to tōgoku nōmin*, pp. 324–28, is the foremost proponent of this theory.

128. Yamada Bunshō, *Shinshū shikō*, pp. 292–93, espouses this view.

129. The year 1156 is the earliest date appearing in Eshinni's letters. The three children mentioned in them are Oguro Nyobō, Shinrenbō Myōshin, and Masukata Ubō. See *Eshinni shōsoku*, *SSZ*, 5:100, 102, 103, 104.

130. There are two letters by Shinran containing the name Imagozen no haha. See *Shūi shinseki goshōsoku*, *SSZ*, 2:725–26. Concerning the theory that this refers to another wife, see Akamatsu Toshihide, *Shinran*, pp. 74, 256–57; and Miyazaki Enjun, *Shinran to sono montei*, pp. 92–94.

131. *Eshinni shōsoku*, *SSZ*, 5:103, 105–106, 111. See also Matsuno Junkō, *Shinran—Sono shōgai to shisō no tenkai katei*, pp. 407–408.

132. Eshinni's wealth is reflected in the fact that she owned at least eight *genin*, or servants, as indicated in the *Eshinni shōsoku*, *SSZ*, 5:99–100.

133. Miyazaki Enjun, *Zoku Shinran to sono montei*, pp. 182–85.

134. *Saishu kyōjū ekotoba*, *SSZ*, 3:824–25.

135. *Kokorozashi* are mentioned in a number of Shinran's letters. See, for example, *Mattōshō*, *SSZ*, 2:671, 688, 689; and *Goshōsokushū*, *SSZ*, 2:698, 705.

136. *Godenshō*, *SSZ*, 3:650–51, 653. See also *Kosha shokan*, *TSSZ*, vol. 3, pt. 2, p. 56; and Yamada Bunshō, *Shinshū shikō*, p. 301.

137. *Iya onna yuzurijō*, *TSSZ*, vol. 4, pt. 1, pp. 177–78.

138. Miyazaki Enjun, *Shinran to sono montei*, pp. 111–113. The word *genin* refers to household servants that were virtual property, though their status was not as abject as outright slaves in that they often acted in behalf of their masters as overseers of their property.

139. *Mattōshō, SSZ,* 2:683. Kasahara Kazuo, *Shinran to tōgoku nōmin,* p. 292, indicates that during this period one *koku* of rice, the average amount needed to feed one person for a year, cost about one *kanmon.*

140. A reproduction of the Anjō no Miei is found in Miyazaki Enjun, *Shinran to sono montei,* p. 174, and a description of the portrait on p. 114.

141. For a list of Shinran's letters and the persons to whom they are addressed, see Miyaji Kakue, *Goshōsokushū kōsan* (Kyoto: Hyakkaen, 1974), pp. 8-9.

142. The precise date that Renni came to Kyoto is not known. It is clear that he was a close protégé of Shinran's, since one of Renni's letters is included with Shinran's in the *Mattōshō, SSZ,* 2:674-80. Also, Renni was apparently given the Bandō copy of the *Kyōgyōshinshō,* for his name is written on the covers of two of the fascicles. See *Kyōgyōshinshō, SSZ,* 2:103, fn.1; and 2:120, fn.1. Renni is best remembered for a dream he had, recorded in the *Godenshō, SSZ,* 3:641-42, in which Shinran was seen as a manifestation of Amida Buddha. Concerning Renni, see Yamada Bunshō, *Shinshū shikō,* pp. 297-98.

143. *Godenshō, SSZ,* 3:651-53.

144. Yamada Bunshō, *Shinshū shikō,* p. 276, cites a 1244 order *(gechijō)* handed down by the Kamakura *bakufu* reprimanding *nembutsu* priests for entering shrines without properly purifying themselves.

145. *Mattōshō, SSZ,* 2:681-83, 686-89.

146. *Bokieshi, SSZ,* 3:783.

147. Miyazaki Enjun, *Shinran to sono montei,* pp. 118-19.

148. *Shūi shinseki goshōsoku, SSZ,* 2:727; and *Kechimyaku monjū, SSZ,* 2:718.

149. *SDJ,* 3:1529-30, s.v. *"Chishiki kimyō."* Ōhara Shōjitsu, *Shinshū kyōgaku no dentō to koshō* (Kyoto: Nagata Bunshōdō, 1965), pp. 96-98, construes Zenran's approach to the Kantō following as emphasizing reliance on one's religious master.

150. *Goshōsokushū, SSZ,* 2:708.

151. *Eshinni shōsoku, SSZ,* 5:105-106; *Godenshō, SSZ,* 3:641-42; and *Kudenshō, SSZ,* 3:20-22.

152. *Tannishō, SSZ,* 2:773-75. Yamada Bunshō, *Shinshū shikō,* pp. 319-20, speculates that this visit occurred in the wake of Zenran's claim to secret teachings.

153. Shinran's disownment letter is found in *Shūi shinseki goshōsoku, SSZ,* 2:727-29. Concerning the authenticity of this letter, see Miyaji Kakue, *Shinran den no kenkyū* (Kyoto: Hyakkaen, 1968), pp. 195-210.

154. According to Shinran's disownment letter, Zenran disparaged the eighteenth vow by "likening it to a wilted flower" *(shibomeru hana ni tatoete)*. *Shūi shinseki goshōsoku, SSZ,* 2:728.

155. Shinran was aware of the great number of illiterate believers among his followers, and he made a conscious effort in his later writings to present ideas simply and clearly so that they could understand. See *Yuishinshō mon'i, SSZ,* 2:638.

156. Concerning the dates and order of composition of Shinran's writings, see Ishida Mitsuyuki, *Shinran kyōgaku no kiso teki kenkyū,* pp. 315-19.

157. Akamatsu Toshihide, *Shinran,* p. 309. One of Shinran's most important discussions of this topic appears in a letter in the *Mattōshō, SSZ,* 2:666-68, probably written during this period.

158. *Kyōgyōshinshō, SSZ,* 2:63, 79. Shinran elaborated on this theme somewhat in 1248 when he composed the *Jōdo wasan, SSZ,* 2:497.

159. *Mattōshō, SSZ,* 2:680-81.

160. *Ichinen tanen mon'i, SSZ,* 2:606-607; and *Mattōshō, SSZ,* 2:684.

161. *Songō shinzō meimon, SSZ,* 2:568-69; and *Mattōshō, SSZ,* 2:684-85. For an English translation of the *Songō shinzō meimon,* see Ueda Yoshifumi, gen. ed., *Notes on the Inscriptions on Sacred Scrolls, A Translation of Shinran's Songō shinzō meimon* (Kyoto: Hongwangi International Center, 1981).

162. Shinran's letters that address this question include *Mattōshō, SSZ,* 2:658-61, 661-

62, 662–63, 666–68, 680–81, 684–85; *Goshōsokushū, SSZ*, 2:711–13; *Goshōsokushū Zenshōbon, SSZ*, 2:714–15; and *Kechimyaku monjū, SSZ*, 2:720–21.

163. Jōshinbō was one follower who was hesitant to accept this idea. See *Mattōshō, SSZ*, 2:680–81.

164. Shinran believed that enlightenment is attained upon birth in Pure Land. While still living in this world, the believer is not yet enlightened, but is assured of enlightenment because of faith. This idea is intimated in the *Mattōshō, SSZ*, 2:674.

165. Shinran's discussion of contrivance (*hakarai*) is found in many of his letters. See, for instance, *Mattōshō, SSZ*, 2:663–64, 669–70. No single letter specifically criticizes licensed evil advocates for pretensions of being "equal to the Tathāgatas," but several intimate that this kind of abuse was occurring. See for example the *Goshōsokushū, SSZ*, 2:712. Among the rules instituted in some Shinshū congregations within a century of Shinran's death is one forbidding members from claiming to be equal to Buddhas. See *Jōkōji nijūikkajō seikin, SSS*, 1:1010. This suggests that there was frequent abuse of this idea in the early Shinshū.

166. *Shōzōmatsu wasan, SSZ*, 2:522, v. 55; *Songō shinzō meimon, SSZ*, 2:576; *Mattōshō, SSZ*, 2:663–64; and *Kechimyaku monjū, SSZ*, 2:720–21.

167. *Mattōshō, SSZ*, 2:658–59, 667; *Goshōsokushū, SSZ*, 2:712; *Goshōsokushū Zenshōbon, SSZ*, 2:715; and *Kechimyaku monjū, SSZ*, 2:720.

168. *Gonengyō no oku ni kiseru onkotoba, HSZ*, p. 1179. This is the only instance in which the words *gi naki o gi to su* appear in Hōnen's writings. Unfortunately there are questions about the authenticity of this particular work. The expression more commonly attributed to Hōnen is: "Not having form is to be the form" (*yō naki o yō to su*). See for example *Hōnen Shōnin gyōjō ezu*, in *Hōnen Shōnin den zenshū*, p. 108; and Kakunyo's biography of Hōnen, *Shūi kotokuden ekotoba, SSZ*, 3:765–66. Concerning this problem, see Wakaki Yoshihiko, "Shinran shokan ni arawareta Hōnen Shōnin," *Shinshūgaku* 45–46 (March 1972): 159–80.

169. This universal applicability of the *nembutsu* is the theme of Hōnen's *Ichimai kishōmon, HSZ*, pp. 415–16, though the phrases "not to have definition" and "not to have form" are not specifically used to describe it there.

170. *Goshōsokushū, SSZ*, 2:712.

171. Nakamura Hajime, *Bukkyōgo daijiten*, 3 vols. (Tokyo: Tōkyō Shoseki, 1975), 1:557–558, s.v. "*Jinen*"; 2:1235, s.v. "*Hōni*"; and *BGJ*, p. 211, s.v. "*Jinen*"; p. 400, s.v. "*Hōni.*" Hereafter *Bukkyōgo daijiten* is cited as *BGDJ*.

172. *Mattōshō, SSZ*, 2:663. The same passage with slight modification is found in *Shōzōmatsu wasan, SSZ*, 2:530.

173. *Mattōshō, SSZ*, 2:664.

174. *Mattōshō, SSZ*, 2:663–64, is dated 1258, when Shinran was eighty-six years old. Only two other letters are dated after this one: *Mattōshō, SSZ*, 2:664–66; and *Shūi shinseki goshōsoku, SSZ*, 2:724–25. Shinran's essay on *jinen hōni* is also recorded in a version dated 1258 written down by Kenchi (1226–1310), *TSSZ*, vol. 3, pt. 2, pp. 54–55, and in a version appended to the *Shōzōmatsu wasan, SSZ*, 2:530–31, done in 1260, two years before Shinran's death.

175. *Shūi shinseki goshōsoku, SSZ*, 2:726.

176. Ibid., 2:725.

177. The letter addressed to the Hitachi followers is dated 11.12. The one to "Imagozen no haha" is dated 11.11. See *Shūi shinseki goshōsoku, SSZ*, 2:725–26. Shinran's death occurred on 1262.11.28.

178. Akamatsu Toshihide, *Kamakura Bukkyō no kenkyū* (Kyoto: Heirakuji Shoten, 1957), pp. 1–28.

179. Miyazaki Enjun is one of the major dissenters from this theory. For his critique of Akamatsu's thesis, see Miyazaki Enjun, *Shinran to sono montei*, pp. 85–103.

180. *Godenshō, SSZ*, 3:653. A more abbreviated account of Shinran's death is found

at the end of some of the early manuscripts of the *Kyōgyōshinshō.* See *TSSZ,* vol. 1, pp. 395–99.

4. LICENSED EVIL

1. Ishida Mitsuyuki, *Ianjin* (Kyoto: Hōzōkan, 1951), pp. 52–68, 74–76; Sumida Chiken, *Igishi no kenkyū* (Kyoto: Chōjiya Shoten, 1960), pp. 16–36, 68–72, 142–65, 206–207; and Kasai Daishū, *Shinshū no igi to sono rekishi* (Osaka: Seibundō, 1977), pp. 12–94. These works all belong to the field of Shin dogmatics concerned with Shin heresy (*ianjin*). They adopt Shinran's teachings axiomatically as a measuring stick for orthodoxy, and apply them ex post facto to the religious controversies of his day to identify what elements in them were heretical. For other works in this genre, see Nakajima Kakuryō, *Ianjinshi* (Tokyo: Mugasanbō, 1912); Suzuki Hōchin, *Shinshū gakushi,* in *Shinpen Shinshū zensho,* 30 vols., ed. Shinpen Shinshū Zensho Kankōkai (Kyoto: Shibunkaku, 1975–77), 20:483–701; Nakai Gendō, *Ianjin no shujusō* (Tokyo: Dōbōsha, 1930); and Ōhara Shōjitsu, *Shinshū igi ianjin no kenkyū* (Kyoto: Nagata Bunshōdō, 1956).

2. Of the three terms, the only one actually used by Shinran is *hōitsu muzan,* in *Mattōshō, SSZ,* 2:682. Both *hōitsu,* self-indulgence, and *muzan,* remorselessness, are mental components which, according to classical Abhidharma Buddhism, obstruct the path to enlightenment. See *BGJ,* p. 150, s.v. *"Zan";* and pp. 393–94, s.v. *"Hōitsu."* The term *hongan bokori,* though not used by Shinran, was current in his day or at least soon thereafter, for it appears in the *Tannishō, SSZ,* 2:782, 785. The term *zōaku muge* was not in common use, but its two components—*zōaku,* meaning "to commit evil," and *muge,* meaning "without obstruction"—were frequent expressions in the Buddhist writings of the period. *Zōaku,* for example, appears in Hōnen's *Shichikajō kishōmon, HSZ,* p. 788, and *muge* is found throughout Shinran's *Kyōgyōshinshō, SSZ,* 2:1, 35, 41, 43, 60, 62, 119, 129, 157, etc.

3. *Juhō yōjinshū,* as cited in Ishida Mitsuyuki, *Ianjin,* p. 35. The author's name is sometimes given as Shinjō and sometimes as Shōjō, depending on the source. See Mikkyō Gakkai, ed., *Mikkyō daijiten,* 6 vols. (Kyoto: Hōzōkan, 1969–70), 3:1096; and Ono Genmyō, *Bussho kaisetsu daijiten,* 13 vols., and *Bekkan,* 1 vol. (Tokyo: Daitō Shuppansha, 1932–35, 1975–78), 5:104, s.v. *"Juhō yōjinshū."* (Hereafter *Bussho kaisetsu daijiten* is cited as *BKDJ.*) For a concise study of the Tachikawa cult, see Mizuhara Gyōei, *Jakyō Tachikawaryū no kenkyū* (Kyoto: Shinbundō, 1931).

4. Ishida Mitsuyuki, *Ianjin,* pp. 35, 59–60.

5. *Nembutsu myōgishū, JZ,* 10:376. Also cited in Ōhara Shōjitsu, *Shinshū igi ianjin no kenkyū,* pp. 81–82; and, in part, in Ishida Mitsuyuki, *Ianjin,* pp. 40–41.

6. *Shichikajō kishōmon, HSZ,* p. 788.

7. *BGDJ,* 2:1094, s.v. *"Hakai muzan,"* cites instances of this term in the *Myōe Shōnin yuikun* and the *Heike monogatari,* both composed in the thirteenth century.

8. Taken from Hōnen's letter entitled *Motochika shin o torite hongan o shinzuru no yō, HSZ,* p. 552. See also *JDJ,* 1:69–70, s.v. *"Ichinengi."*

9. Taken from the *Sanzengi mondō,* by Ryūkan, as quoted in Ishida Mitsuyuki, *Jōdo kyōgaku no kenkyū,* 2 vols. (Tokyo: Daitō Shuppansha, 1979), 1:230. See also *JDJ,* 2:550–51, s.v. *"Tanengi."*

10. For an analysis of the various Pure Land controversies that are aligned with the so-called faith and practice extremes of Pure Land thought, see Tokunaga Michio and Matsui Junshi, "Zenran no igi to sono haikei," *Shūgakuin ronshū* 42 (January 1975): 76, 80.

11. *Ichinengi chōji kishōmon, HSZ,* pp. 800–801, 803–805. This letter is historically linked to another entitled *Etchū no kuni Kōmyōbō e tsukawasu gohenji, HSZ,* pp. 537–39, which indicates that Kōsai's disciples were the ones propagating the single *nembutsu* doctrine in the Hokuriku region. Its postscript says: "The itinerant priest Kōmyōbō in the province of Etchū has written a letter stating that the disciples of Jōkakubō [Kōsai]

put forward the doctrine of the single *nembutsu* and obstruct the repetition of the *nembutsu*." See Sumida Chiken, *Igishi no kenkyū*, pp. 18-23.

12. Inoue Mitsusada, *Shintei Nihon Jōdokyō seiritsushi no kenkyū* (Tokyo: Yamakawa Shuppansha, 1975), pp. 231, 251-53.

13. *Ōjōki, HSZ*, p. 1007. See also *JDJ*, 3:176-77, s.v. "*Hakai ōjō.*"

14. *Zenshōbō densetsu no kotoba, HSZ*, p. 463. See also *JDJ*, 2:11-12, s.v. "*Saitai chikuhatsu.*"

15. Ōno Tatsunosuke, *Shinkō Nihon Bukkyō shisōshi* (Tokyo: Yoshikawa Kōbunkan, 1973), pp. 211, 270. See also *Gaijashō, SSZ*, 2:67-68.

16. *Kyōgyōshinshō, SSZ*, 2:201; and *Tannishō, SSZ*, 2:795.

17. In the *Chinzei myōmoku mondō funjinshō, JZ*, 10:433, written by the Chinzei scholar Myōzui (d. 1787), Shinran is identified along with Kōsai and Gyōkū as an advocate of the single *nembutsu* doctrine. For further discussion of this question, see Sumida Chiken, *Igishi no kenkyū*, pp. 18-23; and Kasai Daishū, *Shinshū no igi to sono rekishi*, pp. 29-37.

18. Brief passages in this section have already appeared in James C. Dobbins, "The Single and the Repeated *Nembutsu* Extremes," in *Jōdokyō no kenkyū*, pp. 1045-60. See that article for a more extensive discussion of the single and repeated *nembutsu* doctrines and of the faith and practice factions of the Pure Land movement.

19. *Tannishō, SSZ*, 2:775.

20. Ibid., 2:775-76.

21. *Mattōshō, SSZ*, 2:682.

22. *Goshōsokushū, SSZ*, 2:703-704.

23. *Mattōshō, SSZ*, 2:686-87.

24. *Goshōsokushū, SSZ*, 2:701-702.

25. *Mattōshō, SSZ*, 2:682.

26. Ibid., 2:691.

27. Ibid., 2:690-91.

28. Ibid., 2:682, 689.

29. *Goshōsokushū, SSZ*, 2:696-97, 700-702, 708. It is unclear exactly where local authorities implemented their suppression of the *nembutsu*. Shinran's primary letter concerning *nembutsu* suppression (*Goshōsokushū, SSZ*, 2:700-703) is addressed to *nembutsu* followers in general rather than to a particular congregation or individual.

30. *Goshōsokushū, SSZ*, 2:682, 288. In certain editions of Shinran's letters, the name Zenshōbō is written differently, either as Zenjōbō or as Zenshōbō (different characters). Some scholars hypothesize that Zenshōbō was actually Kōsai's disciple Zenshō, spreading the single *nembutsu* doctrine in the Kantō region. Others suspect him of Shingon affiliations, perhaps even ties with the Tachikawa cult. See Ōhara Shōjitsu, *Shinshū igi ianjin no kenkyū*, pp. 88-90.

31. There has been considerable controversy over the exact social status of Shinran's early followers. Yamada Bunshō, Hattori Shisō, and Kasahara Kazuo maintain that they were peasant farmers (*nōmin*). Ienaga Saburō believes many were samurai. Akamatsu Toshihide thinks local overseers (*myōshu*), merchants, and artisans were also numerous. See Kitanishi Hiromu, "Shinran to sono kyōdan," in *Nihon Bukkyōshi*, 2:99-102.

32. *Mattōshō, SSZ*, 2:682.

33. Ōhara Shōjitsu, *Shinshū igi ianjin no kenkyū*, pp. 90-91.

34. *Goshōsokushū, SSZ*, 2:700.

35. Matsuno Junkō, "Zōaku muge to Shinran," *Shinshū kenkyū* 3 (1957): 109, points to this as the pivotal issue of the licensed evil problem affecting Shinran's followers in the Kantō.

36. *Ichinen tanen mon'i, SSZ*, 2:613.

37. *Shōzōmatsu wasan, SSZ*, 2:528, v. 101.

38. Shinran alluded to such practices in a long series of quotations near the end of the *Kyōgyōshinshō*, *SSZ*, 2:175–201. For an interpretation of this passage, see Honganjiha Shūgakuin, ed., *Honden kensan jukki*, 2 vols. (Kyoto: Nagata Bunshōdō, 1976), 2:517; and Fugen Daien, *Shinshū gairon* (Kyoto: Hyakkuen, 1950), pp. 280–81.

39. *Kyōgyōshinshō*, *SSZ*, 2:175.

40. Hattori Shisō, *Shinran nōto* (1948; rpt. Tokyo: Fukumura Shuppan, 1970), p. 100, following the theory of Yamada Bunshō, dates this letter 1255. Miyaji Kakue, *Shinran den no kenkyū*, p. 192, dates it one year earlier, 1254.

41. *Goshōsokushū*, *SSZ*, 2:700–701.

42. Shigematsu Akihisa, *Nihon Jōdokyō seiritsu katei no kenkyū* (Kyoto: Heirakuji Shoten, 1964), pp. 596–99; and Sasaki Tesshin, "Nembutsu hihō ni tsuite no ikkōsatsu," *Indogaku Bukkyōgaku kenkyū* 10.1 (January 1962): 209–212.

43. Kasahara Kazuo, *Shinran to tōgoku nōmin*, pp. 379–82, 384–85.

44. Akamatsu Toshihide is one of the few scholars who takes issue with this interpretation. Hattori Shisō and Kasahara Kazuo construe these expressions to be references to the local authorities. Akamatsu claims they refer only to *nembutsu* heretics, not to the authorities. See Akamatsu Toshihide, *Zoku Kamakura Bukkyō no kenkyū*, pp. 4–7.

45. *Kyōgyōshinshō*, *SSZ*, 2:201. This statement was such a harsh indictment of the emperor that the *Shinshū shōgyō zensho* edition of the *Kyōgyōshinshō*, first published in 1940 at a time of patriotic fervor in Japan, omitted the words "the emperor above" (*shujō*) to moderate Shinran's criticism. See Mori Ryūkichi, *Honganji* (Tokyo: San'ichi Shobō, 1973), p. 232.

46. *Goshōsokushū*, *SSZ*, 2:701–702.

47. Ibid., 2:705. Shinran probably borrowed the "worm" analogy from the *Renge mengyō*, *TD*, 12:1072c, or from Hōnen's letter entitled *Etchū no kuni Kōmyōbō e tsukawasu gohenji*, in which the expression is applied to adherents of licensed evil and the single *nembutsu* doctrine. It is certain that Shinran knew of this letter because it is included in Shinran's copy of Hōnen's writings, *Saihō shinanshō*, *SSZ*, 4:162–64.

48. These are the seven singled out in the *Shōshinge* in Shinran's *Kyōgyōshinshō*, *SSZ*, 2:43–46, and in the *Kōsō wasan*, *SSZ*, 2:501–15.

49. Tsuda Sōkichi, *Bungaku ni arawaretaru kokumin shisō no kenkyū*, 5 vols. (Tokyo: Iwanami Shoten, 1965), 1:584–85. The article by Ishida Yoshikazu, "Shinran no kyōsetsu o meguru itan no mondai," *Risō* 569 (October 1980): 31–32, first brought this passage to my attention.

5. THE EARLY SHINSHŪ

1. See for example *Kyōgyōshinshō*, *SSZ*, 2:1, 2. See also Kaneko Daiei, "Kakunyo Shōnin to shūso to no kankei," in *Kakunyo Shōnin no kenkyū*, *Mujintō* 22 (1917): 242.

2. *Senjakushū*, *HSZ*, pp. 311–13.

3. Of Hōnen's major disciples, Ryūkan, Kūamidabutsu, Kōsai, and Shinran are known not to have established temples. Tamura Enchō, *Nihon Bukkyō shisōshi kenkyū*, *Jōdokyōhen*, p. 53.

4. *Tannishō*, *SSZ*, 2:774.

5. Ibid., 2:776; and *Mattōshō*, *SSZ*, 2:684, 685, 688, 692.

6. Ishida Mitsuyuki, *Rennyo* (Kyoto: Jirinsha, 1949), p. 9, ventures only a modest estimate of "several thousand" (*sūsennin*), whereas Kasahara Kazuo, "Shinran to Shinshū kyōdan no keisei," in *Ajia Bukkyōshi*, *Nihonhen*, 3:209–12, places the number around 100,000. The basis of Kasahara's calculation is that one of Shinran's disciples, Chūtarō, is identified in the *Goshōsokushū*, *SSZ*, 2:706, as having over ninety *nembutsu* followers. Shinran had at least fifty disciples in the Kantō. Kasahara hypothesizes that if each of them had twenty additional disciples, and if all had a congregation of approximately one hundred followers each, then the total would be 100,000.

7. *Shinran Shōnin monryo kyōmyōchō*, *SSS*, 1:982–1007. This work dates from the early 1300s, according to Yamada Bunshō, *Shinshūshi no kenkyū*, p. 351.

8. Chiba Jōryū, *Shinshū kyōdan no soshiki to seido* (Kyoto: Dōbōsha, 1978), pp. 3–4.

9. *Gaijashō*, *SSZ*, 3:73.

10. Miyazaki Enjun, *Shinran to sono montei*, pp. 150–51, 153–54, 159–60.

11. Ibid., pp. 156–59. Shinran's handwritten inscriptions of Amida's name survive in three different forms: a six-character version, *Namu Amida Butsu*; an eight-character version, *Namu Fukashigi Kō Butsu*; and a ten-character version, *Kimyō Jin Jippō Mugekō Nyorai*. In Kamakura Buddhism, Nichiren (1222–82) and Ippen (1239–89) are also known to have used religious inscriptions as objects of worship, though at a slightly later period than Shinran's creation of the Amida inscription.

12. Nabata Ōjun, *Shinran wasan shū*, Iwanami bunko, no. 318-3 (Tokyo: Iwanami Shoten, 1976), pp. 340–41.

13. *Zen'en no seikin*, *Jōkōji nijūikkajō seikin*, and *Ryōchi no sadame*, *SSS*, 1:1008–1011. See also Chiba Jōryū, *Shinshū kyōdan no soshiki to seido*, pp. 7–21.

14. *Zen'en no seikin*, *SSS*, 1:1008–1009. See also Chiba Jōryū, *Shinshū kyōdan no soshiki to seido*, pp. 7–10.

15. Chiba Jōryū, *Shinshū kyōdan no soshiki to seido*, pp. 9–10.

16. *Tannishō*, *SSZ*, 2:784.

17. *Haja kenshōshō*, *SSZ*, 3:178. All the occupations mentioned in this passage were forbidden to Buddhist priests under the injunctions of the following Bodhisattva precepts: 10) not to possess weapons, 12) not to deal in commercial activities, and 29) not to make a living by one of the prohibited occupations, which include farming. See Ishida Mizumaro, *Bonmōkyō*, pp. 157–60, 163–66, and 202–204.

18. Chiba Jōryū, *Shinshū kyōdan no soshiki to seido*, p. 15; and Miyazaki Enjun, *Shinran to sono montei*, pp. 162–64.

19. Miyazaki Enjun, *Shinran to sono montei*, pp. 160–61.

20. Ibid., p. 155.

21. Ibid., pp. 149–65. Miyazaki Enjun was one of the first to use the categories of *ritsuryō Bukkyō* and *han ritsuryō Bukkyō* to classify trends in the history of Japanese Buddhism, but they have since been developed more fully by Futaba Kenkō in *Shinran no kenkyū*, pp. 76–122, 257–78; in *Kodai Bukkyō shisōshi kenkyū* (Kyoto: Nagata Bunshōdō, 1962); and in *Shiryō Nihon Bukkyōshi* (Kyoto: Yamazaki Hōbundō, 1971).

22. Futaba Kenkō, *Shinran no kenkyū*, pp. 307–308.

23. *Tannishō*, *SSZ*, 2:773–95. For English translations of the *Tannishō* see: Ryukoku Translation Center, trans., *The Tanni Shō*; Bandō Shōjun and Harold Stewart, trans., "Tannishō: Passages Deploring Deviations of Faith," *Eastern Buddhist* (N.S.) 13.1 (Spring 1980): 57–78; and Dennis Hirota, trans., *Tannishō: A Primer* (Kyoto: Ryukoku University, 1982).

24. *Tannishō*, *SSZ*, 2:773, 778–79, 790–93. For an analysis of these three segments of the *Tannishō*, see Hirose Takashi, "Tannishō no seikaku—Toku ni sanjo o chūshin to shite," *Ōtani gakuhō* 47.1 (June 1967): 1–13.

25. This is the edition of the *Tannishō* contained in *SSZ*, 2:773–95.

26. Concerning early manuscripts and editions of the *Tannishō*, see Kaneko Daiei, *Tannishō*, Iwanami bunko, no. 732 (Tokyo: Iwanami Shoten, 1950), pp. 35–40; and Taya Raishun, "Tannishō no chosaku ni tsuite no mondai," in *GSZ*, 1:126–27.

27. *Tannishō*, *SSZ*, 2:795. For an interpretation of Rennyo's postscript, see Hirose Takashi, *Tannishō no shomondai* (Kyoto: Hōzōkan, 1978), pp. 11–49.

28. Compare *Tannishō*, *SSZ*, 2:773, lines 10–11; 2:775, lines 4–5; and 2:783, lines 2 ff.; with *Kudenshō*, *SSZ*, 3:5, lines 15 ff.; 3:31, lines 11–12; and 3:7, lines 14 ff. These passages were singled out for comparison by the Tokugawa scholar-priest Jinrei, *Tannishō*

kōrinki, in Shinshū Tenseki Kankōkai, ed., *Shinshū taikei*, 37 vols. (1916–25; rpt. Tokyo: Kokusho Kankōkai, 1974–76), 23:1–2. Hereafter *Shinshū taikei* is cited as *ST*.

29. *Tannishō*, *SSZ*, 2:773.

30. Ibid., 2:773–74, 778. The first passage cited states, "Here you have come crossing the borders of more than ten provinces. . . ." The second one says, "We urged [each other] on in our trek to the distant capital. . . ." Ryōshō, *Tannishō monki*, *ZST*, *Bekkan*, 1:2–3, points out that from the tone of the passages the author of the *Tannishō* seems to have been one who made the long journey to Kyoto to see Shinran.

31. *Tannishō*, *SSZ*, 2:777, 782.

32. Ryōshō, *Tannishō monki*, *ZST*, *Bekkan*, 1:2–6, was the first to make this attribution. The vast majority of scholars have accepted his thesis.

33. *Bokieshi*, *SSZ*, 3:780. Yuienbō is also included in the early list of Shinran's disciples, *Shinran Shōnin monryo kyōmyōchō*, *SSS*, 1:982–84. Ryōsho, *Tannishō monki*, *ZST*, *Bekkan*, 1:6–7, distinguishes between Yuienbō of Kawada and another disciple of Shinran's, Yuienbō of Toribami in Musashi province.

34. The Hōbutsuji temple in Ibaragi prefecture claims Yuienbō as its founder. See Teranishi Enen, "Genshi Shinshū kyōdan ni okeru dōjō ni tsuite," *Ōtani gakuhō* 36.1 (June 1956): 70–71.

35. For an overview of the history and development of the *Tannishō*, see Miyazaki Enjun, "Tannishō no seiritsu to kyōdan no dōkō," in *Gendai o ikiru kokoro Tannishō* (Tokyo: Asahi Shinbunsha, 1973), pp. 69–78.

36. For parallel or related passages in Shinran's writings and in other Shinshū works, see Taya Raishun, *Tannishō shinchū* (Kyoto: Hōzōkan, 1973), pp. 41–42, 48–50, 55, 63–67, 75, 79–80, 82–91. One famous quotation found only in the *Tannishō* is: "I, Shinran, have never uttered a single *nembutsu* out of filial devotion to my mother and father" (*SSZ*, 2:776). Others that appeared first in the *Tannishō* and later in other writings are: "Even the good person can be born in Pure Land. How much more so the evil person!" (*SSZ*, 2:775); and "As for me, Shinran, I do not have a single disciple" (*SSZ*, 2:776).

37. *Tannishō*, *SSZ*, 2:775. The expression *akunin shōki* itself does not appear in the *Tannishō* or in any of Shinran's writings. The idea is couched in slightly different terminology in the *Tannisho*, *SSZ*, 2:775, as "the evil person embodying the true cause of birth in Pure Land" (*akunin motomo ōjō no shōin nari*); and in the *Kyōgyōshinshō*, *SSZ*, 2:148, as "the evil person being the object of birth in Pure Land" (*akunin ōjō no ki*).

38. *Tannishō*, *SSZ*, 2:777.

39. Ibid.

40. Ibid., 2:776.

41. Ibid., 2:777.

42. Ibid., 2:776.

43. Some early Shinshū congregations observed this practice, as indicated by *Ryōchi no sadame*, *SSS*, 1:1010–11.

44. *Tannishō*, *SSZ*, 2:776–77.

45. For an outline and brief explanation of the eight, see Umehara Shinryū, "Tanni no kokoro to itanha," in *GSZ*, 1:137–47.

46. *Tannishō*, *SSZ*, 2:779, 783.

47. Ibid., 2:773.

48. Ibid., 2:779, 780, 782, 785, 786, 787, 789, 789.

49. Ibid., 2:784.

50. A few scholars claim that the *Tannishō* is far more fatalistic here about karmic proclivities than Shinran was. Hence, its discussion of wrongdoing is not an accurate portrayal of Shinran's own thought. See Kojima Eijō, "Tannishō no sōten," *Indogaku Bukkyōgaku kenkyū*, 13.1 (January 1965): 75. Nonetheless, the overall theme of this

paragraph is consistent with Shinran's ideas—that is, despite the human inclination to
see good works as beneficial and evil ones as detrimental, it is Amida's vow alone that
ensures salvation. Concerning this question, see also Iwakura Mosaji, "Shukugō ni
tsuite," in *GSZ*, 1:180–93.

51. *Tannishō*, *SSZ*, 2:773.
52. Ibid., 2:783, is a paraphrase of Shinran's statement found in the *Mattōshō*, *SSZ*,
2:691.
53. *Tannishō*, *SSZ*, 2:780–82, 789–90. For further discussion of this point, see
Tanigawa Tetsuzō, "Gakumon to shinkō," in *GSZ*, 1:170–79.
54. *Tannishō*, *SSZ*, 2:785–87.
55. For the locus classicus of this idea, see *Kanmuryōjukyō*, *SSZ*, 1:65.
56. *Tannishō*, *SSZ*, 2:777.
57. Ibid., 2:785. This interpretation of the *nembutsu* as an expression of indebtedness and gratitude can be traced to Shinran's *Goshōsokushū*, *SSZ*, 2:697.
58. *Tannishō*, *SSZ*, 2:786. Concerning this concept, especially in connection with
Shingon Buddhism, see *BGJ*, pp. 307–308, s.v. *"Sokushin jōbutsu."*
59. *Tannishō*, *SSZ*, 2:789. For Nichiren's original assertion, see *Nembutsu muken
jigokushō*, in *Shōwa teihon Nichiren Shōnin ibun*, 1:34–42. For a general discussion of this
entire question, see Ōhara Shōjitsu, "Henji dagoku no igi to nembutsu mukensetsu,"
Indogaku Bukkyōgaku kenkyū, 11.1 (1963): 1–9.
60. *Tannishō*, *SSZ*, 2:786–87, 789.
61. Ibid., 2:779.
62. Concerning this polarization of the Pure Land movement, see James C. Dobbins, "The Single and the Repeated *Nembutsu* Extremes," in *Jōdokyō no kenkyū*, pp. 1045–
60.
63. The *Tannishō*'s treatment of this issue is completely consistent with Shinran's
handling of it in the *Mattōshō*, *SSZ*, 2:669–70. See Taya Raishun, *Tannishō shinchū*, p.
95.
64. *Tannishō*, *SSZ*, 2:782–85.

6. KAKUNYO AND THE CREATION OF THE HONGANJI TEMPLE

1. According to sectarian tradition Shinran, while residing in the Kantō, constructed a small private chapel at Takada in which he enshrined an Amida triad supposedly received from the Zenkōji temple in the province of Shinano. This chapel is
considered the precursor of the Senjuji. See Takadaha Senjuji Onki Hōmuin Monjobu,
ed., *Senjuji shiyō* (Mie: Takadaha Senjuji, 1912), p.16.
2. The *dōjō* of Yuienbō, who is reputed to be the author of the *Tannishō*, also dated
back approximately to Shinran's lifetime, but it did not undergo transformation into a
temple until 1471. His *dōjō*, rather than the Senjuji, typifies the course of congregational development in early Shinshū history. See Teranishi Enen, "Genshi Shinshū kyōdan
ni okeru dōjō ni tsuite," pp. 70–71.
3. According to one legend, the Bukkōji was established by Shinran in 1212, but
scholars commonly agree that it was actually founded in 1324 by Ryōgen (1295–1336)
under the temple name Kōshōji in Yamashina, east of Kyoto. In 1329 it was moved to
Shibutani in Kyoto, only a few minutes' walk from the Honganji, and its name was
changed to Bukkōji. See *SDJ*, 3:1868–70, s.v. "Bukkōji."
4. The story of the Honganji and its rise to power has been recorded in detail in
both Japanese and English sources. Important prewar studies of Honganji history include: Murakami Senjō, *Shinshū zenshi*; Kusaka Murin, *Shinshūshi no kenkyū* (1931; rpt.
Kyoto: Rinsen Shoten, 1975); Yamada Bunshō, *Shinshū shikō*, and *Shinshūshi no kenkyū*;
and Tanishita Ichimu, *Zōho Shinshūshi no shokenkyū* (1941; rpt. Kyoto: Dōbōsha, 1977).

Prominent postwar studies include: Inoue Toshio, *Honganji*; Akamatsu Toshihide and Kasahara Kazuo, eds., *Shinshūshi gaisetsu*; and Honganji Shiryō Kenkyūjo, ed., *Honganjishi*, 3 vols. (Kyoto: Jōdo Shinshū Honganjiha, 1961–69). In English, the early history of the Honganji is summarized in Ira Michael Solomon, "Rennyo and the Rise of Honganji in Muromachi Japan"; and in Stanley Weinstein, "Rennyo and the Shinshū Revival."

5. Miyazaki Enjun, *Shinran to sono montei*, pp. 159–60.

6. Shigematsu Akihisa, *Kakunyo*, Jinbutsu sōsho, no. 123 (Tokyo: Yoshikawa Kōbunkan, 1964), pp. 112–13. The biography that Kakunyo wrote is the *Shūi kotokuden ekotoba*, SSZ, 3:665–768.

7. *Honganjishi*, 1:136–43. Kakushinni held only occupancy rights to the land, which she passed on to Shinran's followers. During this period of Japanese history, property rights were layered and multipartite, rather than controlled by a single individual. Over and above Kakushinni's claim, the Shōren'in imperial temple held absentee proprietorship rights (*honjoshiki*). The Myōkōin temple acted as the Shōren'in's administrator (*kanrei*), and under it the Hōrakuji temple held overseer rights (*ryōshu*) to the land. These three temples were all Tendai, associated in one way or another with Mt. Hiei. See Shigematsu Akihisa, *Kakunyo*, pp. 66–67.

8. Shigematsu Akihisa, *Kakunyo*, pp. 109–10.

9. *Honganjishi*, 1:157–58.

10. For a concise overview of the process of sectarian development in the Shinshū between the time of Shinran and Rennyo, see James C. Dobbins, "From Inspiration to Institution: The Rise of Sectarian Identity in Jōdo Shinshū," pp. 331–43.

11. Kakunyo also went by the name Shūshō, but for consistency's sake I have referred to him only as Kakunyo throughout this study.

12. Anichibō Shōkū should not be confused with the Shōku who founded the Seizan branch.

13. For further details about Kakunyo's early years, see Shigematsu Akihisa, *Kakunyo*, pp. 14–29; and Inaba Enjō, "Kakunyo Shōnin denkō," in *Kakunyo Shōnin no kenkyū*, *Mujintō* 22 (1917): 13–15.

14. Shigematsu Akihisa, *Kakunyo*, pp. 109–110.

15. *Hōonkō shiki*, SSZ, 3:655–60. For a French translation of this work, see Jérôme Ducor, trans., "Hōonkō-shiki: Cérémonial du sermon de reconnaissance," *The Pure Land* (N.S.) 1 (December 1984): 132–41.

16. *Hōonkō shiki*, SSZ, 3:659.

17. *Godenshō*, SSZ, 3:641–42. Kakunyo recorded the same dream in his *Kudenshō*, SSZ, 3:20–22, compiled in 1331, along with a dream of Eshinni's in which she saw Shinran as an incarnation of Kannon. See also *Eshinni shōsoku*, SSZ, 5:105–106. Visions of this sort were not unusual in the Pure Land tradition. According to Hōnen's *Senjakushū*, HSZ, p. 349, Amida appeared in Shan-tao's dreams in the guise of a monk and conveyed to him the contents of the *Hsüan-i fen* section of Shan-tao's *Kuan ching shu*.

18. See, for example, Shinran's statements about Shōtoku Taishi and Hōnen in *Jōdo wasan*, SSZ, 2:500; *Kōsō wasan*, SSZ, 2:513, v. 106; and *Shōzōmatsu wasan*, SSZ, 2:526, v. 84.

19. Kakushinni left three letters bequeathing her rights to the Ōtani property to "master Shinran's followers in the countryside" (*Shinran Shōnin no inaka no godeshitachi*): one dated 1277.10.25, which no longer survives; one dated 1277.11.7; and one 1280.10.25. In a passage appended to the last letter, she designated her descendants (*ama ga kodomo*) as its caretaker (*rusu*). See *Honganjishi*, 1:137–43.

20. The Ōtani memorial was totally dependent on Shinshū followers in the provinces for its economic support. The Kantō congregations supplied the resources to build the first chapel in 1272; to buy an adjoining plot of land and expand the facilities in

1296; to have a petition exempting the Shinshū from *nembutsu* suppression heard before the Kamakura *bakufu* in 1301; to have a succession dispute between Yuizen and Kakunyo heard before the imperial court, the Kyoto constabulary (*kebiishichō*), and the Shōren'in temple beginning in 1307; to have a new image of Shinran sculpted and to rebuild the chapel in 1311, after Yuizen left it in ruins; and to purchase a used temple building and have it reassembled on the Ōtani property in 1338, after the chapel was destroyed during warfare in 1336. See Shigematsu Akihisa, *Kakunyo*, pp. 34–35, 43, 48, 50–51, 65–72, and 148–49.

21. A copy of Kakushinni's letter naming Kakue is contained in *Honganjishi*, 1:143–44.

22. Ibid., 1:170–71.

23. The Shōren'in, an imperial temple of the Tendai school located near the Ōtani memorial, exercised absentee proprietorship rights over the land on which the memorial was located. It therefore assumed adjudicative authority in the dispute between Yuizen and Kakunyo. In 1309 the Shōren'in ruled against Yuizen's claim to property rights of the memorial and upheld Kakushinni's will granting the Kantō followers final say over it. A copy of the Shōren'in's decision is included in *Honganjishi*, 1:161–62. Before the final decision was announced, Yuizen foresaw the outcome and absconded from Kyoto with the image of Shinran from the chapel and with Shinran's ashes. Near Kamakura he set up his own chapel, the Ikkōdō, and there enshrined these treasures. In 1310 Shinran's disciple Kenchi of Takada saw to it that another image of Shinran was sculpted for the Ōtani memorial. Twenty-eight years later, after Yuizen's death, Senkū (d. 1343), also of Takada, was responsible for having the original image returned to Ōtani. It is unclear what happened to Shinran's ashes. According to one legend, they were mixed with lacquer and painted on the sculpture of Shinran that is now enshrined in the Goeidō of the Nishi Honganji. According to another legend, they were hidden inside that sculpture. Concerning the complex question of the original image of Shinran enshrined at Ōtani and the disappearance of his ashes, see Inoue Toshio, *Honganji*, pp. 52–53; and Hattori Shisō, *Rennyo* (1948; rpt. Tokyo: Fukumura Shuppan, 1970), pp. 98–102. The image of Shinran that Yuizen took was not the famous scroll painting called the Kagami no Miei. Kakunyo is known to have carried that portrait to Echizen during a visit in 1311. See Shigematsu Akihisa, *Kakunyo*, pp. 81–82.

24. For the complete text of Kakunyo's letter of entreaty (*konmōjō*) to the Kantō congregations, see *Honganjishi*, 1:172–74. Concerning its contents, see Miyazaki Enjun, "Kakunyo no jūnikajō konmōjō ni tsuite," *Ryūkoku shidan* 49 (1962): 1–8. An English translation of the letter is contained in Ira Michael Solomon, "Rennyo and the Rise of Honganji in Muromachi Japan," pp. 72–74.

25. The early history of the Ōtani memorial is presented in greater detail in *Honganjishi*, 1:123–222; and in Yamada Bunshō, *Shinshūshi no kenkyū*, pp. 24–113, and *Shinshū shikō*, pp. 63–117. It is summarized in English in Ira Michael Solomon, *Rennyo and the Rise of Honganji in Muromachi Japan*, pp. 56–115; and in Stanley Weinstein, "Rennyo and the Shinshū Revival," pp. 337–45.

26. Shigematsu Akihisa, *Kakunyo*, pp. 84–86.

27. A photographic copy of this letter is contained in *Honganjishi*, 1:182.

28. See for example the *Shūjishō*, *SSZ*, 3:37; and the *Gaijashō*, *SSZ*, 3:65, 84.

29. *Honganjishi*, 1:183, 205.

30. Ibid., 1:185–87.

31. For a discussion of all these terms and their implications, see Shigematsu Akihisa, *Kakunyo*, pp. 54–64, 73–77, 151–54. A letter attributed to Kakue, dated 1302.4.22, contains the word *rusushiki* (cf. *Honganjishi*, 1:168–69), but Shigematsu suggests that it is a forgery, since Kakue used the word *gorusu* in all his other writings. Shigematsu believes

that Kakunyo's letter of entreaty (*konmōjō*) to the Kantō followers in 1310 was the first occurrence of the word *rusushiki*. See his *Kakunyo*, pp. 74, 77.

32. *Honganjishi*, 1:206–207.

33. *Kudenshō, SSZ,* 3:36.

34. *Gaijashō, SSZ,* 3:89.

35. Nyoshin is a somewhat shadowy figure in Shinshū history. According to Kakunyo's biography, the *Saishu kyōjū ekotoba, SSZ,* 3:824–25, Nyoshin grew up at Shinran's knee and learned Shinran's teachings directly from him, but at the age of twenty or so Nyoshin is thought to have moved to the Kantō region with his father, Zenran. Little is known about him from the time of Zenran's disownment in 1256 until the establishment of the Ōtani memorial in the 1270s. He did not travel to Kyoto to be with Shinran in 1262 at the time of his death, or soon thereafter, as some of Shinran's important followers did. In his later years Nyoshin was apparently on good terms with the Ōtani memorial, for he corresponded with Kakushinni (cf. *Honganjishi*, 1:191–92), and he made the long trip to Kyoto several times to hold memorial services for Shinran. Unlike most Shinshū adherents, Nyoshin continued to associate with Zenran even after Shinran disowned him. According to the *Bokieshi, SSZ,* 3:781, Nyoshin and Zenran together greeted Kakue and Kakunyo to the Kantō when they traveled there in 1290. Despite this association Nyoshin does not seem to have absorbed Zenran's religious views. Nyoshin was obviously influential among Shinshū followers in the east, for he headed the congregation at Ōami. The contents of his teachings are not fully known, outside of what Kakunyo attributed to him in the *Kudenshō* and the *Gaijashō*. By the early fourteenth century Nyoshin was commonly looked upon as one of Shinran's major disciples, for he is included in the *Shinran Shōnin monryo kyōmyōchō, SSS,* 1:903, 1001. Kakunyo's aggrandizement of Nyoshin undoubtedly inflated his reputation as a major Shinshū figure. Though Nyoshin is traditionally portrayed as the second head priest of the Honganji, after Shinran and before Kakunyo, most scholars agree that he never actually bore that title, nor did he function in that capacity. Concerning Nyoshin, see *Honganjishi*, 1:190–93; Matsuno Junkō, "Shinran shigo no tōgoku kyōdan," in *Shinshūshi gaisetsu*, pp. 80–81; and *SDJ*, 3:1733–36, s.v. "Nyoshin."

36. Inoue Toshio, *Honganji*, p. 66.

37. Zonkaku also went by the name Kōgen, but for consistency's sake I have referred to him only as Zonkaku throughout this study.

38. Concerning Zonkaku's early religious training, see Tanishita Ichimu, *Zonkaku ichigoki no kenkyū narabini kaisetsu* (Kyoto: Nagata Bunshōdō, 1969), pp. 37–93; Shigematsu Akihisa, *Chūsei Shinshū shisō no kenkyū* (Tokyo: Yoshikawa Kōbunkan, 1974), pp. 223–24; and Shigematsu's *Kakunyo*, pp. 172–79.

39. Shigematsu Akihisa, *Kakunyo*, pp. 80–88.

40. Ibid., pp. 186–87.

41. In 1339, during the first brief period of reconciliation, Kakunyo composed a letter naming the line of succession after his death for the office of caretaker of the Honganji. In that letter Kakunyo stated explicitly that Zonkaku was not entitled to the position and that, if he attempted to usurp the office, then the legitimate successor should appeal to the aristocratic and samurai authorities to prevent him. A copy of the letter is contained in *Honganjishi*, 1:208–209.

42. Shigematsu Akihisa, *Chūsei Shinshū shisō no kenkyū*, p. 187.

43. *Rokuyōshō, SSZ,* 2:213.

44. Shigematsu Akihisa, *Chūsei Shinshū shisō no kenkyū*, p. 225.

45. *Jōdo shin'yōshō, SSZ,* 3:120. See also Shigematsu Akihisa, *Chūsei Shinshū shisō no kenkyū*, pp. 217–18.

46. In the *Gaijashō, SSZ,* 3:80, Kakunyo criticized the view that the *nembutsu* is primarily an external act:

So long as one clings to the idea that the utterance of the *nembutsu*, or the act by which one is truly assured, is the true cause of birth in Pure Land, one will not achieve birth in the true Pure Land, for that act is still a human contrivance based on the effort of the unenlightened being.

See also Shigematsu Akihisa, *Chūsei Shinshū shisō no kenkyū*, pp. 217–18. Kakunyo's branding of Zonkaku as a heretic occurs in a letter dated 1339, which is contained in Murakami Senjō, *Shinshū zenshi*, pp. 380–81. Though there is some question about the authenticity of this letter, Shigematsu Akihisa, *Kakunyo*, pp. 157–59, considers it genuine and suggests that it was one of a series of letters written by Kakunyo in 1339 naming his successors at the Honganji.

47. *Haja kenshōshō*, *SSZ*, 3:155–87. An early manuscript edition of the text is published in photographic reproduction in Fugen Kōju, ed., *Haja kenshōshō, Kenmyōshō* (Kyoto: Dōbōsha, 1987).

48. *Gaijashō*, *SSZ*, 3:63–89.

49. Nakajima Kakuryō, "Kakunyo Shōnin to Zonkaku Shōnin to no kyōri kankei," in *Kakunyo Shōnin no kenkyū*, *Mujintō* 22 (1917): 275; and Nakai Gendō, *Ianjin no shujusō*, p. 5.

50. *Gaijashō*, *SSZ*, 3:67.

51. One example of this is the idea that the Shinran's *wasan* hymns must be sung in order for a person to be born in Pure Land, whereas chanting other Pure Land works will result in rebirth in one of the hells. Zonkaku criticized this notion saying that chanting any of these is a subsidiary religious act and that the true act leading to salvation is the *nembutsu*. See *Haja kenshōshō*, *SSZ*, 3:167–70.

52. See for instance the words *gedō* and *jagi* in the *Gaijashō*, *SSZ*, 3:64, 65, 73, 85, 86, 87, and the words *jaken* and *gedō* in the *Haja kenshōshō*, *SSZ*, 3:159, 168, 177, 186.

53. Concerning the idea of lamenting deviations and rectifying heresy, see Terakawa Shunshō, "Tanni to gaija," *Nihon Bukkyō gakkai nenpō* 39 (1974): 267–79. Terakawa argues that both these viewpoints can be found in Shinran's writings, the *Tannishō*, and the *Gaijashō*, but that in Shinshū history after Kakunyo's time the concept of rectifying heresy became dominant and the idea of lamenting deviations became obscured.

54. A catalogue of Shinshū writings compiled by Zonkaku in 1362 indicates that the *Haja kenshōshō* was written in response to a request of Ryōgen's. See *BKDJ*, 9:8, s.v. "*Haja kenshōshō*." The preface to the work indicates that it was submitted to the authorities in the hope that they would give public sanction (*saikyo*) to the practice of the *nembutsu*. See *Haja kenshōshō*, *SSZ*, 3:155. Therefore, the work is sometimes referred to as the *Haja kenshō mōshijō*, "A Petition Assailing Heresy and Revealing Truth." See Takao Giken, "Haja kenshōshō," in *Shinshū seiten kōsan zenshū 7, Zonkaku Shōnin no bu*, ed. Uno Enkū (Tokyo: Kokusho Kankōkai, 1976), p. 281.

55. *Haja kenshōshō*, *SSZ*, 3:155.

56. Ibid., 3:155–57.

57. Ibid., 3:157, 160, 161, 163, 164, 166, 167–68, 170, 171, 173, 175, 177, 178, 179, 180, 181, 182.

58. Ibid., 3:157, 163.

59. Ibid., 3:178–79.

60. Ibid., 3:161–62.

61. Ibid., 3:180–81.

62. Ibid., 3:181–82.

63. Takao Giken, "Haja kenshōshō," in *Shinshū seiten kōsan zenshū 7, Zonkaku Shōnin no bu*, pp. 310–13, 316–17. The idea of guiding deceased relatives through Saṃsāra's realms developed as one form of obligation that people have to their ancestors. If deceased relatives were to fall into one of the hells or into another unfortunate rebirth, then it was incumbent upon their descendants to help them escape from those realms.

Hence, at funerals words of guidance and direction (*indō*) were commonly included in the service to direct the deceased from realms of suffering to enlightenment, or perhaps to Pure Land. Zonkaku maintained that there is no reason for Pure Land adherents to follow those practices. If deceased persons are born in Pure Land, then all their needs are fulfilled. If not, there is little that people here can communicate to them which is not already laid out in the Pure Land teachings known to the deceased. Besides, Zonkaku added, only one-seventh of what people in this world convey to the dead actually reaches them; and such a small amount cannot be consequential in leading them out of Saṃsāra's benighted realms. See *Haja kenshōshō, SSZ*, 3:175–76.

64. *Haja kenshōshō, SSZ*, 3:171–72, 175–76. The passage from the *Nehangyō* cited here is similar to quotations found in Shinran's *Kyōgyōshinshō, SSZ*, 2:175, 191, expressing the same idea.

65. *Haja kenshōshō, SSZ*, 3:172.

66. Ibid., 3:158–59. Another passage highly critical of the monks of Mt. Hiei is found on pp. 174–75.

67. *Haja kenshōshō, SSZ*, 3:170–71, 173–75.

68. For a discussion of Zonkaku's views on Shinto, especially as elucidated in his *Shojin hongaishū, SSS*, 1:697–712, and of their differences from Shinran's, see Fugen Kōju, "Chūsei Shinshū no jingi shisō," *Bukkyō bunka kenkyūjo kiyō* 17 (1978): 31–52.

69. See for example his *Godenshō, SSZ*, 3:651–52.

70. *Goshōsokushū, SSZ*, 2:700.

71. *Haja kenshōshō, SSZ*, 3:167–70.

72. *Guanki, SSS*, 4:719. See also Inoue Toshio, *Honganji*, p.109.

73. *Haja kenshōshō, SSZ*, 3:155.

74. *Gaijashō, SSZ*, 3:64, 66, 67, 68, 69, 70, 71, 72, 73, 74, 76, 77, 78, 79, 80–81, 84, 86, 88.

75. Ibid., 3:79–80.

76. Ibid., 3:75. The word used for faith here is *anjin*, and the words for religious acts and practices are *kigyō* and *sagō*. These are the three components of the Pure Land believer's religious life outlined by Shan-tao in the *Wang-sheng li-tsan chieh, SSZ*, 1:648–51.

77. *Gaijashō, SSZ*, 3:74–75. According to popular belief, a person's good and evil acts are recorded by deities in one of Saṃsāra's heavenly palaces twice a year, during the two equinox seasons. Hence, these periods were frequently set aside to accumulate extra religious merit through intensive practice such as *nembutsu* chanting. Kakunyo considered this practice contrary to the idea of faith, since one's birth in Pure Land is assured without the necessity of generating great stores of religious merit. See Saikō Gijun, "Gaijashō," in *Shinshū seiten kōsan zenshū* 6, *Kakunyo Shōnin no bu*, ed. Uno Enkū (Tokyo: Kokusho Kankōkai, 1976), pp.320–21.

78. *Gaijashō, SSZ*, 3:67–68, 73–74, 80–81.

79. Ibid., 3:78–79. Other popular forms of chanting in the early Pure Land movement were the singing of the Pure Land praises six times a day (*rokuji raisan*)—based on Shan-tao's *Wang-sheng li-tsan chieh, SSZ*, 1:648–83—and singing Shinran's *wasan* hymns.

80. *Gaijashō, SSZ*, 3:72–73.

81. Ibid., 3:76–77.

82. Ibid., 3:64–67, 69–70, 72–73.

83. Ibid., 3:68–69, 71–72.

84. Ibid., 3:70–71.

85. Ibid., 3:84–86.

86. Shigematsu Akihisa, *Chūsei Shinshū shisō no kenkyū*, pp. 207–210; and Sumida Chiken, "Kakunyo Shōnin to igisha," in *Kakunyo Shōnin no kenkyū, Mujintō* 22 (1917): 151–63, 164–68.

87. *Gaijashō, SSZ,* 3:88. Kakunyo criticized the Bukkōji for discouraging Shinshū believers from visiting the Honganji and for pretending to be the foremost temple of the school. He portrayed this as an act of conceit (*kyōman*) going against the grain of Buddhism and against the Pure Land tradition.

88. Kakunyo emphasized the teachings first and foremost, but by no means repudiated the importance of the teacher. He considered the teacher's role to be conveying Amida's message of salvation to the believer. For that reason he interpreted the expression "hearing the name" (*sono myōgō o kikite*), contained in the fulfilled form of the eighteenth vow, to mean hearing the *nembutsu* from a teacher. Hence, a person's experience of faith can only occur as a result of encountering a master propagating the true teachings. The teacher does not displace the teachings, but is instrumental in conveying them to other people. Generally speaking, Kakunyo ascribed greater significance to the teacher than Shinran did. Shinran considered the expression "hearing the name" in the eighteenth vow to mean experiencing faith as a result of the *nembutsu,* whether or not a teacher is involved in the event. In this respect the moment of faith is less circumscribed and less contingent on the agency of a teacher than it is according to Kakunyo. This is one crucial distinction in their two interpretations. See Shigematsu Akihisa, *Chūsei Shinshū shisō no kenkyū,* pp. 213–16.

7. THE SHINSHŪ AND RIVAL SCHOOLS OF BUDDHISM

1. The Kōfukuji's nine accusations against Hōnen's Pure Land movement of 1205 represent a typical response to the new schools in their formative years. Other instances of conflict between the old schools and the new Buddhist movements are cited in Tsuji Zennosuke, *Nihon Bukkyōshi,* 3:345–94.

2. Internally, the old schools attempted to restore rigorous doctrinal studies and adherence to the Buddhist precepts. The most important figures in this revivalist movement were Chōgen (1121–1206), Myōhen (1142–1224), and Gyōnen (1240–1321) of the Tōdaiji; Jōkei (1155–1213) and Ryōhen (1194–1252) of the Kōfukuji; Myōe (1173–1232) of the Kōzanji; Shunjō (1166–1227) of the Sennyūji; and Eison (1201–90) and Ninshō (1217–1303) of the Saidaiji. Externally, the traditional schools sought to popularize forms of Buddhist devotion that would appeal to the general population and that could compete with the teachings of the new schools. The most common forms advocated by the old schools were the chanting of Śākyamuni's name (*Shakuson nembutsu*), esoteric incantations leading to salvation (*kōmyō shingon*), and the veneration of such Bodhisattvas as Miroku, Kannon, and Jizō. See Yoshida Fumio, "Nanto Bukkyō no fukkō," and Hayami Tosuku, "Chūsei shakai to shoshinkō," in *Ajia Bukkyōshi, Nihonhen,* 5:167–220, 229–40.

3. Kanaoka Shūyū, *Koji meisatsu jiten* (Tokyo: Tōkyōdō, 1970), p. 154.

4. Inoue Toshio, *Honganji,* p. 116. Kakunyo received religious instruction at the Ichijōin and Rennyo at the Daijōin. See *Honganjishi,* 1:165, 297–99.

5. Inoue Toshio, *Honganji,* p. 116. Sometimes this status was granted by one of the collateral branches of the Hino, such as the Hirohashi family. See *Honganjishi,* 1:297; and Stanley Weinstein, "Rennyo and the Shinshū Revival," p. 344.

6. Uehara Yoshitarō, *Honganji hōnanshi* (Tokyo: Tōgakusha, 1934), pp. 65–80; and Fukunaga Katsumi, *Shinran kyōdan dan'atsushi* (Tokyo: Yūzankaku, 1972), pp. 35–40.

7. Murayama Shūichi, ed., *Hieizan to Tendai Bukkyō no kenkyū* (Tokyo: Meicho Shuppan, 1975), pp. 27–30.

8. Indirect conflict arose between the Zen school and the Shinshū during Rennyo's proselytization of the Hokuriku seaboard, where a number of major Zen temples were located, such as the Eiheiji, the Sōjiji, and the Daijōji. See Ishida Mitsuyuki, *Rennyo,* p. 83.

9. *Nembutsu muken jigokushō,* in *Shōwa teihon Nichiren Shōnin ibun,* 1:34–42.

10. Fugen Kōju, "Nichiren no Hōnen Jōdokyō hihan to Zonkaku no tachiba," *Shinshūgaku* 56 (1977): 18–19. Speculation about conflict between Nichiren and Shinran's following is based solely on the geographical proximity of the two rather than on documentary evidence.

11. Nichizō (1269–1342) established the *Shichijō monryū* in Kyoto, and Nichijō (1298–1369) the *Rokujō monryū*. Two major Nichiren temples eventually emerged from these groups, the Myōkenji and the Honkokuji. Nichizō's disciple, Daikaku (1297–1364), proselytized extensively in Bizen and Bitchū, converting a number of powerful families there. See Risshō Daigaku Nichiren Kyōgaku Kenkyūjo, ed., *Nichiren kyōdan zenshi* (Kyoto: Heirakuji Shoten, 1964), 1:108–114, 135–37, 151–54.

12. See Kakunyo's *Shusse gan'i*, *SSZ*, 3:63; and Zonkaku's *Ketchishō* and *Hokke mondō*, *SSZ*, 3:188–220, 282–324.

13. Tanishita Ichimu, *Zonkaku ichigoki no kenkyū narabini kaisetsu*, pp. 129–31. Nichiren scholars question this account of the debate. They suggest that, since there is no mention of this event in other historical records, the debate probably took place before a powerful local family (*gōzoku*) rather than before a high official such as the provincial governor. These scholars also point out that, although the Shinshū claimed to have flourished in the region because of this debate, the Nichiren school continued to spread unabated throughout the province of Bingo. See Risshō Daigaku Nichiren Kyōgaku Kenkyūjo, ed., *Nichiren kyōdan zenshi*, 1:138–39.

14. *Shusse gan'i*, *SSZ*, 3:63; *Ketchishō*, *SSZ*, 3:188–220; and *Hokke mondō*, *SSZ*, 3:282–324. The gist of Kakunyo's and Zonkaku's arguments is that the teachings of the "Lotus Sutra" or *Hokekyō*, *TD* 9:1–62, championed by the Nichiren school, and the teachings of the *nembutsu* are not at odds with each other, but are merely two different paths leading to the same end. The *Hokekyō* is suited to the person capable of rigorous religious undertakings, whereas the *nembutsu* is appropriate for the believer of limited ability. Fugen Kōju, "Nichiren no Hōnen Jōdokyō hihan to Zonkaku no tachiba," pp. 48–49, points out that Zonkaku's interpretation of the two paths differs from Shinran's in that Zonkaku saw the two as separate but equal whereas Shinran regarded the *nembutsu* as the true path and the *Hokekyō* as a provisional teaching.

15. *Matsudai nembutsu jushuin*, *JZ*, 10:1–8.

16. Vasubandhu, T'an-luan, and Shan-tao had previously interpreted the *nembutsu* and its attendant religious practices in terms of the *sangō*, the three spheres of activity. See *Jōdoron*, *SSZ*, 1:271; *Wang-sheng lun chu*, *SSZ*, 1:312 ff.; and *Wang-sheng li-tsan chieh*, *SSZ*, 1:648. The Chinzei systematizer Shōgei (1341–1420) later reiterated this theme in his *Jōdo nizō nikyō ryakuju*, *JZ*, 12:8. The idea that the *nembutsu* is manifested in the three spheres of activity also became an important concept in the Seizan branch of the Pure Land school, and it was subsequently absorbed into the Shinshū from the Seizan.

17. Another reason for Benchō to write his *Matsudai nembutsu jushuin* was to admonish his followers against the teachings of Kōsai, Shōkū, and Gyōkū, other disciples of Hōnen's who all advocated faith over practice. Though Benchō did not mention these three by name, he denounced their specific doctrines as heresy (*jagi*) and as "not the teachings of master Hōnen." See *Matsudai nembutsu jushuin*, *JZ*, 10:11; and Etani Ryūkai, *Gaisetsu Jōdoshūshi*, pp. 79–80.

18. In 1258 Ryōchū established a temple in Kamakura, the Goshinji, now known as the Kōmyōji. During his residency there he came into conflict with Nichiren, and in 1271 he and a number of other Pure Land priests complained to the Kamakura government that Nichiren was subjecting them to unwarranted abuse. Subsequently, the government exiled Nichiren to Sado Island in the Japan Sea because of the commotion he had created in Kamakura. See Tsuji Zennosuke, *Nihon Bukkyōshi*, 2:340–42.

19. This postscript is cited in Ōhashi Shunnō, *Hōnen to Jōdoshū kyōdan* (Tokyo: Kyōikusha, 1978), pp. 122–23. Kakunyo, writing fifty years later, used a similar ex-

pression, *sandai denji*, to justify his religious lineage from Hōnen and Shinran. See his *Gaijashō, SSZ*, 3:89.

20. *Kangyōsho denzūki, JZ*, 2:422–32. Ryōchū derived this idea from a passage in Shan-tao's *Kuan ching shu, SSZ*, 1:551–56. Concerning the Chinzei's concept of eliminating evil karma, see Sugi Shirō, *Seichin kyōgi gairon* (1924; rpt. Kyoto: Hyakkaen, 1975), pp. 83–89.

21. Ishii Kyōdō, *Kaitei zōho Jōdo no kyōgi to sono kyōdan* (Kyoto: Fuzanbō, 1972), p. 31.

22. The Zen priest Kokan Shiren (1278–1346) described the Pure Land school as a subordinate school (*fuyōshū*) and an ancillary school (*gūshū*), and the famous Zen master Musō Soseki (1275–1351) in his *Muchū mondō* characterized it as a form of Hīnayāna Buddhism. Shōgei responded by claiming that Pure Land belongs to the same category of immediate teachings (*tongyō*) as Tendai, Shingon, and Zen do, and moreover Pure Land is the most immediate among the immediate (*tonchūton*), for it does not stop at the question of absolute nature in the immediate teachings (*shōton*), but it goes on to address its manifest characteristics (*sōton*) as well. See Ishii Kyōdō, *Kaitei zōho Jōdo no kyōgi to sono kyōdan*, pp. 36–37; and *JDJ*, 2:235–36, s.v. "Shōgei"; and 2:492, s.v. *"Sōtongyō."*

23. *Haja kenshōgi, JZ*, 12:809–13. Also see *JDJ*, 3:178, s.v. *"Haja kenshōgi."*

24. In the Chinzei branch clerical ordination is based on the Tendai's *endonkai* made up of the Bodhisattva precepts, whereas doctrinal transmission consists of Pure Land teachings only, passed on in the form of a *fusatsukai*. See *JDJ*, 1:140–41, s.v. *"Endonkai"*; 2:235–36, s.v. "Shōgei"; and 3:228, s.v. *"Fusatsukai."*

25. *Hōnen Shōnin gyōjō ezu*, in Ikawa Jōkei, *Hōnen Shōnin den zenshū*, p. 302.

26. For example, the twelfth head priest, Seia (d. 1374), is said to have come from the Seizan branch. See Sanda Zenshin, "Jōdoshū to Zonkaku," *Bukkyō ronsō* 17 (1973): 136.

27. Ōhashi Shunnō, *Hōnen to Jōdoshū kyōdan*, pp. 160–61.

28. Up to the mid-fifteenth century, the Chinzei branch was most active in the Kantō region, where there may have been occasional interchanges with the Shinshū. Shōgei, for example, organized a doctrinal study center (*danjō*) at Yokosone, where a strong Shinshū following was located (cf. Ishii Kyōdō, *Kaitei zōho Jōdo no kyōgi to sono kyōdan*, pp. 137–38). Also, in the *Haja kenshōgi*, sometimes entitled *Kashima mondō*, Shōgei denounced *nembutsu* adherents who enshrine images of Shōtoku Taishi as an object of worship, probably in reference to certain Shinshū congregations in the Kantō. See *Haja kenshōgi, JZ*, 12:821–22; and *BKDJ* 9:7, s.v. *"Haja kenshōgi."*

29. *Saishu kyōjū ekotoba, SSZ*, 3:866. See also Yamakami Shōson, "Kakunyo Shōnin to Jōdo iryū ni tsuite," in *Kakunyo Shōnin no kenkyū, Mujintō* 22 (1917): 194.

30. Akamatsu Toshihide, *Kyōto jishikō* (Kyoto: Hōzōkan, 1962), p. 173.

31. Ishida Mitsuyuki, *Rennyo*, pp. 60–65.

32. This event occurred in 1603. See *Honganjishi*, 1:132.

33. Not to be mistaken for Anichibō Shōkū mentioned above.

34. Shōkū's outline of the three paths (*sanmon*) is found in his *Kanmon yōgishō*. See particularly the following passages: *Kanmon yōgishō*, in *Seizan zensho*, 12 vols., ed. Seizan Zensho Kankōkai, (Kyoto: Bun'eidō, 1974), 3:4, 25, 45–46. Shōkū occasionally used the term *yōmon* interchangeably with *kanmon*, the second of the three. For a brief description of the three paths, see Sugi Shirō, *Seichin kyōgi gairon*, pp. 164–73.

35. Mochizuki Shinkō, *Ryakujutsu Jōdo kyōrishi* (Tokyo: Nihon Tosho, 1977), pp. 352–53.

36. *Anjinshō*, in *Seizan Shōnin tanpen shōmotsushū*, ed. Mori Eijun (Kyoto: Bun'eidō, 1980), pp. 181–85.

37. Shōkū conceived of birth in Pure Land in two forms. One is immediate birth (*sokuben ōjō*), and the other is imminent birth (*tōtoku ōjō*). Immediate birth is attained

while still living in this world, and is embodied in the *nembutsu* and other acts through which Amida is at work in the person. Imminent birth occurs at the time of one's death, but the nature of Pure Land into which one is born then is no different from that realized while still living in this world. See Sugi Shirō, *Seichin kyōgi gairon*, pp. 286–87.

38. Mochizuki Shinkō, *Ryakujutsu Jōdo kyōrishi*, pp. 359–66.

39. For a brief discussion of the Seizan's six subbranches, see Sugi Shirō, *Seichin kyōgi gairon*, pp. 140–58.

40. *Saishu kyōjū ekotoba*, *SSZ*, 3:846; and Tanishita Ichimu, *Zonkaku ichigoki no kenkyū narabini kaisetsu*, p. 61.

41. See *Gansanshō*, *SSZ*, 3:46, by Kakunyo; and *Zonkaku hōgo*, *SSZ*, 3:366, and *Rokuyōshō*, *SSZ*, 2:212, 282, by Zonkaku. Also see Fugen Kōju, "Anjin ketsujōshō to Shinshū resso no kyōgaku," *Ryūkoku Daigaku ronshū* 415 (1979): 95, 98–100.

42. *Anjin ketsujōshō*, *SSZ*, 3:615–38. An early manuscript edition of the text is published in photographic reproduction in Fugen Kōju, ed., *Anjin ketsujōshō* (Kyoto: Dōbōsha, 1983). For an English translation of the text, see Eizo Tanaka, trans., "Anjin Ketsujo Sho: On the Attainment of True Faith," *The Pure Land* 2.2—5.2 (December 1980—December 1983). For a discussion of its content, see Winston L. King, "An Interpretation of the *Anjin Ketsujosho*," *Japanese Journal of Religious Studies* 13.4 (December 1986): 277–98.

43. Fugen Kōju, "Anjin ketsujōshō to Shinshū resso no kyōgaku," pp. 81–82, 94; and Hosokawa Gyōshin, "Anjin ketsujōshō no shoshi," *Ōtani gakuhō* 44.3 (March 1965): 64–66. Jōsen is also said to have made a copy of the *Anjin ketsujōshō* in 1338, but that manuscript no longer survives in the original but only as a copy made by Rennyo's son Jitsugo (1492–1581) in 1565.

44. *Zonkaku hōgo*, *SSZ*, 3:366, and *Anjin ketsujōshō*, *SSZ*, 3:625. See Fugen Kōju, "Anjin ketsujōshō to Shinshū resso no kyōgaku," p. 98.

45. A summary of the *Anjin ketsujōshō*'s key concepts is contained in Fugen Kōju, "Anjin ketsujōshō to Shinshū resso no kyōgaku," pp. 82–94.

46. Fugen Kōju, "Anjin ketsujōshō to Shinshū resso no kyōgaku," pp. 95–96, 98–99.

47. Rennyo's utilization of the *Anjin ketsujōshō* has been well documented in Minor Lee Rogers, "Rennyo Shōnin 1415–1499: A Transformation of Shin Buddhist Piety," pp. 234–51, 325–38.

48. Even as recently as the early 1900s some Shinshū scholars maintained that Kakunyo composed the *Anjin ketsujōshō*. See for example Koreyama Ekaku, *Anjin ketsujōshō kōwa* (Kyoto: Kōkyō Shoin, 1925), pp. 1–6. Over the centuries the work has been attributed variously to Kakunyo, Zonkaku, Jōsen, Shinbutsu, Kenchi, Zenran, and Ryōgen, all belonging to the Shinshū, as well as to Shōkū of the Jōdoshū's Seizan branch, to his followers, and to Ippen's followers of the Jishū school. See *BKDJ*, 1:71, s.v. "*Anjin ketsujōshō*."

49. Okumura Gen'yū, *Anjin ketsujōshō: Jōdo e no michi* (Tokyo: Suzuki Gakujutsu Zaidan, 1964), pp. 1–3, associates the *Anjin ketsujōshō* with the Fukakusa subbranch of the Seizan tradition. Others attribute it to the Honzan subbranch. See Uryūzu Ryūō, "Anjin ketsujōshō to Shinshū kyōgaku," *Indogaku Bukkyōgaku kenkyū* 10 (1962): 198–99.

50. Concerning Ippen's life, see Ōhashi Shunnō, *Ippen—Sono kōdō to shisō*, Nihonjin no kōdō to shisō, no. 14 (Tokyo: Hyōronsha, 1971); Kanai Kiyomitsu, *Ippen to Jishū kyōdan* (Tokyo: Kadokawa, 1975); and Kurita Isamu, *Ippen Shōnin: Tabi no shisakusha* (Tokyo: Shinchōsha, 1977). Studies in English concerning Ippen's life and thought are: Yanagi Sōetsu, "Ippen Shōnin," *Eastern Buddhist* (N.S.) 6.1 (October 1973): 33–57; James Harlan Foard, "Ippen Shōnin and Popular Buddhism in Kamakura Japan" (Ph.D. dissertation, Stanford University, 1977); Kondō Tesshō, "The Religious Experience of

Ippen," *Eastern Buddhist* (N.S.) 12.2 (October 1979): 92–116; and Dennis Hirota, trans., *No Abode: The Record of Ippen* (Kyoto: Ryukoku Translation Center, 1986).

51. See, for example, Ippen's letter contained in the *Ippen Shōnin goroku*, in *Jishū zensho*, 2 vols. (Kamakura: Geirinsha, 1974), 2:7.

52. Ippen stated in one of his letters, "It does not matter whether we sentient beings have faith or not (*shin fushin*), whether we are untainted or not, or whether we are burdened with wrongdoings or not. Simply utter *Namu Amida Butsu*." *Ippen Shōnin goroku*, in *Jishū zensho*, 2:8. Concerning the historical incident that brought Ippen to this way of thinking, see *Ippen hijiri e*, in *Jishū zensho*, 1:8; and Ōhashi Shunnō, *Ippen to Jishū kyōdan* (Tokyo: Kyōikusha, 1978), pp. 39–41.

53. Ippen emphasized the present moment in which the Buddha's name is uttered (*tadaima no shōmyō*), and he rejected any distinction between the ten kalpas (*jikkō*) that have passed since Amida's enlightenment and the single instant (*ichinen*) in which the *nembutsu* is spoken. See his brief letter and his poem in *Ippen Shōnin goroku*, in *Jishū zensho*, 2:10, 12.

54. Ippen's strongest tie to Shinto was established at Kumano Hongū shrine where he had a vision in 1274. The *kami* of the shrine, who was widely recognized as a manifestation of Amida Buddha, commissioned Ippen to distribute *nembutsu* amulets to all people, whether they have faith or not and whether they are untainted or not. See *Ippen hijiri e*, in *Jishū zensho*, 1:7–8.

55. The first instance of *nembutsu* dancing in Ippen's career occurred at Odagiri village in Shinano province in 1279. It was a spontaneous event in which all of his entourage, moved by the chanting of the *nembutsu*, broke into dance. See *Ippen hijiri e*, in *Jishū zensho*, 1:13–14. In the later Jishū, *nembutsu* dancing lost much of its spontaneity and became stylized and ritualized.

56. Ippen delegated the responsibility of keeping this register to his foremost disciple Shinkyō (1239–1319). This practice became one of the hallmarks of the Jishū in its development after Ippen's death. See Kanai Kiyomitsu, *Ippen to Jishū kyōdan*, pp. 105, 292–95.

57. It is unclear what Ippen sought to express by the term *jishū*. Some scholars think it might imply performing the *nembutsu* at the six appointed times of the day, or perhaps at the time of one's death. The word is derived from Shan-tao's *Kuan ching shu*, *SSZ*, 1:144, where it refers to believers assembled at a single time. In the seventeenth century, the second character in the word *jishū* was changed, making it Jishū, to indicate the name of the school instead of the word for members. See Ōhashi Shunnō, *Jishū no seiritsu to tenkai*, pp. 39–41.

58. Ōhashi Shunnō, *Jishū no seiritsu to tenkai*, p. 41.

59. The twelve items are: wooden bowl (*hikiire*), chopsticks and case (*hashizutsu*), woven robe (*amiginu*), clerical mantle (*kesa*), undergarment (*katabira*), hand towel sash (*shukin*), waistband (*obi*), paper robe (*kamiko*), rosary (*nenju*), clerical robe (*koromo*), wooden clogs (*geta*), and clerical cap (*zukin*). See *Ippen Shōnin goroku*, in *Jishū zensho*, 2:6–7; and Ōhashi Shunnō, *Jishū no seiritsu to tenkai*, pp. 127–28.

60. Among the eighteen were the following:

> To venerate wholeheartedly the powers of the Shinto *kami*; not to deprecate the virtues of the Buddhist deities from whom they derive (*honji*).
> To undertake wholeheartedly the practice of chanting the Buddha's name; not to engage in any other indiscriminate religious practice.
> To put faith wholeheartedly in the beloved teachings; not to attack other people's teachings.
> To dwell wholeheartedly in discernment of humility; not to arouse a sense of arrogance in oneself.

To control wholeheartedly one's own faults; not to criticize the wrongdoings of other people.

To undertake wholeheartedly the practice leading to enlightenment; not to fraternize with pleasure-seeking (*yuge*) companions.

To follow wholeheartedly the teachings of one's master (*chishiki*); not to indulge wantonly in one's own desires.

See *Ippen Shōnin goroku*, in *Jishū zensho*, 1:5–6. These vows have been translated in full in Ryusaku Tsunoda, ed., *Sources of Japanese Tradition* (New York: Columbia University Press, 1958), pp. 196–98. Except for the passage on worship of Shinto *kami*, the tenor of these vows is similar to Hōnen's *Shichikajō kishōmon* and to the *Zen'en no seikin* congregational rules of the early Shinshū.

61. Ōhashi Shunnō, *Ippen to Jishū kyōdan*, pp. 47–48.

62. The Jishū eventually divided into twelve branches, but around the seventeenth century most of them came under the control of the Shōjōkōji temple. See Nagashima Shōdō, "Jishū," in *Nihon Bukkyō kiso kōza 4, Jōdoshū*, ed. Fujii Masao (Tokyo: Yūzankaku, 1979), pp. 264–68.

63. Ōhashi Shunnō, *Jishū no seiritsu to tenkai*, pp. 165–66.

64. Ōhashi Shunnō, "Jishū," in *Shūkyōshi*, ed. Kawasaki Yasuyuki and Kasahara Kazuo (Tokyo: Yamakawa Shuppansha, 1974), p. 184.

65. Ōhashi Shunnō, *Jishū no seiritsu to tenkai*, pp. 102–103.

66. Ōhashi Shunnō, "Jishū," in *Shūkyōshi*, pp. 188–89.

67. *Gaijashō, SSZ*, 3:67–68.

68. Miyazaki Enjun, "Shoki Shinshū to Jishū," *Ryūkoku Daigaku ronshū* 389–90 (May 1969): 320–21.

69. Akamatsu Toshihide, *Kamakura Bukkyō no kenkyū*, p. 264. Also see pp. 201–202.

70. Ōhashi Shunnō, *Ippen to Jishū kyōdan*, pp. 163–64.

71. Ibid., pp. 164–65. The *Tengu sōshi* scroll is reproduced in Umezu Jirō, *Tengu sōshi, Zegaibōe*, Nihon emakimono zenshū, no. 27 (Tokyo: Kadokawa, 1978). The passage translated here is found on p. 80 of the edited text in Umezu's study.

72. Examples of Raichia's rules are presented in Ōhashi Shunnō, *Banba Jishū no ayumi* (n.p.: Jōdoshūshi Kenkyūkai, 1963), pp. 48–49.

73. *Honganjishi*, 1:157–58, 182 (photographed document).

74. "Ofumi," no. 123 (1490), *RSI*, p. 372.

75. Ōhashi Shunnō, *Jishū no seiritsu to tenkai*, pp. 276–77.

76. Ōhashi Shunnō, *Jishū no seiritsu to tenkai*, pp. 266–81, has done work on Rennyo's proselytization among the Ikkōshū, but not on Ikkōshū doctrinal themes. A few sources such as Inami-chō Shi Hensan Iinkai, ed., *Inami-chō shi* (Toyama: Inami-chō, 1970), 1:276–77, mention the similarity between Rennyo's letters and Raichia's, but do not compare specific ideas such as "relying on the Buddha to please save me."

77. Yamada Yoshio et al., eds., *Konjaku monogatarishū*, vol. 4, Nihon koten bungaku taikei, no. 25 (Tokyo: Iwanami Shoten, 1975), p. 497.

78. Sugi Shirō, *Gobunshō kōwa* (1933; rpt. Kyoto: Nagata Bunshōshō, 1979), pt. 2, pp. 135–38.

79. *Niso Raichia Shōnin shōsoku*, in Ōhashi Shunnō, *Banba Jishū no ayumi*, pp. 182, 183, 185, 186, 187, etc.

80. Compare *Niso Raichia Shōnin shōsoku*, in Ōhashi Shunnō, *Banba Jishū no ayumi*, p. 231, and Rennyo's letter in "Ofumi," no. 64 (1474.7.3), *RSI*, pp. 199–200.

81. One problem in dealing with the *Niso Raichia Shōnin shōsoku* is that the work survives only in a copy made during the Tokugawa period (1600–1867). Hence, there exists the possibility that it is a forgery drawing on Rennyo's letters. Nonetheless, Kanai Kiyomitsu, *Ippen to Jishū kyōdan*, pp. 399–400, and Ōhashi Shunnō, *Banba Jishū no ayumi*, pp. 45–51, both treat it as an authentic work of the thirteenth century.

82. Inoue Toshio, *Honganji*, pp. 219–20.

8. SHINSHŪ FACTIONS

1. *Honpukuji atogaki*, in Kasahara Kazuo, *Shinshū ni okeru itan no keifu* (Tokyo: Tōkyō Daigaku Shuppankai, 1962), p. 254. Concerning the importance of the Honpukuji temple and the historical significance of its records, see Chiba Jōryū, *Honpukujishi* (Kyoto: Dōbōsha, 1980); and Chiba Jōryū, ed., *Honpukuji kyūki* (Kyoto: Hōzōkan, 1980). In the *Honpukuji atogaki* the location of the Bukkōji is written as Shirutani, not Shibutani, perhaps indicating an alternate pronunciation of the place name during this period. This reading is corroborated in Tanishita Ichimu, *Zonkaku ichigoki no kenkyū narabini kaisetsu*, pp. 117–18, where the name is written in characters as Shirutani. I have arbitrarily changed it to Shibutani here to standardize it with other references to the same place in this study.

2. This quotation is taken from Ryōgen's *kanjinchō*, or solicitation register, as cited in Murakami Senjō, *Shinshū zenshi*, p. 300.

3. Kusaka Murin, *Shinshūshi no kenkyū*, pp. 16–19. Ryōgen's gratitude to Zonkaku is reflected in the fact that he built his family a residence in 1327. See Tanishita Ichimu, *Zonkaku ichigoki no kenkyū narabini kaisetsu*, pp. 116–17. Zonkaku was financially dependent on the Bukkōji temple and on other supporters after Kakunyo expelled him from the Honganji in 1322.

4. For Ryōgen's biography, see *Bukkōji chūkō Ryōgen Shōnin den*, *SZ*, 68:347–50, written on the fiftieth anniversary of Ryōgen's death by Yuiryō (1323–1400), tenth head priest of the Bukkōji. In it there are no references to Ryōgen's associations with Kakunyo, Zonkaku, and the Honganji. These are found primarily in Zonkaku's biography. See Tanishita Ichimu, *Zonkaku ichigoki no kenkyū narabini kaisetsu*, pp. 107–108, 114, 116, 117, 121–22, 125.

5. *Gaijashō*, *SSZ*, 3:64–67.

6. For an extensive description of *kōmyō honzon*, see Kusaka Murin, *Shinshūshi no kenkyū*, pp. 39–74.

7. This *myōchō* survives only in the form of a copy made in 1473, but the original one from which it was made was apparently dated 1343. The manuscript was first made public in 1959 by Miyazaki Enjun, "Shoki Shinshū ni okeru monto myōchō no ichirei," in *Uozumi Sensei koki kinen kokushigaku ronsō*, ed. Uozumi Sensei Koki Kinenkai (Suita: Uozumi Sensei Koki Kinenkai, 1959), pp. 629–44. It has also been reproduced in Kasahara Kazuo, *Ikkō ikki no kenkyū* (Tokyo: Yamakawa Shuppansha, 1962), pp. 19–22.

8. Miyazaki Enjun, "Shoki Shinshū to Jishū," p. 320.

9. Miyazaki Enjun, "Shoki Shinshū ni okeru monto myōchō no ichirei," p. 630. Part of this translation was previously published in James C. Dobbins, "From Inspiration to Institution: The Rise of Sectarian Identity in Jōdo Shinshū," p. 339.

10. Miyazaki Enjun, "Shoki Shinshū ni okeru monto myōchō no ichirei," pp. 631–33.

11. Ibid., pp. 637–39.

12. Kasahara Kazuo, *Ikkō ikki no kenkyū*, pp. 23–25.

13. Kasahara Kazuo, "Shinran to Shinshū kyōdan no keisei," in *Ajia Bukkyōshi*, *Nihonhen*, 3:242–45.

14. There are four surviving *ekeizu* from the year 1326, antedating even the Bukkōji's move to Shibutani in Kyoto. They are proof that Ryōgen used *ekeizu* from the very beginning of his ministry. See Kusaka Murin, *Shinshūshi no kenkyū*, pp. 30–31.

15. Ibid., p. 26. There is no mention of Kakunyo or Zonkaku in Ryōgen's lineage, even though he formally received instruction from them as well. This lineage aligns

Ryōgen more with the Senjuji tradition than with the Honganji, since the Senjuji also traced its origins back to Shinbutsu.

16. Kusaka Murin, *Shinshūshi no kenkyū*, p. 26.

17. Ibid., p. 27.

18. Ibid., pp. 34–39; and Chiba Jōryū, *Shinshū kyōdan no soshiki to seido*, pp. 33–34.

19. Kusaka Murin, *Shinshūshi no kenkyū*, pp. 25, 34–39; Mukai Yoshihiko, "Shinshū ekeizu zakkō," *Shirin* 20.1 (January 1935): 106–110; and Chiba Jōryū, *Shinshū kyōdan no soshiki to seido*, pp. 32–35.

20. Kasahara Kazuo, "Shinran to Shinshū kyōdan no keisei," in *Ajia Bukkyōshi, Nihonhen*, 3:247–48. The practice of reverencing *ekeizu* may have been derived from the veneration of *kōmyō honzon*, which also contained graphic representations of Pure Land personages. Kusaka Murin believes that *ekeizu* evolved from *kōmyō honzon* on the one hand and *myōchō* on the other. See his *Shinshūshi no kenkyū*, pp. 25.

21. This document, dated 1334, is entitled the *Ichimi wagō keiyaku no koto*, and is reproduced in Mukai Yoshihiko, "Shinshū ekeizu zakkō," pp. 104–105. Chiba Jōryū, *Shinshū kyōdan no soshiki to seido*, pp. 29–32, points out that it is patterned after fealty oaths used by samurai during this period.

22. Miyazaki Enjun, "Shoki Shinshū to Jishū," pp. 321–23.

23. *Bukkōji chūkō Ryōgen Shōnin den*, SZ, 68:348–49.

24. Kyōen's temple was named the Kōshōji, pronounced the same as the Bukkōji's original name but written with different characters. Zonkaku probably stayed at this temple or at one of its affiliated *dōjō* when he traveled to Bingo province in 1338 and debated members of the Nichiren school. Myōkō is even mentioned in the same entry in Zonkaku's biography as the debate. See Tanishita Ichimu, *Zonkaku ichigoki no kenkyū narabini kaisetsu*, pp. 129–31.

25. Inoue Toshio, *Ikkō ikki no kenkyū* (Tokyo: Yoshikawa Kōbunkan, 1968), pp. 166–67.

26. *Shibutani rekise ryakuden*, SZ, 69:368–69. This work is relatively late—circa early 1800s—but it is the only Bukkōji source dealing with this event.

27. Documents dated 1481 and 1482 indicate that Mt. Hiei's militant priests were threatening attacks against the Bukkōji during this period. See Kusaka Murin, *Shinshūshi no kenkyū*, pp. 105–109.

28. This figure appears in the *Shibutani rekise ryakuden*, SZ, 69:369.

29. *SDJ*, 1:537–39, s.v. "Kōshōji."

30. Concerning the founder of the Kinshokuji, see the *Hogo no uragaki*, SSZ, 3:979, a Shinshū historical work written around 1567 or 1568 by Rennyo's grandson Kensei (1499–1570). For an annotated edition of this work, see Miyazaki Kiyoshi, *Shinshū Hogo uragaki no kenkyū* (Kyoto: Nagata Bunshōdō, 1987). According to legend, the Kinshokuji temple began as a hermitage called the Ten'andō established by Ennin in the 850s and affiliated with Mt. Hiei. Subsequently, it evolved into a chapel devoted to Bishamon, one of Buddhism's four heavenly kings (*shitennō*), who are venerated as protective deities. Shinran is said to have spent the night there during his return to Kyoto from the Kantō, and from that event the temple claims its original tie to the Shinshū tradition. See Hayashima Kyōshō and Bandō Shōjun, eds., *Nihon Bukkyō kiso kōza 5, Jōdo Shinshū*, pp. 295–96. Despite this legend, it is clear that Jikū was the real founder of the temple. See the passage in Tanishita Ichimu, *Zonkaku ichigoki no kenkyū narabini kaisetsu*, pp. 166–67, which uses the expression *kaisan daitoku* ("founder and master") apparently in reference to Jikū.

31. Kusaka Murin, *Shinshūshi no kenkyū*, pp. 76–78.

32. Inscriptions on early religious objects from the Kinshokuji indicate this. See Kusaka Murin, *Shinshūshi no kenkyū*, pp. 78–79, 81.

33. *Hogo no uragaki*, SSZ, 3:979.

34. Most sources indicate only that Nau was a relation (*enja*) of Gutotsu's. See for example Shigematsu Akihisa, *Kakunyo*, p. 199. But Inoue Toshio, *Honganji*, p. 105, states that Gutotsu was her father. Zonkaku married her in 1316, according to Tanishita Ichimu, *Zonkaku ichigoki no kenkyū narabini kaisetsu*, p. 105.

35. Tanishita Ichimu, *Zonkaku ichigoki no kenkyū narabini kaisetsu*, p. 111.

36. Shigematsu Akihisa, *Kakunyo*, pp. 147-49.

37. Shigematsu Akihisa, *Chūsei Shinshū shisō no kenkyū*, p.225.

38. Tanishita Ichimu, *Zonkaku ichigoki no kenkyū narabini kaisetsu*, pp. 144-45. This entry indicates that Zonkaku sent Jikū to study at the An'yōji, the Seizan temple of the Jōdoshū school, where he and Kakunyo had received instruction from Anichibō Shōkū.

39. This account of Jikū's last wishes and of Kōgon's selection for Kinshokuji leadership is found in a work called the *Anjinshō* preserved in the Kinshokuji archives. Relevant passages from it are contained in Kusaka Murin, *Shinshūshi no kenkyū*, pp. 79-80.

40. Tanishita Ichimu, *Zonkaku ichigoki no kenkyū narabini kaisetsu*, p. 172.

41. *Honganjishi*, 1:234-35.

42. *BDJ*, 2:1042-43, s.v. "Kōgon." Kōgon eventually presented this copy to Zennyo, Kakunyo's successor at the Honganji, in 1392.

43. Tanishita Ichimu, *Zonkaku ichigoki no kenkyū narabini kaisetsu*, pp. 2-4. For an early manuscript edition of this text published in photographic reproduction, see Chiba Jōryū, ed., *Zonkaku Shōnin ichigoki, Sode nikki* (Kyoto: Dōbōsha, 1982).

44. Miyazaki Enjun, *Shoki Shinshū no kenkyū* (Kyoto: Nagata Bunshōdō, 1971), pp. 255-63.

45. This is cited in Inoue Toshio, *Honganji*, p. 92.

46. *Gaijashō*, *SSZ*, 3:69-70.

47. Though Zonkaku did not mention religious objects per se in his *Haja kenshōshō*, he defended ardently the importance of the religious teacher in the life of the believer, and he argued that it is natural for the believer to look up to the teacher and to provide for the teacher's material needs with offerings. See the *Haja kenshōshō*, *SSZ*, 3:180-81.

48. Kakunyo admitted the importance of encountering a true religious teacher and considered it one of the crucial events in the life of a believer, but he always upheld the primacy of the teachings over the teacher. See the *Gaijashō*, *SSZ*, 3:86. This was no doubt one reason why he adopted the position he did with respect to religious objects.

49. Gutotsu was the person responsible for these ties. The congregation at Yoshino eventually became large and powerful enough to challenge the political authority of the Kōfukuji temple in Nara which had proprietary rights to many of the estates in the region. See Inoue Toshio, *Honganji*, pp. 105-106.

50. For a summary of these events, see Inoue Toshio, *Honganji*, pp. 105-107; and Hayashima Kyōshō and Bandō Shōjun, eds., *Nihon Bukkyō kiso kōza 5, Jōdo Shinshū*, p. 297. As these sources indicate, Kinshokuji numbers declined even further in the 1570s when the temple repudiated its Shinshū heritage and joined the Chinzei branch of the Jōdoshū school. This was an expedient move aimed at protecting the Kinshokuji from the wrath of Oda Nobunaga, who was determined to crush the power of the Shinshū. Many of the Kinshokuji's affiliated congregations that were devoted to the Shinshū shifted their allegiance to either the Honganji or the Bukkōji. This defection left the Kinshokuji a mere shadow of its former strength. In the early 1700s it was able to revive somewhat after rejoining the Shinshū tradition.

51. Kusaka Murin, *Shinshūshi no kenkyū*, pp. 7-8.

52. Takadaha Senjuji Onki Hōmuin Monjobu, ed., *Senjuji shiyō*, p. 16. According to legend, the image of the Buddha at the Zenkōji was sent to Japan in 552 by the Korean king of Paekche. It was thrown into Naniwa canal by Mononobe no Moriya after epidemics broke out in Japan. Supposedly, the founder of the Zenkōji retrieved it and

built the temple to enshrine it. See *JDJ*, 2:441–42, s.v. "Zenkōji." Replicas of this image became popular in the medieval period, and the Amida triad at the Takada Nyoraidō was presumably one of them.

53. *Mattōshō*, *SSZ*, 2:662–63, 673–74, and *Shūi shinseki goshōsoku*, *SSZ*, 2:726–27. In some editions of the *Mattōshō* the second of these letters is addressed to someone named Shinobu instead of Shinbutsu.

54. *SDJ*, 2:1253–54, s.v. "Shinbutsu."

55. Nakazawa Kenmyō, "Shinbutsu Shōnin densetsu ni tsuite no kōsatsu," *Takada gakuhō* 9 (1934): 345.

56. *SDJ*, 1:504–505, s.v. "Kenchi"; and Hiramatsu Reizō, "Takada monto," in *SSS*, 4:19.

57. Yamada Bunshō, *Shinshū shikō*, p. 90.

58. Inoue Toshio, *Honganji*, p. 64.

59. Matsuno Junkō, "Shinran shigo no tōgoku kyōdan," in *Shinshūshi gaisetsu*, p. 79.

60. Hiramatsu Reizō, "Takada monto," in *SSS*, 4:16–17.

61. *Honganjishi*, 1:186.

62. Matsuno Junkō, "Shinran shigo no tōgoku kyōdan," in *Shinshūshi gaisetsu*, p. 78.

63. Hiramatsu Reizō, "Takada monto," in *SSS*, 4:20; and Kusaka Murin, *Shinshūshi no kenkyū*, p. 6.

64. *Gaijashō*, *SSZ*, 3:88.

65. *Shōzōmatsu wasan*, *SSZ*, 2:529, v. 110.

66. *Kōtaishi Shōtoku hōsan*, *SSZ*, 2:532–41; *Dai Nihon koku zokusan ō Shōtoku Taishi hōsan*, *SSZ*, 4:23–42; and *Shōzōmatsu wasan*, *SSZ*, 2:526–27.

67. *Kyōgyōshinshō*, *SSZ*, 2:77.

68. For a general discussion of this point, see Hiramatsu Reizō, "Takada Senjuji no sōsō to nembutsu hijiri," in *Akamatsu Toshihide Kyōju taikan kinen kokushi ronbunshū*, ed. Akamatsu Toshihide Kyōju Taikan Kinen Jigyōkai (Kyoto: Akamatsu Toshihide Kyōju Taikan Kinen Jigyōkai, 1972), pp. 527–38.

69. Hiramatsu Reizō, "Takada monto," in *SSS*, 4:18.

70. Tanishita Ichimu, *Zonkaku ichigoki no kenkyū narabini kaisetsu*, pp. 97–100.

71. Specifically, Senjuji was the name of an important temple in the Sanmonto branch during its formative period. See Hayashima Kyōshō and Bandō Shōjun, eds., *Nihon Bukkyō kiso kōza 5, Jōdo Shinshū*, pp. 344–46.

72. Hiramatsu Reizō, "Takada monto," in *SSS*, 4:17.

73. Kusaka Murin, *Shinshūshi no kenkyū*, pp. 7–8.

74. *Takada no shōnin daidai no kikigaki*, *SSS*, 4:85.

75. Concerning Shin'e's aristocratic background, see Tanishita Ichimu, *Zōho Shinshūshi no shokenkyū*, pp. 304–336.

76. This biographical information on Shin'e is derived primarily from the *Daidai shōnin kikigaki* and the *Takada no shōnin daidai no kikigaki*, *SSS*, 4:85–89. These two works are variant versions of a history of the Senjuji composed during the mid-1500s. They are the earliest existing biographical sources on Shin'e.

77. Hiramatsu Reizō, "Takada monto," in *SSS*, 4:22.

78. Ibid.

79. Inoue Toshio, *Honganji*, p. 163.

80. *Takada no shōnin daidai no kikigaki*, *SSS*, 4:87–88.

81. Ibid., 4:88.

82. *Honganjishi*, 1:310–11.

83. Takadaha Senjuji Onki Hōmuin Monjobu, ed., *Senjuji shiyō*, p. 38.

84. For an analysis of Rennyo's advantages over Shin'e in attracting followers, see Inoue Toshio, *Honganji*, pp. 161–65.

85. Takadaha Senjuji Onki Hōmuin Monjobu, ed., *Senjuji shiyō*, p. 33–34.

86. See for example *Takada no shōnin daidai no kikigaki*, *SSS*, 4:85–86.

87. Ibid., 4:85.

88. Hiramatsu Reizō, "Takada monto," in *SSS*, 4:21.

89. For a summary of the various arguments in favor of this view, see Hiramatsu Reizō, "Takada monto," *SSS*, 4:21–24.

90. The most extensive description of this is found in the Senjuji biography of Shinran, *Shinran Shōnin shōtōden*, *GSZ*, 4:226, 265–66, 329–31, 345. Though this biography is rather late, written in the early 1700s by Ryōkū, it derives its information from a number of earlier sources, most of them obscure in origin and somewhat questionable in reliability. See *SDJ*, 2:1264–65, s.v. "*Shinran Shōnin shōtōden.*"

91. For a critique of the Senjuji's claim as a form of *hiji bōmon*, see Ōhara Shōjitsu, *Shinshū igi ianjin no kenkyū*, pp. 126–30.

92. These ten secret transmissions are reproduced in Yamada Bunshō, *Shinshūshi no kenkyū*, pp. 155–73.

93. Ōhara Shōjitsu, *Shinshū igi ianjin no kenkyū*, pp. 129–30.

94. Hiramatsu Reizō, "Yuiju ichinin kuketsu sōjō ni tsuite," in *Nihonjin no seikatsu to shinkō*, ed. Ōtani Daigaku Kokushi Gakkai (Kyoto: Dōbōsha, 1979), pp. 190–208; and Hiramatsu Reizō, "Shin'e Shōnin ni kakawaru henzō hijisho o otte," *Takada gakuhō* 69 (1981): 52–73.

95. Most scholars maintain instead that the practice of secret teachings originated in the Senjuji and was later adopted by the Sanmonto branch. See for example Ōhara Shōjitsu, *Shinshū igi ianjin no kenkyū*, pp. 129–30; Shigematsu Akihisa, *Kakunyo*, pp. 203–210; and Kasahara Kazuo, *Rennyo*, Jinbutsu sōsho, no. 109 (Tokyo: Yoshikawa Kōbunkan, 1975), pp. 70–71. Unfortunately, they do not cite early sources in support of their position. Most of them have derived this view from the *Ōtani Honganji tsūki*, *SZ*, 68:152, a historical work written in the late eighteenth century by the Shinshū priest Genchi (1734–94). The earliest instance of the *Shinran'i* concept that they mention is from the *Shinran Shōnin shōtōden* and from other works of Ryōkū's written in the seventeenth century. For lack of earlier evidence, there is reason to question whether the Senjuji's *Shinran'i* concept actually antedates the secret teachings of the Sanmonto branch.

96. Hayashima Kyōshō and Bandō Shōjun, eds., *Nihon Bukkyō kiso kōza* 5, *Jōdo Shinshū*, pp. 343–45. Occasionally, the name Sanmonto was written with another character for *san* meaning "praises." The reason is that they were famous for singing Shinran's *wasan*, or hymns of praise, as a religious practice.

97. Hayashima Kyōshō and Bandō Shōjun, eds., *Nihon Bukkyō kiso kōza* 5, *Jōdo Shinshū*, pp. 345–46. The details of the demise of the Senjuji at Ōmachi are unclear. Supposedly, it was moved to a different location and renamed.

98. Inoue Toshio, *Honganji*, pp. 102–103; and Hayashima Kyōshō and Bandō Shōjun, eds., *Nihon Bukkyō kiso kōza* 5, *Jōdo Shinshū*, pp. 312–13. During this period the Shōjōji looked to the Gōshōji as its main contact in Kyoto from which it received scriptures and religious training.

99. *Guanki*, *SSS*, 4:719. A *kakikudashi* version of this passage with slight variations is found in Inoue Toshio, *Honganji*, p. 109. No specific mention of the Sanmonto is made here, but it is certain that the work was aimed at the Sanmonto, since Nyodō himself wrote a rebuttal of it. The *Guanki* has been preserved in Shinshū temples primarily because it is what Nyodō's rebuttal is directed against.

100. One such condemnation of Nyodō and the Sanmonto is found in the *Hogo no uragaki*, *SSZ*, 3:984.

101. Shigematsu Akihisa, *Chūsei Shinshū shisō no kenkyū*, p. 243. For the *Guanki hensatsu*, see *SSS*, 4:721–31.

102. *Guanki hensatsu*, *SSS*, 4:725; and Shigematsu Akihisa, *Kakunyo*, p.208.

103. For a detailed analysis of the doctrinal content of the *Guanki hensatsu*, see

Shigematsu Akihisa, *Chūsei Shinshū shisō no kenkyū*, pp. 243–60. Defense of the dancing *nembutsu* in Nyodō's writings suggests that he was active in an area where the Jishū school had followers and perhaps that some of them had joined the Sanmonto congregations.

104. *Bokieshi*, *SSZ*, 3:813; Tanishita Ichimu, *Zonkaku ichigoki no kenkyū narabini kaisetsu*, pp. 93–94; and Shigematsu Akihisa, *Kakunyo*, pp. 231–33.

105. *Gaijashō*, *SSZ*, 3:84–85. In the *Kyōgyōshinshō*, *SSZ*, 2:147–48, 156–57, Shinran used the expression "the open and the concealed" (*kenshō onmitsu*) in reference to the apparent meaning and the true meaning of the *Kanmuryōjukyō*.

106. Sumida Chiken, "Kakunyo Shōnin to igisha," pp. 164–65.

107. *Shūi shinseki goshōsoku*, *SSZ*, 2:727.

108. The two temples were the Jōshōji and the Gōshōji. See Hayashima Kyōshō and Bandō Shōjun, eds., *Nihon Bukkyō kiso kōza 5*, *Jōdo Shinshū*, pp. 311–12, 357–58.

109. *Hogo no uragaki*, *SSZ*, 3:984.

110. *Honganjishi*, 1:268–69.

111. *Mattōshō*, *SSZ*, 2:666–68.

112. Ōhara Shōjitsu, *Shinshū igi ianjin no kenkyū*, pp. 141–42. Though it is difficult to substantiate a direct link, there may have been some Zen influence on this belief of the Sanmonto. There were several major Zen temples located in the Hokuriku region—specifically, the Eiheiji, the Sōjiji, and the Daijōji—belonging to the Sōtō branch of the Zen school.

113. *Hogo no uragaki*, *SSZ*, 3:948.

114. Some of the *dangihon* that Zonkaku wrote are *Jimyōshō*, *SSZ*, 3:91–108; *Jōdo shin'yōshō*, *SSZ*, 3:119–54; *Hokke mondō*, *SSZ*, 3:282–324; and *Shojin hongaishū*, *SSS*, 1:697–712.

115. Miyazaki Enjun, *Shoki Shinshū no kenkyū*, pp. 207–208.

116. Matsuno Junkō, "Honganji no seiritsu," in *Shinshūshi gaisetsu*, pp. 92–94.

117. For a detailed account of Shakunyo's role in the founding of the Zuisenji, see *Inami-chō shi*, 1:207–59.

118. *Honganjishi*, 1:260–70.

119. One example of this is that Gyōnyo sent his youngest son Nyojō (1412–60) to become priest of the Zuisenji sometime in the 1430s. See *Inami-chō shi*, 1:262, 264–65.

120. Kakunyo argued for this version of the inscription in the *Gaijashō*, *SSZ*, 3:76. This version is found among the surviving *nembutsu* inscriptions made by Shinran. See Miyazaki Enjun, *Shoki Shinshū no kenkyū*, p. 264.

121. Kitanishi Hiromu, "Zonnyo Rennyo no fukyō," in *Shinshūshi gaisetsu*, p. 127; and *Honganjishi*, 1:313.

122. *Honganjishi*, 1:275–84.

123. Ibid., 1:248–49.

124. Inoue Toshio, *Honganji*, pp. 81–82; and *Honganjishi*, 1:235–37, 241–42, 275–78, 281–82, 285–86.

125. *Honganjishi*, 1:278–79.

126. For an assessment of Zonnyo's impact on the Honganji's development, see Miyazaki Enjun, *Shoki Shinshū no kenkyū*, pp. 197–213.

127. A more extensive discussion of this period in Honganji history is found in Ira Michael Solomon, "Rennyo and the Rise of Honganji in Muromachi Japan," pp. 98–115.

9. RENNYO AND THE CONSOLIDATION OF THE SHINSHŪ

1. Rennyo also went by the name of Kenju, but for consistency's sake I have referred to him only as Rennyo throughout this study.

2. I have borrowed the expression "pastoral letters" as a translation for *Ofumi* from Stanley Weinstein, "Rennyo and the Shinshū Revival," p. 347. Rennyo's surviving *Ofumi* are compiled in Inaba Masamaru, ed., *Rennyo Shōnin ibun* (1937; rpt. Kyoto: Hōzōkan, 1972), cited herein as *RSI*.

3. These collections are assembled in Inaba Masamaru, ed., *Rennyo Shōnin gyōjitsu* (1928; rpt. Kyoto: Hōzōkan, 1948), hereafter cited as *RSG*.

4. This picture of Rennyo comes out most vividly in Hattori Shisō, *Rennyo*, pp. 244–45.

5. Rennyo has been the subject of several studies in English including the following: Stanley Weinstein, "Rennyo and the Shinshū Revival," pp. 331–58; Ira Michael Solomon, "Rennyo and the Rise of Honganji in Muromachi Japan" (Ph.D. dissertation, Columbia University, 1972); "Kinship and the Transmission of Religious Charisma: The Case of Honganji," *Journal of Asian Studies* 33.3 (May 1974): 403–413; and "The Dilemma of Religious Power: Honganji and Hosokawa Masamoto," *Monumenta Nipponica* 33.1 (Spring 1978): 51–65; and Minor L. Rogers, "Rennyo Shōnin 1415–1499: A Transformation in Shin Buddhist Piety" (Ph.D. dissertation, Harvard University, 1972); "Rennyo and Jōdo Shinshū Piety: The Yoshizaki Years," *Monumenta Nipponica* 36.1 (Spring 1981): 21–35; "The Shin Faith of Rennyo," *Eastern Buddhist* (N.S.) 15.1 (Spring 1982): 56–73; and "A View of Rennyo's Early and Middle Years," in *Jōdokyō no kenkyū*, ed. Ishida Mitsuyuki Hakase Koki Kinen Ronbunshū Kankōkai, pp. 1021–44. Many of the bibliographical references used in this chapter were first brought to my attention by their works.

6. The innovations and accomplishments of this period are well documented in John Whitney Hall and Toyoda Takeshi, eds., *Japan in the Muromachi Age* (Berkeley: University of California Press, 1977); and in George Elison and Bardwell L. Smith, eds., *Warlords, Artists, and Commoners: Japan in the Sixteenth Century* (Honolulu: University of Hawaii Press, 1981).

7. Major Buddhist proselytizers who were contemporary with Rennyo include Shōgei (1341–1420) and Shōsō (1366–1440) of the Chinzei branch of the Jōdoshū school; Myōshū (d. 1487) of the Seizan branch; Ikkyū (1394–1481) of the Zen school; Nichishin (1407–88) and Nichichō (1422–1500) of the Nichiren school; Shin'e (1434–1512) of the Senjuji branch of the Shinshū; and Shinshō (1443–95) of the Tendai school. See Miyazaki Enjun, *Shinran to sono montei*, pp. 188–91.

8. Ishida Mitsuyuki, "Rennyo Shōnin jidai no igi shisō to sono hihan," in *Rennyo Shōnin kenkyū*, ed. Ryūkoku Daigaku (Kyoto: Onki Hōyō Jimusho, 1948), pp. 160–62, points out that this period of Shinshū efflorescence was also a time when Shinshū heresies were proliferating.

9. "Ofumi," no. 31 (1473, 9th month), *RSI*, p. 121.

10. Rennyo was married five times and produced twenty-seven children. Many of them assumed positions of authority in Shinshū temples, but twelve of them died before the age of thirty-five. See *Honganjishi*, 1:366–71.

11. Ishida Mitsuyuki, *Rennyo*, pp. 26–28. Concerning Rennyo's search for his mother, see *Kūzenki*, *RSG*, p. 38; and *Jitsugoki*, *RSG*, pp. 144–45. According to the last citation, Rennyo's mother came to be viewed as a manifestation of the Bodhisattva Kannon.

12. *Jitsugoki*, *RSG*, p. 143.

13. *Renjunki*, *RSG*, pp. 62, 64; and *Jitsugo kyūki*, *RSG*, p. 89. Of the six children sent out, most went to live in Zen or Pure Land temples. Several of them later became head priests of major Shinshū temples in the provinces. See Kasahara Kazuo, *Rennyo*, pp. 15–17.

14. For a list of religious texts that Rennyo copied under Zonnyo's direction, see

Honganjishi, 1:282. Concerning Rennyo's travels with Zonnyo, specifically in 1449 to the Hokuriku and the Kantō regions, see Ishida Mitsuyuki, *Rennyo*, p. 47.

15. An account of this succession dispute is found in the *Jitsugoki*, *RSG*, pp. 145–47.

16. *Honpukuji atogaki*, in Kasahara Kazuo, *Shinshū ni okeru itan no keifu*, p. 281, indicates that these merchant converts gave generously to their religion.

17. *Shōshinge taii*, *RSI*, pp. 25–44. The afterword to this manuscript is dated 1458, but the year 1460 is glossed to the side suggesting that there was an error in copying.

18. "Ofumi," no. 1 (1461, 3rd month), *RSI*, p. 47.

19. Ibid., nos. 1–7, *RSI*, pp. 47–61.

20. *Honganjishi*, 1:313–14.

21. Nyokō (d. 1467), head of the major Shinshū temple Jōgūji in Mikawa province, received an inscription from Rennyo in 1461. See Inoue Toshio, *Honganji*, p. 144.

22. An account of the attack is found in the *Honpukuji atogaki*, in Kasahara Kazuo, *Shinshū ni okeru itan no keifu*, pp. 261–62.

23. The letter containing these accusations, which was issued by Mt. Hiei the day before the attack, is reproduced in *Honganjishi*, 1:311.

24. Ibid., 1:314–15.

25. Ibid., 1:320, 340–43. The image of Shinran was entrusted to the Miidera in 1469. The Chikamatsu Bōsha is sometimes referred to as the Kenshōji, which became its temple name in later times.

26. For instance, in 1468 they struck against Katada, accusing the community of acts of piracy on Lake Biwa. Rennyo, who had moved there just the year before, was forced to flee for his life and for the safety of the image of Shinran which he had brought with him. See Kasahara Kazuo, *Rennyo*, pp. 113–14.

27. When Nyokō and the Jōgūji in Mikawa joined Rennyo's following, they brought with them over one hundred *dōjō* that were affiliated with the temple. Rennyo traveled to Settsu in 1466 and to Yoshino in 1469. See Inoue Toshio, *Honganji*, pp. 144, 147, 151.

28. A brief account of Rennyo's visit to the Kantō is contained in the *Jitsugoki*, *RSG*, p. 149.

29. *Honpukuji atogaki*, in Kasahara Kazuo, *Shinshū ni okeru itan no keifu*, p. 270.

30. Rennyo's own impressions of Yoshizaki are recorded in "Ofumi," no. 26 (1473, 9th month), *RSI*, p. 108.

31. Ibid., no. 24 (1473.8.2), *RSI*, p. 104; and no. 25 (1473.8.12), *RSI*, p. 105.

32. *Jitsugoki*, *RSG*, p. 150.

33. *Takada no shōnin daidai no kikigaki*, *SSS*, 4:85.

34. *Mukashi monogatariki*, *RSG*, p. 252.

35. *Kūzenki*, *RSG*, pp. 11, 35–36.

36. *Jitsugo kyūki*, *RSG*, p. 132.

37. For examples of Rennyo's use of the word *Buppō* to refer to Shin teachings, see "Ofumi," nos. 7, 40, 65, 86, 117, *RSI*, pp. 59, 137, 201, 255, 352.

38. For examples in which Rennyo preached against indiscriminate practices (*zōgyō*), see "Ofumi," nos. 9, 19, 32, 50, 57, *RSI*, pp. 68, 93, 124, 168–69, 185–86.

39. "Ofumi," nos. 29, 30, 66, 123, 136, *RSI*, pp. 114–15, 115–16, 203, 372, 403.

40. Ibid., no. 78 (1475.4.28), *RSI*, pp. 233–34.

41. The varieties and origins of the heresies denounced by Rennyo are outlined in Ishida Mitsuyuki, "Rennyo Shōnin jidai no igi shisō to sono hihan," pp. 162–79. Another valuable source on this topic is Umehara Ryūshō, "Rennyo jidai no igi ni tsuite—Jōgai Ofumi o chūshin to shite," in *Nihon shūkyōshi ronshū*, vol. 1, ed. Kasahara Kazuo Hakase Kanreki Kinenkai (Tokyo: Yoshikawa Kōbunkan, 1976), pp. 309–22.

42. *Eigenki*, *RSG*, p. 260

43. Many of Rennyo's surviving letters of thanks for contributions are addressed to *kō*. See "Ofumi," nos. 192–210, *RSI*, pp. 492–506.

44. For a general description of the structure and function of *kō*, see Kasahara Kazuo, *Ikkō ikki* (Tokyo: Shibundō, 1966), pp. 147–53.

45. "Ofumi," no. 28 (1473.9.11), *RSI*, p. 113; no. 32 (1473, 9th month), *RSI*, pp. 123–24; no. 40 (1473.12.8), *RSI*, pp. 136, 139–140; no. 41 (1473.12.12), *RSI*, pp. 142–43; and no. 43 (1473.12.13), *RSI*, pp. 152–53.

46. Ibid., no. 26 (1473, 9th month), *RSI*, p. 108; no. 40 (1473.12.8), *RSI*, p. 140; and no. 48 (1473, 12th month), *RSI*, p. 163.

47. The influx of samurai into Rennyo's following is mentioned, for example, in the *Jitsugoki*, *RSG*, p. 150, describing Rennyo's stop at the Zuisenji in 1473. Rennyo himself had a rather low opinion of samurai, as indicated by the *Eigenki*, *RSG*, p. 262. Nonetheless, they joined Shinshū congregations and took an active role in the political involvements of these groups. See Kasahara Kazuo, *Rennyo*, pp. 228–36.

48. Rennyo upheld this principle of equality even for congregational meetings. He criticized the custom in some congregations of leaders' sitting on a higher level than other members and drinking their cup of sake before others did. See "Ofumi," no. 33 (1473, 9th month), *RSI*, pp. 124–25.

49. Ibid., no. 55 (1474.3.3), *RSI*, p. 182.

50. Ibid., no. 12 (1471.12.18), *RSI*, p. 72.

51. Kasahara Kazuo, *Ikkō ikki—Sono kōdō to shisō*, Nihonjin no kōdō to shisō, no. 5 (Tokyo: Hyōronsha, 1977), pp. 87–95.

52. For one thing, he received the support of the provincial governor (*shugo*) of Echizen, Asakura Toshikage (1428–81), during his years at Yoshizaki. Also, he may have gained access to Yoshizaki in the first place because of its location on an estate claimed by the Daijōin, a subtemple of the Kōfukuji in Nara. Rennyo had close ties with the Daijōin even though it was part of the traditional Buddhist establishment. The reason is that the head priest Keikaku was apparently a relative of Rennyo's. See Inoue Toshio, *Honganji*, pp. 118–19, 153–54.

53. Tsuji Zennosuke, *Nihon Bukkyōshi*, 6:89–90; and Kasahara Kazuo, *Ikkō ikki—Sono kōdō to shisō*, pp. 95–96.

54. "Ofumi," no. 38 (1473, 11th month), *RSI*, pp. 132–33.

55. Ibid., no. 79 (1475.5.7), *RSI*, pp. 238–39, contains ten rules; and no. 83 (1475.7.15), *RSI*, pp. 247–50, contains six rules with explanations. For an overview of the *okite* presented by Rennyo, see Chiba Jōryū, *Shinshū kyōdan no soshiki to seido*, pp. 47–56.

56. "Ofumi," no. 50 (1474.1.11), *RSI*, pp. 167–68.

57. Ibid., no. 84 (1475.11.21), *RSI*, p. 251.

58. Ibid., no. 27 (1473, 9th month), *RSI*, pp. 109–11.

59. *Haja kenshōshō*, *SSZ*, 3:171–72.

60. "Ofumi," no. 59 (1474.5.13), *RSI*, p. 192.

61. Ibid., no. 79 (1475.5.7), *RSI*, p. 238. This is given as one of the *okite* in Rennyo's second version of them.

62. "Ofumi," no. 64 (1474.7.3), *RSI*, p. 199.

63. This is probably why the postscript to Rennyo's copy of the *Tannishō* recommended that the work be shown only to believers mature enough in faith to comprehend accurately its radical meaning. See *Tannishō*, *SSZ*, 2:795.

64. "Ofumi," no. 115 (1483.11.22), *RSI*, p. 347.

65. This theme is reflected in Shinran's *Kyōgyōshinshō*, *SSZ*, 2:44, 55, 59, 166; and in Kakunyo's *Gaijashō*, *SSZ*, 3: 74–75. The *Gaijashō* passage is quoted in Rennyo's "Ofumi," no. 14 (1472.2.8), *RSI*, pp. 77–78.

66. "Ofumi," no. 12 (1471.12.18), *RSI*, p. 72.

67. *Gaijashō, SSZ,* 3:74–75; and "Ofumi," no. 14 (1472.2.8), *RSI,* pp.77–78.

68. Rennyo tacitly equated *anjin* and *shinjin* in "Ofumi," no. 162 (undated), *RSI,* p. 459; and in *Jitsugo kyūki, RSG,* p. 99.

69. Examples of the expression *tōryū no anjin* are found in "Ofumi," no. 16, 28, 36, 64, 66, 78, 105, *RSI,* pp. 83, 111, 128, 199, 204, 234, 309. Rennyo also used the phrase *tōryū no shinjin,* sometimes in a very similar way, indicating that there was no hard and fast distinction in his mind between the two. See "Ofumi," no. 16, 28, 32, 49, 69, 119, *RSI,* pp. 83, 112, 123, 165, 214, 357. Nonetheless, as a general rule he used the word *shinjin* more often to refer to the specific element of faith that is necessary for salvation and the word *anjin* to indicate in a broader sense the entire religious life emerging out of faith.

70. "Ofumi," no. 55 (1474.3.3), *RSI,* p. 182.

71. Ibid., no. 72 (1474.9.6), *RSI,* p. 222.

72. *Jitsugo kyūki, RSG,* p. 119; and *Eigenki, RSG,* p. 265.

73. "Ofumi," no. 76 (1475.2.23), *RSI,* pp. 229–30.

74. For an overview of Rennyo's attitude toward and use of the *Anjin ketsujōshō,* see Terakura Noboru, "Rennyo Shōnin to Anjin ketsujōshō," *Dōbō gakuhō* 3 (1956): 1–34.

75. *Kyōgyōshinshō, SSZ,* 2:22, 33.

76. *Jitsugo kyūki, RSG,* p. 99.

77. Sugi Shirō, *Gobunshō kōwa,* pt. 2, pp. 135–38. Sugi indicates that there are questions about whether Hōnen actually used this phrase. He also identifies isolated instances where Shinran and Zonkaku may have used it as well.

78. For instances of this phrase in *Niso Raichia Shōnin shōsoku,* see Ōhashi Shunnō, *Banba Jishū no ayumi,* pp. 182, 183, 185, 186, 187, 188, 192, 195, 198, 202, 204, 212, 215, 216, 224, 231, 232, 234, 237.

79. An example of the phrase used in this way can be found in the *Konjaku monogatarishū* dating from the early 1100s. See Yamada Yoshio et al., eds., *Konjaku monogatarishū,* vol. 4, p. 497.

80. "Ofumi," no. 1 (1461, 3rd month), *RSI,* p. 47.

81. Ibid., no. 65 (1474.7.5), *RSI,* p. 202.

82. This is a major point in Uryūzu Ryūō, "Rennyo kyōgaku no tasuke tamae ni tsuite," *Indogaku Bukkyōgaku kenkyū* 11.2 (1963): 302–305, and "Rennyo Shōnin yōgojō no mondai—Tasuke tamae o chūshin to shite," *Shinshū kenkyū* 10 (1965): 35–44; Matsuyama Chikō, "Rennyo no shinkō—Goshō tasuke tamae to tanomu kō," *Shinshū kenkyū* 4 (1959): 110–20; and Sugi Shirō, *Gobunshō kōwa,* pt. 2, pp. 135–42. One reason for their concern over this question is that during the *Sangō wakuran* controversy of the late eighteenth- and early nineteenth-century *tasuke tamae* was frequently interpreted according to Chinzei principles. The Shinshū eventually rejected this interpretation as heretical.

83. Sugi Shirō, *Gobunshō kōwa,* pt. 2, p. 136.

84. An account of Rennyo's departure is contained in his "Ofumi," no. 99 (1477.12.29), *RSI,* pp. 293–94.

85. Ibid., nos. 8–83, *RSI,* pp. 62–250.

86. Rennyo recognized that many believers in the provinces around Kyoto claimed affiliation with the Shinshū. See "Ofumi," no. 86 (1477.9.3), *RSI,* p. 254. Ishida Mitsuyuki, "Rennyo Shōnin jidai no igi shisō to sono hihan," pp. 174–76, indicates that some of Rennyo's letters are implicitly critical of Bukkōji beliefs and practices, though they do not mention the Bukkōji by name.

87. "Ofumi," no. 88 (1476.7.18), *RSI,* pp. 261–62; and no. 100 (1478.2.4), *RSI,* p. 297.

88. Ibid., no. 91 (1477, 1st month), *RSI,* p. 269; and no. 105 (1480.6.18), *RSI,* pp.

309–310. In these letters Rennyo singled out for criticism certain individuals in Mikawa and Ise provinces who were proponents of secret teachings.

89. Kasahara Kazuo, *Rennyo*, pp. 281–84.

90. "Ofumi," no. 104 (1479, 12th month), *RSI*, p. 304.

91. By this time Rennyo had gained allies in the Ashikaga *bakufu*. Rennyo's fourth daughter served as a lady-in-waiting in the household of the *shōgun* Ashikaga Yoshimasa (1436–90), and through this connection a rapport developed between them. The *shōgun* was probably instrumental in helping the Honganji gain property rights at Yamashina and perhaps in insuring its safety. See *Honganjishi*, 1:339–40. The Yamashina Honganji was destroyed by attack some fifty years after this time, but that attack was the work of standing armies belonging to regional warlords, not Mt. Hiei. See *Honganjishi*, 1:412.

92. "Ofumi," no. 107 (1480), *RSI*, p. 315. This letter indicates that Shinshū adherents in Kawachi province south of Kyoto transported more than fifty huge logs from the forests of Yoshino to be used as pillars in the building.

93. Details of the problems in reclaiming the image of Shinran from the Miidera in Ōtsu are recorded in *Renjunki*, *RSG*, pp. 65–66.

94. "Ofumi," no. 107 (1480), *RSI*, p. 317.

95. Ibid., no. 113 (1483.8.28), *RSI*, pp. 335–38.

96. Inoue Toshio, *Honganji*, p. 160; and *Honganjishi*, 1:353. This quotation actually dates from several decades later, but the Honganji's appearance at that point was not substantially different.

97. *SDJ*, 3:1907, s.v. "*Hōonkō*."

98. The large number of pilgrims coming to attend the Hōonkō is indicated in "Ofumi," no. 109 (1481), *RSI*, p. 325.

99. The following are the Hōonkō letters written by Rennyo over the course of his career: "Ofumi," *RSI*, no. 18 (1472.11.27), pp. 88–91; no. 39 (1473.11.21), pp. 133–35; no. 74 (1474.11.21), pp. 225–26; no. 75 (1474.11.25), pp. 227–28; no. 84 (1475.11.21), pp. 251–53; no. 96 (1477, 11th month; 1479.11.20), pp. 282–87; no. 108 (1480.11.21), pp. 319–21; no. 111 (1481.11.24), pp. 332–33; no. 112 (1482. 11.21), pp. 333–34; no. 115 (1483.11.22), pp. 344–47; no. 117 (1484.11.21), pp. 350–52; no. 119 (1485.11.23, 1486. 11.26), pp. 354–63; no. 126 (1494.11.21), pp. 377–79; no. 130 (1496.11.21), pp. 386–87; no. 134 (1497.11.21), pp. 398–99; no. 135 (1497.11.25), pp. 401–402; and no. 156 (1498. 11.21), pp. 444–46.

100. For a fuller discussion of the Hōonkō as it developed in Rennyo's time, see Minor Lee Rogers, "Rennyo Shōnin 1415–1499: A Transformation in Shin Buddhist Piety," pp. 255–79.

101. "Ofumi," no. 106 (1480.8.23), *RSI*, p. 313.

102. *Honganji sahō no shidai*, *RSG*, p. 194.

103. *Kūzenki*, *RSG*, p. 13.

104. The primacy of the *nembutsu* inscription over other objects of worship is indicated in the *Jitsugo kyūki*, *RSG*, p. 71.

105. Chiba Jōryū, *Shinshū kyōdan no soshiki to seido*, pp. 150–56.

106. *Eigenki*, *RSG*, p. 259.

107. "Ofumi," no. 192 (7th month, 28th day) *RSI*, pp. 492–93, indicates one contribution of five thousand *hiki*.

108. Most information about contributions to the Honganji in Rennyo's time is derived from his notes thanking congregations for them. See "Ofumi," nos. 192–210, *RSI*, pp. 492–506.

109. For example, see "Ofumi," no. 115 (1483.11.21), *RSI*, p. 346; no. 117 (1484.11.21), *RSI*, p. 351; and no. 119 (1485.11.23), *RSI*, p. 357. All of these are Hōonkō letters containing passages critical of priests who lack faith, who become angry at followers that do have faith, and who act in ways adverse to the Buddhist teachings.

110. "Ofumi," no. 214 (1468.3.28), *RSI*, p. 509; and no. 215 (1489.10.28), *RSI*, p. 510.

111. A rationalization of excommunication by Rennyo's son Jitsugo can be found in the *Jitsugoki*, *RSG*, pp. 167-68. Also see pp. 168-69 concerning Rennyo's opposition to execution.

112. For a more detailed discussion of the *ikkeshu*, see Michael Solomon, "Kinship and the Transmission of Religious Charisma: The Case of Honganji," pp. 403-413; and "Rennyo and the Rise of Honganji in Muromachi Japan," pp. 258-75.

113. *Honganji sahō no shidai*, *RSG*, pp. 219-20.

114. This did not take place until the seventeenth century. See Chiba Jōryū, *Shinshū kyōdan no soshiki to seido*, pp. 150-56.

115. *Honganji sahō no shidai*, *RSG*, p. 201.

116. *Jitsugo kyūki*, *RSG*, p. 94. The quotation is drawn from the *Lao Tzu*, Chap. 9.

117. *Jitsugo kyūki*, *RSG*, p. 85. In the early 1500s eighty of Rennyo's *Ofumi* were singled out as the letters of greatest import and were edited into a five-fascicle collection, ordered more or less chronologically, entitled the *Gobunshō*, *SSZ*, 3:402-518. Concerning its compilation, see Izumoji Osamu, ed., *Ofumi*, Tōyō bunko, no. 345 (Tokyo: Heibonsha, 1978), pp. 366-69. Several other letters, such as the *Gozokushō*, *SSZ*, 3:519-21, and the *Natsu ofumi*, *SSZ*, 3:522-28, were considered significant enough to merit separate titles of their own.

118. The letter mentioned here, "Ofumi," no. 96 (1477, 11th month), *RSI*, pp. 282-84, was later named the *Gozokushō*, *SSZ*, 3:519-21. During Hōonkō services in local Shinshū temples each year, it is more common today to hear this text read than Kakunyo's *Hōonkō shiki*, *SSZ*, 3:655-60.

119. *Jitsugo kyūki*, *RSG*, p. 97.

120. For a discussion of village formation during the medieval period, see Nagahara Keiji, "Village Communities and Daimyo Power," in *Japan in the Muromachi Age*, ed. John Whitney Hall and Toyoda Takeshi, pp. 107-21.

121. For an overview of the Honganji's political involvements during this period, see Neil McMullin, *Buddhism and the State in Sixteenth-Century Japan* (Princeton: Princeton University Press, 1984).

122. For an account of the Honganji's partition, see Inoue Toshio, *Honganji*, pp. 210-17.

123. For example, Chiba Jōryū, "Seiji to Bukkyō," in *Nihon Bukkyōshi*, 3:60, cites a derogatory comment made of recalcitrant Pure Land adherents by Ikeda Mitsumasa (1609-82) of Okayama-han.

124. *Honganjishi*, 1:311.

125. Chiba Jōryū, *Shinshū kyōdan no soshiki to seido*, p.90.

126. For a list and explanation of the twenty-five *anjin rondai*, which are the backbone of orthodoxy in the Nishi Honganji today, see Takagi Akiyoshi, *Anjin rondai kaisetsu* (Kyoto: Nagata Bunshōshō, 1982).

127. *Ryōgemon*, *SSZ*, 3:529. This is the basic text adopted by the Nishi Honganji. The version used by the Higashi Honganji is the same except that it is entitled the *Gaikemon*, or "Statement of Confession," and the second article begins, "We rejoice that our birth. . ." leaving out the words "in knowing" (*zonji*). In a few smaller branches of the Shinshū, there are more substantive differences in the content of this creed. Concerning them, see Umehara Ryūshō, "Jōdo Shinshū ni okeru shinkō kokuhakumon no seiritsu," in *Shinshūshi no kenkyū*, ed. Miyazaki Enjun Hakase Kanreki Kinenkai (Kyoto: Nagata Bunshōdō, 1966), pp. 110-14.

128. Rennyo is traditionally cited as the author of the creed, but present-day scholars agree that it was pieced together from his writings sometime after his death. Four versions of the *Ryōgemon* are included in Rennyo's collected writings, *RSI*, pp. 515-18, but

they are listed as works of questionable authenticity (*shingi mitei*). Concerning the composition of this statement, see Tokushi Yūshō, "Ryōgemon seiritsu kō," in *Rennyo Shōnin kenkyū*, ed. Ryūkoku Daigaku, pp. 345–48; and Umehara Ryūshō, "Jōdo Shinshū ni okeru shinkō kokuhakumon no seiritsu," pp. 90–99.

AFTERWORD

1. This general argument can be found throughout the writings of Shinran and Rennyo. See for example *Mattōshō*, *SSZ*, 2:656–58, 658–60; and "Ofumi," no. 110 (1481.11.14), *RSI*, p. 328–31. Rennyo's letter cited here contains extensive quotations from the *Anjin ketsujōshō*.

2. The eschatology of *mappō* was introduced into the Pure Land tradition by Tao-ch'o, *An-lo chi*, *SSZ*, 1:378–79, 427–28, and became a central element in Shinran's and Rennyo's teachings. See for example *Shōzōmatsu wasan*, *SSZ*, 2:516–23; and "Ofumi," no. 68 (1474.8.5), *RSI*, pp. 208–12.

3. Daisetz T. Suzuki, *Collected Writings on Shin Buddhism*, p. 31, describes Pure Land as "not a world existing in space-time but an idealistic world of enlightenment." Yoshifumi Ueda, gen. ed., *Letters of Shinran, A Translation of Mattōshō*, p. 14, and *Notes on Essentials of Faith Alone, A Translation of Shinran's Yuishinshō-mon'i*, p. 4, associates Amida with the "supreme Buddha[who] is formless" and the "formless and nameless Tathagata."

4. Ishida Mitsuyuki, *Ianjin*, pp. 117–18, explicates the Shin concept of heresy, *ianjin*, in terms of the affirmation of egoism (*jiga aisei*) and religious faith in terms of the repudiation of egoism.

5. Universal salvation is a theme in such major Mahāyāna sutras as the *Nehangyō*, *TD*, 12:554–60, and the *Hokekyō*, *TD*, 9:5–10.

6. The eighteenth vow in particular, *Muryōjukyō*, *SSZ*, 1:9, 24, is framed in such a way that Amida would have refused enlightenment if sentient beings were to be denied access to his Pure Land.

7. This kind of argument is presented in greater detail in the review article by Luis O. Gómez, "Shinran's Faith and the Sacred Name of Amida," *Monumenta Nipponica* 38.1 (Spring 1983): 73–84. See also the response to his article by Ueda Yoshifumi and Dennis Hirota, as well as Gómez's reply to them, in *Monumenta Nipponica* 38.4 (Winter 1983): 413–27.

Bibliography

I. PRIMARY SOURCES

Amidakyō ("Smaller Pure Land Sutra"). *SSZ*, vol. 1.

Amidakyō shūchū ("Collected Comments on the 'Smaller Pure Land Sutra'"). *TSSZ*, vol. 7.

Anjin ketsujōshō ("Notes on the Firm [Abode] of Faith"). *SSZ*, vol 3.

Anjinshō ("Notes on Faith"). In *Seizan Shōnin tanpen shōmotsushū*. Ed. Mori Eijun.

An-lo chi ("Collection on the Land of Bliss"). *SSZ*, vol. 1.

Bokieshi ("Illustrated Account of Our Beloved Departed [Master]"). *SSZ*, vol. 3.

Bonmōkyō ("Brahma's Net Sutra"). *TD*, vol. 24.

Bukkōji chūkō Ryōgen Shōnin den ("Biography of Master Ryōgen, Restorer of the Bukkōji"). *SZ*, vol. 68.

Chinzei myōmoku mondō funjinshō ("Rousing Notes of Questions and Answers Concerning Chinzei Topics"). *JZ*, vol.10.

Ch'ün-i lun ("A Treatise [Dispelling] Myriad Doubts [on Pure Land]"). *TD*, vol. 47.

Dai Nihon koku zokusan ō Shōtoku Taishi hōsan ("Hymns of Praise to Shōtoku Taishi, Minor Ruler of the Great Kingdom of Japan." *SSZ*, vol. 4.

Daidai shōnin kikigaki ("Recorded Sayings on the Generations of Masters [at the Senjuji]"). *SSS*, vol. 4.

Daihōdō daranikyō ("Great Vaipulya Dhāraṇī Sutra"). *TD*, vol. 21.

Dainichikyō ("Great Vairocana Buddha Sutra"). *TD*, vol. 21.

Eigenki ("Eigen's Record"). *RSG*.

Eshinni shōsoku ("Letters of Eshinni"). *SSZ*, vol. 5.

Etchū no kuni Kōmyōbō e tsukawasu gohenji ("A Reply Sent to Kōmyōbō of Etchū Province"). *HSZ*.

Fa-shih tsan ("Praises for [Pure Land] Services"). *SSZ*, vol.1.

Gaijashō ("Notes Rectifying Heresy"). *SSZ*, vol. 3.

Gaikemon ("Statement of Confession"). *RSI*.

Ganganshō ("Notes on the Vows"). *SSZ*, vol. 3.

Gengibunshō ("Notes on the 'Profound Principles Chapter' [of Shan-tao's 'Commentary on the Pure Land Meditation Sutra']"). *Zōho kaitei Nihon daizōkyō*, vol. 90.

Gobunshō ("The Letters"). *SSZ*, vol. 3.

Godenshō ("The Biography"). *SSZ*, vol. 3.

Gokuraku jōdo shūgi ("Essential Principles on the Pure Land Paradise"). *Zōho kaitei Nihon daizōkyō*, vol. 90.

Gonengyō no oku ni kiseru onkotoba ("Words Recorded at the End of the 'Protective [Buddhist Deities] Sutra' [i.e., 'Smaller Pure Land Sutra']"). *HSZ*.

Goshōsokushū ("Collection of Letters"). *SSZ*, vol. 2.

Goshōsokushū Zenshōbon ("Collection of Letters, Zenshō's Version"). *SSZ*, vol. 2.

Gozokushō ("Personal History"). *SSZ*, vol. 3.

Guanki ("Record of Foolishness and Darkness"). *SSS*, vol. 4.

Guanki hensatsu ("Reply to 'Record of Foolishness and Darkness'"). *SSS*, vol. 4.

Gukanshō ("Notes of My Foolish Views"). *Nihon koten bungaku taikei* (Iwanami Shoten), vol. 86.

Gusanshingi ("Principles of the Three States of Mind United"). In *Ryūkan Risshi no Jōdokyō*. Hirai Shōkai.

Haja kenshō mōshijō ("A Petition Assailing Heresy and Revealing Truth"). *SSZ*, vol. 3.

Haja kenshōgi ("Principles Assailing Heresy and Revealing Truth"). *JZ*, vol. 12.

Haja kenshōshō ("Notes Assailing Heresy and Revealing Truth"). *SSZ*, vol. 3.

Heike monogatari ("Tale of Heike"). *Nihon koten bungaku taikei* (Iwanami Shoten), vols. 32–33.

Hino ichiryū keizu ("Genealogy of the Hino Lineage"). *SSS*, vol. 7.

Hogo no uragaki ("Scribblings on Discarded Paper"). *SSZ*, vol. 3.

Hokekyō ("Lotus Sutra"). *TD*, vol. 9.

Hokke mondō ("Questions and Answers on the Lotus"). *SSZ*, vol. 3.

Hōnen Shōnin denki ("Biography of Master Hōnen"). *JZ*, vol. 17.

Hōnen Shōnin gyōjō ezu ("Illustrated Account of the Deeds of Master Hōnen"). *JZ*, vol. 16.

Honganji no Shōnin Shinran denne ("Illustrated Biography of Master Shinran of the Honganji"). *SSZ*, vol. 3.

Honganji sahō no shidai ("Order of Honganji Observances"). *RSG*.

Honpukuji atogaki ("Surviving Writings on the Honpukuji"). In *Shinshū ni okeru itan no keifu*. Ed. Kasahara Kazuo.

Hōonkō shiki ("Liturgy of Gratitude"). *SSZ*, vol. 3.

Ichimai kishōmon ("Single Page Testament"). *HSZ*.

Ichimi wagō keiyaku no koto ("Covenant Binding Allies Together"). In "Shinshū ekeizu zakkō." Ed. Mukai Yoshihiko.

Ichinen tanen funbetsuji ("Discernment of the Single and the Repeated Nembutsu"). *SSZ*, vol. 2.

Ichinen tanen mon'i ("Notes on the Single and the Repeated Nembutsu"). *SSZ*, vol. 2.

Ichinengi chōji kishōmon ("Pledge to Prohibit the Single Nembutsu Doctrine"). *HSZ*.

Igyōbon ("Chapter on Easy Practices"). *SSZ*, vol. 1.

Ippen hijiri e ("Illustrated [Account] of the Holy Man Ippen"). *Jishū zensho*, vol. 1.

Ippen Shōnin goroku ("Recorded Sayings of Master Ippen"). *Jishū zensho*, vol. 2.

Iya onna yuzurijō ("Letter of Transference of the Woman [Named] Iya"). *TSSZ*, vol. 4.

Jimyōshō ("Notes on Holding Fast to the Name"). *SSZ*, vol. 3.

Jitsugo kyūki ("Jitsugo's Early Record"). *RSG*.

Jitsugoki ("Jitsugo's Record"). *RSG*.

Jōdo hōmon genrushō ("Essay on the Origins of the Pure Land Teachings"). *TD*, vol. 84.

Jōdo nizō nikyō ryakuju ("Verses Summing up [the Place of] Pure Land in the Two Collections and the Two Teachings"). *JZ*, vol. 12.

Jōdo sangyō ōjō monrui ("Selected Passages on Birth in Pure Land from the Three [Pure Land] Sutras"). *SSZ*, vol. 2.

Jōdo shin'yōshō ("Notes on the True Essentials of Pure Land"). *SSZ*, vol. 3.

Jōdo wasan ("Hymns on Pure Land"). *SSZ*, vol. 2.

Jōdoron ("Treatise on Pure Land"). *SSZ*, vol. 1.

Jōkōji nijūikkajō seikin ("Twenty-one Regulations of the Jōkōji"). *SSS*, vol. 1.

Juhō yōjinshū ("Collection on the State of Mind for Receiving the Dharma"). *Misshū gakuhō*, vols. 99–102.

Jūjikyōron ("Treatises on the 'Ten Stages Sutra'"). *TD*, vol. 26.

Jūjū bibasharon ("Treatise on the Ten Abodes"). *TD*, vol. 26.

Kakuzenshō ("Notes by Kakuzen"). *Dai Nihon Bukkyō zensho*, vols. 45–51.

Kangyōsho denzūki ("Record of the Transmitted [Teachings] of the 'Commentary on the Pure Land Meditation Sutra'"). *JZ*, vol. 2.

Kanmon yōgishō ("Notes of Essential Principles on the Path of Cognizing [Pure Land]"). *Seizan zensho*, vols. 3–4.

Kanmuryōjukyō ("Pure Land Meditation Sutra"). *SSZ*, vol.1.

Kanmuryōjukyō shūchū ("Collected Comments on the 'Pure Land Meditation Sutra'"). *TSSZ*, vol. 7.

Kashima mondō ("Questions and Answers Concerning the Kashima [Kami]"). *JZ*, vol. 12.

Kechimyaku monjū ("Collection of Writings from the Lineage"). *SSZ*, vol. 2.

Kegonkyō ("Flower Garland Sutra"). *TD*, vol. 9.

Ken jōdo shinjitsu kyōgyōshō monrui ("Selected Passages Revealing the True Teaching, Practice, and Enlightenment of Pure Land"). *SSZ*, vol. 2.

Ketchishō ("Notes on the Establishment of Wisdom"). *SSZ*, vol.3.

Kōfukuji sōjō ("Kōfukuji's Petition to the Emperor"). *Nihon shisō taikei* (Iwanami Shoten), vol. 15.

Konjaku monogatarishū ("A Collection of Tales of Past and Present"). *Nihon koten bungaku taikei* (Iwanami Shoten), vols. 22–26.

Kosha shokan ("Letters [Found] in Early Copies"). *TSSZ*, vol. 3.

Kōsō wasan ("Hymns on the Patriarchs"). *SSZ*, vol. 2.

Kōtaishi Shōtoku hōsan ("Hymns of Praise to Prince Shōtoku"). *SSZ*, vol. 2.

Kuan ching shu ("Commentary on the Pure Land Meditation Sutra"). *SSZ*, vol. 1.

Kuan-nien fa-men ("Methods in [Pure Land] Meditation"). *SSZ*, vol. 1.

Kudenshō ("Notes of Oral Transmissions"). *SSZ*, vol. 3.

Kūzenki ("Kūzen's Record"). *RSG*.

Kyōgyōshinshō ("Teaching, Practice, Faith, and Enlightenment"). *SSZ*, vol. 2.

Lao Tzu. In *Lao Tzu chiao-ku.* Ed. Ma Hsü-lun.

Lo-pang wen-lei ("Selected Passages on the [Pure Land] Paradise"). *TD*, vol. 47.

Mappō tōmyōki ("Record of the Lamp in [the Age of] the Dharma's Decline"). *SZ*, vol. 58.

Matsudai nembutsu jushuin ("Personal Seal [Attesting] to the Transmission of the Nembutsu in the Latter Days"). *JZ*, vol. 10.

Mattōshō ("Notes on the Lamp in the [Age of the Dharma's] Decline"). *SSZ*, vol. 2.

Mo-ho chih-kuan ("Great Meditation"). *TD*, vol. 46.

Motochika shin o torite hongan o shinzuru no yō ("Concerning Motochika's Adoption of Faith and his Faith in the Principal Vow"). *HSZ*.

Muchū mondō ("Questions and Answers Within a Dream"). *Zengaku taikei*, vol. 6.

Mukashi monogatariki ("Record of Tales of Old"). *RSG*.

Muryōjukyō ("Larger Pure Land Sutra"). *SSZ*, vol. 1.

Muryōjukyō ubadaisha ganshōge ("Verses on the Aspiration to Be Born in Pure Land: A Treatise on the Pure Land Sutra"). *SSZ*, vol. 1.

Myōe Shōnin yuikun ("Instructions Left by Master Myōe"). *Nihon koten bungaku taikei* (Iwanami Shoten), vol. 83.

Natsu ofumi ("Summer Letters"). *SSZ*, vol. 3.

Nehangyō ("Nirvāṇa Sutra"). *TD*, vol. 12.

Nembutsu muken jigokushō ("Notes on the Nembutsu [Leading] to the Hell of Incessant Suffering"). *Shōwa teihon Nichiren Shōnin ibun*, vol. 1.

Nembutsu myōgishū ("Collection on the Significance of [Amida's] Name in [the Form of] the Nembutsu"). *JZ*, vol. 10.

Niso Raichia Shōnin shōsoku ("Letters of the Second Patriarch, Master Raichia"). In *Banba Jishū no ayumi.* Ōhashi Shunnō.

Nyonin ōjō kikigaki ("Recorded Sayings on the Birth of Women in Pure Land"). *SSZ*, vol. 3.

Ofumi ("Pastoral Letters"). *RSI*.

Ōgo no kakochō ("Register of the Past"). In *Jishū kakochō.* Ed. Ōhashi Shunnō.

Ōjōki ("Record of Birth in Pure Land"). *HSZ*.

Ōjōyōshū ("Collection [of Scriptural Passages] on the Essentials for Birth in Pure Land"). *SSZ*, vol. 1.

Ōtani Honganji tsūki ("Comprehensive Account of the Ōtani Honganji"). *SZ*, vol. 68.

Renge mengyō ("Lotus Blossom Countenance Sutra"). *TD*, vol.12.

Renjunki ("Renjun's Record"). *RSG*.

Rennyo Shōnin itokuki ("Record of Master Rennyo's Enduring Virtue"). *SSZ*, vol. 3.

Rokuyōshō ("Notes of Essentials on the Six [Fascicles]"). *SSZ*, vol. 2.

Ryōchi no sadame ("Rules of Ryōchi"). *SSS*, vol. 1.

Ryōgemon ("Statement of Conviction"). *SSZ*, vol. 3.

Saihō shinanshō ("Notes of Guidance to the Western Direction"). *SSZ*, vol. 4.

Saishu kyōjū ekotoba ("Illustrated Account of Utmost Reverence"). *SSZ*, vol. 3.

Sange gakushōshiki ("Procedures for Scholar-Monks of the Mountain [Tendai] School"). *TD*, vol. 74.

San-lun hsüan-i ("Profound Principles of the Three Treatises"). *TD*, vol. 45.

Sanzengi mondō ("Questions and Answers on 'Principles of Nonmeditative Practices'"). In *Ryūkan Risshi no Jōdokyō*. Hirai Shōkai.

Senjaku hongan nembutsushū ("Collection [of Scriptural Passages] on the Nembutsu of the Principal Vow Singled Out [by Amida]"). *HSZ*.

Senjakushū ("Singled-Out Collection"). *HSZ*.

Shasekishū ("Sand and Pebbles"). *Nihon koten bungaku taikei* (Iwanami Shoten), vol. 85.

Shibunritsu ("Vinaya in Four Sections"). *TD*, vol. 22.

Shibutani rekise ryakuden ("Abbreviated Biographies of Successive Generations at the Shibutani [Bukkōji]"). *SZ*, vol. 69.

Shichikajō kishōmon ("Seven Article Pledge"). *HSZ*.

Shinran muki ("Record of Shinran's Dreams"). *TSSZ*, vol.4.

Shinran Shōnin monryo kyōmyōchō ("Register of Master Shinran's Disciples"). *SSS*, vol. 1.

Shinran Shōnin shōtōden ("Orthodox Biography of Master Shinran"). *GSZ*, vol. 4.

Shojin hongaishū ("Collection on the Original Intent of the [Shinto] Kami"). *SSS*, vol. 1.

Shōshin nembutsuge ("Verses on the Nembutsu of True Faith"). *SSZ*, vol. 2.

Shōshinge ("Verses on True Faith"). *SSZ*, vol. 2.

Shōshinge taii ("Great Significance of the 'Verses on True Faith'"). *RSI*.

Shoshū jiin hatto ("Laws for Temples of All Schools"). In *Shinshū kyōdan no soshiki to seido*. Chiba Jōryū.

Shōzōmatsu wasan ("Hymns on the True, the Imitated, and the Declining [Dharma]"). *SSZ*, vol. 2.

Shūi kotokuden ekotoba ("Illustrated Biographical Account of the Venerable Priest [Hōnen] from Collected Materials"). *SSZ*, vol. 3.

Shūi shinseki goshōsoku ("Authentic Letters from Collected Materials"). *SSZ*, vol. 2.

Shūjishō ("Notes on Holding Fast"). *SSZ*, vol. 3.

Shusse gan'i ("Fundamental Meaning of Transcending the World"). *SSZ*, vol. 3.

Songō shinzō meimon ("Notes on Inscriptions on Sacred Scrolls"). *SSZ*, vol. 2.

Takada no shōnin daidai no kikigaki ("Recorded Sayings on the Generations of Masters at the Takada [Senjuji]"). *SSS*, vol. 4.

Tannishō ("Notes Lamenting Deviations"). *SSZ*, vol. 2.

Tannishō kōrinki ("Record from the Lecture Hall on 'Notes Lamenting Deviations'"). *ST*, vol. 23.

Tannishō monki ("Recorded Sayings on 'Notes Lamenting Deviations'"). *ZST*, *Bekkan*, vol. 1.

Ta-sheng ch'i-hsin lun ("Treatise on the Awakening of Faith in Mahāyāna"). *TD*, vol. 32.

Tengu sōshi ("Book of Goblins"). *Nihon emakimono zenshū* (Kadokawa Shoten), vol. 27.

Ushū Kōgan gokyōkai ("Ecclesiastical Judgments on Kōgan of Dewa Province"). *ZST*, vol. 18.

Wang-sheng li-tsan chieh ("Verses of Worship and Praise on Birth in Pure Land"). *SSZ*, vol. 1.

Wang-sheng lun chu ("Commentary on the 'Treatise on Birth in Pure Land'"). *SSZ*, vol. 1.

Yuishinshō ("Essentials of Faith Alone"). *SSZ*, vol. 2.

Yuishinshō mon'i ("Notes on 'Essentials of Faith Alone'"). *SSZ*, vol. 2.

Zaijarin ("Pivotal [Points] Shattering Heresy"). *JZ*, vol. 8.

Zen'en no seikin ("Regulations of Zen'en"). *SSS*, vol.1.

Zenshōbō densetsu no kotoba ("Words [of Hōnen] According to Zenshōbō"). *HSZ*.

Zonkaku hōgo ("Words of Religious Instruction by Zonkaku"). *SSZ*, vol. 3.

Zonkaku ichigoki ("Record of the Life of Zonkaku"). In *Zonkaku ichigoki no kenkyū narabini kaisetsu.* Tanishita Ichimu.

II. SECONDARY SOURCES

A. Works in English

Andrews, Allan A. *The Teachings Essential for Rebirth.* Tokyo: Sophia University, 1973.

Anesaki, Masaharu. *History of Japanese Religion.* 1930; rpt. Tokyo: Charles E. Tuttle Company, 1963.

Bandō Shōjun. "Myōe's Criticism of Hōnen's Doctrine." *Eastern Buddhist* (N.S.) 7.1 (May 1971).

_____ and Stewart, Harold, trans. "Tannishō: Passages Deploring Deviations of Faith." *Eastern Buddhist* (N.S.) 13.1 (Spring 1980).

Bloom, Alfred. "The Life of Shinran Shōnin: The Journey to Self-Acceptance." *Numen* 15 (1968).

_____ . *Shinran's Gospel of Pure Grace.* Tucson: University of Arizona Press, 1965.

Brown, Delmer M., and Ishida Ichirō. *The Future and the Past.* Berkeley: University of California Press, 1979.

Chappell, David W. "Chinese Buddhist Interpretations of the Pure Lands." In *Buddhist and Taoist Studies.* Ed. Michael Saso and David W. Chappell. Honolulu: University of Hawaii Press, 1977.

_____ . "Tao-ch'o (562–645): A Pioneer of Chinese Pure Land Buddhism." Ph.D. dissertation, Yale University, 1976.

Coates, Harper Havelock, and Ishizuka, Ryugaku, trans. *Hōnen, The Buddhist Saint,* 5 vols. 1925; rpt. Kyoto: Society for the Publication of Sacred Books of the World, 1949.

Corless, Roger Jonathan. "T'an-luan's Commentary on the Pure Land Discourse: An Annotated Translation and Soteriological Analysis of the *Wang-sheng lun chu* (T. 1819)." Ph.D. dissertation, University of Wisconsin, 1973.

Dobbins, James. C. "Buddhism in Japan." In *A Thousand Cranes: Treasures of Japanese Art.* Seattle: Seattle Art Museum, 1987.

_____ . "The Concept of Heresy in the Jōdo Shinshū." *Transactions of the International Conference of Orientalists in Japan* 25 (1980).

_____ . "From Inspiration to Institution: The Rise of Sectarian Identity in Jōdo Shinshu." *Monumenta Nipponica* 41.3 (Autumn 1986).

_____ . "The Single and the Repeated *Nembutsu* Extremes." In *Jōdokyō no kenkyū.* Ed. Ishida Mitsuyuki Hakase Koki Kinen Ronbunshū Kankōkai. Kyoto: Nagata Bunshōdō, 1982.

Ducor, Jérôme, trans. "Hōonkō-shiki: Cérémonial du sermon de reconnaissance." *The Pure Land* (N.S.) 1 (December 1984). French translation.

Eliade, Mircea, gen. ed. *The Encyclopedia of Religion,* 16 vols. New York: Macmillan and Free Press, 1987.

Eliot, Sir Charles. *Japanese Buddhism.* 1935; rpt. London: Routledge & Kegan Paul, 1959.

Elison, George, and Smith, Bardwell L., eds. *Warlords, Artists, and Commoners: Japan in the Sixteenth Century.* Honolulu: University of Hawaii Press, 1982.

Foard, James Harlan. "Ippen Shōnin and Popular Buddhism in Kamakura Japan." Ph.D. dissertation, Stanford University, 1977.

Fujikawa, Asako. *Daughter of Shinran.* Tokyo: Hokuseido Press, 1964.

Fujiwara, Ryosetsu. *The Way to Nirvana: The Concept of the Nembutsu in Shan-tao's Pure Land Buddhism.* Tokyo: Kyoiku Shincho Sha, 1974.

Gómez, Luis O. "Shinran's Faith and the Sacred Name of Amida." *Monumenta Nipponica* 38.1 (Spring 1983). Rejoinder by Ueda Yoshifumi and Dennis Hirota, and surrejoinder by Gómez: "Correspondence." *Monumenta Nipponica* 38.4 (Winter 1983).

Groner, Paul. *Saichō: The Establishment of the Japanese Tendai School*. Berkeley: Berkeley Buddhist Studies Series, 1984.

Hall, John Whitney, and Toyoda Takeshi, eds. *Japan in the Muromachi Age*. Berkeley: University of California Press, 1977.

Hirota, Dennis, trans. *No Abode: The Record of Ippen*. Kyoto: Ryukoku University, 1986.

_____ , trans. *Tannishō: A Primer*. Kyoto: Ryukoku University, 1982.

Honpa Hongwanji Mission of Hawaii, comp. *The Shinshu Seiten: The Holy Scripture of Shinshu*. Honolulu: Honpa Hongwanji Mission of Hawaii, 1955.

Hori Ichiro. *Folk Religion in Japan: Continuity and Change*. Chicago: University of Chicago Press, 1974.

_____ . "On the Concept of the Hijiri." *Numen* 5 (1958).

Inagaki, Hisao. *A Dictionary of Japanese Buddhist Terms*. Kyoto: Nagata Bunshōdō, 1984.

_____ , trans. *Zendo's Exposition on the Merit of the Samādhi of Meditation on the Ocean-like Figure of Amida Buddha*. Ryukoku Translation Pamphlet Series, no. 2. Kyoto: Ryukoku University, 1966.

Kikumura, Norihiko. *Shinran: His Life and Thought*. Los Angeles: Nembutsu Press, 1972.

King, Winston L. "An Interpretation of the *Anjin Ketsujōshō*." *Japanese Journal of Religious Studies* 13.4 (December 1986).

Kitagawa, Joseph M. *Religion in Japanese History*. New York: Columbia University Press, 1966.

Kondō Tesshō. "The Religious Experience of Ippen." *Eastern Buddhist* (N.S.) 12.2 (October 1979).

Malalasekera, G.P., gen. ed. *Encyclopedia of Buddhism*. Colombo: Government of Ceylon, 1964-.

Matsunaga, Daigan and Alicia. *Foundation of Japanese Buddhism*, 2 vols. Los Angeles and Tokyo: Buddhist Books International, 1974–76.

McMullin, Neil. *Buddhism and the State in Sixteenth-Century Japan*. Princeton: Princeton University Press, 1984.

Morrell, Robert E. *Sand and Pebbles*. Albany: State University of New York Press, 1985.

Müller, F. Max, gen. ed. *Sacred Books of the East*. Vol. 49: *Buddhist Mahāyāna Texts*. Oxford: Clarendon Press, 1894.

Nagahara Keiji. "Village Communities and Daimyo Power." In *Japan in the Muromachi Age*. Ed. John Whitney Hall and Toyoda Takeshi.

Ohtani, Lady Yoshiko. *Eshin-ni: The Wife of Shinran Shonin*. Kyoto: Honpa Hongwanji, 1970.

Pas, Julian. "Shan-tao's Commentary on the *Amitāyur-Buddhānusmṛti-sūtra*." Ph.D. dissertation, McMaster University, 1973.

_____ . "Shan-tao's Interpretation of the Meditative Vision of Buddha Amitāyus." *History of Religions* 14.2 (November 1974).

Rhodes, Robert F., trans. "Saichō's *Mappō Tōmyōki*: The Candle of the Latter Dharma." *Eastern Buddhist* (N.S.) 13.1 (Spring 1980).

Rogers, Minor Lee. "Rennyo and Jōdo Shinshū Piety: The Yoshizaki Years." *Monumenta Nipponica* 36.1 (Spring 1981).

_____ . "Rennyo Shōnin 1415–1499: A Transformation of Shin Buddhist Piety." Ph.D. dissertation, Harvard University, 1972.

_____ . "The Shin Faith of Rennyo." *Eastern Buddhist* (N.S.) 15.1 (Spring 1982).

_____ . "A View of Rennyo's Early and Middle Years." In *Jōdokyō no kenkyū*. Ed. Ishida Mitsuyuki Hakase Koki Kinen Ronbunshū Kankōkai. Kyoto: Nagata Bunshōdō, 1982.

Ryukoku Translation Center, trans. *The Jōdo Wasan.* Kyoto: Ryukoku University, 1965.

_____, trans. *The Kōsō Wasan.* Kyoto: Ryukoku University, 1974.

_____, trans. *The Kyō Gyō Shin Shō.* Kyoto: Ryukoku University, 1966.

_____, trans. *The Shoshin Ge.* Kyoto: Ryukoku University, 1966.

_____, trans. *The Shōzōmatsu Wasan.* Kyoto: Ryukoku University, 1980.

_____, trans. *The Sūtra of Contemplation on the Buddha of Immeasurable Life as Expounded by Śākyamuni Buddha.* Kyoto: Ryukoku University, 1984.

_____, trans. *The Tanni Shō.* Kyoto: Ryukoku University, 1962.

Solomon, Ira Michael. "The Dilemma of Religious Power: Honganji and Hosokawa Masamoto." *Monumenta Nipponica* 33.1 (Spring 1978).

_____. "Kinship and the Transmission of Religious Charisma: The Case of Honganji." *Journal of Asian Studies* 33.3 (May 1974).

_____. "Rennyo and the Rise of Honganji in Muromachi Japan." Ph.D. dissertation, Columbia University, 1972.

Suzuki, Daisetz T. *Collected Writings on Shin Buddhism.* Kyoto: Shinshū Ōtaniha, 1973.

_____. *Shin Buddhism.* New York: Harper and Row, 1970.

_____, trans. *The Kyōgyōshinshō.* Kyoto: Shinshū Ōtaniha, 1973.

Takahatake, Takamichi. *Young Man Shinran: A Reappraisal of Shinran's Life.* Waterloo, Ontario: Wilfred Laurier University Press, 1987.

Tanabe, George Joji, Jr. "Myōe Shōnin (1173–1232): Tradition and Reform in Early Kamakura Buddhism." Ph.D. dissertation, Columbia University, 1983.

Tanaka Eizo, trans. "Anjin Ketsujo Sho: On the Attainment of True Faith." *The Pure Land* 2.2–5.2 (December 1980–December 1983).

Tri-State Buddhist Temples, comp. *Shinshū Seiten: Jōdo Shin Buddhist Teaching.* San Francisco: Buddhist Churches of America, 1978.

Tsunoda, Ryusaku, ed. *Sources of Japanese Tradition.* New York: Columbia University Press, 1958.

Ueda Yoshifumi, gen. ed. *Letters of Shinran, A Translation of Mattōshō.* Kyoto: Hongwanji International Center, 1978.

_____, gen. ed. *Notes on Essentials of Faith Alone, A Translation of Shinran's Yuishinshō-mon'i.* Kyoto: Hongwanji International Center, 1979.

_____, gen. ed. *Notes on Once-calling and Many-calling, A Translation of Shinran's Ichinen-tanen mon'i.* Kyoto: Hongwanji International Center, 1980.

_____, gen. ed. *Notes on the Inscriptions on Sacred Scrolls, A Translation of Shinran's Songō shinzō meimon.* Kyoto: Hongwanji International Center, 1981.

_____, gen. ed. *Passages on the Pure Land Way, A Translation of Shinran's Jōdo monrui jushō.* Kyoto: Hongwanji International Center, 1982.

_____, gen. ed. *The True Teaching, Practice, and Realization of the Pure Land Way, A Translation of Shinran's Kyōgyōshinshō,* 4 vols. Kyoto: Hongwanji International Center, 1983-.

Weinstein, Stanley. "The Concept of Reformation in Japanese Buddhism." In *Studies in Japanese Culture,* vol. 2. Ed. Saburō Ōta. Tokyo: Japan Pen Club, 1973.

_____. "Rennyo and the Shinshū Revival." In *Japan in the Muromachi Age.* Ed. John Whitney Hall and Toyoda Takeshi.

Yamamoto Kosho. *An Introduction to Shin Buddhism.* Ube: Karinbunko, 1963.

_____, trans. *The Kyogyoshinsho.* Ube: Karinbunko, 1975.

_____, trans. *The Words of St. Rennyo.* Ube: Karinbunko, 1968.

Yanagi Sōetsu. "Ippen Shōnin." *Eastern Buddhist* (N.S.) 6.1 (October 1973).

B. Works in Japanese

Ajia Bukkyōshi, Nihonhen. See Nakamura Hajime, Kasahara Kazuo, and Kanaoka Shūyū, eds. *Ajia Bukkyōshi, Nihonhen.*

Akamatsu Toshihide. *Kamakura Bukkyō no kenkyū.* Kyoto: Heirakuji Shoten, 1957.

_____ . *Kyōto jishikō*. Kyoto: Hōzōkan, 1962.

_____ . *Shinran*. Jinbutsu sōsho, no. 65. Tokyo: Yoshikawa Kōbunkan, 1961.

_____ . *Zoku Kamakura Bukkyō no kenkyū*. Kyoto: Heirakuji Shoten, 1966.

_____ and Kasahara Kazuo, eds. *Shinshūshi gaisetsu*. Kyoto: Heirakuji Shoten, 1963.

BDJ. See Mochizuki Shinkō, ed. *Bukkyō daijiten*.

BGDJ. See Nakamura Hajime. *Bukkyōgo daijiten*.

BGJ. See Taya Raishun, Ōchō Enichi, and Funabashi Issai, eds. *Bukkyōgaku jiten*.

BKDJ. See Ono Genmyō, ed. *Bussho kaisetsu daijiten*.

Bussho Kankōkai, ed. *Dai Nihon Bukkyō zensho*, 151 vols. Tokyo: Bussho Kankōkai, 1912-22.

Chiba Jōryū, ed. *Honpukuji kyūki*. Kyoto: Hōzōkan, 1980.

_____ . *Honpukujishi*. Kyoto: Dōbōsha, 1980.

_____ . *Shinshū kyōdan no soshiki to seido*. Kyoto: Dōbōsha, 1978.

_____ , ed. *Zonkaku Shōnin ichigoki, Sode nikki*. Kyoto: Dōbōsha, 1982.

Dobbins, James. C. "Shinshūshi ni okeru itan ni taishite no mikata." *Shinshūgaku* 63 (February 1981).

Etani Ryūkai. *Gaisetsu Jōdoshūshi*. Tokyo: Ryūbunkan, 1978.

Fugen Daien. *Shinshū gairon*. Kyoto: Hyakkuen, 1950.

Fugen Kōju, ed. *Anjin ketsujōshō*. Kyoto: Dōbōsha, 1983.

_____ . "Anjin ketsujōshō to Shinshū resso no kyōgaku." *Ryūkoku Daigaku ronshū* 415 (1979).

_____ . "Chūsei Shinshū no jingi shisō." *Bukkyō bunka kenkyūjo kiyō* 17 (1978).

_____ , ed. *Haja kenshōshō*. Kyoto: Dōbōsha, 1987.

_____ . "Nichiren no Hōnen Jōdokyō hihan to Zonkaku no tachiba." *Shinshūgaku* 56 (1977).

Fujishima Tatsurō. *Eshinni Kō*. Kyoto: Hōzōkan, 1984.

Fujita Kōtatsu. *Genshi Jōdo shisō no kenkyū*. Tokyo: Iwanami Shoten, 1970.

Fukuma Kōchō and Ōkuwa Hitoshi, eds. *Shiryō Shinshū kyōdanshi*. Kyoto: Bun'eidō, 1978.

Fukunaga Katsumi. *Shinran kyōdan dan'atsushi*. Tokyo: Yūzankaku, 1972.

Fukushima Kazuto. *Kindai Nihon no Shinran*. Kyoto: Hōzōkan, 1973.

Furuta Takehiko. *Shinran shisō—Sono shiryō hihan*. Tokyo: Fuzanbō, 1975.

Futaba Kenkō. *Kodai Bukkyō shisōshi kenkyū*. Kyoto: Nagata Bunshōdō, 1962.

_____ . *Shinran no kenkyū*. Kyoto: Hyakkaen, 1970.

_____ , ed. *Shiryō Nihon Bukkyōshi*. Kyoto: Yamazaki Hōbundō, 1971.

GSZ. See Yūki Reimon, gen. ed. *Gendaigoyaku Shinran zenshū*.

Haga Yaichi. *Kuyaku Gobunshō*. Tokyo: Kōyūkan, 1916.

Hattori Shisō. *Rennyo*. 1948; rpt. Tokyo: Fukumura Shuppan, 1970.

_____ . *Shinran nōto*. 1948; rpt. Tokyo: Fukumura Shuppan, 1970.

_____ . *Zoku Shinran nōto*. 1950; rpt. Tokyo: Fukumura Shuppan, 1970.

Hayashima Kyōshō and Bandō Shōjun, eds. *Nihon Bukkyō kiso kōza* 5, *Jōdo Shinshū*. Tokyo: Yūzankaku, 1979.

Hirai Shōkai. *Ryūkan Risshi no Jōdokyō*. 1941; rpt. Tokyo: Kokusho Kankōkai, 1984.

Hiramatsu Reizō. "Shin'e Shōnin ni kakawaru henzō hijisho o otte." *Takada gakuhō* 69 (1981).

_____ . "Takada monto." In *SSS*, vol. 4.

_____ . "Takada Senjuji no sōsō to nembutsu hijiri." In *Akamatsu Toshihide Kyōju taikan kinen kokushi ronbunshū*. Ed. Akamatsu Toshihide Kyōju Taikan Kinen Jigyōkai. Kyoto: Akamatsu Toshihide Kyōju Taikan Kinen Jigyōkai, 1972.

_____ . "Yuiju ichinin kuketsu sōjō ni tsuite." In *Nihonjin no seikatsu to shinkō*. Ed. Ōtani Daigaku Kokushi Gakkai. Kyoto: Dōbōsha, 1979.

Hirose Takashi. "Tannishō no seikaku—Toku ni sanjo o chūshin to shite." *Ōtani gakuhō* 47.1 (June 1967).

_____. *Tannishō no shomondai.* Kyoto: Hōzōkan, 1978.

Honganji Shiryō Kenkyūjo, ed. *Honganji nenpyō.* Kyoto: Jōdo Shinshū Honganjiha, 1981.

_____, ed. *Honganjishi,* 3 vols. Kyoto: Jōdo Shinshū Honganjiha, 1961–69.

_____, ed. *Honganjishi sakuin.* Kyoto: Jōdo Shinshū Honganjiha, 1984.

Honganjiha Shūgakuin, ed. *Honden kensan jukki,* 2 vols. Kyoto: Nagata Bunshōdō, 1976.

Honganjishi. See Honganji Shiryō Kenkyūjo, ed. *Honganjishi.*

Horigome Yōzō. *Seitō to itan.* Tokyo: Chūō Kōronsha, 1964.

Hoshino Genpō, Ishida Mitsuyuki, and Ienaga Saburō, eds. *Shinran.* Nihon shisō taikei, no. 11. Tokyo: Iwanami Shoten, 1976.

Hosokawa Gyōshin. "Anjin ketsujōshō no shoshi." *Ōtani gakuhō* 44.3 (March 1965).

HSZ. See Ishii Kyōdō, ed. *Shōwa shinshū Hōnen Shōnin zenshū.*

Ienaga Saburō. *Chūsei Bukkyō shisōshi kenkyū.* 1947; rpt. Kyoto: Hōzōkan, 1976.

_____, Akamatsu Toshihide, and Tamamuro Taijō, eds. *Nihon Bukkyōshi,* 3 vols. Kyoto: Hōzōkan, 1967.

Ikawa Jōkei. *Hōnen Shōnin den zenshū.* Osaka: Hōnen Shōnin Den Zenshū Kankōkai, 1967.

Inaba Enjō. "Kakunyo Shōnin denkō." In *Kakunyo Shōnin no kenkyū, Mujintō* 22 (1917).

Inaba Masamaru, ed. *Rennyo Shōnin goichidai kikigaki.* Iwanami bunko, nos. 3034–35. Tokyo: Iwanami Shoten, 1942.

_____, ed. *Rennyo Shōnin gyōjitsu.* 1928; rpt. Kyoto: Hōzōkan, 1948.

_____, ed. *Rennyo Shōnin ibun.* 1937; rpt. Kyoto: Hōzōkan, 1972.

Inami-chō Shi Hensan Iinkai, ed. *Inami-chō shi.* Toyama: Inami-chō, 1970.

Inoue Mitsusada. *Nihon kodai no kokka to Bukkyō.* Tokyo: Iwanami Shoten, 1971.

_____. *Shintei Nihon Jōdokyō seiritsushi no kenkyū.* Tokyo: Yamakawa Shuppansha, 1975.

Inoue Tetsuo. *Shinshū honpa gakusō itsuden.* Kyoto: Nagata Bunshōdō, 1979.

_____. *Shinshū sōmei jiten.* 1926; rpt. Kyoto: Hyakkaen, 1977.

Inoue Toshio. *Honganji.* Tokyo: Shibundō, 1962.

_____. *Ikkō ikki no kenkyū.* Tokyo: Yoshikawa Kōbunkan, 1968.

Ishida Mitsuyuki. *Ianjin.* Kyoto: Hōzōkan, 1951.

_____. *Jōdo kyōgaku no kenkyū,* 2 vols. Tokyo: Daitō Shuppansha, 1979.

_____. *Jōdokyō kyōrishi.* Kyoto: Heirakuji Shoten, 1977.

_____. *Nihon Jōdokyō no kenkyū.* Kyoto: Hyakkaen, 1963.

_____. *Rennyō.* Kyoto: Jirinsha, 1949.

_____. "Rennyo Shōnin jidai no igi shisō to sono hihan." In *Rennyo Shōnin kenkyū.* Ed. Ryūkoku Daigaku.

_____. *Senjakushū kenkyū josetsu.* Kyoto: Hyakkaen, 1976.

_____. *Shinran kyōgaku no kiso teki kenkyū.* Kyoto: Nagata Bunshōdō, 1970.

_____. *Shinran kyōgaku no kiso teki kenkyū 2.* Kyoto: Nagata Bunshōdō, 1977.

_____. "Shinran no shinkegi hihan no shūkyō teki igi." *Shūkyō kenkyū* 39 (1965).

Ishida Mitsuyuki Hakase Koki Kinen Ronbunshū Kankōkai, ed. *Jōdokyō no kenkyū.* Kyoto: Nagata Bunshōdō, 1982.

Ishida Mizumaro. *Bonmōkyō.* Tokyo: Daizō Shuppan, 1971.

_____. *Genshin.* Nihon shisō taikei, no. 6. Tokyo: Iwanami Shoten, 1970.

_____. *Jōdokyō no tenkai.* Tokyo: Shunjūsha, 1967.

_____. *Shinran shisō to shichikōsō.* Tokyo: Daizō Shuppan, 1976.

_____. *Shinran to sono tsuma no tegami.* Tokyo: Shunjūsha, 1968.

_____. *Tannishō Shūjishō Kudenshō Gaijashō.* Tōyō bunko, no. 33. Tokyo: Heibonsha, 1964.

Ishida Yoshikazu. "Kinsei Shinshū kyōgaku no seiritsu to tenkai o meguru ikkōsatsu." *Kinsei Bukkyō* 3 (February 1961).

_____. "Shinran no kyōsetsu o meguru itan no mondai." *Risō* 569 (October 1980).

———. "Shinshū ni okeru igi ianjin to itan no mondai." *Kyōto joshi daigaku jinbun ronsō* 7 (1962).

Ishii Kyōdō. *Kaitei zōho Jōdo no kyōgi to sono kyōdan.* Kyoto: Fuzanbō, 1972.

———, ed. *Shōwa shinshū Hōnen Shōnin zenshū.* 1955; rpt. Kyoto: Heirakuji Shoten, 1974.

Itō Yuishin. *Jōdoshū no seiritsu to tenkai.* Tokyo: Yoshikawa Kōbunkan, 1981.

Iwakura Mosaji. "Shukugō ni tsuite." In *GSZ*, vol. 1.

Izumoji Osamu, ed. *Ofumi.* Tōyō bunko, no. 345. Tokyo: Heibonsha, 1978.

JDJ. See Jōdoshū Daijiten Hensan Iinkai, ed. *Jōdoshū daijiten.*

Jishū zensho, 2 vols. Kamakura: Geirinsha, 1974.

Jōdoshū Daijiten Hensan Iinkai, ed. *Jōdoshū daijiten*, 4 vols. Tokyo: Sankibō, 1974–82.

Jōdoshū Shūten Kankōkai, ed. *Jōdoshū zensho*, 20 vols. Tokyo: Jōdoshū Shūten Kankōkai, 1908–14.

JZ. See Jōdoshū Shūten Kankōkai, ed. *Jōdoshū zensho.*

Kageyama Haruki. *Hieizan to Kōyasan.* Tokyo: Kyōikusha, 1980.

Kakunyo Shōnin no kenkyū. Mujintō 22 (1917).

Kamata Shigeo and Tanaka Hisao, eds. *Kamakura kyū Bukkyō.* Nihon shisō taikei, no. 15. Tokyo: Iwanami Shoten, 1971.

Kanai Kiyomitsu. *Ippen to Jishū kyōdan.* Tokyo: Kadokawa, 1975.

Kanaoka Shūyū. *Koji meisatsu jiten.* Tokyo: Tōkyōdō, 1970.

Kaneko Daiei. "Kakunyo Shōnin to shūso to no kankei." In *Kakunyo Shōnin no kenkyū, Mujintō* 22 (1917).

———, ed. *Shinshū seiten.* Kyoto: Hōzōkan, 1979.

———. *Tannishō.* Iwanami bunko, no. 732. Tokyo: Iwanami Shoten, 1950.

———, Ōhara Shōjitsu, and Hoshino Genpō, eds. *Shinshū shinjiten.* Kyoto: Hōzōkan, 1983.

Kasahara Kazuo. *Ikkō ikki.* Tokyo: Shibundō, 1966.

———. *Ikkō ikki no kenkyū.* Tokyo: Yamakawa Shuppansha, 1962.

———. "Ikkō ikki no shisō teki kiban." *Rekishi to bunka* 10 (March 1972).

———. *Ikkō ikki—Sono kōdō to shisō.* Nihonjin no kōdō to shisō, no. 5. Tokyo: Hyōronsha, 1977.

———. *Rennyo.* Jinbutsu sōsho, no. 109. Tokyo: Yoshikawa Kōbunkan, 1975.

———. *Shinran to Rennyo—Sono kōdō to shisō.* Nihonjin no kōdō to shisō, no. 40. Tokyo: Hyōronsha, 1978.

———. *Shinran to tōgoku nōmin.* Tokyo: Yamakawa Shuppansha, 1975.

———. *Shinshū ni okeru itan no keifu.* Tokyo: Tōkyō Daigaku Shuppankai, 1962.

——— and Inoue Toshio, eds. *Rennyo Ikkō ikki.* Nihon shisō taikei, no. 17. Tokyo: Iwanami Shoten, 1972.

Kasai Daishū. *Shinshū no igi to sono rekishi.* Osaka: Seibundō, 1977.

Kashiwabara Yūgi. *Jōdo sanbukyō kōgi, Kaitei shinpan.* Kyoto: Heirakuji Shoten, 1980.

Kashiwabara Yūsen. "Shinran ni okeru jingikan no kōzō." In *Shinran Shōnin.* Ed. Ōtani Daigaku.

———, Chiba Jōryū, Hiramatsu Reizō, and Mori Ryūkichi, gen. eds. *Shinshū shiryō shūsei*, 13 vols. Kyoto: Dōbōsha, 1974–83.

Kawasaki Yasuyuki and Kasahara Kazuo, eds. *Shūkyōshi.* Tokyo: Yamakawa Shuppansha, 1974.

Keika Bunka Kenkyūkai, ed. *Kyōgyōshinshō senjutsu no kenkyū.* Kyoto: Hyakkaen, 1954.

Kikumura Norihiko and Nishina Ryū. *Shinran no tsuma Eshinni.* Tokyo: Yūzankaku, 1981.

Kitanishi Hiromu. *Kakushinni no shōgai.* Kyoto: Higashi Honganji Shuppanbu, 1984.

Kojima Eijō. "Tannishō no sōten." *Indogaku Bukkyōgaku kenkyū* 13.1 (January 1965).

Kono Hōun and Kumoyama Ryūju, eds. *Shinshū jiten.* 1935; rpt. Kyoto: Hōzōkan, 1978.

Koreyama Ekaku. *Anjin ketsujōshō kōwa.* Kyoto: Kōkyō Shoin, 1925.

Kurita Isamu. *Ippen Shōnin: Tabi no shisakusha.* Tokyo: Shinchōsha, 1977.

Kuroda Toshio. *Jisha seiryoku.* Iwanami shinsho, no. 117. Tokyo: Iwanami Shoten, 1980.

Kusaka Murin. *Shinshūshi no kenkyū.* 1931; rpt. Kyoto: Rinsen Shoten, 1975.

Kyōke Kenkyūjo, ed. *Shinshū gaiyō.* Kyoto: Hōzōkan, 1953.

Ma Hsü-lun, ed. *Lao Tzu chiao-ku.* 1924; rpt. Peking: Ku-chi Ch'u-pan-she, 1956. Chinese annotated edition.

Masutani Fumio. *Shinran Dōgen Nichiren.* Tokyo: Shibundō, 1956.

Matsubara Yūzen. *Mappō tōmyōki no kenkyū.* Kyoto: Hōzōkan, 1978.

―――. *Shinran to mappō shisō.* Kyoto: Hōzōkan, 1968.

Matsuno Junkō. "Shinran monka no ichi kyōgaku." *Indogaku Bukkyōgaku kenkyū* 3.1 (September 1954).

―――. *Shinran―Sono kōdō to shisō.* Nihonjin no kōdō to shisō, no. 2. Tokyo: Hyōronsha, 1971.

―――. *Shinran―Sono shōgai to shisō no tenkai katei.* Tokyo: Sanseidō, 1959.

―――. "Zōaku muge to Shinran." *Shinshū kenkyū* 3 (1957).

Matsuyama Chikō. "Rennyo no shinkō―Goshō tasuke tamae to tanomu kō." *Shinshū kenkyū* 4 (1959).

Mibu Taishun. *Eizan no shinpū.* Tokyo: Chikuma Shobō, 1967.

Mikkyō Gakkai, ed. *Mikkyō daijiten,* 6 vols. Kyoto: Hōzōkan, 1969–70.

Miyaji Kakue. *Goshōsokushū kōsan.* Kyoto: Hyakkaen, 1974.

―――. *Shinran den no kenkyū.* Kyoto: Hyakkaen, 1968.

Miyasaka Yūshō et al., eds. *Kana Hōgoshū.* Nihon koten bungaku taikei, no. 83. Tokyo: Iwanami Shoten, 1964.

Miyazaki Enjun. *Honganji no Shōnin Shinran denne shiki.* Kyoto: Nagata Bunshōdō, 1983.

―――. "Kakunyo no jūnikajō konmōjō ni tsuite." *Ryūkoku shiden* 49 (1962).

―――. "Shinran denki ni tsuite." In *GSZ,* vol.4.

―――. "Shinran no tachiba to Kyōgyōshinshō no senjutsu." In *Kyōgyōshinshō senjutsu no kenkyū.* Ed. Keika Bunka Kenkyūkai.

―――. *Shinran to sono montei.* Kyoto: Nagata Bunshōdō, 1956.

―――. "Shoki Shinshū ni okeru monto myōchō no ichirei." In *Uozumi Sensei koki kinen kokushigaku ronsō.* Ed. Uozumi Sensei Koki Kinenkai. Suita: Uozumi Sensei Koki Kinenkai, 1959.

―――. *Shoki Shinshū no kenkyū.* Kyoto: Nagata Bunshōdō, 1971.

―――. "Shoki Shinshū to Jishū." *Ryūkoku Daigaku ronshū* 389–90 (May 1969).

―――. "Tannishō no seiritsu to kyōdan no dōkō." In *Gendai o ikiru kokoro Tannishō.* Tokyo: Asahi Shinbunsha, 1973.

―――. *Zoku Shinran to sono montei.* Kyoto: Nagata Bunshōdō, 1961.

Miyazaki Kiyoshi. *Shinshū Hogo no uragaki no kenkyū.* Kyoto: Nagata Bunshōdō, 1987.

Mizuhara Gyōei. *Jakyō Tachikawaryū no kenkyū.* Kyoto: Shinbundō, 1931.

Mochizuki Shinkō, ed. *Bukkyō daijiten,* 10 vols. Tokyo: Sekai Seiten Kankō Kyōkai, 1960.

―――. *Ryakujutsu Jōdo kyōrishi.* Tokyo: Nihon Tosho, 1977.

Mori Eijun, ed. *Seizan Shōnin tanpen shōmotsushū.* Kyoto: Bun'eidō, 1980.

Mori Ryūkichi. *Honganji.* Tokyo: San'ichi Shobō, 1973.

_____ . *Rennyo*. Kōdansha gendai shinsho, no. 390. Tokyo: Kōdansha, 1979.

Mukai Yoshihiko. "Shinshū ekeizu zakkō." *Shirin* 20.1 (January 1935).

Murakami Senjō. *Shinshū zenshi*. Tokyo: Heigo Shuppansha, 1916.

Murayama Shūichi, ed. *Hieizan to Tendai Bukkyō no kenkyū*. Tokyo: Meicho Shuppan, 1975.

Nabata Ōjun. *Shinran wasanshū*. Iwanami bunko, no. 318-3. Tokyo: Iwanami Shoten, 1976.

_____ et al., eds. *Shinranshū Nichirenshū*. Nihon koten bungaku taikei, no. 82. Tokyo: Iwanami Shoten, 1964.

Nagashima Shōdō. "Jishū." In *Nihon Bukkyō kiso kōza 4, Jōdoshū*. Ed. Fujii Masao. Tokyo: Yūzankaku, 1979.

Nakai Gendō. *Ianjin no shujusō*. Tokyo: Dōbōsha, 1930.

Nakajima Etsuji. *Gukanshō zenchūkai*. Tokyo: Yūseidō, 1969.

Nakajima Kakuryō. *Ianjinshi*. Tokyo: Mugasanbō, 1912.

_____ . "Kakunyo Shōnin to Zonkaku Shōnin to no kyōri kankei." In *Kakunyo Shōnin no kenkyū, Mujintō* 22 (1917).

Nakamura Hajime. *Bukkyōgo daijiten*, 3 vols. Tokyo: Tōkyō Shoseki, 1975.

_____ , Kasahara Kazuo, and Kanaoka Shūyū, eds. *Ajia Bukkyōshi, Nihonhen*, 9 vols. Tokyo: Kōsei Shuppansha, 1972-76.

Nakazawa Kenmyō. *Shijō no Shinran*. 1922; rpt. Kyoto: Hōzōkan, 1983.

_____ . "Shinbutsu Shōnin densetsu ni tsuite no kōsatsu." *Takada gakuhō* 9 (1934).

Nihon Bukkyōshi. See Ienaga Saburō, Akamatsu Toshihide, and Tamamuro Taijō, eds. *Nihon Bukkyōshi*.

Ōe Junjō. "Kyōgyōshinshō Shinkan bessensetsu no hihan." In *Kyōgyōshinshō senjutsu no kenkyū*. Ed. Keika Bunka Kenkyūkai.

_____ and Ōhara Shōjitsu, eds. *Shinshū seiten*. Kyoto: Nagata Bunshōdō, 1977.

Ōhara Shōjitsu. "Henji dagoku no igi to nembutsu mukensetsu." *Indogaku Bukkyōgaku kenkyū* 11.1 (1963).

_____ . *Shinshū igi ianjin no kenkyū*. Kyoto: Nagata Bunshōdō, 1956.

_____ . *Shinshū kyōgaku no dentō to koshō*. Kyoto: Nagata Bunshōdō, 1965.

Ōhashi Shunnō. *Banba Jishū no ayumi*. N.p.: Jōdoshūshi Kenkyūkai, 1963.

_____ , ed. *Hōnen Ippen*. Nihon shisō taikei, no. 10. Tokyo: Iwanami Shoten, 1971.

_____ . *Hōnen—Sono kōdō to shishō*. Nihonjin no kōdō to shishō, no. 1. Tokyo: Hyōronsha, 1970.

_____ . *Hōnen to Jōdoshū kyōdan*. Tokyo: Kyōikusha, 1978.

_____ . *Ippen*. Jinbutsu sōsho, no. 183. Tokyo: Yoshikawa Kōbunkan, 1983.

_____ . *Ippen—Sono kōdō to shisō*. Nihonjin no kōdō to shisō, no. 14. Tokyo: Hyōronsha, 1971.

_____ . *Ippen to Jishū kyōdan*. Tokyo: Kyōikusha, 1978.

_____ , ed. *Jishū kakochō*. Fujisawa: Jishū Sōhonzan Shōjōkōji Kyōgaku Kenkyūjo, 1964.

_____ . *Jishū no seiritsu to tenkai*. Tokyo: Yoshikawa Kōbunkan, 1973.

_____ . *Odori nembutsu*. Tokyo: Daizō Shuppan, 1974.

_____ . *Sanso Ryōchū Shōnin*. Kamakura: Kanagawa Kyōku Kyōmusho, 1984.

_____ . *Yugyō hijiri*. Tokyo: Daizō Shuppan, 1971.

Okabe Shūjō. "Ryōgemon." In *Shinshū seiten kōsan zenshū 8, Rennyo Shōnin no bu*. Ed. Uno Enkū. Tokyo: Kokusho Kankōkai, 1976.

Okami Masao and Akamatsu Toshihide, eds. *Gukanshō*. Nihon koten bungaku taikei, no. 86. Tokyo: Iwanami Shoten, 1967.

Okamura Shusatsu, ed. *Shinshū daijiten*, 3 vols. 1936; rpt. Kyoto: Nagata Bunshōdō, 1972.

Okumura Gen'yū. *Anjin ketsujōshō: Jōdo e no michi*. Tokyo: Suzuki Gakujutsu Zaidan, 1964.

Ono Genmyō. *Bussho kaisetsu daijiten*, 13 vols.; *Bekkan*, 1 vol. Tokyo: Daitō Shuppan-sha, 1932–35, 1975–78.

Ōno Tatsunosuke. *Shinkō Nihon Bukkyō shisōshi*. Tokyo: Yoshikawa Kōbunkan, 1973.

Ōtani Daigaku, ed. *Shinran Shōnin*. Kyoto: Hōzōkan, 1961.

―――, ed. *Shinshū nenpyō*. Kyoto: Hōzōkan, 1973.

Risshō Daigaku Nichiren Kyōgaku Kenkyūjo, ed. *Nichiren kyōdan zenshi*. Kyoto: Heirakuji Shoten, 1964.

RSG. See Inaba Masamaru, ed. *Rennyo Shōnin gyōjitsu.*

RSI. See Inaba Masamaru, ed. *Rennyo Shōnin ibun.*

Ryūkoku Daigaku, ed. *Bukkyō daijii*, 6 vols. Tokyo: Fuzanbō, 1935–36.

―――, ed. *Rennyo Shōnin kenkyū*. Kyoto: Onki Hōyō Jimusho, 1948.

―――, ed. *Shinshū yōron*. Kyoto: Hyakkaen, 1953.

Ryūkoku Daigaku Shinshūgaku Kenkyūkai, ed. *Jōdo sanbukyō sakuin*. Kyoto: Ryūkoku Daigaku Shinshūgaku Kenkyūkai, 1979.

―――, ed. *Senjakushū sakuin*. Kyoto: Nagata Bunshōdō, 1981.

―――, ed. *Shinran Shōnin chosaku yōgo sakuin, Kyōgyōshinshō no bu*. Kyoto: Ryūkoku Daigaku Shinshūgaku Kenkyūkai, 1966.

―――, ed. *Shinran Shōnin chosaku yōgo sakuin, Wakan senjutsu no bu*. Kyoto: Ryūkoku Daigaku Shinshūgaku Kenkyūkai, 1971.

Saikō Gijun. "Gaijashō." In *Shinshū seiten kōsan zenshū* 6, *Kakunyo Shōnin no bu*. Ed. Uno Enkū. Tokyo: Kokusho Kankōkai, 1976.

Sanda Zenshin. "Jōdoshū to Zonkaku." *Bukkyō ronsō* 17 (1973).

―――. *Seiritsushi teki Hōnen Shōnin shoden no kenkyū*. Kyoto: Kōnenji Shuppanbu, 1966.

Sasaki Tesshin. "Nembutsu hihō ni tsuite no ikkōsatsu." *Indogaku Bukkyōgaku kenkyū* 10.1 (January 1962).

Satō Tetsuei. "Rennyo Shōnin to Kudenshō." In *Rennyo Shōnin kenkyū*. Ed. Ryūkoku Daigaku.

SDJ. See Okamura Shusatsu, ed. *Shinshū daijiten.*

Seizan Zensho Kankōkai, ed. *Seizan zensho*, 12 vols. Kyoto: Bun'eidō, 1974.

Shigaraki Takamaro. *Gendai Shinshū kyōgaku*. Kyoto: Nagata Bunshōdō, 1979.

Shigematsu Akihisa. *Chūsei Shinshū shisō no kenkyū*. Tokyo: Yoshikawa Kōbunkan, 1974.

―――. *Kakunyo*. Jinbutsu sōsho, no. 123. Tokyo: Yoshikawa Kōbunkan, 1964.

―――. *Nihon Jōdokyō seiritsu katei no kenkyū*. Kyoto: Heirakuji Shoten, 1964.

Shinran Shōnin Zenshū Kankōkai, ed. *Teihon Shinran Shōnin zenshū*, 9 vols.; *Bessatsu*, 1 vol. Kyoto: Hōzōkan, 1969–70.

Shinshū Shōgyō Zensho Hensanjo, ed. *Shinshū shōgyō zensho*, 5 vols. Kyoto: Kōkyō Shoin, 1940–41.

Shinshū Tenseki Kankōkai, ed. *Shinshū taikei*, 37 vols. 1916–25; rpt. Tokyo: Kokusho Kankōkai, 1974–76.

―――, ed. *Zoku Shinshū taikei*, 24 vols.; *Bekkan*, 4 vols. 1936–41; rpt. Tokyo: Kokusho Kankōkai, 1976–77.

Shinshūshi gaisetsu. See Akamatsu Toshihide and Kasahara Kazuo, eds. *Shinshūshi gaisetsu.*

Shōwa teihon Nichiren Shōnin ibun, 4 vols. Minobu: Sōhonzan Minobu Kuonji, 1952–59.

Shūkyōshi. See Kawasaki Yasuyuki and Kasahara Kazuo, eds. *Shūkyōshi.*

SSS. See Kashiwabara Yūsen et al., gen. eds. *Shinshū shiryō shūsei.*

SSZ. See Shinshū Shōgyō Zensho Hensanjo, ed. *Shinshū shōgyō zensho.*

ST. See Shinshū Tenseki Kankōkai, ed. *Shinshū taikei.*

Sugi Shirō. *Gobunshō kōwa*. 1933; rpt. Kyoto: Nagata Bunshōdō, 1979.

―――. *Seichin kyōgi gairon*. 1924; rpt. Kyoto: Hyakkaen, 1975.

Sugihira Gichi. "Gi naki o gi to su to iu koto." In *Shinran Shōnin*. Ed. Ōtani Daigaku.

Sumida Chiken. *Igishi no kenkyū*. Kyoto: Chōjiya Shoten, 1960.

―――. "Kakunyo Shōnin to igisha." In *Kakunyo Shōnin no kenkyū*, *Mujintō* 22 (1917).

Suzuki Gakujutsu Zaidan, ed. *Zōho kaitei Nihon daizōkyō*, 100 vols. Tokyo: Suzuki Gakujutsu Zaidan, 1973-78.

Suzuki Hōchin. *Shinshū gakushi*. In *Shinpen Shinshū zensho*, vol. 20. Ed. Shinpen Shinshū Zensho Kankōkai. Kyoto: Shibunkaku, 1977.

SZ. See Tsumaki Jikiryō, ed. *Shinshū zensho*.

Taga Munehaya. *Jien*. Jinbutsu sōsho, no. 15. Tokyo: Yoshikawa Kōbunkan, 1959.

Taira Masayuki. "Chūsei teki itan no rekishi teki igi—Itan kyōgaku to shōensei teki shihai ideorogii." *Shirin* 63.3 (May 1980).

――――. "Hōnen no shisō kōzō to sono rekishi teki ichi—Chūsei teki itan no seiritsu." *Nihonshi kenkyū* 198 (February 1979).

Takachiho Tetsujō. "Jōdoshū to no taiketsu." In *Rennyo Shōnin kenkyū*. Ed. Ryūkoku Daigaku.

Takadaha Senjuji Onki Hōmuin Monjobu, ed. *Senjuji shiyō*. Mie: Takadaha Senjuji, 1912.

Takagi Akiyoshi. *Anjin rondai kaisetsu*. Kyoto: Nagata Bunshōdō, 1982.

――――. *Sanjō wasan no iyaku to kaisetsu*. Kyoto: Nagata Bunshōdō, 1966.

Takagi Ichinosuke et al., eds. *Heike monogatari*. Nihon koten bungaku taikei, nos. 32-33. Tokyo: Iwanami Shoten, 1969-70.

Takakusu Junjirō and Watanabe Kaikyoku, eds. *Taishō shinshū daizōkyō*, 85 vols. Tokyo: Taishō Issaikyō Kankōkai, 1924-32.

Takao Giken. "Haja kenshōshō." In *Shinshū seiten kōsan zenshū 7, Zonkaku Shōnin no bu*. Ed. Uno Enkū. Tokyo: Kokusho Kankōkai, 1976.

Takeda Eishō. *Honganjiha gonshiki no genryū*. Kyoto: Honganji Shuppanbu, 1982.

Tamaki Kōshirō. *Shōtoku Taishi to Shinran, Hitotsu no suitei no kokoromi*. Tokyo: Shōtoku Taishi Hōsankai, 1980.

Tamura Enchō. *Hōnen*. Jinbutsu sōsho, no. 36. Tokyo: Yoshikawa Kōbunkan, 1959.

――――. *Hōnen Shōnin den no kenkyū*. Kyoto: Hōzōkan, 1972.

――――. *Nihon Bukkyō shisōshi kenkyū, Jōdokyōhen*. Kyoto: Heirakuji Shoten, 1959.

Tamura Yoshirō. *Kamakura shin Bukkyō shisō no kenkyū*. Kyoto: Heirakuji Shoten, 1965.

Tanaka Hisao. *Myōe*. Jinbutsu sōsho, no. 60. Tokyo: Yoshikawa Kōbunkan, 1961.

Tanigawa Tetsuzō. "Gakumon to shinkō." In *GSZ*, vol 1.

Tanishita Ichimu. *Zōho Shinshūshi no shokenkyū*. 1941; rpt. Kyoto: Dōbōsha, 1977.

――――. *Zonkaku ichigoki no kenkyū narabini kaisetsu*. Kyoto: Nagata Bunshōdō, 1969.

Taya Raishun. "Tannishō no chosaku ni tsuite no mondai." In *GSZ*, vol 1.

――――. *Tannishō shinchū*. Kyoto: Hōzōkan, 1973.

――――, Ōchō Enichi, and Funabashi Issai, eds. *Bukkyōgaku jiten*. Kyoto: Hōzōkan, 1974.

TD. See Takakusu Junjirō and Watanabe Kaikyoku, eds. *Taishō shinshū daizōkyō*.

Terakawa Shunshō. "Tanni to gaija." *Nihon Bukkyō gakkai nenpō* 39 (1974).

Terakura Noboru. "Rennyo Shōnin to Anjin ketsujōshō." *Dōbō gakuhō* 3 (1956).

Teranishi Enen. "Genshi Shinshū kyōdan ni okeru dōjō ni tsuite." *Ōtani gakuhō* 36.1 (June 1956).

Tokunaga Michio and Matsui Junshi. "Zenran no igi to sono haikei." *Shūgakuin ronshū* 42 (January 1975).

Tokushi Yūshō. "Ryōgemon seiritsu kō." In *Rennyo Shōnin kenkyū*. Ed. Ryūkoku Daigaku.

TSSZ. See Shinran Shōnin Zenshū Kankōkai, ed. *Teihon Shinran Shōnin zenshū*.

Tsuda Sōkichi. *Bungaku ni arawaretaru kokumin shisō no kenkyū*, 5 vols. Tokyo: Iwanami Shoten, 1965.

Tsuji Zennosuke. *Nihon Bukkyōshi*, 10 vols. Tokyo: Iwanami Shoten, 1960-61.

Tsumaki Jikiryō, ed. *Shinshū zensho*, 74 vols. Kyoto: Zōkyō Shoin, 1913-16.

Tsunetani Hōryū. *Honganji fūbutsushi*. Kyoto: Nagata Bunshōdō, 1978.

Tsutsumi Genryū. "Shinshū shoki kyōdan no keisei to igi." *Shūkyō kenkyū* 51.3 (1977).

Uehara Yoshitarō. *Honganji hōnanshi*. Tokyo: Tōgakusha, 1934.

Umehara Ryūshō. "Jōdo Shinshū ni okeru shinkō kokuhakumon no seiritsu." In *Shinshūshi no kenkyū.* Ed. Miyazaki Enjun Hakase Kanreki Kinenkai. Kyoto: Nagata Bunshōdō, 1966.

———. "Rennyo jidai no igi ni tsuite—Jōgai Ofumi o chūshin to shite." In *Nihon shūkyōshi ronshū,* vol. 1. Ed. Kasahara Kazuo Hakase Kanreki Kinenkai. Tokyo: Yoshikawa Kōbunkan, 1978.

Umehara Shinryū. "Tanni no kokoro to itanha." In *GSZ,* vol. 1.

Umezu Jirō. *Tengu sōshi, Zegaibōe.* Nihon emakimono zenshū, no. 27. Tokyo: Kadokawa, 1978.

Uryūzu Ryūō. "Anjin ketsujōshō to Shinshū kyōgaku." *Indogaku Bukkyōgaku kenkyū* 10 (1962).

———. "Rennyo kyōgaku no tasuke tamae ni tsuite." *Indogaku Bukkyōgaku kenkyū* 11.2 (1963).

———. "Rennyo Shōnin yōgojō no mondai—Tasuke tamae o chūshin to shite." *Shinshū kenkyū* 10 (1965).

Wakaki Yoshihiko. "Shinran shokan ni arawareta Hōnen Shōnin." *Shinshūgaku* 45–46 (March 1972).

Washio Junkyō. *Zōtei Nihon Bukka jinmei jisho.* 1911; rpt. Tokyo: Tōkyō Bijutsu, 1979.

Watanabe Tsunaya, ed. *Shasekishū.* Nihon koten bungaku taikei, no. 85. Tokyo: Iwanami Shoten, 1966.

Yamabe Shūgaku and Akanuma Chizen. *Kyōgyōshinshō kōgi,* 3 vols. 1914; rpt. Kyoto: Hōzōkan, 1967–68.

Yamada Bunshō. *Shinshū shikō.* 1934; rpt. Kyoto: Hōzōkan, 1968.

———. *Shinshūshi no kenkyū.* 1934; rpt. Kyoto: Hōzōkan, 1979.

Yamada Yoshio et al., eds. *Konjaku monogatarishū,* vol. 4. Nihon koten bungaku taikei, no. 25. Tokyo: Iwanami Shoten, 1975.

Yamakami Shōson. "Kakunyo Shōnin to Jōdo iryū ni tsuite." In *Kakunyo Shōnin no kenkyū, Mujintō* 22 (1917).

Yamamoto Ryōshin. "Rennyo no goshō no ichidaiji ni tsuite." *Ōtani gakuhō* 39 (March 1960).

Yamazaki Ryūmyō. "Rennyo no kenkyū—Nyonin ōjō ni tsuite." *Indogaku Bukkyōgaku kenkyū* 31.2 (March 1983).

Yūki Reimon, gen. ed. *Gendaigoyaku Shinran zenshū,* 10 vols. Tokyo: Kōdansha, 1974.

———. "Kyōgyōshinshō Shinkan bessensetsu no yōshi." In *Kyōgyōshinshō senjutsu no kenkyū.* Ed. Keika Bunka Kenkyūkai.

Zengaku Taikei Hensankyoku, ed. *Zengaku taikei,* 8 vols. Tokyo: Ikkatsusha, 1910–15.

ZST. See Shinshū Tenseki Kankōkai, ed. *Zoku Shinshū taikei.*

Index